HIDDEN®
Salt Lake City
& Beyond

HIDDEN®
Salt Lake City & Beyond

Kurt Repanshek

Ulysses Press®
BERKELEY, CALIFORNIA

Published by:
ULYSSES PRESS
P.O. Box 3440
Berkeley, CA 94703
www.ulyssespress.com

ISSN 1535-8372
ISBN 1-56975-272-9

Printed in Canada by Transcontinental Printing

10 9 8 7 6 5 4 3 2 1

MANAGING EDITOR: Claire Chun
EDITOR: Lily Chou
EDITORIAL ASSOCIATES: Marin Van Young, David Archer
TYPESETTER: Lisa Kester
CARTOGRAPHY: Pease Press
COVER DESIGN: Sarah Levin, Leslie Henriques
INDEXER: Sayre Van Young
COVER PHOTOGRAPHY:
    FRONT: Corbis Corporation/David Stoecklein
    CIRCLE & BACK: Cheyenne Rouse (Backpackers)
ILLUSTRATOR: Doug McCarthy

Distributed in the United States by Publishers Group West, in
Canada by Raincoast Books, and in Great Britain and Europe by
World Leisure Marketing

For the athletes of the Salt Lake Games,
who have focused their lives on the pursuit of being the very best they can be
in sports that most of us can only sit back and marvel at.

Acknowledgments

This book would not have been possible without help from the Utah State Parks and Recreation staff, particularly Delores Badley and Deena Loyola. Ken Kraus at the Utah Travel Council provided unflagging input on Utah's out-of-the-way nooks and crannies, while Tracie Cayford provided a steady stream of memorable events from around the state. Chamber bureaus throughout the state were an invaluable resource. In particular, thanks go to Barbara McConvill at the Ogden/Weber Convention and Visitors Bureau, Loretta King at the Utah County Convention and Visitors Bureau, Shawn Stinson at the Park City Chamber of Commerce–Convention and Visitors Bureau, and Maridene Alexander Hancock at the Logan Convention and Visitors Bureau. Additionally, kudos to the Salt Lake Organizing Committee's media relations staff for tracking down the obscure, and the obvious, in terms of event schedules, transportation plans, and venue trivia. Finally, I'd like to thank my wife, Marcelle, for her patience and support throughout this project, although I'm not sure she ever really came to view my traipsing about Utah's fabulous countryside, eating in its best restaurants, and staying in some of its finer lodgings as work.

What's Hidden?

At different points throughout this book, you'll find special listings marked with a hidden symbol:

◀ HIDDEN

This means that you have come upon a place off the beaten tourist track, a spot that will carry you a step closer to the local people and natural environment of Salt Lake City.

The goal of this guide is to lead you beyond the realm of everyday tourist facilities. While we include traditional sightseeing listings and popular attractions, we also offer alternative sights and adventure activities. Instead of filling this guide with reviews of standard hotels and chain restaurants, we concentrate on one-of-a-kind places and locally owned establishments.

Our authors seek out locales that are popular with residents but usually overlooked by visitors. Some are more hidden than others (and are marked accordingly), but all the listings in this book are intended to help you discover the true nature of Salt Lake City and put you on the path of adventure.

Write to us!

If in your travels you discover a spot that captures the spirit of Salt Lake City, or if you live in the region and have a favorite place to share, or if you just feel like expressing your views, write to us and we'll pass your note along to the author.

We can't guarantee that the author will add your personal find to the next edition, but if the writer does use the suggestion, we'll acknowledge you in the credits and send you a free copy of the new edition.

ULYSSES PRESS
P.O. Box 3440
Berkeley, CA 94703
E-mail: ulysses@ulyssespress.com

Contents

Maps

OUTDOOR ADVENTURE SYMBOLS

The following symbols accompany national, state and regional park listings, as well as beach descriptions throughout the text.

▲	Camping			Snorkeling or Scuba Diving
	Hiking			Water Skiing
	Biking			Windsurfing
	Horseback Riding			Canoeing or Kayaking
	Downhill Skiing			Boating
	Cross-country Skiing			Boat Ramps
	Swimming			Fishing

ONE

Salt Lake City and Beyond

Seven decades ago they came to a Rocky Mountain foothill in northern Utah, strapped long wooden boards to their feet, and launched themselves off a snowy ramp in a friendly competition to see who could soar farther through the crisp mountain air. More often than not it was one of the Engen brothers, a trio of transplanted Norwegians who helped put Ecker Hill and its ski-jumping pioneers on the map. The Olympic Winter Games were in their infancy when Alf, Sverre and Corey Engen, and dozens of others began thrilling thousands of Utahns who gathered in the cold at the base of Ecker Hill to watch those hardy men defy gravity in jumps that took them nearly 300 feet through the air. During the 1930s Ecker Hill, a tiny knob north of Park City, produced world record after world record. And more often than not it was Alf Engen who garnered the glory with his leaps. While Engen's official hill record jump stands at 296 feet, it's said that on one unofficial jump he soared 311 feet.

It's against this background that the 2002 Olympic Winter Games descend on Salt Lake City and its surrounding Wasatch Mountains. Although Ecker Hill is just a memory overgrown by scrub brush these days, its glories marked only by a plaque honoring the 300 or so men who jumped from the hill during its competitive days, less than two miles away today's best jumpers will vie for Olympic gold at the Utah Olympic Park's state-of-the-art jumps. Just as Ecker Hill landed Utah on the world's winter sports map in the 1930s, the Salt Lake Games are returning the state to that prominence. From the Utah Olympic Park to the Utah Olympic Oval in the Salt Lake Valley, the 2002 Winter Games are showcasing Salt Lake City, the ten venues where the world's best winter athletes will compete, and the Wasatch Mountains. For 17 days in February 2002 the Games will make Salt Lake City the winter-sports capital of the world, an honor Utahns hope will long be remembered. After all, they'll let you know, their state is home to The Greatest Snow on Earth.

Those unfamiliar with Utah often think first of Mormons—members of the Church of Jesus Christ of Latter-day Saints—when talk turns to the state. And while the 84,916-square-mile state is indeed the headquarters for the LDS Church, the church is not the only religion practiced in the state nor does it define Utah. True, Temple Square in the heart of Salt Lake City is Utah's number-one tourist draw, and its magnificent temple and renowned tabernacle justify that designation. Still, there are those who would argue, and justifiably so, that southern Utah's labyrinthine canyon country, or the state's frothy whitewater, or its snow heavy mountains, or its five national parks, could easily claim that honor.

For three weeks in February 2002, the state will point to its snow-laden mountains as its greatest tourist draw. Head up into the Wasatch in winter and you'll be confronted by so much snow and so many alpine resorts that it can be hard to decide where to park your car and unload your skis or snowboards. From the Brian Head Resort (surrounded by the stunning red-rock beauty that defines much of southern Utah) on the southern end of the Wasatch to Beaver Mountain (a "mom-and-pop" ski area barely a stone's throw from Idaho), the mountains offer 14 alpine resorts to test your skills while sampling Utah's famously dry snow. Salt Lake City, Utah's capital and the host to the 2002 Winter Games, is the gateway to these resorts and more.

Although it's intended to help you get the most out of your trip to northern Utah, *Hidden Salt Lake City & Beyond* is not an encyclopedia on Utah's capital, nor is it intended to be. Rather, it's designed to help you negotiate the northern half of the state. In the following three chapters you'll learn about northern Utah's highlights, the places you should definitely consider visiting. Sprinkled liberally throughout them are "hidden" spots—sights, accommodations and eateries not heavily publicized nor usually included on group tours. They're the kind of places you usually discover after spending a number of days in one area and learning where the locals like to go.

Along with pointing out these places, the text touches on the history of the various corners of Utah. You'll learn about the Mormons' flight from religious persecution that brought them to the state, the rough-and-tumble miners who played a key role in settling the state, and a bit about Utah's trademark snow and why it's so dry. This guide will also help you get the most out of the 2002 Olympic Winter Games.

So whether you're heading to the Olympics, are in Utah for a vacation, or are merely looking for adventure, *Hidden Salt Lake City & Beyond* can make your trip to the Beehive State more enjoyable and productive.

After dispatching helpful introductory information such as the state's geology, history and wildlife, sections that paint a portrait of Utah, this book delves into three geographic regions, starting with Salt Lake City and its surroundings (covered in Chapter Two). From there the book meanders, as any good trav-

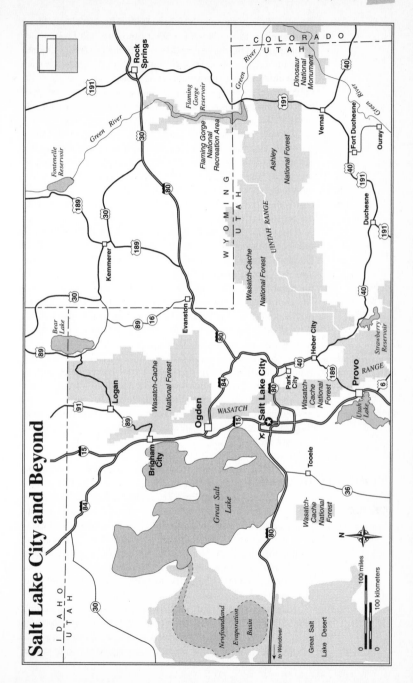

Salt Lake City and Beyond

eler should, moving on to Northern Utah (Chapter Three). Here, Utah's ties to the taming of the West can be seen at Promontory Summit, where the "golden spike" was driven in 1869 to knit the transcontinental railroad together, and where the state's connection with America's space industry is rooted.

Northeastern Utah (Chapter Four) is perhaps the most geologically diverse region of the state, running from the seismically sculpted Wasatch Range that is the heart of the state's ski industry to Dinosaur National Monument (truly a Jurassic park) along the Utah–Colorado border. Just as you'll recognize world-class skiing and snowboarding at Park City's three alpine resorts, you'll appreciate first-rate dinosaur digs north of Vernal in the national monument. For those interested in bucking whitewater, the Green and Yampa rivers that flow through the monument offer some of the state's best rapids.

Once you've reviewed these chapters, or perhaps before you even consider them, delve into the chapter devoted to the Salt Lake Games (Chapter Five). Here you'll find a section on how to survive the Games, providing tips on what to pack for standing in the mountains while watching alpine ski racing, biathlon or perhaps bobsledding, and what to expect in terms of transportation bottlenecks. The chapter also details the Cultural Olympiad, the Games' official arts festival, and points you to non-venue ski resorts where you can escape the Olympic crowds for some turns.

The Salt Lake Games and the best of Salt Lake City and surrounding northern and northeastern Utah—places widely known as well as some largely unknown—are packaged into this book. Whether you plan on visiting the Salt Lake area for only a few days or for a month, this book will make it easier to chart your course. If southern Utah is on your agenda, pick up a copy of *Hidden Utah* (Ulysses Press, 2000).

▼▼▼▼▼▼▼▼▼▼▼▼▼

The Story of Utah

GEOLOGY

Utah, perhaps more than any other state, is a portal into the past. Sandstone and coal beds from Vernal to Price are vaults for Jurassic fossils, preserving the remains and footprints of some of the most voracious dinosaurs that trod the earth. Cliff faces were *pleine aire* easels to American Indians, beginning with the ancient Anasazi and continuing on through the Ute Nation, whose medicine men detailed their tribes' annals on the rocky walls. More recently, miners literally burrowed into Utah, first to extract coal, silver and gold, and more recently in search of oil and gas, uranium and copper.

Squeezed, tugged and buckled by North America's tectonic plates, Utah is an amalgamation of geologic provinces. Northern Utah's landscape reflects this remarkable geology. Its jagged, steeply pitched mountains, which are still enjoying their youth, tower over much of the landscape. Impossible to overlook, of course, is the Great Salt Lake, a massive inland sea.

The Great Basin province (also known as the Basin and Range) lies west of a line drawn north to south from Idaho to Nevada through Ogden, Salt Lake City and Provo. This oft-parched high-desert landscape was once inundated by prehistoric Lake Bonneville, which in its prime left parts of Utah, Idaho and Nevada awash under a freshwater inland ocean nearly 350 miles long and 145 miles wide. East of a diagonal line drawn from Vernal southwest through Price sprawls the northern tip of the Colorado Plateau, a tabletop of sedimentary rocks that erosion has sculpted into a magnificent matrix of canyons, buttes, draws and mesas.

Sandwiched between the Basin and Range and Colorado Plateau lies the high country of the Wasatch and High plateaus and the east–west running Uinta Mountain Range. Here rise the thickest of Utah's forests, as stands of conifer, aspen, oak, maple and juniper shroud much of the mountains. Bejeweled alpine lakes and tumbling mountain streams add a lushness to the landscape that's largely missing in southern Utah.

Although it's mostly unseen, the state's most significant geologic landmark, due to its active status beneath the heavily populated Wasatch Front, is the Wasatch Fault. This geologic worm is responsible for having ratcheted up its namesake mountains over the millennia. The fault, however, has long been quiescent, not having unleashed its signature magnitude 7 quake in more than six centuries.

Hoisted ever upward by the periodic shudders of this deep-seated geologic fault, the north-to-south-running Wasatch Range is a monument to the fault's energy. And unlike the East Coast's Appalachians, whose ancient age is reflected by gently rounded summits and deep forests, the Wasatch carries all the angular

SLIPPING AND SLIDING

How does the Wasatch Fault, which has been pushing up its namesake mountains for 15 million years, work? Unlike California's more famous San Andreas fault (a "slip-strike" fault in which blocks of rock slip sideways during quakes), the Wasatch is one of the world's longest and most active "normal" faults (a "dip-slip" fault in which the blocks slip mostly vertically as the earth's crust pulls apart). To picture how this works, imagine holding three bricks in front of you by squeezing them together. If you relax this pressure, the center brick slides down. In the case of the Wasatch Fault, the Salt Lake Valley is the center brick that sinks while the adjoining mountains rise.

blemishes, mannerisms and rumblings of geologic puberty. Erosion has yet to soften the gray, granitic spires that scrape the sky; rocky escarpments left by the fault's previous subterranean grindings gash the mountains' flanks; tiny swarms of earthquakes, usually unnoticed, reverberate through the range each year.

HISTORY   **NATIVE PEOPLE**   Utah is an open book, its geologic and cultural history readily available to anyone who takes the time to read the landscape. For more than 10,000 years people have roamed across Utah. They learned how to live in the state's mountains, deserts and canyonlands, finding nourishment in the streams, fields and forests.

Storytelling was an integral part of these cultures and the tribal shaman often bore the responsibility of recounting these tales through images. Painstakingly etched into rock panels throughout Utah's backcountry are symbols, characters, animals and warriors—images that ask many questions of their creators but offer few direct answers. Scattered across the state in places such as Nine Mile Canyon, these petroglyphs and pictographs paint a picture of both Utah's prehistoric past, a time when ancient hunters and gatherers known as the Fremont and Anasazi roamed the state, and the more recent past of Indian tribes such as the Utes, Paiutes and Shoshones, who added their own scenes to some of the rock panels first touched by the Fremont and Anasazi. At times overlapping the cultures, these exquisite patches of art often tell stories that are not always easily comprehended. While it's easy to interpret a warrior astride a horse with bow drawn, not so understandable are the asexual, anthropomorphic entities that seem to be clutching balloons or tossing lightning bolts.

> The Great Salt Lake is so salty that early mountain men mistook it for the Pacific Ocean.

Utah's first prehistoric groups to be given names by today's historians were the Fremont and Anasazi. While the Anasazi, also known as "ancestral Puebloans," arose around A.D. 200 in southern Utah near the Four Corners region, surviving by growing crops like corn, beans and squash, the Fremont arrived just to the north in the Great Basin and Uinta Basin by at least A.D. 500. The two cultures seemingly coexisted in Utah until around A.D. 1300. While the Fremont, who supplemented their hunting and gathering with farming of corn, beans and squash, lived in pit houses, the Anasazi lived in cliff dwellings in addition to pit houses, many of which remain today and can be seen by sharp-eyed tourists or those on guided tours.

For reasons still unclear today, these two cultures seemed to vanish from the landscape around 1300, possibly because of a long-lasting drought, perhaps due to assimilation by other peoples.

Historically, Utah was then populated by the Goisute, Navajo, Shoshone, Southern Paiute and Ute peoples, who, like the Fremont and Anasazi before them, engaged in hunting, gathering and fishing. These tribes, endemic to the Great Basin and Rocky Mountain regions, roamed the state, which is named after the Ute tribe. While the Utes lived in structures familiar to most today as tepees, the Southern Paiute, who ranged across southern Utah as well as parts of Nevada and Arizona, fashioned ice-cream-cone-shaped "wickiups" from poles and brush.

The tribes can still be found in Utah. While the Ute have a reservation that covers nearly four and a half million acres in northeastern Utah (tribal headquarters are in Fort Duchesne), the Goisute, whose ancestors roamed the West Desert and Nevada, live on the Skull Valley Reservation southwest of Tooele. Another tribe still in northern Utah is the Northwestern band of the Shoshone, which has small holdings in northern Utah, with an office in Brigham City.

EXPLORERS AND MOUNTAIN MEN   Spanish explorers are believed to have found their way into Utah in the 1700s, although somewhat more romantic tales date to the mid-1600s, a time when Spaniards supposedly roamed the Uinta Mountains and enslaved Utes during their search for gold ore and caches of gold they thought had been hidden there by the Aztecs.

Spaniard Juan Maria Rivera reached the state in 1765, entering Utah in the southeastern corner near today's Hovenweep National Monument and working his way as far north as Moab. More famous was the 1776 journey of Atanasio Dominguez and Silvestre Velez de Escalante, two Franciscan priests searching for a route from Sante Fe, New Mexico, to Monterey, California. They sallied into the Uinta Basin near present-day Jensen and drifted as far west as Utah Lake before turning back to the southeast and Santa Fe. Their journals provided extensive notes on Utah's native peoples, vegetation and landscape.

Jim Bridger, Jedediah Smith, Miles Goodyear and scores of other mountain men hunted and trapped their way through northern Utah between 1807 and 1840. It was Bridger, then a stalwart 20-year-old, who worked his way down Logan Canyon from 1825–26 and reached the Great Salt Lake, thinking it was the Pacific Ocean.

These trappers rambled wherever beaver led them. Bear Lake in extreme northern Utah was a popular gathering spot for their annual "rendezvous," as was Blacksmith Canyon south of Logan. Goodyear found the present-day site of Ogden to be a comfortable, logical place to build a trading post and erected Fort Buenaventura along the banks of the Ogden River in 1844 with hopes of growing rich from passing wagon trains en route to California.

Just as the era of the mountain man was ending in the 1840s, Congress' determination to gain a better understanding of this country brought explorer John C. Fremont into Utah on his way across the West. Fremont visited the Great Salt Lake and Antelope Island, which he named for the game he and his men shot, and explored the Great Basin.

MORMON SETTLEMENT   The influx of Mormons in 1847 ushered in the widespread settlement of Utah by whites. Under Brigham Young the church latched onto an ambitious colonization effort that established isolated communities in the state's far-flung corners and rugged interior. By 1850, just three years after the Mormons had arrived in Salt Lake City, outposts known as Bountiful, Farmington, Manti, Ogden, Provo and Tooele sprang up; hundreds more around the state would soon follow.

In addition to spreading the word of their gospel, the Mormons also tamed the landscape. Elaborate irrigation systems nourished parched and dusty fields, orchards flourished and communities grew.

While the Mormons decided in 1849 to create their own state, a place called "Deseret," Congress withheld statehood and instead named the area the Utah Territory. Tensions between the Mormons and Congress grew heated in the 1850s, when Washington politicians condemned the Mormon practice of polygamy. Though President Buchanan sent the U.S. Cavalry to Utah in 1857 in a show of force, no battles broke out. The federal presence, however, continued during the Civil War, as President Lincoln, fearful that Utahns might side with the South, maintained a garrison of soldiers on Salt Lake City's eastern bench in the form of Fort Douglas.

The soldiers not only kept an eye on the Mormons but also took to the mountains to search for valuable ores that might spur a mining boom and draw non-Mormons into the state. The move succeeded grandly: silver, gold, copper, lead and other deposits were found in Wasatch Range and mountains southwest of Provo and generated a fevered rush to the ore fields.

Among the towns that flourished under this mining boom was one nestled in a small valley on the eastern slopes of the Wasatch Range, a place called Park City. While Park City was not Utah's first ski town—Alta lays claim to that distinction, having entered the snow business in 1938—it perfected the concept and helped place Utah's ski industry on the globe.

MODERN TIMES   Utah joined the rocket age in 1957 when Thiokol Chemical Corporation came to Brigham City with plans to build a solid fuel rocket propellant plant, which it did to the west of town. The center remains today, with NASA being one of its main customers, while nearby Utah State University in Logan has developed a nationally recognized rocket curriculum through its Space Dynamics Lab.

To the south, while skiing was making the Wasatch Range fashionable, another revolution was taking placing in the Salt Lake Valley that put that part of the state on the technological map. In Salt Lake City, medical advances such as artificial hearts were being pioneered, and the state capital also became a financial center for the Intermountain West.

These technological and financial advances spurred a significant influx of people to the state throughout the 1980s and 1990s, though Utahns' high birth rate has remained the primary factor behind the state's booming population.

FLORA

Considering the kaleidoscopic landscape, from snow-capped peaks to arid deserts, is it any surprise that Utah's vegetative province is equally diverse? A range of elevations and varied moisture conditions result in an incredible array of vegetation, from ancient bristlecone pines and unusual Joshua trees to hanging gardens and old-growth pine forests.

Utah is easily divided into three vegetative regions: the Wasatch and Uinta mountain ranges, the Basin and Range province, and the Colorado Plateau.

A quick glance across the Basin and Range and the Colorado Plateau generates the impression that these parts of the state are arid, desolate and generally inhospitable for both plants and animals. But a closer look reveals a vivid collection of plants that dab color and texture to the landscape.

Plants that overlap in the Basin and Range and Colorado Plateau areas include shrubs such as rabbitbrush, blackbrush and greasewood. Single-leaf ash trees also seem to enjoy the canyon country, often finding niches where runoff collects.

Juniper and piñon dominate the mountain landscape. Pine, fir, spruce, aspen, maple, scrub oak and willow are among the trees found throughout the Wasatch and Uinta ranges. Though there are open meadows that burst in spring with wildflowers such as

FLOCKING TOGETHER

Three national wildlife refuges—Fish Springs southwest of Tooele, Bear River west of Brigham City, and Ouray south of Vernal—along with the shores of the Great Salt Lake are tremendous lures for migratory birds such as avocets, stilts, white pelicans, herons, cranes, egrets, ducks, Canada geese and many more waterfowl and shorebird species. During the winter months Fish Springs is a good area to spot and photograph bald eagles, as is Willard Bay along the eastern shore of the Great Salt Lake between Ogden and Brigham City.

asters, penstemons and sego lilies, patches of south-facing slopes within the mountains might also harbor sweet-scented sagebrush.

FAUNA   Though grizzly bears no longer wander Utah's mountains, long ago having been hunted out, other remnants of the "wild West" can still be found in the state. Wild mustangs continue to gallop across the prairie in areas such as the West Desert and Book Cliffs, while deer, elk and moose all graze in substantial numbers in the northern forests. On occasion, moose have stumbled out of the Wasatch Mountains and into Salt Lake City's neighborhoods, only to be rounded up by state wildlife personnel and returned to the mountains.

Black bears mainly prowl the Uinta Range, although they and cougars can be found in the Book Cliffs area.

Bighorn sheep, with their magnificently curved horns, can be found in several areas of Utah, ranging from the northeastern corner of the state near Flaming Gorge National Recreation Area to Antelope Island and the Wasatch Range. Not as numerous nor quite as visible are mountain goats. Some of these shaggy, bearded creatures live around Mount Timpanogos and near the mouth of Little Cottonwood Canyon, while another herd clatters around the Tushar Mountains east of Beaver.

Nearly 3000 wild horses still cluster in parts of the state, notably the West Desert, the Uinta Basin south of Vernal and north of Green River, and the San Rafael Swell. While most of these horses are thought to have descended from mares and stallions that escaped ranches in the late 1800s, some think that many can be traced back to horses brought to the region by Spanish explorers.

Elk, plentiful throughout much of northern Utah, can be spotted at the state-run Hardware Ranch near the head of Blacksmith Fork below Logan.

Wolves have not yet returned to the state, but wildlife biologists expect offspring from those released in Yellowstone National Park to one day reach parts of northern Utah.

Utah's skies harbor many bird species, from buzzing hummingbirds to raucous magpies to graceful raptors such as red-tail hawks and golden and bald eagles. A reliable spotting area for bald eagles is the Weber River near Henefer along Route 84 northeast of Park City. The eagles roost in the trees along the river throughout the winter, pulling fishy meals from the stream. When summer arrives the eagles head north while great blue herons arrive to use the area for a rookery. Wild turkeys frequent some areas of the state, too.

Where to Go   A vacation to the Salt Lake area can entail as little or as much travel as you desire. You can sequester yourself within the capital and browse its museums, antique shops and historic neighborhoods, or roam the Salt Lake Valley and head up into the mountains to sample the skiing. Practically throughout the year golf is played in the valley, and road and mountain bikers spin their wheels year-round. Looking for something a bit more leisurely? Then visit Hogle Zoo or Red Butte Garden on the east side of the capital, paddle a canoe through Jordan River State Park, or attend a concert at Abravanel Concert Hall or a Broadway play at the Capitol Theatre. During the 17-day run of the Olympic Winter Games a myriad of activities and events will beckon you, from the Cultural Olympiad's offerings to Park City's street fairs.

If you're flying to Utah, most likely you'll arrive in the **Salt Lake Valley** at Salt Lake City International Airport. On the jet's approach to the airport, you receive a panoramic view of the valley that Brigham Young and his fellow Mormons reached in July 1847 in their bid to escape religious persecution. The rugged and angular Wasatch Range defines the eastern border of the valley, while the Oquirrh Mountains do the same for the western edge. Just north of the airport is the Great Salt Lake, the largest inland lake west of the Mississippi. Salt Lake City is the spiritual center for the LDS Church. Ever since Brigham Young established the church's headquarters here, the city has served as the base of the church's world-wide operations, which today emanate from the beautiful and well-kept grounds and buildings of the Temple Square complex. But Salt Lake City is more than just a religious center—it also offers a lively cultural scene thanks to its theaters, playhouses, art galleries and restaurants, as well as the University of Utah, and is a growing business center for the Intermountain West.

Northern Utah is a veritable wilderness compared to the Salt Lake Valley. Steep and thickly forested mountains rim Ogden and Brigham City to the east, while the Great Salt Lake shimmers just to the west of these cities. At Promontory Summit west of Brigham City and atop the northern tip of the lake lies the Golden Spike National Historic Site, the spot where the transcontinental railroad was bound together. Closer to Brigham City is the Bear River Migratory Bird Refuge, a sanctuary for millions of waterfowl and shorebirds who rest here on their migrations north and south. Although Ogden is farther away from Promontory Summit than Brigham City, it is Utah's true railroad town, and the Union Station that anchors the city's historic district is a landmark rich in railroad history.

Logan, the region's only other major city, lies in the lush Cache Valley that's cupped by mountains to the east, south and west. Bear Lake, 40 miles east of Logan, is a popular and refreshing summer retreat, drawing boaters, anglers and even scuba divers to its waters, while fruit lovers arrive for the late-summer raspberry festival.

Both ski resorts and dinosaur bones are scattered throughout **Northeastern Utah,** a sprawling slice of the state that stretches from Park City's alpine slopes to Dinosaur National Monument, which straddles the Utah–Colorado border. The backside of the Wasatch Range cradles the Deer Valley, Park City and Canyons ski resorts as well as the tony resort town of Park City, which is home to the U.S. Ski and Snowboard Association as well as dozens of top-notch restaurants. The east-to-west-running Uinta Mountains provide a more rugged recreational experience for backcountry skiers, hikers and anglers who don't mind trekking miles to access high-country lakes and tumbling streams teeming with trout. Although off the beaten path, Dinosaur National Monument is a rich treasure of this country's Jurassic past, and the Green and Yampa rivers that flow through the monument and its surrounding landscape sate the souls of many recreationalists.

Park City arguably will be the hub of activity during the Games, with 26 medal events and more than 78 competitions scheduled for the Deer Valley and Park City resorts as well as the Utah Olympic Park.

When to Go

SEASONS

Summers in the northern mountains are downright enjoyable (high temperatures are typically in the mid-80s and overnight lows in the 50s) with little precipitation aside from the random afternoon thunderstorm. However, Salt Lake Valley temperatures can surpass the century mark repeatedly during summer. Come winter, the northern half of the state braces for heavy snows and cold, below-freezing weather.

The worst time to visit northern Utah is between mid-April and early June, a time derisively, and descriptively, known as the "mud season" thanks to melting snows and spring rains. This is the most unpredictable time of year, weather-wise, in the region, as sunny, mild weather one week can be replaced by snowstorms and body-numbing temperatures the next. In Park City and other ski areas, many restaurants and resort facilities shut down for several weeks when the snows are gone but the slopes are not yet dried out to handle mountain-bike and hiking traffic.

Utah's summer tourist season typically runs from Memorial Day through Labor Day, and the weather generally cooperates in grand design. Meadows swell with wildflowers well into July, scant rainfall makes for optimum conditions to enjoy the outdoors, and the lack of humidity makes the warm mountain temperatures generally bearable. Thunderstorms do arise, but not as often as in neighboring Wyoming.

Statewide, July is Utah's hottest month, followed closely by August. Of course, to many the 82° that is Park City's average high in July is quite pleasant, unlike the 101° average July high of St. George, in the southern part of the state.

Unless you're a skier, autumn—which usually arrives by mid-September—offers Utah's best weather, in all parts of the state. The changing season paints the mountains with yellow, orange and red aspen, maple and scrub oak in the north and funnels in cooler, occasionally crisp air that's perfect for biking and hiking. It also marks harvest time in places such as Brigham City, Bear Lake and Provo.

The weather largely remains dry in the fall, even in the high country, which is a perfect retreat for the year's last backpacking trek, camping outing or fishing foray. It's not entirely out of the question, though, for the high country to witness a snowstorm in October. Generally, heavy snows don't arrive before Thanksgiving, which is the traditional kickoff to ski season in the Wasatch Range; heavy, reliable snows, in fact, often do not arrive before year's end, forcing resorts to rely on their snowmaking systems.

> To assure a thick snow-pack for your ski vacation, it's best to plan a Utah visit between January and early April.

Winters can bring short bursts of exceptionally cold weather in the state's mountainous areas, but as a rule Utah's winters are on the mild side when compared with those in Wyoming and Montana. Sub-zero readings in the state's ski country are few and far between; instead, most winter days see high temperatures climb into the 30s in Park City as well as Little and Big Cottonwood canyons.

CALENDAR OF EVENTS

Festivals serve dual purposes in Utah—they lure tourists to the state and give the locals an excuse to get together. Glancing over the list of events, it's clear that Utahns have extensive tastes: music and art festivals, re-enactments of mountain-man rendezvous and settler celebrations, harvest jubilees and, in a state where the snow is widely accepted as the greatest on Earth, even a winter carnival or two. Utah's Western heritage isn't overlooked, either, as there are pow-wows, rodeos and chili cookoffs. Below is a sampling of some of the leading annual events. Check with local chambers of commerce (listed in the regional chapters of this book) to see what will be going on when you are in the area.

JANUARY

Salt Lake Valley, Northern Utah and Northeastern Utah The **Utah Winter Games,** a cornucopia of winter-sports competitions, lures thousands of Utahns to the slopes, cross-country courses and ice rinks in a bid to see who are the best athletes. Chocoholics and snow sliders converge at Solitude Ski Resort each January to mix and match their passions during the **Chocolate Lovers Tour,** which allows you to both ski the slopes and take breaks to melt chocolate in your mouth at various booths.

Northeastern Utah   Late in the month Robert Redford presents **The Sundance Film Festival**, a marketing orgy of independent film projects that draws Hollywood actors, actresses, producers and moguls to Park City in the one mid-winter event that can overshadow Utah's snow season.

FEBRUARY   **Salt Lake Valley, Northern Utah and Northeastern Utah**   The **2002 Olympic Winter Games** bring athletes from around the world together to show their mettle and earn their medals. The Games run from February 8–24.

MARCH   **Salt Lake Valley**   Spring can't be far off once the **Home and Garden Show** kicks off in Salt Lake City with its gardening and home-improvement exhibits. Snowbird is the backdrop for the NFL **Celebrity Classic**, a charitable ski race that draws notable gridiron warriors to the slopes. Irish eyes are smiling in Salt Lake City for the **St. Patrick's Day Parade**, which runs down 200 East Street. **Northern Utah**   The railroads largely created Ogden, which honors its past with the **Railroad Festival** that features model-train layouts in Union Station.

APRIL   **Salt Lake Valley**   Snowbird Ski and Summer Resort welcomes the season with its **Easter Sunrise Service and Easter Egg Hunt**. **Northern Utah**   Ogden, which traces its origin to a mountain man who decided to open a trading post, celebrates its history with the **Mountain Man Rendezvous**, where black-powder musketry is demonstrated along with Dutch-oven cooking and a trader's row.

MAY   **Salt Lake Valley**   The **Great Salt Lake Festival** appreciates the briny lake as well as the shorebirds and waterfowl that flock to its shores on their migratory flights with birding outings and naturalist talks.

SALT LAKE CITY SPORTS

When the IOC voted in June 1995 to give the 2002 Winter Games to Salt Lake City, Utah's capital and its roughly 1.5 million residents became the largest city to ever host a Winter Games. Salt Lake City will boast the largest sports program to date for a Winter Games, with 7 sports, 15 disciplines and 78 medal events. New to Winter Games are women's bobsleigh, men's and women's skeleton, men's and women's 1500-meter short-track speed skating, men's Nordic combined sprint, men's and women's cross-country skiing sprint, and men's and women's biathlon pursuit.

Northern Utah   America's railroad heritage is celebrated at Golden Spike National Historic Site during the **Wedding of the Rails Anniversary and Commemoration**, when the driving of the golden spike that symbolically tied the transcontinental rail line together is re-enacted.

Salt Lake Valley   The Pony Express is recalled at **Simpson Springs** during a re-enactment of the horse-powered mail system, while the **Utah Arts Festival** arrives in downtown Salt Lake City. Runners head for the **Salt Lake City Classic**, which features both 5K and 10K road races.

JUNE

Northeastern Utah   The **Northern Utah Indian Pow Wow** is held at Fort Duchesne on the Uintah and Ouray Indian Reservation. Sponsored by the Northern Ute Tribe, the pow-wow includes traditional dance and drum contests.

Statewide   Bigger than the Fourth of July celebration in Utah is July 24th's **"Days of '47"** celebration, also known as **Utah Pioneer Day**, which commemorates the arrival of Brigham Young and his followers in the Salt Lake Valley on July 24, 1847.

JULY

Salt Lake Valley   Jazz aficionados head into the mountains to attend the **Jazz and Blues Festival** at Snowbird Ski and Summer Resort. In conjunction with the "Days of '47" celebration is the **Deseret News Marathon and 10K** races, which cut through the heart of Salt Lake City. Antelope Island is taken over by cyclists during the **Moonlight Bike Ride** across the causeway that ties the island to the state.

Northern Utah   The **Cache Valley Cruise-In** lures some of the hottest cars, hot rods, motorcycles and trucks in the West to Logan for a long weekend of activities such as the Broom Sweep, in which drivers hang a broom out their windows to sweep balls along the road. The **Utah Festival Opera Company** opens shop with three classic operas that are performed at Logan's Ellen Eccles Theater. Staged several times a week, the shows continue on a revolving basis into August.

Northeastern Utah   The **Oakley Rodeo**, the best little rodeo in Utah, brings members of the Professional Rodeo Cowboy Association to this sleepy Summit County community in the days leading up to the Fourth of July. The **Utah Symphony** fills the mountains with music when it begins its summer run of performances in the open-air, slope-side band shell at Deer Valley Resort.

Statewide   County fairs abound during this summer month.

AUGUST

Salt Lake Valley   Belly dancing, not skiing or snowboarding, is the focus at Snowbird Ski and Summer Resort when the **Utah Belly Dance Festival** opens its doors.

Northern Utah   Raspberries are served up in shakes, jams and pancakes during **Bear Lake Raspberry Days** at Garden City on the shores of Bear Lake. The **Festival of the American West** near Wellsville recalls and re-enacts the Old West, featuring the **World Championship Dutch Oven Cookoff**. The **Annual Railroaders Festival**, offering steam-locomotive demonstrations, is held at the Golden Spike National Historic Site on the second Saturday in August.

Northeastern Utah   The ski town turns into an arts colony when Park City hosts the **Park City Arts Festival**, luring artists, craftsmen and thousands of shoppers looking for bargains. Bluegrass wafts through the air at Deer Valley Resort during the **Folk and Bluegrass Festival**. The **Park City International Jazz Festival** also begins at Deer Valley Resort this month.

SEPTEMBER   **Salt Lake Valley**   The **Utah State Fair** sets up shop at Salt Lake City's state fairgrounds for ten days of pie contests, flower contests, rides and other fair-related activities. The city's **Greek Festival** offers ethnic foods, dancing and crafts. The Bonneville Salt Flats turn into the world's fastest race course when the **World of Speed** is staged. Oom-pah bands, brauts and beer are in abundance at Snowbird Ski and Summer Resort during **Oktoberfest**, held weekends through the month and into October.

Northern Utah   Harvest time means it's time for Brigham City's **Peach Days Festival**, Utah's oldest continuing harvest festival, with a parade, an antique car show, a Dutch-oven cookoff and a carnival.

Northeastern Utah   The hamlet of Midway in the Heber Valley recalls its heritage with the **Swiss Days** festival, which features authentic Scandinavian foods, music and dancing.

OCTOBER   **Salt Lake Valley**   Cowboys head to Antelope Island for the **Bison Roundup**. At historic Gardner Village in West Jordan you'll find the **Scarecrow Festival**, which offers pumpkin sales and decoration exhibits. The **Scottish Festival**, featuring traditional music, food and dancing, comes to Salt Lake City.

Northern Utah   To celebrate the coming of fall, Logan stages its **Pumpkin Walk**. Just south of Logan the American West Heritage Center offers a **corn maze**.

Northeastern Utah   The **Great Pumpkin Festival** is held in Jensen's town park in time for Halloween.

NOVEMBER   **Statewide**   If the snow gods are willing, the state's **ski resorts** start to open.

Salt Lake Valley   The Christmas holidays can't be far off once the **Temple Square Holiday Lights** are lit during Thanksgiving weekend.

Northeastern Utah   Wine lovers head to Deer Valley Resort for the **Beaujolais Festival,** when the season's favorite is paired with some of the tastiest foods found in ski country. Deer Valley is also the setting for the **Navajo Rug Show,** a charitable event that raises money for the Adopt-a-Native Elder program on the Navajo Indian Reservation. Christmas lights that have been strung throughout the **Dinosaur Gardens** at Vernal's Utah Field House are turned on late in the month. Barring unseasonably warm weather, the Park City Mountain Resort hosts the **America's Opening World Cup** ski races.

Salt Lake Valley   Salt Lake City stages its **First Night** New Year's Eve celebration in the heart of downtown with entertainment and fireworks. The **Dickens Festival** makes its week-long run at the Utah State Fairgrounds in Salt Lake City, complete with roaming characters out of Charles Dickens' best-known works. The **Winterfest** celebration at Snowbird Ski and Summer Resort features the country's best wines, beers and foods over a weekend of cooking seminars. The **Nutcracker** is a seasonal mainstay of the Ballet West troupe, which performs the Christmas classic in the Capitol Theater.

DECEMBER

Northern Utah   Over at Golden Spike National Historic Site west of Brigham City the **Railroad Film Festival and Winter Steam Train Demonstrations** are staged between Christmas and New Year's Day. **Elk Feeding** begins at the Hardware Ranch located near the head of Blacksmith Fork Canyon south of Logan. Once the snow covers the ground, sleigh rides are conducted through the refuge.

Northeastern Utah   In Helper the **Electric Light Parade** revolves around an evening parade through downtown to celebrate the season with lighted floats.

HEIDEN'S HAUL

An unforgettable performance at the 1980 Winter Games in Lake Placid was American Eric Heiden's haul of five gold medals in speed skating (500-, 1000-, 1500-, 5000- and 10,000-meter races)—more than half the eight medals the U.S. contingent won. Heiden's performance was the most productive for an individual athlete in any Olympics, winter or summer. While American Mark Spitz returned home from the 1972 Summer Games with seven gold medals in swimming, three of those were won in relay events. Heiden's achievement was even more impressive when you consider that in previous Winter Olympic history Americans had won but eleven gold medals, and Heiden needed just ten days to win five.

Before You Go

VISITORS CENTERS

Free visitor information packages, which include guides to accommodations throughout the state, a state highway map and details to special events, can be obtained by contacting the **Utah Travel Council**. ~ Council Hall, Salt Lake City, UT 84114; 801-538-1030, 800-200-1160, fax 801-538-1399. Much of the information is also available at the council's web site: www.utah.com.

A good place to go for Games-related information is the organizing committee's website, **www.saltlake2002.com**, where you can find a rundown on the events and venues and find links for tickets and lodging.

Another great resource is the **Visitor Information Services Coalition** (VIS), an amalgamation of chamber bureaus and tourist-related entities from around the state. VIS is also a clearinghouse for accommodations, so if you're looking for lodging this is a great place to start. ~ 888-222-5562; www.saltlakeinfo.org.

Northern Utah is divided into five travel regions. You can obtain detailed information from their respective websites and offices.

The **Golden Spike Empire** covers a portion of northern Utah, including the cities of Ogden and Brigham City. ~ 2501 Wall Avenue, Ogden, UT 84401; 801-627-8288, 800-255-8825; www.ogdencvb.org, e-mail info@ogdencvb.org.

Bridgerland comprises the rest of northern Utah, including Logan and Bear Lake. ~ 160 North Main Street, Logan, UT 84321; 435-752-2161, 800-882-4433; www.bridgerland.com, e-mail btr@sunrem.com.

Great Salt Lake Country encompasses Salt Lake City and the Bonneville Salt Flats. ~ 90 South West Temple Street, Salt Lake City, UT 84101; 801-521-2822, 800-541-4955; www.slc.org, e-mail slcvb@saltlakecvb.com.

Mountainland covers Park City, Provo and Heber City. ~ 586 East 800 North, Orem, UT 84097; 801-229-3800.

Dinosaurland entails northeastern Utah, including Vernal, Flaming Gorge National Recreation Area and Dinosaur National Monument. ~ 25 East Main Street, Vernal, UT 84078; 435-789-6932, 800-477-5558; www.dinoland.com, e-mail dinoland@easilink.com.

PACKING

Packing for a trip to Utah is pretty easy. While winter requires a suitcase packed with clothes you can wear in layers—sweaters, shirts and undershirts that wick sweat away from your body; fleece shirts, jackets and pants to wear under outer shell garments while skiing; gloves and headwear—come summer short-sleeved shirts, casual slacks, jeans and shorts will get you by. Men might want to add a sports jacket to their attire and women a nice dress or smart-looking ensemble for dinners at some of the capital's trendier restaurants.

In general, though, Utahns are an informal lot, as typified by "Park City formal." What's that? Jeans go very well with your tuxedo jacket, thank you very much. For the most part, Utahns are either dressed to play, to go to church, or somewhere in between. There's no need for a coat and tie in the state.

Cool temperatures often lull newcomers into forgetting that thin, high-altitude air filters out far less of the sun's ultraviolet rays; above timberline, exposed, unprotected skin will sunburn faster than it would on a Hawaiian beach.

Other essentials to pack or buy along the way include a good sunscreen, high-quality sunglasses, and a wide-brimmed hat.

For outdoor activities, tough-soled hiking boots are more comfortable than running shoes on slickrock. Don't forget cycling shorts and shirts, a hydration system and a fanny pack or daypack if you plan to bike or hike. You'd be wise to pack some light rain gear as well, to deal with the sudden cloudbursts that tend to punctuate northern Utah's summer afternoons. Even RV travelers and those who prefer to spend most nights in motels may want to take along a backpacking tent and sleeping bag in case the urge to sleep under the starry skies becomes irresistible. A canteen, first-aid kit, flashlight and other routine camping gear are also likely to come in handy. Both cross-country and downhill ski rentals are available in resort areas during the winter. In summer, mountain bikes replace skis in most of the rental shops. Other outdoor recreation equipment—canoes, fishing tackle, golf clubs— can be rented, too.

A camera, of course, is essential for capturing your travel experience; of equal importance is a good pair of binoculars to bring wildlife up close or merely pan distant landscapes from scenic overlooks. And don't, for heaven's sake, forget your copy of *Hidden Salt Lake City & Beyond*.

LODGING

Utah accommodations run the gamut from tiny one-room cabins to luxury resorts that blend traditional alpine-lodge ambience with contemporary elegance. Bed-and-breakfast establishments are found in most of the larger or more tourist-oriented towns, and even in some more remote locations such as Vernal. Typical of the genre are lovingly restored Victorian-era mansions comfortably furnished with period decor; these usually have fewer than a half-dozen rooms.

The abundance of motels in towns along all major highway corridors presents a range of choices, from name-brand motor inns to traditional ma-and-pa establishments that have endured for the half-century since motels became a part of American culture. While ordinary motels in the vicinity of major tourist destinations can be pricey, lodgings in small towns away from major resorts and interstate routes can offer friendliness, quietude and comfort at ridiculously low rates.

At the other end of the price spectrum, high-season (winter) rates in Park City, Snowbird and Alta can be frightfully exorbitant. These resort areas justify an "ultra-ultra-deluxe" notation on prices, as choice properties can command tariffs upwards of $1000 a night, particularly over Christmas week and Presidents' Day weekend. At the same time, a number of new hotels in Salt Lake City can deliver quite a blow to your budget, with year-round room rates starting at $150 a night and quickly moving past $200.

Whatever your preference and budget, you can probably find something to suit your taste. Just remember that rooms can be scarce and prices may rise during peak season, which is summer in most of the state, Park City and the Cottonwood Canyons during winter. Travelers planning to visit a place in peak season should either make advance bookings or arrive early in the day, before the No Vacancy signs start lighting up.

Lodging prices in this book focus on high-season rates; you can expect lesser rates during the off-season. *Budget* hostelries generally run less than $55 per night for two people and are clean but modest. *Moderate* motels and hotels range from $55–$100; what they have to offer in the way of luxury often depends on their location, but they usually have larger rooms and more attractive surroundings than their budget counterparts. For *deluxe*-priced accommodations, expect to spend between $100 and $150 for a homey bed and breakfast or a double in a hotel or resort; you'll commonly find spacious rooms, a fashionable lobby, a restaurant and often a bar or nightclub. *Ultra-deluxe* facilities, priced above $150, are among the finest in the state, offering all the amenities of a deluxe hotel, plenty of extras and great locations; these places for the most part are limited to Utah's ski resort areas and the heart of Salt Lake City's downtown.

As noted above, there are *ultra-ultra-deluxe* accommodations in Park City and at Snowbird and Alta that surpass $500 a night and can even go beyond $1000.

DOLLAR-SAVING TIPS

To save money, consider avoiding ski trips during Christmas, New Year's and Presidents' Day weekend, or stay in more affordable lodging in Salt Lake City. Also good to know is that resorts offer multiday ticket packages that are cheaper than buying a series of day tickets, and that early-season lodging packages often offer free or reduced-price skiing privileges. Another way to save money on ski trips is to come early or late in the season. Summer is much more affordable in Utah's ski country, as accommodations are in surplus and room rates often drop to less than half the winter rates.

Room rates vary as much with locale as with quality. Some of the trendier destinations have no rooms at all in the budget price range. In other communities and small towns, just about every motel falls into the budget category.

DINING

Utah offers a delicious spectrum of possibilities, ranging from regional cuisine such as beef and trout to elaborate creations utilizing seafood and wild game. Most cities have Italian, Mexican and Chinese restaurants, and you can choose from a wide selection of gourmet foods in Salt Lake City, Ogden, Logan and Park City. If your idea of an ideal vacation includes savoring epicurean delights, then by all means seize the opportunity whenever it arises.

One Utah staple that seems to appear on most menus is Utah trout; another is rack of lamb. In northern Utah during the summer and fall, fresh fruits and berries from the region appear in desserts.

Restaurants listed in this book offer lunch and dinner unless otherwise noted. Dinner entrées at *budget* eateries cost $12 or less. The ambience is informal, service usually speedy and the crowd often a local one. *Moderate*-priced restaurant entrées range between $12 and $21 at dinner; surroundings are casual but pleasant, the pace slower, and the menu more varied than at budget restaurants. *Deluxe* establishments tab their entrées from $21; presentation is typically sophisticated, decor plusher and the service more personalized than at moderate-priced restaurants.

Restaurants in resort towns often close for a period during the off-season. And because restaurants change hands often, efforts have been made in this book to include places with established reputations. Compared to evening dinners, breakfast and lunch menus vary less in price from restaurant to restaurant.

LIQUOR

Utah's conservatism has led to somewhat confusing liquor laws, in which you need a membership (essentially a cover charge good for two weeks) to enter a private club that serves hard liquor. There are "beer bars," though, where you don't need a membership to quaff a brew, and most restaurants have liquor licenses that allow you to enjoy a drink with your meal.

Wherever you drink, however, it's illegal in Utah to nurse two drinks (such as a shot of whiskey and a beer chaser) at the same time.

Smoking, which is banned in most buildings throughout Utah, *is* allowed within private clubs. As a result, you can expect a smoky environment in these establishments.

DRIVING

Utah is a rugged state and there are some important things to remember when driving. Its 84,916 square miles present a wide variety of road conditions, from Salt Lake City's heavy interstate traffic typical of that found in East and West Coast urban areas, to narrow, twisting mountain roads leading to the ski resorts, to long, straight stretches of highway through the Great Salt Lake Desert and central portions of the state that can be dangerously mesmerizing. Mountainous areas in the northern part of the state can be potentially hazardous for inattentive or inexperienced drivers.

In the mountains, don't be surprised by the lack of guardrails separating motorists from precipitous dropoffs. The fact is, highway safety studies have found that far fewer accidents occur where there are no guardrails. Statistically, edgy, winding mountain roads are much safer than straight, fast interstate highways.

In winter it is wise to travel with a shovel, gravel or cat litter for traction, blankets or sleeping bags, and a long-burning candle in your car.

Unpaved roads are another story. While many are wide and well-graded, weather and/or the wear and tear of heavy seasonal use can create unexpected road conditions. Some U.S. Forest Service and Bureau of Land Management roads are designated for four-wheel-drive or high-clearance vehicles only. If you see a sign indicating four-wheel-drive only, believe it. These roads can be very dangerous in a standard passenger car without the high ground clearance and extra traction afforded by four-wheel drive . . . and there may be no safe place to turn around if you get stuck.

Away from the heavily urbanized Wasatch Front, many roads—interstates and state highways alike—take you far from civilization, so be sure to have a full radiator and a tank of gas. If you're heading into the rugged outback of the San Rafael Swell or the West Desert, it's a good idea to carry extra fuel, food and water. Should you become stuck, local people are usually helpful, offering stranded vehicles assistance, but in case no one else is around, a CB radio or car phone is a handy travel companion for long back-country drives. Don't place too much faith in cell phones, as coverage can be spotty.

Utah gets its share of snow in the winter months—upwards of 500 inches in some places. Mountain passes frequently become snow-packed or suffer from ground blizzards. Under these conditions, tire chains are always advised, even on main highways. State patrol officers may make you turn back if your car is not equipped with chains or four-wheel drive. At the very least, studded tires are recommended.

The maximum speed limit on interstate highways is 75 miles per hour, while on other roads limits typically range from 55 to 65 mph, and 35 or even 25 mph in construction zones. Violators are subject to fines, of course.

You can get full information on statewide road conditions for Utah any time of the year by calling 800-492-2400. You may also contact the Utah Highway Patrol at 801-965-4505.

Any place that has cowboys and Indians, rocks to climb and limitless room to run is bound to be a hit with youngsters. Plenty of family adventures await in Utah, from tackling rivers and hiking through the backcountry to rockhounding and visiting manmade attractions. A few guidelines will help make travel with children easier.

TRAVELING WITH CHILDREN

Book reservations in advance, making sure that the places you stay accept children. Many bed and breakfasts do not. If you need a crib or extra cot, arrange for it ahead of time. A travel agent can be of help here, as well as with most other travel plans.

If you are traveling by air, try to reserve bulkhead seats, where there is plenty of room. Take along extras you may need, such as diapers, changes of clothing, snacks and toys or small games. When traveling by car, be sure to take along the extras, too. Pack plenty of water and juices to drink; dehydration can be a subtle but serious problem. Most towns, as well as some national parks, have stores that carry diapers, baby food, snacks and other essentials, though they usually close early. Larger towns often have all-night groceries or convenience stores.

A first-aid kit is a must for any trip. Along with adhesive bandages and antiseptic and anti-itch creams, include any medicines your pediatrician might recommend to treat allergies, colds, diarrhea or any chronic problems your child may have.

Utah's sunshine is intense. Take extra care by using sunscreen or sunblock with an SPF of 15 or higher, long-sleeve shirts and wide-brimmed hats. Children's skin is usually more tender than adult skin and can burn severely before you realize it.

Parts of Utah can be harsh and unforgiving—on pets as well as humans. While kennels exist throughout the state for boarding your animals overnight, and some lodgings even permit your pets in your room, it's best to leave your pets behind at home. That said, pets are permitted on leashes in virtually all campgrounds.

TRAVELING WITH PETS

Make sure the dog gets adequate shade, ventilation and water. Fortunately, dogs are free to run everywhere else in national forests, and leashes are required only in designated camping and picnic areas.

Wildlife such as mountain lions can pose special hazards in the backcountry of northern Utah. While there are no grizzly bears in the state, there are black bears that, if sufficiently provoked, may attack dogs. Porcupines, common in conifer forests, are tempting to chase and slow enough to catch, but if you dog latches on to one of them, a mouthful of quills means painfully pulling them out one by one with pliers, or making an emergency visit to a veterinary clinic in the nearest town.

Text continued on page 26.

Winter Games Rundown

The modern Olympic Games date to 1896, when Frenchman Pierre de Coubertin pulled together a global group of sport and philosophy leaders (the forerunners of the International Olympic Committee) who agreed to have a modern Games similar to those held in ancient Greece. But a winter version didn't debut until 1924, when the IOC decided to make a trial run at staging a Winter Olympics. Those Games were held in Chamonix, France, and attracted 258 athletes from 16 countries. Here are some highlights of past Winter Games.

- Charles Jewtraw won America's first gold medal in Winter Olympic competition at the 1924 Chamonix Games when he won the 500-meter speed-skating race. He covered the distance in 44 seconds, a far cry from today's world record of 34.32 seconds.

- American William Fiske was just 16 years old at the 1928 Games in St. Moritz, but that didn't prevent him from claiming the bobsleigh gold medal. Fiske returned to win another gold at the 1932 Games. During World War II he joined the Royal Air Force as a pilot and became the first American pilot to die during the conflict when he was shot down on August 16, 1940.

- The U.S. hosted its first Winter Games in 1932 when the tiny upstate New York hamlet of Lake Placid staged the third Olympic Winter Games. The Games, the first held outside of Europe, gave the U.S. an opportunity to shake off the blues of the Depression; it spent three-quarters of a million dollars to ready Lake Placid for the athletes. The most popular event in these Games was the bobsleigh, which drew 14,000 spectators.

- Canada's ice hockey team was dealt a blow at the 1936 Games in Garmisch-Partenkirchen when it lost the gold medal to a British team that included eight players who, although born in Britain, lived and played hockey in Canada. Also in 1936, Norway's Sonja Henie won her third, and last, gold medal in figure skating, having previously won gold at the 1928 and 1932 Games.

- The 1948 Winter Games were staged in St. Moritz, Switzerland. Choosing the site was relatively easy for the IOC—due to Switzerland's neutrality during World War II, the country, and St. Moritz, did not suffer from bombing raids during the war. Evidence that politics influence sports, neither Germany nor Japan were invited to these Games.

- Dick Button, well-known today for his TV commentary during figure-skating competitions, was propelled to stardom by the 1948 Games. He won the men's figure-skating title with a performance that featured the Olympic debut of the "double axel."

- When the 1956 Winter Games opened in Italy at Cortina d'Ampezzo, the Soviet Union made an impressive first appearance in international winter sports competitions, winning 16 medals. American men swept the medals in the figure-skating competition: Hayes Jenkins won gold, Ronald Robertson silver, and David Jenkins, Hayes' younger brother, bronze.

- When the IOC awarded the 1960 Games to Squaw Valley, it boosted the number of medal sports by adding women's speed skating and biathlon to the event list. Bobsleigh, however, wasn't conducted because the organizing committee couldn't justify spending three-quarters of a million dollars on a track. Though St. Moritz, Lake Placid and Garmisch-Partenkirchen offered to stage the event, the IOC opted to cancel bobsleigh for these Games.

- When the 1964 Winter Games opened in Innsbruck, Austria, luge was introduced on the medal list. Sadly, these Games also witnessed tragedy: unusually warm weather and poor snow cover played a role in the deaths of an Australian alpine skier as well as a British bobsleigh athlete.

- Proving that you *can* go home again, the IOC decided that the 1980 Winter Games should return to picturesque Lake Placid. It was at these Games that the U.S. men's hockey team performed the "Miracle on Ice" by defeating the powerful Russian team for the gold medal.

- A Soviet athlete claimed three gold medals at the Lake Placid Games. Nikolai Zinjatov won both the 30K and 50K races and was a member of the Soviet Union's 4 x 10K relay race.

- Ice dancing infused sensuality to the 1984 Sarajevo Games when the British team of Jayne Torvill and Christopher Dean used the music of *Bolero* as a backdrop to their steamy gold-medal performance. Their dance recounted a story of lovers who jumped into a lava pit rather than spend life apart.

- American speedskater Bonnie Blair won the 500-meter gold medal in three consecutive games—1988, 1992 and 1994. Her gold medals in the 500- and 1000-meter races at the 1992 Games in Albertville, France, made Blair the first American woman to win three gold medals in Winter Games competition.

- Bulgaria finally had an athlete win a Winter Olympics gold medal in 1998 when biathlete Yekaterina Dafovska won the 15K individual event.

- During Georg Hackl's successful run for gold in men's luge at the 1998 Nagano Games, the U.S. and Canadian teams filed a protest, arguing that the German was wearing a new boot that was not available to other athletes. The protest, which was denied, claimed the boot also was illegal in that its angle made it more aerodynamic than boots worn by other lugers.

**GAY &
LESBIAN
TRAVELERS**
The rugged beauty of Utah is appealing to many: the wide open spaces stretching for miles and miles and the sprawling mountains invite people who are looking to get away from it all. It's a state that gives people a lot of space, literally, and encourages you to do your own thing, which allows gays or lesbian travelers to feel comfortable here.

That notwithstanding, Utah is a conservative state and has no openly gay communities. Information and support on gay and lesbian issues in Utah, however, can be obtained from the **Gay and Lesbian Community Center of Utah** in Salt Lake City. ~ 361 North 300 West; 801-539-8800.

**WOMEN
TRAVELING
ALONE**
Traveling solo grants an independence and freedom different from that of traveling with a partner, but single travelers are more vulnerable to crime and should take additional precautions.

While Utah's crime rate is lower than those found in more urbanized states, don't let that give you a false sense of security or override common sense. It's unwise to hitchhike and probably best to avoid inexpensive accommodations on the outskirts of town; the money saved does not outweigh the risk. Bed and breakfasts and youth hostels are generally your safest bet for lodging, and they also foster an environment ideal for bonding with fellow travelers.

Keep all valuables well-hidden and hold onto cameras and purses. Avoid late-night treks or strolls through questionable sections of town, but if you find yourself in this situation, continue walking with a confident air until you reach a safe haven. A fierce scowl never hurts.

These hints should by no means deter you from seeking out adventure. Wherever you go, stay alert, use your common sense and trust your instincts.

If you are hassled or threatened in some way, never be afraid to scream for assistance. It's a good idea to carry change for a phone call and a number to call in a case of emergency. For more hints, get a copy of *Safety and Security for Women Who Travel* (Travelers Tales, 1998).

**SENIOR
TRAVELERS**
Utah is a hospitable place for older vacationers. Many private sightseeing attractions give significant discounts to seniors.

The **American Association of Retired Persons** (AARP) offers membership to anyone over 50. AARP's benefits include travel discounts with a number of firms. ~ 601 E Street NW, Washington, DC 20049; 800-424-3410; www.aarp.org.

Elderhostel provides educational courses that are all-inclusive packages at colleges and universities, some in Utah. ~ 11 Avenue de Lafayette, Boston, MA 02111; 877-426-8056, fax 617-426-0701; www.elderhostel.org.

Be extra careful about health matters. In Utah's changeable climate and elevation, seniors are more at risk for suffering hypothermia. High altitudes may present a risk to persons with heart or respiratory conditions; ask your physician for advice when planning your trip. Also, Utah's summers can be quite hot, with temperatures surpassing 100°F, so it's important to drink plenty of water and avoid hiking during the height of the day.

In addition to the medications you ordinarily use, it's a good idea to bring along the prescriptions for obtaining more. Consider carrying a medical record with you, including your history and current medical status as well as your doctor's name, phone and address. Make sure that your insurance covers you while you are away from home.

DISABLED TRAVELERS

Utah is striving to make public areas fully accessible to persons with disabilities. Parking spaces and restroom facilities for the handicapped are provided according to both state law and national park regulations.

There are many organizations offering information for travelers with disabilities, including the **Society for the Advancement of Travel for the Handicapped** (SATH) at 347 5th Avenue, Suite 610, New York, NY, 10016, 212-447-7284, fax 212-725-8253, www.sath.org; and the **MossRehab ResourceNet** at MossRehab Hospital, 1200 West Tabor Road, Philadelphia, PA 19141, 215-456-9600, www.mossresourcenet.org.

For general travel advice, contact **Travelin' Talk**, a networking organization. ~ P.O. Box 1796, Wheat Ridge, CO 80034; 303-232-2979; www.travelintalk.net. **Access-Able Travel Source** provides traveling information online. ~ www.access-able.com.

> The emphasis on strong family values and large families explains why Utah claims one of the largest birth-rates in the U.S.

FOREIGN TRAVELERS

Passports and Visas   Most foreign visitors need a passport and tourist visa to enter the United States. Contact your nearest U.S. Embassy or Consulate well in advance to obtain a visa and to check on any other entry requirements.

Customs Requirements   Foreign travelers are allowed to carry in the following: 200 cigarettes (1 carton), 50 cigars or 2 kilograms (4.4 pounds) of smoking tobacco; one liter of alcohol for personal use only (you must be 21 years of age to bring in alcohol); and US$100 worth of duty-free gifts that can include an additional quantity of 100 cigars. You may bring in any amount of currency, but must fill out a form if you bring in over US$10,000. Carry any prescription drugs in clearly marked containers (you may have to produce a written prescription or doctor's statement for the customs officer). Meat or meat products, seeds, plants, fruits and narcotics are not allowed to be brought into the United States. Contact the **United States Customs Service** for further information. ~ 1300 Pennsylvania Avenue NW, Washington, DC 20229; 202-927-6724; www.customs.treas.gov.

Driving   If you plan to rent a car, an international driver's license should be obtained before arriving in the United States. Some car-rental agencies require both a foreign license and an international driver's license. Many also require a lessee to be at least 25 years of age; all require a major credit card. Seat belts are mandatory for the driver and all passengers. Children under the age of five or under 40 pounds should be in the back seat in approved child-safety restraints.

Currency   United States money is based on the dollar. Bills come in denominations of $1, $2, $5, $10, $20, $50 and $100. Every dollar is divided into 100 cents. Coins are the penny (1 cent), nickel (5 cents), dime (10 cents), quarter (25 cents), half-dollar (50 cents) and dollar, although half-dollar and dollar coins are rarely used. You may not use foreign currency to purchase goods and services in the United States. Consider buying traveler's checks in dollar amounts. You may also use credit cards affiliated with an American company, such as Interbank, Barclay Card, VISA and American Express.

Electricity and Electronics   Electric outlets use currents of 110 volts, 60 cycles. To operate appliances made for other electrical systems, you need a transformer or other adapter. Travelers who use laptop computers for telecommunications should be aware that modem configurations for U.S. telephone systems may be different from their European counterparts. Similarly, the U.S. format for videotapes is different from that in Europe; National Park Service visitors centers and other stores that sell souvenir videos often have them available in European format on request.

Weights and Measures   The United States uses the English system of weights and measures. American units and their metric equivalents are: 1 inch = 2.5 centimeters; 1 foot (12 inches) = 0.3 meter; 1 yard (3 feet) = 0.9 meter; 1 mile (5280 feet) = 1.6 kilometers; 1 ounce = 28 grams; 1 pound (16 ounces) = 0.45 kilogram; 1 quart (liquid) = 0.9 liter.

Outdoor Adventures

CAMPING

Tent or RV camping is a great way to tour Utah's national and state parks and forests during the spring, summer and fall months. Besides probably saving substantial sums of money, campers enjoy the freedom to watch sunsets from beautiful places, spend nights under spectacular starry skies, and wake up to find themselves in lovely surroundings that few hotels can match.

It's not hard to find a place to pitch your tent or park your RV. Plus, most towns have some sort of commercial RV park, and long-term mobile-home parks often rent spaces to RVers by the night. But unless you absolutely need cable television, none of these places can compete with the wide array of public campgrounds available in government-administered sites.

Federal campgrounds are typically less developed; you usually won't find electric, water or sewer hookups in campgrounds at national forests, monuments or recreation areas. However, Utah state parks feature a wide range of campsites, from rustic sites with no amenities to campgrounds with RV hookups, showers and electricity.

For a list of state parks with camping facilities, contact **Utah State Parks and Recreation**. ~ 1634 West North Temple, Suite 116, Salt Lake City; 801-538-7221, 800-322-3770. For information on camping in Utah's national forests, contact **National Forest Service-Intermountain Region**. ~ 2501 Wall Avenue, Ogden; 801-625-5306; www.fs.fed.us/r4. Camping and reservation information for national parks, monuments and recreation areas is available from the parks and monuments listed in this book or from the **National Park Service–Rocky Mountain Regional Headquarters**. ~ P.O. Box 25287, Denver, CO 80225; 303-969-2000. For information on camping in public lands administered by the **Bureau of Land Management**, contact the BLM's Salt Lake office. ~ 324 South State Street, Suite 301, Salt Lake City; 801-539-4001.

Roughly 65 percent of Utah is owned by the federal government, either in the form of a national park, monument or forest, or lands overseen by the U.S. Bureau of Land Management.

Fishing, camping, boating and hunting are allowed on the roughly four-and-a-half-million-acre **Uintah and Ouray Indian Reservation** in northeastern Utah. For information and permits, contact the Northern Ute Indian Tribe's Fish and Wildlife Office. ~ P.O. Box 190, Fort Duchesne, UT 84026; 435-722-5511.

Tent camping is allowed in the backcountry of all national forests except in a few areas where signs are posted prohibiting it. You may need a permit to hike or camp in national forest wilderness areas, so contact specific forests for more information. Ranger stations provide trail maps and advice on current conditions and fire regulations. In dry seasons, emergency rules may prohibit campfires and sometimes ban cigarette smoking, with stiff enforcement penalties.

For backcountry hiking in national parks and monuments, you must first obtain a permit from the ranger at the front desk in the visitors center. The permit procedure is simple, although there might be a nominal fee. The permit system helps park administrators measure the impact on sensitive ecosystems and distribute use evenly among major trails to prevent overcrowding.

PERMITS

Text continued on page 32.

Alpine Gold

Although alpine ski events didn't arrive on the Winter Olympics scene until the 1936 Games in Garmisch-Partenkirchen, Germany, and then only with the Nordic combined event, these ski events quickly captured the public's attention. They revolved around speed and were spectator-friendly and easily understood. Down through the years many of the Games' memorable events were played out on the slopes.

- In 1952 the Winter Games headed to Oslo, Norway, where a Norwegian skier, who years later would be highly visible in Salt Lake City's Olympic efforts, rose to fame. Stein Eriksen, the son of an Olympic gymnast, reached the pinnacle of Olympic skiing when he won both a gold and a silver medal in the Oslo Games.

- Austria's Anton "Toni" Sailer won gold in the men's downhill, giant slalom and slalom at the 1956 Winter Games in Italy at Cortina d'Ampezzo—the first athlete to claim first place in all three events.

- A developer was behind the IOC's decision to stage the VIII Olympic Winter Games in the United States. Alec Cushion was on a ski vacation in California when he became enamored with the mountains along the California–Nevada border. After buying some of the land, he got the U.S. Olympic Committee to make the little-known community of Squaw Valley the U.S. candidate for the 1960 Winter Games.

- At the 1964 Games in Innsbruck, Austria, skiers Billy Kid and Jimmie Heuga rose to prominence by claiming the U.S.'s first alpine skiing medals. Norway's Sixten Jernberg concluded his Olympic career at the 1964 Games, where he won the gold medal in the 50K cross-country race. During that career Jernberg collected nine medals—four golds, three silvers and two bronzes.

- Frenchman Jean-Claude Killy became just the second athlete in Winter Olympic history to sweep the gold medals in the downhill, giant slalom and slalom races at the 1968 Grenoble Games.

- Sapporo, Japan, made history in 1972 when it became the first Asian city to host a Winter Games. Japanese athletes rose to the occasion, too: Yukio Kasaya, Akitsugu Konno and Kiyogi Aochi won gold, silver and bronze in the 70-meter ski jump.

- Spain finally won an Olympic gold medal when Francisco Fernandez Ochoa won the men's slalom ski race at Sapporo.

- Bill Koch, a little-known Vermonter, made U.S. Olympic history at the 1976 Games in Innsbruck when he won the silver medal in the 30K cross-country race. It was the first time in 12 Olympics that an American had won a cross-country medal. "We knew the American was strong, but we were surprised to see him finish second," said Ivan Garanin of the Soviet Union, who won the bronze medal.

- American twins Phil and Steve Mahre won gold and silver, respectively, in the men's slalom race at the 1984 Sarajevo Games. Cocky Bill Johnson gave the American delegation another gold medal when he won the downhill.

- Italian Alberto Tomba used the Calgary Games in 1988 to launch himself to the top of the alpine ski world, winning gold in both the slalom and giant slalom races. His slalom victory over West Germany's Frank Woerndl by just six-hundredths of a second marked the closest men's slalom race in Olympic history.

- Kenya, which is not normally known for its snow, sent an athlete to the Winter Games in Nagano in 1998. Phillip Boit competed in the 10K cross-country race ... and finished last, 20 minutes behind gold medalist Bjorn Daehlie of Norway.

- Italy's Deborah Compagnoni became the first alpine skier to win gold medals in three Olympics when she won the giant slalom at the Nagano Games.

- Fifty years after Norway's Thorleif Haug won the bronze medal in ski jumping at the Chamonix Games, a scoring mistake was discovered that cost him that medal. The corrected score moved American Ander Haugen, who was 83 years old in 1974, into third place. He received his medal in a special ceremony in Oslo, Norway.

BOATING   Most of Utah's large lakes are surrounded by corresponding state parks, where you can find a campground and boat ramp, as well as fish-cleaning stations. State boating regulations can be obtained from the **Utah State Parks and Recreation**. ~ 1594 West North Temple, Suite 116, Salt Lake City, UT 84114; 801-538-7220; www.nr.state.ut.us. Aside from Lake Powell in the Glen Canyon National Recreation Area, lakeside boat rentals in Utah can be hard to find, although they are available at Great Salt Lake, Utah Lake and Flaming Gorge National Recreation Area. Two good web sites with Utah boating information are www.utahrec.com and www.boatingutah.com.

River rafting is a very popular sport in northeastern Utah, notably on the Green and Yampa rivers. Independent rafters, kayakers and canoeists are welcome once they obtain permits from the Bureau of Land Management or National Park Service, but because of the bulky equipment and specialized knowledge of river hazards involved, most adventurous souls stick with group trips offered by any of the many rafting companies located in Green River and Jensen. Rafters, as well as people using canoes, kayaks, windsurfers or inner tubes, are required by state and federal regulations to wear life jackets.

FISHING   In a land as arid as Utah, many residents have an irresistible fascination with water. During the warm months, especially on weekends, lake shores and readily accessible portions of streams are often packed with anglers. Vacationers can beat the crowds to some extent by planning their fishing days during the week.

Utah fish hatcheries keep busy stocking streams with trout, particularly rainbows, the most popular game fish throughout the West. The larger reservoirs feature an assortment of sport fish, including crappie, carp, white bass, smallmouth bass, largemouth bass and walleye pike.

For copies of state fishing regulations, inquire at a local fishing supply store or marina. Utah's regulations can also be obtained by contacting the **Utah Division of Wildlife Resources**. ~ 1596 West North Temple, Salt Lake City; 801-538-4700; www.nr.state.ut.us.

State fishing licenses are required for fishing in national parks and recreation areas, but not on Indian reservations, where daily permits are sold by the tribal governments.

WINTER SPORTS   In winter, downhill and cross-country skiing are all very popular. Utah has 14 downhill ski resorts; the largest are the Park City Mountain Resort, The Canyons and Snowbasin Resort, all within an hour's drive of Salt Lake City. There are seven commercially run cross-country trail systems in the state, as well as countless miles of trails that weave through national forests. Maps and brochures are available from the **Utah State Parks and Recreation**. Information on Utah's ski resorts can be obtained from the resorts listed throughout this book, or from **Ski Utah**. ~ 150 West 500 South, Salt Lake City; 801-534-1779; www.skiutah.com, www. rideutah.com.

GUIDES & OUTFITTERS

The best way to assure the reliability of the folks guiding you into the wilderness by horse, raft or cross-country skis is to choose someone who has met the standards of a statewide organization of their peers. For a membership list, contact the **Utah Guides and Outfitters Association**. ~ 775 Dahlia Street, Denver, CO 80220; 303-333-5781, fax 303-333-6218; www.utahguidesand outfitter.com. A comprehensive list of guides, outfitters and dude ranches is available from the **Utah Travel Council**. ~ Council Hall, Salt Lake City; 801-538-1030, 800-200-1160; www.utah.com.

TWO

Salt Lake Valley

Gazing out across the Salt Lake Valley today, it's hard to envision the rugged wilderness that confronted Brigham Young in late July of 1847 when he and 147 pilgrims arrived in search of a nourishing land where they could enjoy religious freedom. Where scrub-covered foothills once rambled and fingers of creeks drained out of the overshadowing Wasatch Mountains, there now stands a thriving metropolis with residential neighborhoods, a business core, industrial sectors and a supporting infrastructure of bridges and highways. Stretching north and south of Salt Lake City proper, chains of smaller communities that were once isolated islands now bind the Wasatch Front in a sea of suburbia from Ogden south through Salt Lake City and on to Provo and Orem.

While young, wiry Pony Express riders once blazed a trail westward towards Sacramento, Route 80, a ribbon of interstate highway that runs into the setting sun, now leads the way west. On its way, the interstate squeezes between the alkaline southern shores of the Great Salt Lake and the northern tip of Tooele, once a ranching and mining outpost that now serves as a bedroom community to Utah's capital, before cutting the desolate Great Salt Lake Desert and the Bonneville Salt Flats in half.

Today's metropolis of Salt Lake City in large part is testament to the industrious nature of Brigham Young and his followers. It's said that on the very day that they reached the valley—July 24, 1847—they dug into the soil and planted gardens, and soon thereafter laid out the checkerboard grid that would become their city.

Not all was milk and honey for the pilgrims, though—the U.S. Cavalry arrived in Salt Lake City during the Civil War. (President Lincoln, worried that Young, his growing church and the fledgling Utah Territory would side with the Confederates, dispatched the troops.) While the war never reached Utah, the soldiers' presence left an indelible mark on the state as they roamed into the canyons surrounding Salt Lake City in search of valuable ores. Their successes not only spawned the state's mining industry, but also lured thousands of non-LDS settlers to Utah.

These days the sprawling Salt Lake Valley harbors roughly three-quarters of Utah's 2.2 million residents, making the 84,990-square-mile state one of the nation's most urban—an ironic distinction in a land of open spaces, rugged canyons and lofty mountain peaks. The valley is home to the world-wide headquarters of the Church of Jesus Christ of Latter-day Saints and the University of Utah, the state's flagship public institution of higher education, and is *the* cultural center on the western flanks of the Rocky Mountains.

As much as the city and its embracing valley invest in business through hard work and entrepreneurship, more than a few of their residents make their homes here because of the recreational cornucopia that lies minutes away. Seven alpine resorts and six wilderness areas lie within an hour's drive of downtown, while the canyons gnawed into the Wasatch Range by time and weather offer some of the region's finest climbing and hiking routes. The Provo River is a renowned trout stream, one of the state's best, and the number of golf courses in the valley suggest that links, not skiing, should be the unofficial state sport.

Salt Lake City

As the rising sun's rays crest the Wasatch Mountains in north-central Utah, they illuminate the "New West" metropolis of Salt Lake City. Hard against the mountains' rumpled flanks, with the Great Salt Lake shimmering just off to the west, Utah's capital is an evolving educational, financial, technological and cultural center determined to capture and reflect the vibrancy of the Rocky Mountain West.

Salt Lake's future certainly seems boundless with the hard-work mentality that has produced one of the nation's best business climates. It's a city with an envious quality of life thanks to the surrounding mountains, visiting Broadway shows, resident ballet and symphony, and professional sports. It's a city that, after hosting the world during the 2002 Olympic Winter Games, aspires to become the recognized winter training grounds for the western United States.

While Salt Lake City was conceived by the LDS Church, it is not a one-religion enclave. In fact, only about half of the city's population is Mormon. The rich diversity is found not only in the other religions that have footholds through churches in the city, but in the wide array of cuisines served in the city's restaurants, in the global student body population at the University of Utah, and in the cultural offerings that highlight the nightlife throughout the year.

The Salt Lake Valley can easily be split in two, with Salt Lake City a world of its own and the burgeoning southern half of the valley, with its chic ski resorts and restaurants, a land of its own.

SIGHTS

Hand-hewn from a high-desert wilderness in the mid-1800s by religious refugees seeking Zion, Salt Lake City rapidly evolved from a far-flung outpost into a bustling Western city. Between the 1850s and the early 1900s, Salt Lake City grew rapidly and beautifully as architects drew from the latest vogues sweeping the eastern half of the country. Many of these ornate and elaborate buildings remain, salted among more contemporary high-rises.

HIDDEN ▶ Not far north of downtown is **The Children's Museum of Utah**, a fun, hands-on museum with dozens and dozens of kid-delighting interactive exhibits. Along with displaying more than 400 artifacts from around the state, the museum offers workshops and performances spanning the arts, sciences and humanities. Late in 2001 the museum is scheduled to move into the Gateway Center (see "Shopping" below). Closed Sunday. Admission. ~ 840 North 300 West; 801-328-3383, fax 801-328-3384; www.child museum.org.

Utah's **Capitol Building** arose in 1915 and was designed to resemble the nation's capitol. The dome carries an outer layer of copper, while inside the rotunda is laid with Georgia marble. Standing within recessed alcoves in the rotunda are important figures from Utah's past, while the walls hold murals reflecting the state's trapper and explorer history. Tours are offered daily. ~ 400 North State Street; 801-538-3000.

Today, across the street to the south of the capitol, you'll find **Council Hall**. But back in 1866, when it was built to house the city council and serve as the territorial capitol, the structure was located several blocks to the south. In the 1960s the sandstone block building was dismantled and moved north to its present location. Today the 60-foot-square structure houses the **Utah Travel Council**. Information on state and national parks and forests can be obtained here. There's also a natural-history bookstore inside. ~ 300 North State Street; 801-538-1030, 800-200-1160.

A nice morning, afternoon or evening stroll can be had by heading up **City Creek Canyon** just northeast of the capitol. At the mouth of the canyon lies Memory Grove, which pays tribute to the men and women from Utah who served in the country's military forces. Individual memorials to World War I, World War II, Vietnam and other conflicts, as well as a meditation chapel, are surrounded by grassy lawns that border City Creek. Following the paved road north through Memorial Grove will take you deeper into City Creek Canyon, which offers hiking and biking trails as well as picnic grounds. The canyon is open to vehicles on even-numbered days and legal holidays, open to bikes on odd-numbered days, and opened to pedestrians every day. ~ Approximately 250 North Canyon Road; 801-483-6797.

The **Pioneer Memorial Museum**, overseen by the local chapter of Daughters of Utah Pioneers, provides a broad picture of Utah and pioneer history. While the second floor offers a wonderful collection of dolls, the basement tugs at the hearts of military historians with its exhibit of uniforms and weapons. In the carriage house, reached through a subterranean passage, 19th-century

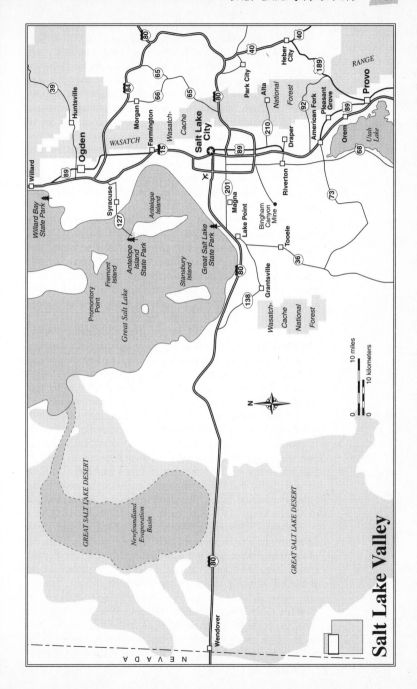

Salt Lake Valley

wagons, sleighs and surreys are on display, as is a blacksmith shop and a late-1800s fire engine. Closed Sunday except from June through August. ~ 300 North Main Street; 801-538-1050.

Just as the Vatican in Rome is the spiritual center for Catholics, **Temple Square** in Salt Lake City is the heart of the Latter-day Saints religion. Located at the geographic center of the city, this is where Brigham Young's home, the church's administrative buildings, elaborate temple, tabernacle, and history and archives are located. While only faithful church members may enter the temple, the other buildings are open to visitors. The one-block by two-block area makes for a wonderful day-long or half-day tour. With five million visitors a year, Temple Square is Utah's biggest tourist attraction. Please see "Walking Tour" for details. ~ 50 West North Temple; 801-240-2534.

A quick stroll northeast from Eagle Gate leads to the one-acre **Brigham Young Historic Park**, which honors Young for his work as a pioneer, settler, territorial governor and head of the LDS Church. An oval-shaped pathway circles a small grassy area and leads past exhibits showing how the Mormons tamed the arid state with innovative irrigation systems, cut rock from nearby canyons for their buildings, and funneled streams with wooden flumes to millworks. ~ 50 North 2nd Avenue.

A short walk east on 1st Avenue leads to **Mormon Pioneer Memorial Monument**, a small, tidy graveyard that is the final resting place of Brigham Young and several other Mormon pioneers and church leaders. Rising just inside the grounds is "All is Well," a statue of a pioneer husband and wife with their daughter that stands as a tribute to all Utah settlers. ~ 140 East 1st Avenue.

Societal stature wasn't overlooked in Salt Lake City, as evidenced by the stuffy **Alta Club** located across from Temple Square. Founded in 1883 by prominent Utah businessmen, the members'-only club continues to flourish. The Italian Renaissance architecture was in keeping with the style of East Coast men's clubs of the day. While the Alta Club initially excluded members of the Latter-day Saints Church, that slight vanished with the arrival of the 20th century. ~ 100 East South Temple; 801-322-1081.

Although Mormonism is Utah's predominant religion, it's by no means the only religion practiced in the state. The **Cathedral of the Madeleine**, located just a few blocks east of Temple Square, was built by the Roman Catholic Church. Construction on the church's Romanesque exterior began in 1900 and was finished nine years later; the interior, a rich Spanish Gothic environment reflective of the late Middle Ages, was completed in 1918. Lining the walls of the towering cathedral are beautiful, two-story-tall stained-glass windows made in Munich. While bat gargoyles jut from the exterior walls just below the roof line, the interior shows off masterful woodwork, frescoes and an intricate tabernacle. Today the ornate structure is included on the National Register of Historic Places. The church is open daily, and 45-minute tours are offered Friday and Sunday afternoons. ~ 331 East South Temple; 801-328-8941.

The **Governor's Mansion**, also known as the Kearns Mansion, is a Chateauesque-influenced limestone mansion built in 1902 for Thomas Kearns, who made his fortune in mining and later served in the U.S. Senate. The mansion, now the governor's official residence, is bookended by twin, three-story circular towers. Built into the home are vaults for both jewelry and wine. Tours are offered Tuesday and Thursday afternoons from April through November. ~ 603 East South Temple Street; 801-538-1005.

Amateur astrologists enjoy the **Hansen Planetarium**. Housed in a building that began life in 1905 as the Salt Lake City Public Library, the planetarium offers tours of the heavens and a hands-on space science museum children enjoy. Admission. ~ 15 South

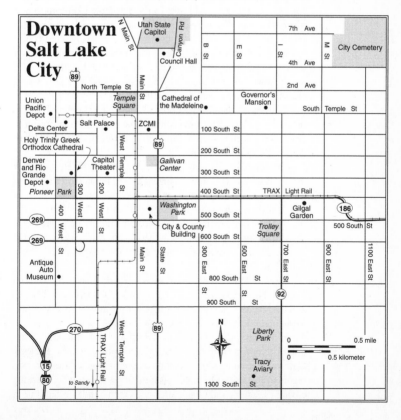

State Street; 801-538-2104, fax 801-531-4948; www.hansen planetarium.com.

To peer into Salt Lake City's past, descend into the **Social Hall Heritage Museum**, a subterranean gallery that houses the remains of Utah's first public building—a 350-seat Greek Revival theater. Displayed behind glass walls are sections of the building's walls and other artifacts found on the site in 1990 during excavations for a walkway passing beneath State Street. The walkway is open throughout the day; tours can be arranged by appointment. ~ 39 South State Street; 801-321-8745.

Some of the West's best music can be heard in the **Maurice Abravanel Concert Hall**. The spacious hall is a lasting legacy to the memory of the Greek-born Abravanel, who long conducted the Utah Symphony. Built in 1976, the hall is renowned for its impeccable acoustics. ~ 123 West South Temple; 801-355-2787, 888-451-2787.

The **Salt Palace Convention Center** is the lifeblood of the city's convention industry and home to the **Salt Lake Convention and Visitors Bureau**. The bureau contains rack after rack after rack of brochures and pamphlets highlighting Salt Lake City's and Utah's tourist attractions, lodgings and restaurants. Also available is a walking-tour guide that encompasses the entire downtown. ~ 90 South West Temple; 801-521-2822, fax 801-355-9323; www. visitsaltlake.com, e-mail slcvb@saltlake.org.

Adjacent to the visitors bureau is the **Salt Lake Art Center**, a two-story gallery displaying some of the best artworks from the city and the region. ~ 20 South West Temple; 801-328-4201, fax 801-322-4323.

City officials refer to it as "19th-century street furniture," but most folks see it as simply an ornate **clock**. Erected on the south-western corner of 100 South and Main Street in 1873, the four-faced clock was initially powered by a water wheel beneath the street. Then large springs that had to be wound once a week enabled it to keep time. Finally, in 1912, the clock was wired for electricity, which continues to drive it nowadays. ~ 100 South and Main Street.

Built in 1913 to entertain growing Salt Lake City, today's **Capitol Theater** was originally known as the Orpheum Theater and trod regularly by vaudeville acts. It now hosts a variety of per-formances. ~ 50 West 200 South; 801-323-6800.

HIDDEN ►   In the basement of the Holy Trinity Greek Orthodox Cathe-dral, Utah's Greek immigrants are remembered at the **Hellenic Cultural Museum**, which documents their struggles and achieve-ments in the state. On display is a mining exhibit, videos, ethnic costumes, letters and Greek artifacts. Open Sunday after church and Wednesday from 9 a.m. to noon or by appointment. ~ 279 South 300 West; 801-359-4163.

A small cultural and recreational oasis in the heart of the city, the **Gallivan Center** boasts an ice-skating rink, a pond, water fountains, grassy areas, an aviary, an outdoor chess board with three-foot-tall pieces, artworks and a 1000-seat amphitheater. ~ 239 South Main Street; 801-532-0459, fax 801-521-8329.

When riding the rails was a popular form of public transportation, the **Denver and Rio Grande Depot** was the jumping-off point in Salt Lake City. Located on the west side of downtown, this sprawling depot was designed as the crown jewel of the Denver and Rio Grande and Western Pacific railroads. A blend of Renaissance Revival and Beaux Arts classicism architecture, the depot cost $750,000 when it was built in 1910. Since 1981 the depot has housed the **Utah State Historical Society**, which sponsors a permanent exhibit on Utah history and a variety of revolving exhibits. Also inside the depot is the **Utah History Information Center**, a public research facility that contains a wealth of information on Utah and the West in general. Closed Sunday. ~ 300 South 455 West; 801-533-3500 (museum), 801-533-3535 (information center), fax 801-533-3503; www.history.utah.org.

One of Salt Lake City's most famous and statuesque landmarks is the **Salt Lake City and County Building**, which dates to the early 1890s and is thought to be located on the grounds where Brigham Young and his followers first camped in 1847 when they

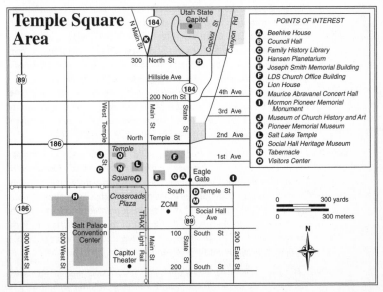

Temple Square Area

POINTS OF INTEREST

Ⓐ Beehive House
Ⓑ Council Hall
Ⓒ Family History Library
Ⓓ Hansen Planetarium
Ⓔ Joseph Smith Memorial Building
Ⓕ LDS Church Office Building
Ⓖ Lion House
Ⓗ Maurice Abravanel Concert Hall
Ⓘ Mormon Pioneer Memorial Monument
Ⓙ Museum of Church History and Art
Ⓚ Pioneer Memorial Museum
Ⓛ Salt Lake Temple
Ⓜ Social Hall Heritage Museum
Ⓝ Tabernacle
Ⓞ Visitors Center

Text continued on page 44.

Temple Square

For a taste of the state's history, and to behold the beauty held in some of the most gorgeous flower gardens in Utah, nothing compares with Temple Square. In an area running just one block north to south and two blocks east to west is a rich collection of modern and beautifully restored historic buildings.

MUSEUM OF CHURCH HISTORY AND ART   This building, located across from the northwestern corner of Temple Square, is where questions about the history of the LDS Church can be answered. Inside you'll find a gallery honoring the church's past presidents, exhibits detailing the plight of Brigham Young and his followers who fled to Utah to leave behind religious intolerance, and pioneer artifacts. ~ 45 North West Temple; 801-240-3310.

FAMILY HISTORY LIBRARY   Just south of the church museum, this facility houses one of the world's best genealogical libraries. Within its extensive computerized collections are hundreds of millions of families. The collections are open to public use and guides stand ready to help you get started. Closed Sunday. ~ 35 North West Temple; 801-240-2331.

TEMPLE SQUARE   Across the street to the east of the library is historic Temple Square, the heart of the LDS Church and Utah's number-one tourist attraction. Covering ten downtown acres, the square contains the six-spired **Salt Lake Temple** and the **Tabernacle** that serves as the backdrop for the Mormon Tabernacle Choir. The temple is open only to church members in good standing. In the 8000-seat tabernacle, choir rehearsals on Thursday evenings are open to the public, as are the Sunday morning performances. Spring and summer are the best times to visit the square, which is covered with fragrant flower gardens and pools, cascades and fountains of water. Tours of the square are offered daily. ~ 50 West North Temple; 801-240-2534, 801-537-9703.

ASSEMBLY HALL   Constructed between 1877 and 1880 as a meeting hall, the hall was built from leftover granite taken from Little Cottonwood Canyon for the Salt Lake Temple. Essentially a miniature tabernacle, the building houses a 650-pipe organ. Inside the benches and columns, which are original, are made from white pine but painted, in the case of the benches, to resemble oak, and in the case of the columns, marble. Today the building continues to serve as a meeting place and host concerts. ~ 50 West North Temple; 801-240-2534.

JOSEPH SMITH MEMORIAL BUILDING   Continue east along South Temple Street and you'll come to this building, where more history on the LDS Church and its followers is available. There are free, regular showings of *The Testaments,* a large-format (think IMAX) church documentary film tracing the Mormons' flight to Utah. The building was originally the Hotel Utah. The front doors open to the old hotel's massive lobby, complete with marble pillars holding up the second-floor balcony with its ornately carved railing. There is also a genealogical center for the public to research their family history. The tenth floor holds two restaurants. Closed Sunday. ~ 15 East South Temple; 801-240-1266.

LION HOUSE   This adobe-block building a block and a half east of the memorial building was built in 1855 for Brigham Young and his extensive family. Young, who was married to more than two dozen women, partitioned the home according to whether his wives had children: The main floor was reserved for mothers and their children, the second for Young's childless wives, and the third for children. Young died here in 1877 from appendicitis. The home's name stems from the statute of a lion resting atop the front portico. There are no tours of the home, but a restaurant located in the building's original kitchen and dining room on the lower level is open to the public for cafeteria-style lunches (Monday through Saturday) and dinners (Friday and Saturday). ~ 63 East South Temple; 801-363-5466.

BEEHIVE HOUSE   Just east and adjacent to Young's home is the Beehive House, which he used as his official residence when he was president of the Mormon Church and governor of the Utah Territory. The church used the house for its headquarters until 1917. The house's name stems from the wooden beehive that sits atop the roof as a testament to the hard-working nature of Utah's pioneers. Listed on the National Register of Historic Places, tours of the house and its pioneer furnishings are offered daily. ~ 67 East South Temple; 801-240-2671.

LDS CHURCH OFFICE BUILDING   On the north end of the block, separated from the Lion and Beehive houses by lush, colorful gardens, this 28-story building has some of the best views of Salt Lake City. The base of world-wide operations for the church, the office building is the tallest structure in Salt Lake City. Observation decks on the 26th floor offer panoramic views of both the Wasatch Range and the Salt Lake Valley. Tours of the church's beautiful gardens start here. ~ 50 East North Temple; 801-240-2190.

EAGLE GATE   Spanning State Street and South Temple just south of the Beehive and Lion houses, this arch was originally erected in 1859 to serve as the entrance to Brigham Young's home. The first eagle to perch atop the archway was carved from wood. The current eagle is bronze, weighs 4000 pounds and has a wingspan of 20 feet. ~ State Street and South Temple.

reached the valley. Exquisitely detailed carvings of Indian chiefs, Spanish explorers and pioneers grace the building's exterior, while inside there are 40 fireplaces with polished marble hearths. In the late 1980s a massive renovation, driven by fears that the Wasatch Fault that passes beneath Salt Lake City was primed for a jolt, saw the installation of hundreds of "base isolators" that would act something like shock absorbers during a quake; the entire building had to be severed from its foundation and jacked up in order to put in the isolators. Today the building houses the offices of the mayor and the city council. Closed weekends. ~ 451 South State Street; 801-535-6333.

In an earlier day **Trolley Square** held the barns that housed the city's trolley fleet. Dating to 1907, the barns marked the beginning and the end of the day for nearly 150 trolley cars that rolled through the city, powered by overhead electrical cables. Today the site holds an eclectic array of antique shops, restaurants, boutiques and theaters. ~ 602 East 500 South; 801-521-9877.

HIDDEN ► One of the city's most eclectic pieces of backyard art can be found at **Gilgal Garden**, which occupies a small, half-acre lot hidden away in downtown Salt Lake City. The site contains a collection of sculptures created by the late Thomas Child, an LDS stonemason who used quartz and granite to turn his yard into a memorial of sorts to the church. The likeness of Mormon founder Joseph Smith's face can be found atop a sphinx's body, while quotes from Emerson, Sophocles and Brigham Young can be seen inscribed into pavement stones. ~ 749 East 500 South.

Car buffs will want to head to the west side of town for a tour of the **Antique Auto Museum,** home to 100 or so automobile antiques and classics, such as a 1926 Pierce-Arrow Roadster convertible and a 1926 Stutz Bearcat. The museum, run by Classic Cars International, donates its admission price to the Utah Boys Ranch. Closed Sunday. Admission. ~ 355 West 700 South; 801-322-5509.

Not far south of the heart of the downtown area lies **Liberty Park** with its 16 wooded acres, the **Chase Home Museum of Utah Folkart,** and the **Tracy Aviary** (801-596-8500), where more than 240 species of birds from around the world are on display. The park also contains tennis courts, jogging paths, a children's playground and a small lake with paddle boats. An unusual attraction is the **Seven Canyons Fountain**, which covers an acre and depicts a section of the Wasatch Front. Each of the front's canyons is labeled and water flowing from the fountain represents the streams that cut the canyons. ~ 600 East 1300 South.

Franklin Covey Field just might offer the most picturesque setting of any baseball stadium in the country. Home to the Salt Lake Stingers of the Triple-A Pacific Coast League, the stadium faces the craggy Wasatch Range, which must be an intoxicating view difficult for opposing batters to ignore when they step up to the plate. ~ 77 West 1300 South; 801-485-3800.

LODGING

From sumptuous hotels and historic bed and breakfasts to resort complexes and chain properties, Salt Lake City and its suburbs offer more than 17,500 beds. The arrival of light rail in the downtown area in 1999 and the 2002 Olympic Winter Games combined to spur the revival of some historic properties and the debut of new properties. Some of these newer properties are quite elaborate in terms of furnishings and amenities, so be prepared to pay a bit extra to stay at them.

◄ HIDDEN

A piece of Salt Lake City's history has been preserved in the **Saltair Bed and Breakfast**, a quaint Victorian home that once belonged to Fortunato Anselmo, an Italian vice counsel for Utah and Wyoming. Due to his diplomatic role, Anselmo's home was considered to stand on foreign soil, and so while Prohibition shut down most breweries and wineries in the country, he continued to make *vino* in his basement. In addition to five rooms in the house, there is a two-bedroom bungalow and two cottages that sleep up to four. Gay-friendly. ~ 164 South 900 East; 801-533-8184, 800-733-8184, fax 801-595-0332; www.saltlakebandb.com, e-mail saltair@saltlakebandb.com. DELUXE TO ULTRA-DELUXE.

The **Anton Boxrud Bed and Breakfast** lies within Salt Lake City's historic district, located just a half-block from the governor's mansion. Built in 1901 (and largely maintained in that style), the home might be too stuffy for children, but adults appreciate the hand-woven lace works, polished wood trims and columns, and thick terry robes. Complementing seven bedrooms (five with private baths) is a parlor fireplace to relax next to, a hot tub out back surrounded by a grape arbor for slow simmering, and a covered porch in front for watching the world go by. Gay-friendly. ~ 57 South 600 East; 801-363-8035, 800-524-5511, fax 801-596-1316; www.bbiu.org/antonbox rud, e-mail antonboxrud@home.com. MODERATE TO DELUXE.

Of the 50 U.S. states, Utah boasts the healthiest population and the second lowest death rate.

The **Inn on Capitol Hill** is on the National Historic Register and dates to 1906, when it was built for a doctor who worked for the Union Pacific Railroad. A large, sprawling, four-story brick home—some would call it a mansion—on a hillside, the inn's 13 guest rooms reflect a different aspect of Utah's early days. One room honors the Ute Indians, another the state's mountain men, and still another the railroad era. A full breakfast is included. ~ 225 North State Street; 801-575-1112, 888-884-3466, fax 801-933-4957; www.utahinn.com, e-mail reservations@utahinn.com. DELUXE TO ULTRA-DELUXE.

Text continued on page 48.

The Great
Salt Lake

Jim Bridger thought he had reached the Pacific Ocean when he stumbled upon the Great Salt Lake in the early 1800s. Considering the saltiness of the water, that's probably not too surprising. A remnant of the prehistoric Lake Bonneville that covered 20,000 square miles in parts of today's Utah, Idaho and Nevada, the Great Salt Lake takes in the water from four rivers and numerous creeks and streams.

Outside of the Great Lakes, the lake is America's largest inland body of water, measuring 92 miles north to south and 48 miles east to west. Despite its size, the lake has an average depth of just 13 feet.

Its saltiness, which makes it impossible for swimmers to sink, is attributed to the fact that the lake has no outlets and thereby collects all the salts and minerals washed into it by rivers and streams. Due to fluctuations in annual precipitation and the resulting runoff from the mountains, the lake's salinity changes from year to year. It has ranged from a low of 5.5 percent all the way up to 27.3 percent.

The water level also varies greatly. In 1963, when the lake reached its recorded low, eight of the ten islands were landlocked. In 1983, when high snowfalls and rainfalls pushed the lake up 12 feet, the waters submerged access to Antelope Island and threatened to flood portions of Salt Lake City and Ogden. In response to the rising waters the state installed huge pumps on the lake's western shores to shunt some of the waters into the West Desert.

Although the rise and fall of the lake's waters have deterred development along the shoreline, the wetlands that wrap the lake make it a key stop-over for migratory birds. Between two and five million feathered creatures enjoy the marshes, relishing the feast of brine shrimp and a variety of insects. Among the birds you might see are white pelicans, snowy plovers, eared grebes, bank swallows, bald eagles and peregrine falcons.

Of the lake's ten islands, **Antelope Island** is the largest, covering 28,463 acres. Reached via a seven-and-a-half-mile-long causeway extending from Syracuse, a small community 30 miles north of Salt Lake City via Route 15, the island today is a state park with sandy beaches, rugged mountain trails and a resident herd of roughly 700 bison descended from a small number introduced in 1893. Mixing with the shaggy buffalo are mule deer, big-horn sheep and pronghorn antelope. ~ From Salt Lake City, take Route 15 north for 16 miles to Exit 335, then west 14 miles to the island; 801-773-2941.

Mormons first explored Antelope Island in 1848, a year after reaching the Salt Lake Valley. Among the initial explorers was Fielding Garr, who returned later that year to establish a ranch near freshwater springs on the southeastern edge of the island. The ranch went on to become one of the West's largest, with 10,000 sheep once roaming Antelope Island.

Today the **Garr Ranch** is a time capsule preserving late-19th- and 20th-century ranching practices. The few buildings that remain housed the ranch superintendent's family and the hired hands; during the winter months potbelly stoves and fireplaces warmed both the main house and the bunkhouse. The main house (the oldest pioneer structure in Utah still in its original location) is an interesting amalgamation of architecture, as it was built in three phases. The first two stages involved adobe bricks made on the island; the third employed concrete blocks. Nearby, the 1880s spring house kept meats and milk from spoiling under the hot summer sun. Across the yard is the blacksmith's shop, which stayed busy keeping the horses shod and the ranch equipment running. ~ 4528 West 1700 South, Syracuse; 801-773-2941; parks.ut.us/parks/ www1/ante.htm.

Antelope Island offers mile after mile of cycling terrain for both road bikes and mountain bikes. The nine-mile-long White Rock Bay Loop offers a scenic ride for mountain bikers, who will curse the uphills on the way out but enjoy the downhills on the return. Road bikers are frequently seen on the seven-and-a-half-mile causeway that links the island to the mainland, and the six-mile-long loop around the northern end of the island is good for family rides. Late each summer cyclists flock to the causeway to tour "Antelope By Moonlight," an invigorating ride out and back across the causeway that starts at 10 p.m.

Twenty minutes west of Salt Lake City by car, the lake is readily accessed at both Antelope Island State Park and Great Salt Lake State Park.

Arriving in the heart of downtown Salt Lake City in late 2000, the **Salt Lake City Marriott City Center** packs 359 rooms, 15 meeting rooms, a restaurant, a lounge, an indoor pool and a health club into its 12 stories. The guest rooms are complete with data-port phones, speaker phones and safes. Minutes away are such attractions as Temple Square, the Delta Center and countless restaurants. ~ 220 South State Street; 801-961-8700, 800-228-9290, fax 801-961-8703; www.marriotthotels.com. ULTRA-DELUXE.

The Hilton hotel chain is represented by the **Hilton Salt Lake City Center**, an 18-story downtown complex with 499 rooms, 24,000 square feet of meeting space, and two restaurants. Along with a complimentary continental breakfast, the Hilton sets out complimentary evening hors d'oeuvres that include fresh fruits, cheeses and desserts. The second-floor business center offers computers, fax machines and copiers. There's also a heated indoor pool, saunas and a fitness center with free weights and stationary bikes. ~ 255 South West Temple; 801-328-2000, fax 801-238-4888. ULTRA-DELUXE.

The **New Peery Hotel**, which first opened its doors in 1910 and is listed on the National Register of Historic Places, today has something of a European feel, with rich carpeting and period furnishings throughout. There are basically two varieties of rooms —smallish queen rooms and deluxe king, double queen and suite rooms. The latter three feature separate parlor areas with plush couches, armoires and coffee tables. All rooms boast canopy beds and furnishings carrying early-20th-century lines. Although a bit off the city's beaten path these days, when it first opened the hotel easily handled railway passengers arriving in the nearby Rio Grande train depot. Located near the heart of downtown, the Peery is close to the Capitol Theater, Abravanel Hall and the Salt Palace Convention Center, as well as Temple Square. The hotel features a workout room and two restaurants. Gay-friendly. ~

AUTHOR FAVORITE

Traveling on business can be a lonely mission, a malady the 230-room **Hotel Monaco** tries to cure by offering you a "loaner" goldfish for your room. While the fish are nice, what I really like about the hotel are its eclectic furnishings as well as its great location in downtown Salt Lake City. Across the street is the Capitol Theater with its Broadway shows, and barely two blocks away is Abravanel Hall with its concerts. You don't need to look far for a meal, either—the Bambara Restaurant is just down the hall from the hotel lobby. ~ 15 West 200 South; 801-595-0000, 877-294-9710, fax 801-532-8500; www.monaco-saltlakecity.com. DELUXE TO ULTRA-DELUXE.

110 West 300 South; 801-521-4300, 800-331-0073, fax 801-575-5014; www.peeryhotel.com. DELUXE TO ULTRA-DELUXE.

Little America Hotel and Towers long has been a Salt Lake City mainstay. Although owned by the same company that owns the Snowbasin ski resort, the site of the downhill and Super-G races for the 2002 Olympic Winter Games, the hotel and its 850 rooms and suites might be a bit much for ski vacationers. When you spend your days on the slopes, do you really need data-port phones and work desks? Still, the Italian marble baths are nice for an après-ski or -hike soak, and downstairs you'll find a full-service restaurant, coffee shop and lounge. ~ 500 South Main Street; 801-363-6781, 800-453-9450, fax 801-596-5911; www.littleamerica.com. MODERATE TO ULTRA-DELUXE.

No room at Little America? Then head across the street to the **Grand America Hotel**, a lavish lodging that in mid-2001 became the flagship property of the Little America chain of hotels dotting Wyoming, Utah and Arizona. Five years in the making, the Grand America offers the most sumptuous accommodations in Utah. Owner Earl Holding, who also owns Idaho's Sun Valley resort and the Snowbasin ski resort that will host the downhill and Super-G ski races during the 2002 Salt Lake Games, spared no expense in building the Grand America on a 20-acre parcel in downtown Salt Lake City. Though stuffy looking from the street, inside the Grand America is opulent. Holding handpicked the Italian marble from Italy and white Vermont granite that are used freely throughout the 24-story hotel, as well as the centuries-old tapestries draping some of its walls and the crystal chandeliers hanging from its ceilings. The hotel has its own butcher shop and bakery, guaranteeing the freshest meals possible. Of course, these materials and amenities didn't come cheaply, and neither will your room. Rates start at $235 and run to $4,500 for one of the 3000-square-foot presidential suites. ~ 555 South Main Street; 801-258-6000, 800-533-3525; www.grandamerica.com. ULTRA-DELUXE.

Standing between Temple Square and the Salt Palace Convention Center, **The Inn at Temple Square** is an elegant time capsule in the heart of downtown, just a short walk from Salt Lake City's cultural mainstays and shopping district. The 90 rooms and suites offer a mix of traditional elegance with modern conveniences. Four-poster beds are standard, as are comfy robes. A plus for the health-conscious is the hotel's strict no-smoking policy; guests are asked to sign a pledge not to smoke within the hotel. ~ 71 West South Temple; 801-531-1000, 800-843-4668, fax 801-536-7272; www.theinn.com. DELUXE TO ULTRA-DELUXE.

Another downtown lodging mainstay is **West Coast Salt Lake Hotel**, which offers nearly 400 rooms within walking distance of the Salt Palace Convention Center, Abravanel Hall, the Capitol Theater and even Temple Square. The tastefully decorated rooms come with either queen- or king-sized beds and balconies, some with sweeping views of the Wasatch Range. You'll also find a swimming pool, a fitness center, a business center, two restaurants and two lounges on the premises. ~ 161 West 600 South; 801-521-7373, 800-325-4000, fax 801-524-0354; www.coasthotels.com. MODERATE TO DELUXE.

The **Crystal Inn** is on the southern edge of the heart of downtown. Its 175 rooms are larger than most competitors' and feature either a king- or queen-sized bed. Its rates include a hot buffet breakfast, free airport shuttle, and an indoor pool with hot tub and fitness facility. Rooms are partitioned to provide a sitting area and come with microwave ovens and refrigerators. ~ 230 West 500 South; 801-328-4466, 800-366-4466, fax 801-328-4072; www.crystalinns.com. MODERATE TO DELUXE.

Got a tight budget but want to stay close to downtown but not on a park bench? Try the **Avenues Hostel**. This no-frills hostel located just five blocks from Temple Square delivers warm, dry rooms with wood-frame bunks and mattresses. You can opt for a spot in the dormitory and use the shared bathrooms, or go after one of the private rooms with their own bathrooms. Beyond the sleeping space, the hostel offers two complete kitchens, an outdoor kitchen with a grill, and two living rooms, one of which holds a large-screen TV and a fireplace. Not only are local phone calls free, but there's a computer with internet access for guests, and they'll pick up from the airport for just $10. Needless to say, this place is popular with the budget-conscious, and reservations are highly recommended for the winter and summer seasons. ~ 107 F Street; 801-359-3855, fax 801-532-0182; www.hostels.com/slchostel. BUDGET.

Another clean, inexpensive and generally no-frills place to hang your hat is the **Ute Hostel**. Located in a converted store, the hostelry is a relatively short walk from downtown and offers free transportation from the airport, Amtrak station or Greyhound bus depot. The hostel also can arrange ski, bike or even golf club

HEAVENLY VOICES

The Mormon Tabernacle Choir claims its roots in the hardy pioneers who flocked west with Brigham Young in search of a land where they could practice their religion without persecution. At night the church members would raise their voices to the heavens around their campfires. A month after Brigham Young led his followers into the Salt Lake Valley the Tabernacle Choir was officially formed. The dome-shaped Tabernacle was first used in 1867. Its acoustics are so fine that it's said you can hear a pin dropped 170 feet away.

rentals for you. The dorm rooms all share a bathroom, but what did you expect for $15 a night? There's also kitchen facilities, and both smoking and no-smoking common areas. ~ 21 East Kelsey Avenue; 801-595-1645; www.infobytes.com/utehostel, e-mail ute hostel@infobytes.com. BUDGET.

Salt Lake City's dining scene befits a metropolitan city. In fact, while Denverites might take exception to the claim, some Salt Lake chefs will tell you that Utah's capital has become the Rocky Mountains' culinary capital. Interspersed among the traditional standard-American eateries is a highly diverse range of international flavors, including Middle Eastern, Spanish, French, Japanese, Mexican, Chinese, Indian and more. You can dine in elegance or show up after a day on the slopes or the golf course without changing your attire.

DINING

The **Blue Iguana** serves up a wide range of Mexican dishes, but is particularly known for its *moles*. Ensconced in a below-street-level nook on a back alley next door to the Dead Goat Saloon and not far from the Capitol Theater, the restaurant's list of *moles* ranges from the green chile *verde* and nuts and habaneros chile *amarillo* to the chocolate-based *negro* and *de almendras*, an almond *mole*. ~ Arrow Press Square, 165 South West Temple; 801-533-8900, fax 801-531-6690; www.blueiguana.citysearch.com, e-mail blueiguana@deadgoat.com. BUDGET TO MODERATE.

◀ HIDDEN

Prominent in Salt Lake City's old hotel district, the **New Yorker** cuts some of the city's best steaks and offers lamb, veal and seafood, too. The setting is out of the city's railroading heyday, with thick leaded-glass windows, mirrors on the salmon-hued walls that hold framed covers of *New Yorker* magazine covers, and linen-draped tables. The only drawback is it's a private club (which lets non-members in with a temporary membership for a nominal fee) that can get smoky at times. Closed Sunday. ~ 60 West Market Street; 801-363-0166, fax 801-363-0588; www.gastron omyinc.com. MODERATE TO DELUXE.

The dining experience at the **Market Street Grill** is a step into the past: the restaurant tries to maintain a 1930s ambience with blond-wood wainscoting, a long counter, and black-and-white checkered flooring. The menu is heavy with seafood, such as crab-stuffed shrimp, Pacific Northwest salmon and Maine lobster, all of which is flown in daily. There is also a wide selection of beef and poultry as well as pasta dishes. Breakfast and Sunday brunch are available if you're out and about early. ~ 48 Market Street; 801-322-4668, fax 801-531-0730; www.gastronomyinc.com. MODERATE TO DELUXE.

Salt Lake's ever-maturing dining scene means there's always a new restaurant or two to sample. One of 2001's newcomers is the highly acclaimed **Au Bon Appetit**, a French bistro that complements Market Street's other culinary offerings with its hearty menu. Not sure what to try? The "Pierrade" is a house speciality in which you cook strips of thinly sliced Angus beef on a hot lava stone delivered to your table with the meat. Once cooked to your desire, dip the morsels into a variety of sauces ranging from garlic to dijon. For something lighter, perhaps the salmon filet with sautéed spinach and rice will do. Arrive for breakfast and you can choose from the creations fresh out of the restaurant's patisserie. Show up Wednesday evening and you'll be treated to live jazz. During the Winter Olympics the Swiss Olympic Committee will transform the restaurant into the "House of Switzerland." ~ 18 West Market Street; 801-519-9595. BUDGET TO MODERATE.

Lamb's Restaurant is a Salt Lake City institution, dating to 1919 and thus the oldest continually operating eatery in the capital. The 1930s-style café ambience still reigns, and power lunches featuring some of the city's power elite still take place. The rice pudding is renowned. Breakfast is served here, too. Closed Sunday. ~ 169 South Main Street; 801-364-7166, fax 801-355-1644. MODERATE.

Belly dancers spice up meals on Friday and Saturday at **The Cedars of Lebanon**, where Middle Eastern and Lebanese foods crowd the menu. Tabbouleh, *baba ghanoush*, hummus and, of course, baklava are served, along with chicken, lamb, beef and chicken kabobs. ~ 152 East 200 South; 801-364-4096; www.cedars oflebanon.citysearch.com. BUDGET TO MODERATE.

The end of the 20th century brought a restoration of some of Salt Lake City's historic buildings, including an extensive renovation of the Continental Bank built in 1924. While much of the building was transformed into a hotel, **Bambara** took over the lobby and quickly won local culinary awards with its American regional cuisine. The open kitchen anchors the middle of the lobby so you can watch as the chefs prepare pan-roasted and grilled meats, seafood and game dishes such as quail with rabbit sausage. Breakfast, lunch and dinner are served. ~ 202 South Main Street; 801-363-5454, fax 801-363-5888. MODERATE TO DELUXE.

Salt Lake City has a growing number of sushi eateries, and **Shogun** has a loyal following in the heart of the capital. The chefs work with ahi tuna, mackerel and amberjack tuna, among other sea creatures, in crafting their sushi. If raw fish isn't your dish, they have other Japanese entrées on the menu. ~ 321 South Main Street; 801-364-7142. MODERATE TO DELUXE.

Despite being housed in the old Salt Lake City High School building, the setting for **Baci Trattoria** is somewhat nouveau—arched ceilings, splashes of bright colors and glass artwork that stirs art-deco memories. During warm weather, tables move out onto the sidewalk. The meals, however, aren't overwhelmed by the surroundings. You can go simple with pizza baked in a wood-fired oven, or choose a more elaborate Mediterranean or Italian dish. Closed Sunday. ~ 134-140 West Pierpont; 801-328-1500, fax 801-539-8783; www.gastronomyinc.com. MODERATE TO DELUXE.

At the **Metropolitan**, which has been nominated for a James Beard Award, you'll find "hand-crafted new American cooking." Examples are appetizers such as Pacific oyster soup and wild-mushroom ragout and entrées such as organic beet ravioli, saddle of rabbit, and seared diver scallops. The cosmopolitan ambience—clean lines, lots of glass, an open kitchen trimmed in copper—mirrors the food. ~ 173 West Broadway; 801-364-3472, fax 801-364-8671. MODERATE TO DELUXE.

Can't sleep? Need to check your e-mail? Then head to **Orbit**,   ◄ HIDDEN
an eclectic all-night internet café on Salt Lake City's west side. From 11 p.m. until 10:30 a.m. weekdays you can order breakfast; lunch and dinner are served from 11 a.m. to 11 p.m. While the "late night" menu features such breakfast standbys as pancakes, eggs, French toast and Belgian waffles, it is also stacked with burgers, sandwiches, pizzas and calzones. As for the decor, think art deco with a dash of cosmic tossed in. ~ 540 West 200 South; 801-322-3808, fax 801-322-3821. BUDGET.

P. F. Chang's China Bistro may be a chain restaurant, but you don't get that feeling when seated inside this spacious restaurant that evokes pre-colonial China with its hand-painted murals and towering statues. The "lettuce wraps," which feature either diced and spiced chicken or vegetarian fillings that you spoon onto a leaf of lettuce, are the bistro's signature appetizer, and worth a sampling. The rest of the menu comprises Chinese dishes revolving around meat, poultry, seafood and vegetables. ~ 174 West 300 South; 801-539-0500; www.pfchangs.com. BUDGET TO MODERATE.

If you're heading into the mountains for the day and want to pack a picnic, stop at **Tony Caputo's Market and Deli** on the way out of town. Housed in a brick building that once was a Firestone tire outlet, this Italian deli offers fresh meats and cheeses like

AUTHOR FAVORITE

Handcrafted ales and lagers brewed on site, creative dishes that fill your stomach but don't drain your wallet, relaxing surroundings—that's one of my favorite recipes for dining out, and the folks at **Squatters** have perfected such an atmosphere. You needn't enjoy brews to dine here, either, as they also have a wide-ranging wine list to match the tasty menu that ranges from buffalo wings and burgers to steak and chicken to stir-fried tofu and spicy jambalaya. ~ 147 West Broadway; 801-363-2739; www.squatters.com. MODERATE.

prosciutto, wine-cured salami, capocollo, Swiss cheese, smoked gouda and provolone as well as a hearty variety of marinated vegetables. Not into building your own meal? Then order one of Tony's hot or cold sandwiches or perhaps some lasagna, roasted pork loin or poached salmon. And don't forget some biscottis. ~ 308 West 300 South; 801-531-8669, fax 801-532-2930. BUDGET.

HIDDEN ▶   **3rd West Bistro** shares the old Firestone building with Tony Caputo's and offers an off-the-beaten-path dining atmosphere that's not too far from the heart of downtown Salt Lake City. Servers in smartly pressed white shirts tend to diners seated at linen-covered tables surrounding the bistro's open kitchen, which churns out such dinner entrées as beef Wellington with a wild-mushroom bordelaise and Tagliatelle with Fiery Seafood, a concoction of assorted seafood cooked with crushed chilies, spinach and asiago cheese. ~ 300 West 300 South; 801-328-3463; www. 3rdwestbistro.com. MODERATE TO DELUXE.

Ensconced in an old church that still retains its beautiful stained-glass windows, you would expect a heavenly experience when you enter **Ichiban Sushi**, which *Gourmet* magazine calls one of the country's top sushi bars. If you love sushi, you'll understand that recognition when you sample one of the creations of chef Peggy Whiting, an American trained in Japan. Beginners often go with the crab or salmon sushi, while more advanced palates crave the sea urchin or squid varieties. The kitchen also dishes out four varieties of sukiyaki; seafood and chicken dishes; and combination platters that might mix different types of sushi, salmon or chicken teriyaki. Complementing the food is the ambience—warm wood floors and ceilings, private rooms in the loft, and, fittingly, a salt-water aquarium just inside the entrance. ~ 336 South 400 East; 801-532-7522. BUDGET TO MODERATE.

> Only the Dead Sea is saltier than the Great Salt Lake.

Spicy tandoori dishes, curries and other traditional Indian cuisine can be found at **Taj India**. Not far from the heart of downtown, this restaurant focuses on Northern Indian cooking such as the tandoori chicken, marinated in yogurt and roasted on a skewer in tandoor, and the Rogan Josh—cubed lamb braised in a garlic sauce. ~ 73 East 400 South; 801-596-8727. BUDGET TO MODERATE.

HIDDEN ▶   Vegetarian cuisine is the hallmark of the **Oasis Café**, although it also serves seafood. In addition to featuring a wide selection of imported teas and roasting its own coffee beans, the café is next door to the Golden Braid bookstore, where you can sate your literary soul. Breakfast, lunch and dinner are offered. ~ 151 South 500 East; 801-322-0404, fax 801-322-3902. MODERATE TO DELUXE.

For a relaxed, kid-friendly setting, try **The Old Spaghetti Factory** located in the Trolley Square complex on the east side of town. Inexpensive pasta dishes are king here. ~ 189 Trolley Square; 801-521-0424, fax 801-521-0953. BUDGET TO MODERATE.

"Handmade gourmet Mexican cuisine" can be found at **Rico Mexican Market,** a thriving outlet that evolved from Jorge Fierro's peddling of pinto beans at one of Salt Lake City's farmers' markets. Though there are no tables for dining at, you can order enchiladas, burritos or tamales to go or shop for your own ingredients: The market's shelves are stocked with a dozen or so salsas of varying spiciness, chipotles, whole green chiles, jalapeño peppers, pink beans, baby lima beans, black-eyed beans, chile puya, and corn and flour tortillas. Closed Sunday. ~ 779 South 500 East; 801-533-9923. BUDGET.

Stop at **Granato's** and you can order cappocola ham, turkey, salami, one of several varieties of prosciutto or a variety of other cold cuts and cheeses from the deli cases to build your own sandwich, or order a hot or cold sandwich to go. Don't forget to order a side of pasta salad with feta cheese, tortellini and veggies or some baklava or cannoli. You can even place an order by phone and they'll deliver. ~ 1391 South, 300 West; 801-486-5643, fax 801-486-6069. BUDGET.

Although more than a century old, Salt Lake City is still evolving; evidence can be found in the neighborhoods that are sprouting their own restaurants and shopping outlets.

Hidden away in a nook of the growing "9th and 9th" neighborhood, **Wasabi Sushi** has established a reputation for its "sushi to go." There's no dining-in here—just order your meal and stand by while the chefs create it. You can find a seaweed-based soup, rice bowls, and a variety of sushi "rolls" similar to the California and Seattle rolls. ~ 865 East 900 South; 801-328-3474, fax 801-521-6372. BUDGET TO MODERATE.

◄ HIDDEN

Around the corner from Wasabi's is **The Coffee Garden,** a bohemian college hangout that cranks out espresso, tea, chai tea, granita and hot chocolate to go with its quiches, salads, modest selection of deli sandwiches, and fresh-made cakes and pies. With order in hand retreat to one of the shop's armchairs, couches or tables to read the day's news. ~ 898 South 900 East; 801-355-3425. BUDGET.

Like bread? Then stop by the **Great Harvest Bread Company.** Each day of the week offers a different specialty bread. One day it might be fresh-baked pesto sun-dried tomato bread or tomato herb, another cinnamon burst, orange apricota almond, Oregon herb or blueberry streusel. Come warm weather you don't have to go far to sample these breads, as there's a great patio outside. ~ 905 East 900 South; 801-328-2323. BUDGET.

At **Guru's,** an eatery with a New Age feel, you can order tacos, burritos, salads, pasta dishes, rice bowls and desserts such as the Karma Apple Square. You can eat knowing that you're doing a

good deed, too, as the restaurant's owners have created a phil-
anthropic foundation that gives to such charities as the Cancer
Wellness House, the American Brain Tumor Association and the
Homeless Youth Resource Center. Closed Sunday. ~ 912 East
900 South; 801-355-4878, fax 801-352-4875. BUDGET.

SHOPPING   Shopping is a spectator sport in the Salt Lake Valley. Dozens of
unique shops and antique stores, and even a few malls, lie within
the heart of downtown, while the suburbs offer more malls, stand-
alone stores and factory outlets.

Scheduled to debut in November 2001, the **Gateway Center**
is a sprawling one-block-wide-by-three-blocks-deep development
designed to breathe life into the capital's west side. The 2.4-million-
square-foot project will blend retail, hotel, residential and cultural
destinations into one area. Among the attractions are a 13-screen
theater, restaurants, nightclubs and museums. Part of the project
entails renovating the historic Union Pacific depot, which will serve
as the center's entrance. ~ Located between North Temple, 200
South, 400 West and 500 West.

You could shop nearly all day long under one roof at **Crossroads Mall**, which boasts nearly 150 stores. Located in the heart
of downtown, the mall offers well-known department stores such
as Nordstrom and Mervyn's as well as boutique outlets such as
Godiva Chocolatier, Papyrus and Turquoise Connection. ~ 50
South Main Street; 801-531-1799.

Across the street from Crossroads stands the **ZCMI Center
Mall** with its 90-plus shops. Among the stores is an Eddie Bauer
outlet, Meier & Frank, the Metro Sports Club and an expansive
food court. Closed Sunday. ~ 47 South Main Street; 801-321-8745.

HIDDEN ▶   A renowned, locally owned bookstore that sells new and used
books is **Sam Weller's Books**. The shop, which has been in the
Weller family since 1929, features three stories of new, used and
rare books. Can't find what you want? They'll special order it.
Closed Sunday. ~ 254 South Main Street; 801-328-2586, 800-
333-7269; www.samwellers.com.

Salt Lake City has a wealth of antique shops that offer everything from fine furniture to cowboy artifacts and Persian rugs.
Anthony's Antiques offers not only French Country pieces from
the 17th, 18th and 19th centuries, but also fine art from local
artists and Black Forest decorative items. Closed Sunday. ~ 401
East 200 South; 801-328-2231.

The **Beehive Collectors Gallery** specializes in Mormon memorabilia, books, military items, Indian art, rugs and Western photographs. Open Friday and Saturday or by appointment. ~ 368
East 300 South; 801-533-0119.

Creative and eclectic crafts and jewelry made by local and regional artists, as well as Alessi kitchenware imported from Italy,

can be found at **Q Street Fine Crafts**. Closed Sunday and Monday. ~ 88 Q Street; 801-359-1899.

Metaphysical and other New Age literary works can be found at the **Golden Braid** bookstore. Texts on detoxifying your body, vegetarian diets, and Zen are among the subjects broached. ~ 151 South 500 East; 801-322-1162.

Mission- and Arts and Crafts–style light fixtures can be found, or made to order, at **Restrospect Water & Light**. Within this tiny shop you can find vintage chandeliers, ornate sconces, glass, mica and clip-on shades, reproduction sinks, clawfoot bathtubs and retro hardware for your doors and drawers. ~ 68 East 700 South; 801-517-3876.

Just as the "9th and 9th" neighborhood has a modest variety of eateries, so too does it have its own shopping options.

In the need for a bouquet or fresh roses to mend a broken heart? Head to **Twigs and Company**, which some think has the best roses in all of Utah. ~ 888 South 900 East; 801-596-2322.

At **The Southwest Shop** you can find items with a Southwestern flavor. Jewelry, artworks, furniture, pottery, glassware, baskets and rugs, as well as kokopellis, are among the goods sold here. ~ 914 East 900 South; 801-531-8523.

Stop by **The Children's Hour Book and Toy Store** and you'll be overwhelmed by children's books, children's jewelry and children's clothing. ~ 928 East 900 South; 801-359-4150.

Art galleries can be found throughout the downtown area. The **Dolores Chase Fine Art Gallery** presents contemporary paintings from Utah artists. In the heart of downtown near several restaurants, it's a perfect stop before or after dinner on the two nights (Thursday and Friday) that it's open. Closed Sunday. ~ 260 South 200 West; 801-328-2787.

The **Tivoli Gallery** is one of Salt Lake City's oldest galleries, and with 25,000 square feet of display space, also one of the city's largest. American and European artworks from the 19th and 20th centuries are joined by a collection of contemporary works from

AUTHOR FAVORITE

As a fan of the American West, I love stepping into **Ken Sanders Rare Books** (and hopefully not kick up too much dust) and entering this literary museum that chronicles our nation's westward expansion. Specializing in Western Americana, first editions and Mormon books, it's also a great source for old maps, prints and paper ephemera. ~ 268 South 200 East; 801-521-3819; www.ksb.com.

Utah artists. Open Saturday by appointment. Closed Sunday and Monday. ~ 255 South State Street; 801-521-6288.

An interesting morning or afternoon can be spent shopping at the **Trolley Square** complex on the east side of Salt Lake City. On this site that once housed the city's trolley barns you'll find restaurants, a brewpub, antiques, artworks jewelry stores, Pottery Barn and Restoration Hardware outlets, a Williams-Sonoma shop and more. ~ 602 East 500 South; 801-521-9877.

> The 11,623 pipes that funnel the sound of the Tabernacle organ are made from round, hand-carved wood staves ranging in length from one-half inch to 32 feet. Organ recitals are held daily and are open to the public.

Another pocket of Salt Lake City that has evolved its own identity is the Sugarhouse section at the south end of the capital. Visit and you'll find interesting shops bearing everything from antiques to artworks to books to even tattoos.

The **Bingham Gallery** houses, and sells, a wonderful sampling of American fine arts, including paintings by Maynard Dixon, Charles Muench and Oscar E. Berninghaus. ~ 1074 East 2100 South; 801-832-9220; www.binggallery.com.

Arrive in town without a book or magazine for passing what spare time might arise? Then head over to **Barnes & Noble's** two-story Sugarhouse literary emporium. ~ 1104 East 2100 South; 801-463-2610.

Wild Oats Market is a purveyor of organic foods. Enter this sprawling grocery and you'll find everything from vitamins to range-free chickens, organic lamb chops and Atlantic salmon to sprouts and cheeses to a full-service deli. ~ 1131 East Wilmington Avenue, The Commons at Sugarhouse; 801-359-7913; www.wildoats.com.

Is your body taking a beating from Utah's dry air? Then head over to **Mountain Body**, an "Herbal Cosmetic Deli" where you can find "mountain glows" (a concoction of oils, extracts, minerals and emollients that will recharge your skin), "mountain balms" (for healing chapped skin) and a wide variety of bath additives and aromatherapy products. ~ 1155 East Wilmington, The Commons at Sugarhouse; 801-474-2331, 800-417-2365; www.mountainbody.com.

Forget something for your ski trip or mountain outing? Stop by **Evolution Outfitters**, a spinoff of Salt Lake City's Evolution Ski Company. A self-described "mountain sports specialist," this shop offers everything from skis to hiking gear. Closed Sunday and Monday. ~ 2146 South Highland Drive; 801-983-8001.

At **Ten Thousand Villages** you'll find a wide and interesting assortment of handicrafts collected from throughout the world. The store boasts potteries, woven goods and carvings among its stock. Closed Sunday. ~ 2186 South Highland Drive; 801-485-8827.

Robert Redford's merchandising arm has reached into Sugarhouse, where you can find a **Sundance Catalog Outlet Store** offering many of the same items you'll find in the catalog—furniture, knickknacks, clothing and jewelry with the Sundance brand. ~ 2201 South Highland Drive; 801-487-3400.

Although some folks are confused by Utah's liquor laws, you can certainly have fun in the capital, with or without a drink. For starters, there usually are shows and concerts to be taken in or sporting events featuring the National Basketball Association's Utah Jazz, the Women's National Basketball Association's Utah Starzz, the International Hockey League's Utah Grizzlies, or the Pacific Coast League's Salt Lake Stingers. Beyond these options are dozens of nightclubs and saloons where you can wet your whistle and catch a touring musical act. **NIGHTLIFE**

Throughout the fall and winter months many locals take in one or more of the performances of the **Utah Symphony**, which makes its home in the acoustically impeccable **Maurice Abravanel Concert Hall** in the heart of downtown. Guest artists such as Bernadette Peters and The Chieftans frequently perform with the symphony. During the summer months the symphony goes on the road, playing in outdoor arenas such as the Deer Valley Resort. ~ 123 West South Temple; 801-355-2787 (tickets), 888-451-2787.

Sports fans and concert enthusiasts flock to the **Delta Center** throughout the year. When the NBA's Utah Jazz or the WNBA's Utah Starzz isn't in action, the 20,000-plus-seat arena is center stage for some of the best in rock-and-roll and country music, as well as the occasional tractor pull. ~ 301 West South Temple; 801-325-2000.

Since Salt Lake City's lights make it hard to study the night sky, head to **Hansen Planetarium**, where you'll find plenty of stars to behold during one of the planetarium's astrological shows. Those who live with tunes in their heads won't want to miss one of the planetarium's laser shows set to music. Admission. ~ 15 South State Street; 801-538-2104; www.hansenplane tarium.com.

The **Capitol Theater** may be old, but it remains a lively place. Throughout the year this theatrical grand dame is the setting for touring Broadway shows, the Utah Opera Company, Ballet West and the Ririe-Woodbury Dance Company. ~ 50 West 200 South; 801-355-2787 (tickets).

Want to catch a movie and a cold brew at the same time? Check out **Brewvies**, which has two 153-seat cinemas, a restaurant that cooks up appetizers, burgers, sandwiches and pizza, and a bar that serves locally brewed beers on tap as well as a collection of bottled brews. Drinks and munchies can be taken to your seat in the theater. ~ 677 South 200 West; 801-355-5500.

Don't let the goat skull over the bar intimidate you. The **Dead Goat Saloon** has been around since 1965 as a private club that showcases regional and national rock-and-roll acts. A nominal "membership fee" (essentially a cover charge) gets you in. ~ Arrow Press Square, 165 South West Temple; 801-328-4628; www.dead goat.com.

Another hot spot in town is **The Zephyr Club**, another private club that lures national rock acts into Salt Lake City. ~ 301 South West Temple; 801-355-5646.

At **Papiyons**, a private club, the crowd dances Thursday through Saturday from 8 p.m. to 1:30 a.m. ~ 145 West Pierpont Avenue; 801-328-0868.

Sports-bar fans can find a game and a wide range of domestic and international brews at the **Port O'Call Social Club**, which employs 15 satellites to feed its 32 televisions. Pool and foosball tables are other entertainment options. ~ 400 South West Temple; 801-521-0589, fax 801-521-7177; www.portocall.com.

"Wasatch" is a American Indian word that means "mountains of many waters," while "Oquirrh" means "shining mountains."

The **Hard Rock Café** in Trolley Square is just like those found in other major cities—plenty of rock-and-roll memorabilia and tunes along with your meal. ~ 505 South 600 East; 801-532-7625.

The atmosphere at **Fats Grill** might not be the most intoxicating, but you won't find a better place in Salt Lake City to shoot a game or two of billiards. Not only does Fats offer 14 pool tables, but there's a decent kitchen that serves up nachos, quesadillas, pasta salads, hot and cold sandwiches, wraps and pizzas; all can be washed down with one of the eight beers on tap or one of the bottled brews in stock. The place is also smoke-free and caters to adults 21 and older. ~ 2182 South Highland Drive; 801-484-9467.

PARKS

WASATCH-CACHE NATIONAL FOREST 🏃 🚴 🐎 ⛺ ♨️ 🚤 🛥️ ⛵ If it's not the busiest forest in the country in terms of recreation, you can be sure the Wasatch-Cache National Forest is not far from the top. Its snow-covered peaks attract skiers and snowboarders in winter, hikers, campers and climbers in the warmer months. Sprawled across 1.2 million acres from the northeastern corner of the state through the Salt Lake Valley and north to the Idaho border, the national forest on Salt Lake City's doorstep claims four alpine resorts within 30 minutes of downtown. Wilderness areas near the capital include the **Lone Peak Wilderness**, a 30,088-acre parcel in the central Wasatch Range co-managed with the Uinta National Forest; the **Twin Peaks Wilderness**, an 11,4630-acre tract close to Salt Lake City; and the **Mount Olympus Wilderness**, a 16,000-acre preserve just north of the Twin Peaks

Wilderness. ~ The most direct forest access from Salt Lake City is via Routes 190 and 210 southeast of the city. Millcreek, Emigration and City Creek canyons are the other main access routes from Salt Lake City. Salt Lake Ranger District: 6944 South 3000 East, Salt Lake City; 801-943-1794. Winter users can call 801-364-1581 for avalanche conditions in the forest.

▲ From Farmington and Bountiful just north of Salt Lake City to Big and Little Cottonwood canyons and a slice of the forest southwest of Grantsville, there are 18 campgrounds with 376 sites in this section of the forest, some with hookups; free to $12; most have a 14-day maximum stay.

UINTA NATIONAL FOREST 🥾 🚴 🐎 🛶 ⛵ Adjoining the Wasatch-Cache National Forest near the southern end of the Salt Lake Valley is the Uinta National Forest, which encompasses 958,258 acres of high desert, rugged canyons and lofty peaks reaching to 11,877 feet. The **Lone Peak Wilderness** along the forest's northern boundary covers 30,088 acres and attracts many day-users. Facilities include picnic areas and restrooms. ~ The major access from the Salt Lake Valley is via Route 92. Uinta National Forest: 88 West 100 North, Provo, 801-377-5780; Pleasant Grove Ranger District: 390 North 100 East, Pleasant Grove, 801-785-3563.

▲ Forest-wide, there are 29 campgrounds in the three ranger districts with 1314 RV/tent sites, some with hookups; the bulk of the sites are in the Heber Ranger District; free to $12 for individual sites; most have a 14-day maximum stay.

ANTELOPE ISLAND STATE PARK 🥾 🚴 🐎 🛶 ⛵ Antelope Island State Park not only attracts humans but is popular with hundreds of species of shorebirds and wading fowl. The island is also home to bison and a herd of bighorn sheep, which was introduced in 1997. Pronghorn antelope, which were spied on the island when explorer John C. Fremont and guide Kit Carson visited in 1845, had vanished by the 1930s; in 1993 a small herd was reintroduced by the state. Swimmers and campers head to the two miles of sandy beaches rimming Bridger Bay while hikers trek to Elephant Head, Split Rock Bay or the top of 6595-foot Frary Peak. Facilities include swimming beaches, restrooms, showers, group pavilions, a marina, hiking and mountain biking trails and concessions. Day-use fee, $5; $2 causeway toll. ~ From Salt Lake City, take Route 15 16 miles north to Exit 335, then head west 14 miles on Routes 108/127 to the island; 4528 West 1700 South, Syracuse; 801-773-2941; parks.state.ut.us/parks/www1/ante.htm.

▲ There is one campground with 64 RV sites and 13 tent sites; $10 per night; 14-day maximum stay. For reservations, call 800-322-3770.

Text continued on page 64.

The Mormon
Faith

Although Utah is universally accepted as the headquarters for the Church of Jesus Christ of Latter-day Saints, the religion's birthplace is far to the east, in New York state. And while the church flourished under the leadership of Brigham Young, the faith was originally given life in the early 1800s by Joseph Smith, who as a young man was uncertain which religion to follow.

In 1820 Smith, troubled by this dilemma, headed into a forest and prayed for God to tell him which church to join. Instead of hearing an answer, though, Smith claimed to have been visited by God and his son, Jesus Christ, and told that none of the existing religions was worthy. Three years later God was said to have dispatched the angel Moroni to lead Smith to a book of golden plates that contained the religious gospel of an alleged, long-forgotten American culture. This gospel, Smith was told, was the one true religion that he should follow. Using these writings, Smith in 1827 wrote the Book of Mormon. Three years later he organized the LDS Church.

But just as the pilgrims fled England in the 1600s because of religious persecution, Smith and his followers continually found themselves moving in search of a place where they could peacefully practice their faith. From New York the Mormons went to Ohio and then Missouri before moving on in 1839 to Nauvoo, Illinois. It was while defending his religion in 1844 that Smith and his brother, Hyrum, were killed by a mob in Carthage, Illinois, that opposed his church.

Upon Smith's death Brigham Young, who had joined the church in 1832, rose to become church president and convinced his congregation to flee to the West. On July 24, 1847, after a nearly 1300-mile-long pilgrimage, Young and a group of 148 followers found themselves near the mouth of today's Emigration Canyon on the eastern rim of the Salt Lake Valley. Although feverish and bed-ridden, Young managed to gaze down on the valley and proclaim that it was the place they would settle.

In the valley the Mormons quickly displayed a knack for taming the harsh land, building extensive irrigation systems that ferried water from the mountains to their fields. After laying out the grid that would become Salt Lake City, Young focused on spreading the church's word by dispatching missionaries to settle Utah and convert whomever they could. Young's dream of strengthening his church has been carried on by successive church presidents who continue to dispatch missionaries, not just throughout Utah but throughout the world.

Today, by sending most young male church members out on two-year missions after high school, the LDS Church has built a worldwide following of more than ten million members.

Just as Brigham Young relied on divine revelations from God to help him lead his congregation, so, too, do today's church leaders. And just as Smith and Young were viewed by their followers as prophets, so, too, is the current church president.

Roughly three-quarters of Utah's nearly two million residents members are of the LDS Church, so its substantial influence on the state should come as no surprise. Despite the generally accepted constitutional division between church and state, in Utah it's not unusual for legislative leaders to discuss proposed legislation with church leaders. The church's conservative, strait-laced nature is also reflected throughout the state and its residents.

The world-wide headquarters for the LDS Church can be found at Temple Square in the heart of downtown Salt Lake City. The church's gleaming six-towered temple, constructed over a 40-year period with quartzite, copper and gold leaf, is the centerpiece of the square, which is also home to the church's administrative buildings, the dome-shaped Tabernacle, the LDS Assembly Hall and beautiful gardens that radiate with color from spring into fall.

GREAT SALT LAKE STATE PARK 🛶 ⛵ 🚤 🛥️ 🚤 Although this inland sea covers more than 2000 square miles, you won't find any fishing here since it's too salty for fish. But this doesn't deter summer crowds that come to enjoy the white-sand beaches and the steady breezes that make for good sailing. You'll find outdoor showers, restrooms, picnic crowds and a 300-slip marina. ~ Route 80, 16 miles west of Salt Lake City; 801-250-1898; parks.state.ut.us/parks/www1/grea.htm.

JORDAN RIVER STATE PARK 🚶 🚴 🚣 🚤 🛥️ Not far from downtown Salt Lake City, Jordan River State Park offers something for just about everyone. This nearly-five-mile stretch of highly versatile parkland caters to canoeists, golfers and even model-airplane enthusiasts who benefit from the scale-sized runway. Paths winding along the Jordan River are popular with joggers, strollers and cyclists. Facilities include picnic grounds, group pavilions and restrooms. ~ Located in north Salt Lake City between North Temple and 2200 North, 1084 North Redwood Road; 801-533-4496; parks.state.ut.us/parks/www1/jorr.htm.

The East Bench

▼▼▼▼▼▼▼▼▼▼▼▼▼ Salt Lake City's eastern border is a well-defined series of benches that stair-step up into the Wasatch Range thanks to the relentless tidal work of ancient Lake Bonneville. These levels make obvious building locations, as demonstrated by the homes, businesses and roads that straddle them.

SIGHTS The **University of Utah**, the state's oldest university, sprawls across the lower levels of these benches. The campus includes Presidents Circle, where you'll find Kingsbury Hall and the Utah Museum of Natural History, as well as the Utah Museum of Fine Arts and Rice Stadium, which will stage the opening and closing ceremonies of the 2002 Olympic Winter Games. ~ 801-581-6515.

Envisioned initially to serve the needs of the University of Utah's theatrical students, over the decades **Kingsbury Hall** has become a significant stop on the nation's cultural highway. Dedicated in 1930 and renovated in the late 1990s, the assembly hall has seen the likes of Maude Adams, Basil Rathbone, Vincent Price, George C. Scott and Roddy McDowell grace its stage; Robert Frost and Carl Sandburg recite poetry; and balladeer Burl Ives sing his stories. More recently, the hall has been the backdrop for Carol Channing, pianist Michael Feinstein, Willie Nelson and other performers. ~ Presidents Circle, University of Utah; 801-581-6261, 801-581-7100 (tickets).

Dark and dusty like all good museums should be, the **Museum of Natural History** at the University of Utah displays dinosaur fossils found in Utah as well as state mammals, minerals and other natural-history topics. The main dinosaur room is crowded with towering skeletons of all manner of 'saurs, including a stegosaurus and allosaurus. Admission. ~ Presidents Circle, University of Utah; 801-581-6927, fax 801-585-3684.

In the spring of 2001 the **Utah Museum of Fine Arts** moved into a sprawling new building, one that replaced a much smaller facility that was able to display only a small fraction of the museum's 17,000-piece collection. Among the museum's holdings are paintings and sculptures from around the world. It also has a variety of rotating temporary exhibits in addition to educational programs for young and old, concerts and lectures. ~ 370 South 1530 East, University of Utah; 801-581-7049; www.utah.edu/umfa.

Fort Douglas was established on a bench overlooking the city by President Lincoln in 1862 in response to the LDS Church's refusal to allow the Union Army to enlist recruits from the Utah Territory. Although the rhetoric between Brigham Young and Washington grew hot and LDS faithfuls prepared to battle Union troops, no shots were ever traded. The 120-acre site served as a prisoner-of-war camp for captured German soldiers during both World Wars. Among the buildings and sites worth visiting are the **Fort Douglas Museum**, which recounts the fort's past as well as

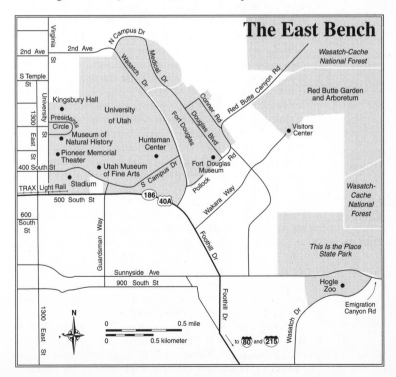

early military history in Utah; the officers' quarters located along **Officers Circle**; and the **Post Chapel**. The military grounds are just east of the University of Utah. The museum is closed Sunday and Monday. ~ 32 Potter Street, Fort Douglas; 801-581-1710.

Literally growing up the east bench of Salt Lake City, not far from Fort Douglas, is the **Red Butte Garden and Arboretum**, a 150-acre sanctuary for plants, shrubs, trees and wildlife that is the largest botanical and ecological center in the Intermountain West. Overseen by the University of Utah, the arboretum features fragrant butterfly and herb gardens, wildflower meadows, waterfalls, ponds, a whimsical children's garden complete with a 150-foot-long vegetative rattlesnake tunnel covered with ivy, and hiking trails. During the summer months the garden hosts a concert series. Closed Monday in winter. Admission. ~ 300 Wakara Way; 801-581-4747, fax 801-585-6491; www.redbutte.utah.edu.

Near the mouth of Emigration Canyon, **This Is the Place Heritage Park** lies on the east side of Salt Lake City, where it's thought that Brigham Young uttered those now-famous words, "This is the right place," when he first viewed the expansive valley. A monument marking the alleged spot can be found in the park just south of **Old Deseret Village**, a living-history park where guides in mid-19th-century garb recall the times of Young and his followers. The village, which is open Memorial Day through Labor Day weekend and then briefly in December for "Candlelight Christmas," includes an apple orchard, "shaving parlor," ice cream shop, gristmill and other pioneer shops. While entering the park itself is free, admission is charged for the village. ~ 2601 Sunnyside Avenue; 801-582-1847; parks.state.ut.us/parks/www1/this.htm.

Just past the park lies **Hogle Zoo**, the home of polar bears, snow leopards, Siberian tigers, apes, Capuchin monkeys, giraffes and hundreds of other animals. Unfortunately, most of the enclosures are dusty, unimaginative crowded spaces. Admission. ~ 2600 East Sunnyside Avenue; 801-582-1631, fax 801-584-1770; www.hoglezoo.org.

DINING

HIDDEN ▶

Located close to the University of Utah, Red Butte Gardens and Hogle Zoo, the **Red Butte Café** specializes in quick and delicious yet unpretentious meals. On the edge of a strip mall, the café features booths and wood tables surrounded by earth-toned walls inlaid with windows that provide a somewhat airy atmosphere on sunny days. The menu is filled with Southwestern entrées as well as cold and grilled sandwiches if you're in a rush. ~ 1414 Foothill Drive; 801-581-9498. BUDGET TO MODERATE.

Colleges always seem to engender interesting restaurants hidden away in nooks, and **W.H. Brumby's** is one of those eateries. On the flanks of the University of Utah, Brumby's starting commercial life as a bakery before expanding into table service. A good variety of sandwiches are at the heart of the lunch menu, while dinner menus offer a variety of vegetarian and seafood items in addition to daily specials. Desserts, as might be expected from the restaurant's roots, are worth saving room for. And if you're in a hurry, order something to go. ~ 224 South 1300 East; 801-581-0888, fax 801-581-0889. BUDGET TO MODERATE.

If your vision of an Italian bistro is a small, quaint eatery off the beaten path with a rich variety of pasta and meat dishes and a hearty wine list, try the **Fresco Italian Café**. Tucked away not   ◄ HIDDEN
far from the heart of downtown behind the King's English bookstore, this cozy restaurant features pasta and vegetarian dishes as well as lamb and veal. A fireplace heats the small dining room while the tables wear linen tablecloths, the walls are white plaster and the floors heavy terra-cotta tiles. Summertime is perfect for dinners served out back on the patio. Dinner only. ~ 1513 South 1500 East; 801-486-1300. MODERATE TO DELUXE.

Visually, there's nothing high-end about **Mazza,** a tidy nine-table nook that produces delicious Middle Eastern meals such as falafel patties and a variety of sandwiches as well as side dishes of hummus, *baba ghanoush* and basmati rice. So what if you have to eat it off of plastic plates with plastic utensils? While you're munching, check out the intriguing photos of 1930s "Beyrouth" or the sketches of an even earlier Beirut and Tyr. ~ 1515 South 1500 East; 801-484-9259. BUDGET.

For rustic Southwestern dining, head ten minutes up Emigration Canyon to the **Santa Fe Restaurant**. Away from the down-   ◄ HIDDEN
town crowds, this eatery whips up entrées such as salmon Santa Fe, a charbroiled piece of fish with brown butter hollandaise and toasted hazelnuts, chicken roulade and sweet corn tamale, and pork chops de la Santa Fe, which is a double chop coated with Macintosh maple glaze. The interior, as you'd expect from its name,

AUTHOR FAVORITE

When it's time to note a special occasion with my wife over a romantic dinner, I often head southeast of Salt Lake City to **Log Haven** in the upper reaches of Millcreek Canyon. There, in the elegantly rustic setting of a log mansion surrounded by towering evergreens and waterfalls, it's easy to escape stress over a bottle of wine and a delicious meal. Imaginative entrées such as coriander-rubbed ahi tuna and whiskey syrup–glazed prawns grace the menu, and in summer the restaurant's concert series lets us enjoy a sumptuous dinner while being serenaded by local artists. ~ Located four miles up Millcreek Canyon Road; 801-272-8255, fax 801-272-6315; www.log-haven.com, e-mail loghaven@aol.com. MODERATE TO DELUXE.

is infused with cacti, images of coyotes, and blazing fireplaces. In the summer, ask for a table on the deck. Sunday brunch is served. ~ 2100 Emigration Canyon; 801-582-5888, fax 801-583-0928. BUDGET TO MODERATE.

Orson Welles and Sir John Gielgud are just two of the many notables who have tread the boards at Kingsbury Hall.

Adjacent to the Santa Fe is a throwback to 1950s eatery style—**Ruth's Diner**. Built around the heart and soul of a trolley car, the diner is a great spot for Sunday brunch or a casual dinner. Come the warm-weather months the back patio is opened for meals and customers flock to it to enjoy the invigorating Wasatch Mountain air. Meals are pretty much what you'd expect from a roadside diner—hearty breakfasts built around omelets and pancakes, while burgers, sandwiches and enchiladas are on the lunch and dinner menus. ~ 2100 Emigration Canyon; 801-582-5807. BUDGET TO MODERATE.

SHOPPING   At the colorfully named **The Blue Cockatoo** gift shop you can find local artworks such as hand-blown glass bird feeders, photography revealing southern Utah, and eclectic metal creations featuring over-sized flies, spiders and dragonflies. There's even a beetle of sorts whose body is a World War II soldier's helmet. ~ 1506 South 1500 East; 801-467-4023.

A bookstore worthy of a visit is the **King's English**, which specializes in current fiction and children's selections. Located in an old house and adjacent service station that has been converted into book space, the shop divides its genres into different rooms. Linked to the Fresco Italian Café by a doorway found in the mystery section, diners can browse while waiting for a table. ~ 1511 South 1500 East; 801-484-9100.

NIGHTLIFE   Throughout the year plays, modern dance and concerts are presented within **Kingsbury Hall** on the University of Utah campus. The hall, which turned 70 in 2000, was renovated from top to bottom in the late 1990s and continues to draw national acts. ~ Presidents Circle, University of Utah; 801-581-6261.

PARKS   **EAST CANYON STATE PARK**   Located a short drive northeast of Salt Lake City in a gap in the mountains, East Canyon State Park is known for its boating and fishing in East Canyon Reservoir. Raptors and great blue herons are frequently spotted near the shorelines. Open year-round, the park is popular with boaters and anglers during the warm-weather months and ice-fishers come winter. Facilities include picnic grounds, boat ramps, a group pavilion, showers and fish-cleaning stations. Day-use fee, $5. ~ From Salt Lake City, head east about 5.5 miles on Route 80 to Exit 143, then north 14 miles on Route 65 to the park;

5535 South Route 66, Morgan; 801-829-6866; parks.state.ut.us/parks/www1/east.htm.

▲ There are two campgrounds with 60 RV and 15 tent sites; $12 per night; 14-day maximum stay. For reservations, call 800-322-3770.

▼▼▼▼▼▼▼▼▼▼▼▼

South Valley and Mountain Resorts

The South Valley, more a suburban extension of Salt Lake City than a separate entity, is best known for being the gateway to the recreational bonanzas that lie within the steep, granitic Big and Little Cottonwood canyons.

At the mouths of the canyons are Murray and Sandy, towns that were developed here because of the streams that spilled out of the canyons and the silver ore nestled within. Although Murray, settled in 1849, got its start as an agrarian settlement, a smelter arrived in 1869 to turn silver ore into bars and the mining industry remained rooted in the community for nearly a century. These days the city enjoys a mix of industrial, office and service businesses.

Sandy, homestead in the 1860s, enjoyed a similar start in life as smelters rolled in to minister the ore pulled from Little Cottonwood Canyon while hotels, saloons and brothels catered to the miners' needs and, ahem, desires. When the mining industry stumbled in the 1890s, the community quickly turned its efforts to agriculture, a move that kept Sandy from turning into a ghost town. Service businesses, malls and offices today feed the city's economy.

West of the cities the South Valley sweeps broadly across to the Oquirrh Mountain range, which has proven to be one of Utah's richest mining beds thanks to the long history of the Bingham Canyon mine that continues to produce copper, gold, lead, silver and other ores.

It takes only minutes to leave Murray and Sandy and head into the resorts of one or the other of the Cottonwood canyons. While Alta and Brighton date to the 1930s, Snowbird and Solitude are relative newcomers, arriving in 1971 and 1956 respectively. The four arguably enjoy the most and the best snow in Utah, as the ridgeline that divides them from the Park City resorts has a nasty habit of stalling storms over Alta, Bright, Snowbird and Solitude.

Though Snowbird does the most year-round business, drawing a steady crowd of summer vacationers to its hiking and biking trails, Solitude is moving in that direction with the ongoing build-out of its base village; Alta and Brighton seem largely content to focus on winter.

Fifteen minutes from the heart of Salt Lake City via Routes 80 and 215 lie Big and Little Cottonwood canyons, two long, west-running gorges cut into the Wasatch Range that have been per-

SIGHTS

fectly sculpted for ski resorts with dramatically jutting, angular peaks, steep slopes, thick forests and intermittent meadows. Clustered on the western flanks of the Wasatch Range, the canyons' four resorts are blessed with ridiculous amounts of snow, in large part due to the prevailing winds that usually stall winter storms along the north–south ridgeline and directly over the resorts, and in part due to moisture from the Great Salt Lake that gets sucked up by these storms and then laid down in prodigious quantities of snow on the slopes.

Taking the 6200 South exit from Route 215 and then heading east, you'll first encounter Big Cottonwood Canyon, with its hiking trails, a gushing stream that roars during spring runoff, and two ski resorts.

Brighton, at the canyon's head, isn't the Wasatch's steepest resort, but its heavily forested slopes offer an intimate experience for skiers and snowboarders. There also are a few bowls that are packed with powder throughout the winter. With free skiing for kids under ten, Brighton has a solid reputation as a family-oriented resort. What this resort lacks, though, are après-ski lounges, restaurants and beds. In summer this resort sleeps, although its parking lots are used by hikers heading into the high country. ~ Route 190, 25 miles from Salt Lake City, Star Route, Brighton; 801-532-4731, 800-873-5512, fax 435-649-1787; www.skibrighton.com.

So close to Brighton that you can ski over to it is the **Solitude Mountain Resort**, a blossoming destination that somehow continues to offer, well, solitude for skiers and snowboarders; its sprawling, picturesque terrain sates the soul. (The resort is currently developing an intimate pedestrian village complete with hotels, restaurants and shops.) Come summertime, Solitude is popular with hikers and mountain bikers. ~ Route 210, 23 miles from Salt Lake City, 12000 Big Cottonwood Canyon, Salt Lake City; 801-534-1400, 800-748-4754, fax 435-649-5276; www. skisolitude.com.

The next canyon south of Big Cottonwood Canyon is Little Cottonwood Canyon, a name that in no way impugns the year-round recreation you'll experience there. As with Big Cottonwood Canyon, here you'll find trout streams and trailheads that lead off into the wilderness areas of Wasatch-Cache National Forest.

Skiing is foremost in this canyon, though, and to skiers the **Alta Ski Lifts Company** is hallowed ground. Cradled by the mountains near the canyon's head, this skiers-only resort shuns high-tech in favor of the yesteryear romanticism of an isolated mountain resort. A handful of slow-speed lifts distribute skiers around the mountain, which receives 500 inches and more of snow each year. At the base, a small handful of cozy lodges hang on the lip of the ski area, ready to provide a quaint, intimate stay for overnight guests. With lift prices nearly half of what most destination

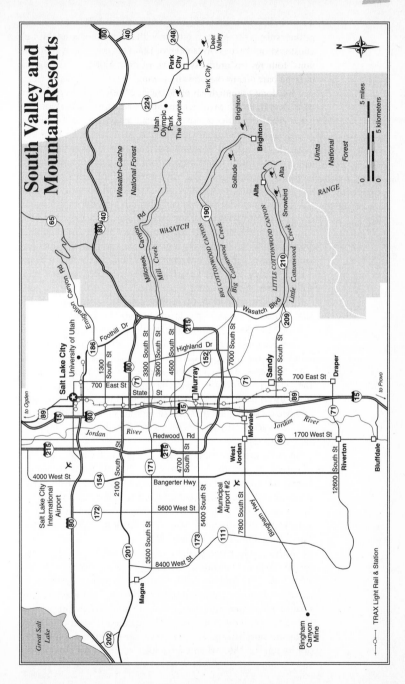

South Valley and Mountain Resorts

N

5 miles

5 kilometers

Wasatch-Cache National Forest

Uinta National Forest

WASATCH   RANGE

Park City

Deer Valley

Park City

Utah Olympic Park

The Canyons

Brighton

Brighton

Solitude

Alta

Alta

Snowbird

BIG COTTONWOOD CANYON

Big Cottonwood Creek

LITTLE COTTONWOOD CANYON

Little Cottonwood Creek

Wasatch Blvd

Emigration Canyon Rd

Millcreek Canyon Rd

Mill Creek

Salt Lake City

University of Utah

Foothill Dr

Highland Dr

1300 South St

3300 South St

3900 South St

4500 South St

7000 South St

9400 South St

700 East St

State St

Sandy

Draper

Murray

to Ogden

Jordan   River

Midvale

Jordan   River

Redwood   Rd

4700 South St

West Jordan

1700 West St

Riverton

Bluffdale

Salt Lake City International Airport

4000 West St

2100 South St

Bangerter Hwy

5600 West St

Municipal Airport #2

5400 South St

7800 South St

12600 South St

700 East St

3500 South St

8400 West St

Magna

Bingham Hwy

Bingham Canyon Mine

Great Salt Lake

to Provo

TRAX Light Rail & Station

resorts charge these days, Alta is ski country's best bargain. In summer the resort is much quieter, with hikers wandering through its forests and wildflower-strewn meadows on their way to the high country. ~ Route 210, 25 miles from Salt Lake City, Alta; 801-359-1078; www.altaskiarea.com.

Just west and adjacent to Alta is the **Snowbird Ski and Summer Resort**, which lacks its neighbor's romantic yesteryear ambience but more than makes up for it with ter-

In 1864 a group of soldiers enjoying a picnic near the head of Little Cottonwood Canyon stumbled across silver in the area of present-day Alta.

rain that's best suited for advanced and expert skiers. Dominating the resort base is the monolithic Cliff Lodge, which is the heart of a small, self-contained village that covers all the bases with retail shops, restaurants and even a delicatessen. Whereas Alta focuses on winter, Snowbird, as its full name implies, doesn't let summer slip away quietly. Once the snow melts from the slopes the resort opens its hiking and mountain biking trails, climbing wall, ropes course and pools. It also features summer concerts, star gazing and outdoor theater. ~ Route 210, 24 miles from Salt Lake City; 801-933-2222, fax 801-933-2298; www.snowbird.com.

Surprising only in that it took so long to arrive is a lift ticket that will get you into both Alta and Snowbird. The *Alta Snowbird Pass* lets skiers—sorry 'boarders, you're still *non gratis* at Alta—enjoy these two resorts with one lift ticket. With the pass, skiers are allowed to make tracks across the combined resorts' 4700 acres. The connection between the two resorts was made possible during the summer of 2001 when Snowbird installed a second high-speed quad lift in Mineral Basin. The lift runs to the saddle on Sugarloaf Mountain, a point that lets skiers drop down into either resort.

Outside the canyons, life for travelers mellows but doesn't totally disappear.

Not far from the mouth of Big Cottonwood Canyon is a slice of early-20th-century life. Throughout the year **Wheeler Historic Farm** stages dances, Victorian teas, wagon rides and farm and garden shows. Visitors can try their hand at milking cows or take a hay-wagon ride. School kids often camp overnight at the farm, which harbors a "haunted" woods. Admission. ~ 6351 South 900 East, Salt Lake City; 801-264-2212.

Although the western edge of the south Salt Lake Valley holds no ski resorts, it has one of the wonders of the industrial world. About the time Antelope Island was being explored, so too was a canyon 25 miles southwest of Salt Lake City. Thomas and Sanford Bingham were ranchers, but their surname has forever been linked to one of the mining industry's greatest feats: the **Bingham Canyon Mine**. The mine, nicknamed "the richest hole on Earth," got its start in 1863 when Union soldiers from Fort Douglas detected lead ore in the canyon. A decade later discoveries of gold and silver spurred a boom that ran for 20 years. Though the site was considered spent in 1893, two engineers thought the relatively sparse copper ores buried there could be profitably mined if done on a large scale. Thus open-pit mining was born.

Today the mine operated by Kennecott Utah Copper is two and a half miles wide and roughly a half-mile deep. Through the years more than 15 million tons of copper have been pulled from the mine, making it the most productive copper mine in history. In 1972 it was listed as a National Historic Landmark. On one rim of the mine sits a visitors center with mining artifacts, videos, displays of copper's effect on our lives, and 3-D microscopes for viewing ore samples. The center is closed November through March. Admission. ~ Take Route 15 south to the 9000 South exit and head west to the mine, Bingham; 801-252-3234.

Between the ski resorts on the eastern side of the valley and the Bingham Mine on the western side are two quieter attractions that provide some meditative space.

A tribute to the world can be found at the **International Peace Gardens**, the floral centerpiece of a 21-acre park featuring botanical displays in honor of two dozen countries; it's located near the southwestern corner of Salt Lake City. Closed December through April. ~ 1060 South 900 West, Salt Lake City; 801-974-2411.   ◄ HIDDEN

Veterans and their families are drawn to **Veterans Memorial State Park**, a 30-acre memorial commemorating those who fought for the United States. In addition to a cemetery, the grounds contain a chapel as well as a military museum. ~ 17111 Camp Williams Road, about 23 miles south of Salt Lake City via Routes 15, 71 and 68, Riverton; 801-254-9036.

Shoppers and history buffs will find that their interests overlap at **Gardner Village**, which offers a step back into the 19th century. Located on a parcel of land where Brigham Young directed Archibald Gardner to build a gristmill in 1853, the village today contains a collection of quaint shops connected by meandering walkways. Soon after Gardner built his mill, which was fed by water from the West Jordan Canal he developed, the site grew to include a mattress factory, broom factory, blacksmith shop and general store. After the first mill burned down, Gardner replaced it in 1877. The site's only original building remaining today, the mill has been converted into a restaurant and furniture shop. There are other historic buildings on the grounds, but they were moved in from other locations in Utah. There is a museum on the grounds that opens a window on Gardner's life and times. ~ From Salt Lake City, take Route 15 south about seven miles to Exit 301 and then west on 7800 South, 1100 West 7800 South, West Jordan; 801-566-8903; www.gardnervillage.com.   ◄ HIDDEN

LODGING

Up the Cottonwood canyons, most of the lodging possibilities surround Alta and Snowbird, although a base village arising at the bottom of Solitude Mountain Resort promises badly needed rooms. Be prepared for sticker shock during ski season; bargains are prevalent in summer.

HIDDEN ►

One of the more intriguing properties outside of the two canyons is **La Europa Royale**, a refined cross between an intimate B&B and a lavish hotel. Not far from the entrances to Big and Little Cottonwood canyons, this self-described "elegant small hotel" is surrounded by two acres of carefully tended grounds perfect for evening strolls. The nine rooms and suites feature two-person whirlpool baths and showers, fireplaces and soundproof walls. Meals are served in the dining room, on the patio or in your room. ~ 1135 East Vine Street, Salt Lake City; 801-263-7999, 800-523-8767, fax 801-263-8090; www.laeuropa.com, e-mail tflynn@laeuropa.com. DELUXE TO ULTRA-DELUXE.

Over the ridge in Big Cottonwood Canyon, the growing base at Solitude offers another place to stay. There are a number of options at The Village at Solitude, ranging from a hotel to time-share rentals.

The Inn at Solitude offers 46 hotel rooms at the base of the slopes in a European-style structure complete with a living room and library, an exercise center, a wine cellar, a heated outdoor pool and hot tub, and ski lockers. There's even a small movie theater, a club and a restaurant on the premises. ~ 12000 Big Cottonwood Canyon, Salt Lake City; 801-536-5700, 800-748-4754, fax 801-535-4135. DELUXE TO ULTRA-DELUXE.

Across the courtyard, **Creekside at Solitude** offers 18 two- and three-bedroom condos that rise over the Creekside restaurant. Each of the units has a wood-burning fireplace to fight off the chill, full kitchens, living and dining rooms, a private deck and a spot in the underground parking garage. ~ 12000 Big Cottonwood Canyon, Salt Lake City; 801-536-5700, 800-748-4754, fax 801-535-4135. ULTRA-DELUXE.

Close by, but not close enough to be classified as ski-in, ski-out accommodations, **The Crossings** is a collection of three- and four-bedroom townhomes. Each comes with two fireplaces, a full kitchen, a private deck, and a one-car garage. ~ 12000 Big Cottonwood Canyon, Salt Lake City; 801-536-5700, 800-748-4754, fax 801-535-4135. ULTRA-DELUXE.

Over at Brighton, accommodations are decidedly more spartan. There's just one lodge—the **Brighton Lodge**—and it offers just 20 rooms, of which five are essentially hostel-style rooms (yes, with ultra-deluxe price tags) with a shared bathroom down the hall. The room rates include a complimentary continental breakfast, and there's also a large jacuzzi outside for mingling with the other guests. ~ Star Route, Brighton; 800-873-5512. ULTRA-DELUXE.

The immediate area near Alta has a good number of properties with a wide range of ambience. Being slopeside, these accommodations are quite expensive in general. Not all lodges take credit cards, so be sure to check on payment options. Also, there is extremely limited parking at Alta, and after storms you may find you have to dig out your rig. If you're flying into Utah for a ski vacation, it's best to take a shuttle from the airport directly to your lodge.

The Lodge at Snowbird offers a mix of condominium-type rooms, from hotel-style units to studios with lofts. All have fireplaces and full kitchens, which help contain the cost of a ski vacation, and balconies with grand mountains views. The lodge also features a heated pool and hot tub and a ground-level restaurant. ~ Little Cottonwood Canyon Road, Snowbird; 801-947-8220, 800-453-3000, fax 801-742-2211; www.snowbird.com. DELUXE TO ULTRA-DELUXE.

Snowbird provides more lodging possibilities, thanks to the **Cliff Lodge** and its outlying condominium properties. Combined, they offer more than 900 rooms at the resort base. The Cliff Lodge is an imposing ten-story structure that towers over the resort base. Outwardly, this blocky, battleship-gray concrete edifice struggles to blend in with the canyon's craggy peaks and rugged walls. But inside you'll find one of the country's most extensive oriental rug collections draped across the lobby walls, comfortable rooms, and a varied collection of restaurants. Atop the hotel is a 25-meter outdoor pool with adjoining hot tub and a spa where you can get rubbed down or wrapped in seaweed. In summer, the climbing wall that runs up the west-facing side of the lodge tests climbers' skills. ~ Little Cottonwood Canyon Road, Snowbird; 801-947-8220, 800-453-3000, fax 801-742-2211; www.snowbird.com. DELUXE TO ULTRA-DELUXE.

While the mountains overshadowing the Salt Lake Valley just to the east average 500 inches of snow each winter, the valley floor receives an average of 59 inches of snow.

Conveniently located between Alta and Snowbird, for those skiers who want to sample both resorts, are the **Hellgate Condominiums**. The 12 units come with full kitchens, fireplaces, cable television and nearby laundry facilities. There is limited garage parking. ~ Little Cottonwood Canyon Road, Alta; 801-742-2020. ULTRA-DELUXE.

There are other lodging possibilities in Little Cottonwood Canyon. The **Blackjack Condominium Lodge**, which draws its name from an old mine, offers studio and one-bedroom units equipped with fireplaces and full kitchens. Guests also have access to exercise rooms, saunas and laundry facilities. ~ Superior Bypass Road, Alta; 801-742-3200, 800-343-0347, fax 801-742-3201; www.blackjacklodge.com, e-mail blackjack@webguymail.net. DELUXE TO ULTRA-DELUXE.

A heated swimming pool with adjoining hot tub, situated between the **Alta Peruvian Lodge** and its ski slopes, makes for a wonderful après-ski soak. Within the lodge's walls are dorms and rooms with private and shared baths. You can warm yourself at day's end in front of several fireplaces or with hot chocolate or apple cider. Breakfast, lunch and dinner are included in the rates. While winter is definitely the busy season, the lodge is open and less expensive during the summer months. ~ Little Cottonwood Canyon Road, Alta; 801-742-3000, 800-453-8488, fax 801-742-3007; www.altaperuvian.citysearch.com. MODERATE TO ULTRA-DELUXE.

The **Travis Home** is a modified A-frame home that comes fully furnished and stands across the street from the Alta resort. The home has three bedrooms, a loft, two baths, a complete kitchen, a fireplace and laundry facilities. ~ P.O. Box 8076, Alta, UT 84092; 801-942-5219. MODERATE TO ULTRA-DELUXE.

Open only during the ski season, the 94-room **Goldminer's Daughter Lodge** is located next to the Alta Lodge and across from the Wildcat and Collins lifts. There's no pretentiousness in this property, where tight hallways lead to rooms that come in a variety of sizes and furnishings. All rooms—except dorm rooms—have private bathrooms, television and phones. While the smaller rooms hold one double bed, the larger bedrooms feature either a king-sized bed or two double beds. Breakfast and dinner are included. ~ Little Cottonwood Canyon, Alta; 801-742-2300, 800-453-4573. MODERATE TO DELUXE.

During its 19th-century boom days Alta proudly laid claim to 26 bars on its main street.

Owned and overseen by Alta's venerable mayor, Bill Levitt, the **Alta Lodge** has been opening its doors to guests—many of them repeat visitors—for more than six decades. The rooms—refined college dormitory style is an apt description—are nothing to rave about but the breakfasts and dinners (included in your room rate) are delicious and filling. The lodge's location across from the Collins and Wildcat lifts is convenient. If you're not interested in paying full-freight for a room with bath, less-expensive dorm rooms are available. Upstairs is the Sitzmark Club, a cozy lounge with a roaring fireplace for recounting the day's war stories. A special kids' program includes après-ski activities, dinner and a movie. If the lodge is full, inquire about the two-bedroom condominium that can sleep up to six. Winter isn't the only season here. With the area's enjoyable summers and great hiking possibilities, the lodge is a good base of operations from June to October. ~ Little Cottonwood Canyon Road, Alta; 801-742-3500, 800-707-2582, fax 801-742-3504; www.altalodge.com, e-mail info@altalodge.com. DELUXE TO ULTRA-DELUXE.

The oldest and smallest lodge at Alta is the **Snowpine Lodge**, which lies across from the Albion and Sunnyside lifts. Like the Alta

Lodge, the interior is simple and rustic with a mix of wood planks and stone walls dating to the late 1800s; a wall of glass lining the dining room provides a gorgeous view of the ski area. With space for just 50, the lodge definitely has an intimate feel; it's a place where you get to know your fellow guests. The rooms (some with private baths) are cozy and clean and carry a Western motif with exposed wood and Western art. There is an outdoor hot tub, and you'll also find a sauna on the grounds. Unlike some of its neighboring lodges, Snowpine shuts down for the summer months. ~ Little Cottonwood Canyon, Alta; 801-742-2000, fax 801-742-2244. MODERATE TO DELUXE.

Next door to the Snowpine is **Alta's Rustler Lodge**, an eight-floor complex ready to pamper one after a powder day. If the heated pool and jacuzzi don't get out the kinks, try a spell in the eucalyptus steam room. There's also a fitness center if the slopes didn't provide enough of a workout. As with the other lodges, the 87 rooms range in size and furnishings, while the common areas offer comfortable chairs and couches. Breakfast and dinner are included in the room rates. Credit cards are not accepted, but cash and personal checks are. During the summer months, this lodge caters to groups only. ~ Little Cottonwood Road, Alta; 801-742-2200, 888-532-2582, fax 801-742-3832; www.rustlerlodge.com. DELUXE TO ULTRA-DELUXE.

A number of high-end condominium and townhouse properties in the canyon, ranging from one-bedroom units to sprawling five-bedroom houses, are managed by **Canyon Services**. ~ P.O. Box 920025, Snowbird, UT 84092; 801-943-1842, 800-562-2888, fax 801-943-4161; www.canyonservices.com. ULTRA-DELUXE.

Although not quite as mature as those found in the heart of Salt Lake City, dining options in this part of the valley are growing quite nicely, thank you.

DINING

While some might question **Lugano's** ambience—its L-shaped dining room wraps around an open kitchen, the tables are closely aligned to each other—executive chef Greg Nevill makes up for it with his delicious northern Italian cooking. Starters such as Tuscan white-bean soup with prosciutto, basil oil and parmesan or "clay pot" mussels swimming in a broth of saffron and picholine olives and cooked in a wood-burning oven can be followed by a risotto dish made daily, red wine–braised chicken "osso bucco" with soft polenta and grilled portobello mushroom, or perhaps grilled Atlantic salmon with lobster broth and winter root vegetable medley. ~ 2300 East 3364 South, Salt Lake City; 801-412-9994, fax 801-412-9257. MODERATE TO DELUXE.

On the border of Salt Lake City and the south end of the Salt Lake Valley is **Café Madrid**, where you'll find authentic Spanish cuisine, not some Americanized knock-off or Mexican hybrid,

◀ HIDDEN

thanks to the chef who hails from Spain. Don't let the surrounding shopping center fool you. Inside the café you'll find a menu with potato-onion frittatas, squid in ink, chicken marsala and a paella that must be ordered a day ahead. Closed Sunday. ~ 2080 East 3900 South, Salt Lake City; 801-273-0837. MODERATE.

Outside of the canyons, one of the valley's best Italian restaurants is **Tuscany**, which is found not far from the mouth of Big Cottonwood Canyon. The restaurant feels like a northern Italian hunting lodge, and the flagstone patio garden, interspersed with towering conifers, offers some of the best dining seats in the summer. Linguini with clams in garlic sauce, oven-roasted pesto-crusted salmon filet and various meat dishes are among the menu items. Dinner nightly; no lunch Saturday through Monday. ~ 2832 East 6200 South, Salt Lake City; 801-277-9919, fax 801-277-0980. MODERATE TO DELUXE.

The atmosphere at **Lone Star Taqueria** is decidedly Tex-Mex: The wooden split-rail fence that rims the restaurant's patio proudly bears hubcaps and cowboy boots while the interior is festive with colorful banners streaming from the ceiling. Some say the best fish tacos in the Salt Lake Valley are found here; you'll have to be the judge of that. If tacos aren't your thing, you'll also find overstuffed burritos crammed with beef, roasted pork, broiled chicken or vegetables. ~ 2265 East Fort Union Boulevard, Salt Lake City; 801-944-2300. BUDGET TO MODERATE.

HIDDEN ▶   The ambience is rich and the food French at **La Caille**, where the setting is a replica of a French chateau and the food is served by waitresses and waiters in 18th-century costumes. Located just beyond the mouth of Little Cottonwood Canyon, the restaurant grounds features a winery; in the warm months peacocks stroll the yards. ~ 9565 Wasatch Boulevard, Sandy; 801-942-1751, fax 801-944-8990. MODERATE TO DELUXE.

The warm ambience created at **Emilia Ristorante** through the use of heavy terra-cotta tiles, stained glass, belt-driven ceiling fans, and warm woods highlighted by brass ensures a relaxing meal of northern Italian cuisine. The wood-burning ovens employed by the chefs were imported from Italy. You can eat simply by ordering a calzone or go hearty with a wood-fired half chicken with a side of chunky caesar smashed potatoes drizzled with a sweet veal reduction or perhaps the braised beef shortrib with diced, roasted vegetables served in a port reduction sauce. ~ 75 East 9400 South, Sandy; 801-304-4075. MODERATE TO DELUXE.

In the canyons, since all of the lodges at Alta offer meal plans for their guests, the lack of demand for independent restaurants has resulted in the existence of just one in the immediate vicinity of that resort. Snowbird, meanwhile, offers eight sit-down eateries at the base and one mid-mountain, although not all are open year-round.

Alta's lone independent, the **Shallow Shaft**, is a cozy affair, living proof that one shouldn't judge a book by its cover. Some consider the restaurant's interior, which is lined with mining memorabilia, a bit funky, but the food belies the setting. Once known for its Southwestern fare, the Shallow Shaft's menu now reads like one out of downtown Salt Lake, with appetizers such as stuffed mushrooms and smoked-salmon-and-avocado quesadillas followed by rack of lamb, house-smoked Atlantic salmon with a honey-lime-chipotle glaze and fresh grapefruit, and linguini with pesto. ~ Alta Road, Alta; 801-742-2177, fax 801-742-2914; www.shallowshaft.com, e-mail tgarling@shallowshaft.com. MODERATE TO DELUXE.

During the hiking season, the Kickstand, a sandwich and snack kiosk, opens for business in the parking lot below the Albion Basin.

Down the road at Snowbird the options run from steaks and seafood to pizza and Southwestern.

The **Steak Pit** is the resort's steak house. Beef shares the menu, however, with Alaskan king crab, Australian lobster tail and other denizens of the deep. As befits a steakhouse, the ambience is rustic. The cedar-plank walls are lined with photos of the resort and its mountains, as well as celebrities such as former NFL great Steve Young, while diners are seated around oak tables in booths. ~ Snowbird Center Level 1, Snowbird; 801-933-2260. MODERATE TO DELUXE.

Skiers and shredders in a hurry graze at **The Rendezvous**, a cafeteria that features a variety of hot and cold entrées for a quick meal. Open in winter only. ~ Snowbird Center Level 2, Snowbird; 801-742-2222 ext. 4086. BUDGET.

Fast-food burger joints haven't yet surfaced in the canyons, but there's a **Pier 49 San Francisco Pizza** outlet at Snowbird where you can build a gourmet pizza. ~ Snowbird Center Level 2, Snowbird; 801-742-3222. BUDGET.

A relaxed, family-friendly atmosphere reigns at **The Forklift**, where breakfasts can be built around pancakes or omelets, and lunches over burgers or pasta dishes. Located across from the tram dock, the restaurant offers patio dining during the summer months. ~ Snowbird Center Level 3, Snowbird; 801-933-2240. BUDGET TO MODERATE.

High atop the Cliff Lodge rests **The Aerie**, the resort's top-of-the-line restaurant, where the meals are nearly as intoxicating as the views. Game, beef and seafood are splashed across the menu in forms such as crab salad cake and jumbo shrimp, rabbit ravioli, filet mignon and seared ahi tuna, while in the adjoining lounge one can order sushi. ~ Cliff Lodge, Level 10, Snowbird; 801-933-2160. MODERATE TO DELUXE.

The **Atrium** offers quick summer breakfast buffets and hearty winter lunch buffets, along with a large espresso bar sure to keep the energy levels up. ~ Cliff Lodge, Level B, Snowbird; 801-933-2140. BUDGET TO MODERATE.

Quick, healthy meals are the hallmark of the **Summit Café**, located next to the Cliff Spa. Fruit smoothies, vegetable juices, salads and vegetarian dishes are the mainstays here. Open in winter only. ~ Cliff Lodge, Level 10, Snowbird; 801-933-2175. BUDGET TO MODERATE.

You'd be wise to keep a cold beverage by your side while eating at **Keyhole Junction**, where spiciness is a mainstay of its Southwestern and Mexico dishes. If you need proof, try the grilled flank steak. Vegetarians will enjoy the wild-mushroom enchiladas, which are topped with *queso fresco*, roasted chiles, onions and cilantro. Margarita lovers will find a soul mate in the Twisted Shrimp, which are doused in a tequila, garlic and lime marinade. ~ Cliff Lodge, Level A, Snowbird; 801-933-2025. BUDGET TO DELUXE.

During 1942 members of the 503rd Parachute Battalion practiced winter warfare in the mountains surrounding Alta.

Over at The Lodge, the **Lodge Club Bistro** whips up entrées ranging from meats such as beef tenderloin and rack of lamb, to fowl, seafood and pasta dishes. Through the restaurant's windows you can watch the Snowbird tram crawl across the sky to the top of the resort. Inside, flower-filled vases sit atop the white linen–covered tables. In summer the tables are moved out onto the patio. ~ The Lodge at Snowbird, Pool Level, Snowbird; 801-933-2145. MODERATE TO DELUXE.

The Iron Blosam Lodge is home to the **Wildflower Ristorante**, where candle-lit meals are served. Mediterranean food, such as olive-crusted duck breast, molasses-cured double thick pork chops, and pastas dressed with lobster, grace the menu. ~ Iron Blosam Lodge, Level 3, Snowbird; 801-933-2230. MODERATE TO DELUXE.

If you don't want to leave the mountain for a meal, head over to the **Mid-Gad Restaurant**, found on the mountain right off the aptly named Lunch Run in the Gad Valley. Meals are quick, revolving around sandwiches, burgers, pizzas and chili. ~ Gad Valley, Snowbird; 801-933-2245. BUDGET.

SHOPPING   Malls and furniture stores dominate the shopping scene in the southern reaches of the Salt Lake Valley, but there are a few exceptions.

In a state where recreation ranks high, it's no surprise that Salt Lake City includes a **Patagonia** outlet store stocked to the rafters with fleece goods, sweaters and other outdoorsy apparel. ~ 3267 South Highland Drive, Salt Lake City; 801-466-2226.

The **Cottonwood Mall**, Utah's first indoor mall, claims more than 140 stores and a theater. ~ 4835 South Highland Drive, Salt Lake City; 801-278-0416.

With skiing, hiking, biking, boating and camping luring count-less Utahns out of doors, there's an REI store where you can buy the latest gear or rent some for a weekend outing. ~ 3285 East 3300 South, Salt Lake City; 801-486-2100.

The **Fashion Place Mall** offers more than 100 stores, including 15 food outlets. ~ 6191 South State Street, Murray; 801-265-0504.

Gardner Village mixes history with shopping. Located on the grounds where a grist mill was erected in 1877 at the request of Brigham Young, the village today is a cluster of quaint shops selling everything from fudge to metalworks. Throughout the year the village stages a number of events such as Easter egg hunts, gardening workshops and scarecrow festivals. ~ 1100 West 7800 South, West Jordan; 801-566-8903; www.gardnervillage.com.

The **South Towne Center** claims not only chain department stores under its roof but also more than 70 speciality stores and a ten-screen cinema. There's also a food court. ~ 10450 South State Street, Sandy; 801-572-1516; www.southtownecenter.com.

Roughly three dozen factory outlet stores, including Adidas, Samsonite and Bass Shoes, exist at the **Factory Stores of America** complex 13 miles south of Salt Lake City in Draper. ~ 12101 South Factory Outlet Drive, Draper; 801-571-2933.

With Salt Lake City's nightclubs and theaters a short ride north, the southern end of the valley is not particularly known for its after-dark activities. However, **The Comedy Circuit** showcases some of the country's top comedians. The shows, offered Wednesday through Saturday at 8 p.m., with two shows on Friday, run two hours and are for adult audiences. ~ 7720 South 700 West, Midvale; 801-561-7777.

NIGHTLIFE

Utah is actually considered to be an urban state since the bulk of its population is clustered around the Wasatch Range, but you don't have to head too far west before wide open spaces become the dominant landscape. Tooele County, just 15 miles west of Salt Lake City, represents the last bastion of humanity before the Nevada border is reached, and its population is roughly 20,000.

Tooele and the Great Salt Lake Desert

Tooele and Grantsville, which sit side by side in a small valley bordered on the east by the Oquirrh Mountains, on the west by the Stansbury Mountains, and on the north by the southern shore of the Great Salt Lake, are small, sleepy agricultural towns that increasingly are becoming bedroom communities for Salt Lake City.

Just west of Tooele and Grantsville, the Stansbury Range rises to 11,031 feet and then quickly gives way to the Great Salt Lake Desert, which not only holds a bombing range for the Air Force but also the Salt Flats that sate Hollywood's need for desolate landscapes and race-car drivers' need for speed.

The county's only other substantial town huddles on Utah's far western border in the form of Wendover, another sleepy town that is overshadowed by its sister community of Wendover, Nevada, which thrives with its casinos and nightclubs.

Settled by ranchers in 1849, Tooele County landed on the map in 1864 when soldiers found profitable silver, lead, zinc and gold ores in the Rush Valley, just south of Tooele. The initial discovery led to 500 claims being logged in the first year alone. While the town of Ophir's population climbed to roughly 6000 in the boom days of the 1870s, Mercur's population once hit 10,000.

Today the mining towns have mostly vanished; those that remain do so largely as ghost towns. The major economic impetus comes from the military, which arrived during World War II and erected an air base in Wendover, next to the Nevada border, where the *Enola Gay* was hangered before making its infamous bombing run on Hiroshima. The Tooele Army Depot was also established during the war and served as a supply, storage and repair center. The Dugway Proving Grounds, built in a remote area of Tooele County in 1942 to serve as a testing grounds for weaponry, gained controversy during the Vietnam War when it functioned as a biological and chemical warfare center.

The Great Salt Lake Desert, born some 20,000 years ago when prehistoric Lake Bonneville began to recede, remains today like it almost always has—a large, mostly barren stretch of flat land interrupted by a few wrinkles of mountains.

SIGHTS

Despite its out-of-the-way location, the town of Tooele and the county of the same name hold interesting insights into the hardy souls who settled this part of Utah, those who forged their way across the state en route to presumably greener pastures in California, and those who came to develop America's military might.

When the **Benson Gristmill** earned a spot on the National Register of Historic Sites in 1972, it was said to be the most significant structural landmark between Salt Lake City and Reno, Nevada. The structure's integrity comes from 24-inch beams that were held together with wooden pegs pounded into holes lined with "green" leather; when the leather dried out, it shrank and provided a tight fit for the pegs. Handmade nails were used to secure the wooden planks onto the building's exterior. The two-story mill was built in 1854 to grind grain grown by Tooele County's settlers. A year later the growing community around the mill was named "Richville," which served as the county seat until 1861. Open Tuesday through Saturday from May 1 to Labor Day. ~ About eight miles north of Tooele at the junction of Routes 138 and 36, Stansbury Park; 435-882-7678.

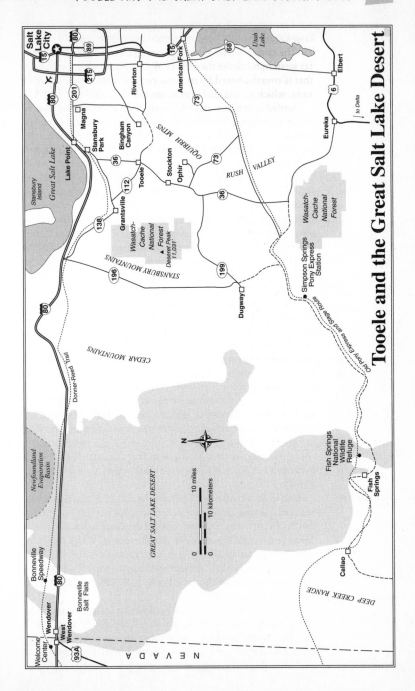

Tooele and the Great Salt Lake Desert

A whirlwind of activity usually can be found at the **Deseret Peak Complex**, a growing recreation center that currently boasts baseball fields, a demolition derby arena, a horse track, a BMX bike track, an outdoor pool and soccer fields. Plans call for a fine-arts center, an archery park and a convention center to be added in the years ahead. ~ 2930 West Route 112, Tooele; 435-843-4000.

Tooele County's mining past comes alive at the **Barrick Mining Museum**, where a visitors center at the Deseret Peak Complex displays ore cars, tools and other items from Barrick's mining past. Closed Labor Day to Memorial Day. ~ 2930 West Route 112, Tooele; 435-843-4000.

The railroad played a central role in Utah, hauling freight, mail and people across the sprawling state. At the **Tooele County Railroad and Mining Museum** a piece of railroading history exists in the form of a steam engine, some cabooses and a dining car. A miniature railroad on the grounds provides rides for kids on Saturday, while the museum details some of the county's mining history. Closed Sunday and Monday, and from Labor Day to Memorial Day. ~ Broadway and Vine Street, Tooele; 435-882-2836.

A tiny rock building in downtown Tooele houses the **Daughters of Utah Pioneers Museum**, which contains pioneer artifacts and early-day photos of the region. Along with the unique 1867 building is an 1855 log cabin. ~ 35 East Vine Street, Tooele.

Eight miles northwest of Tooele via Route 112 lies **Grantsville**, another agrarian outpost that contains a few surprises for travelers. For instance, remnants of an ill-fated group of pioneers who struggled across the Great Salt Lake Desert and then perished in the High Sierra can be found in the **Donner-Reed Museum**. A limited number of guns, furnishings and other items the California-bound settlers tossed out onto the desert in an effort to lighten their wagons' loads are housed in the museum along with other pioneer and American Indian artifacts. Tours by appointment. ~ Corner of Cooley and Clark streets, Grantsville; 435-884-3411.

HIDDEN ►   Sharks in Grantsville? They can be found at the **Bonneville Seabase**, a diving center that operates out of natural hot springs that bubble to the surface just south of the Great Salt Lake. Scuba diving and snorkeling are allowed in the springs, which also teem with shrimp, puffers, angel fish and other salt-water denizens. Open Thursday through Monday and by appointment. ~ Five miles northwest of Grantsville along Route 138; 435-884-3879, 800-840-3874.

Heading west toward the Nevada border from Grantsville on Route 80, the Great Salt Lake Desert quickly fills the windshield, and then some, sparkling alkali white to the south, west and north. Sharp-eyed motorists along Route 80 will spy the 85-foot-

HIDDEN ►   tall **"Tree of Life,"** also known as "The Tree of Utah" and "The

Metaphor," rising above the glaringly white salt flats on the north side of the interstate 26 miles east of Wendover. The unusual artwork arose in 1981 under the direction of Karl Momen, a Swedish artist who couldn't resist using the flats as his palette. Littering the flats beneath the tree are several "leaves" appearing to have fallen from the tree. Parking is not allowed along the interstate. ~ On Route 80, 59 miles west of Grantsville.

On Route 80, closing in on the Utah–Nevada border is a rather strange but famous spot. Hollywood often visits the **Bonneville Salt Flats** for its movie-making needs. Both *Independence Day* and *Con-Air* shot some scenes there. The flats also attract car racers intent on setting land-speed records down the seven-mile-long Bonneville Speedway. The flats, made up of a sodium compound similar to common table salt, cover more than 30,000 acres in extreme western Utah, just east of Wendover. They typically rejuvenate themselves each year through a succession of flooding from the Great Salt Lake and evaporation; gusting winds keep the surface flat. The racing season on the Bonneville Speedway is usually July through October, when the surface of the salt flats is particularly hard. ~ Route 80 Exit 4, ten miles east of Wendover; for information, contact the U.S. Bureau of Land Management; 801-977-4300; www.ut.blm.gov/recsite.html.

> The first unofficial land-speed record established on the Bonneville Salt Flats came in 1914 when Teddy Tetzlaff drove his *Blitzen Benz*: 141.73 mph.

Today the **Wendover Army Air Field** is a military ghost town, but in 1945 it was a top-secret facility where the crew for the *Enola Gay* trained for the nuclear bombing run on Japan. During World War II the base was home to nearly 20,000 soldiers and airmen. The air field's deserted buildings are on the grounds of the Wendover (Utah) Airport found on the south end of town. Brochures for self-guided tours of the airbase can be picked up at the Nevada Welcome Center off Exit 410 of Route 80. ~ To reach the airbase, head south on 2nd Street in Wendover.

Fifty-one miles southwest of Tooele on the Old Pony Express and Stage Route lies the **Simpson Springs Pony Express Station**, a replica of the original station here on the southeastern edge of the Great Salt Lake Desert. Due to the remote and isolated location of Simpson Springs, the setting is pretty darn near what existed back in the 1860s when the Pony Express was in business. ~ From Tooele, go south 25 miles on Route 36 then head about 26 miles west on the Old Pony Express and Stage Route.

◄ HIDDEN

Located 42 miles west of Simpson Springs and almost 93 miles southwest of Tooele, the **Fish Springs National Wildlife Refuge** is the most isolated national wildlife refuge in the lower 48 states. Due to the fact that it's the only wetland of any size within 30 miles, it's long been a desert oasis for humans and wildlife. While pre-Columbian Indian tribes frequented the area, the Pony Express

◄ HIDDEN

maintained a station here in 1860–61; the transcontinental telegraph line also came through the area, as did the Lincoln Highway when it was constructed in the early 20th century. These days birds are the main visitors, with nearly 270 species having been spotted at the refuge. An 11-mile-long auto route follows the dikes around the refuge's nine ponds and offers great views of some of the rookeries. ~ Head south from Tooele 25 miles on Route 36, then west on the gravel Old Pony Express and Stage Route for 63 miles; 435-831-5353.

LODGING

Tooele is an overnight waystation for Route 80 travelers, and as such offers two chain motels, an independent and not much more in the way of lodgings.

The **Oquirrh Motor Inn** along Route 80 north of Tooele has 41 rooms. Nothing fancy here, just clean, comfortable rooms. ~ Route 80, Lake Point; 801-250-0118. MODERATE.

The **Best Western** in town offers 31 traditional motel rooms equipped with phones and a swimming pool. ~ 365 North Main Street, Tooele; 435-882-5010, 800-448-5010. MODERATE.

Just up the street is the **Comfort Inn**, which has 60 rooms, an outdoor pool and a hot tub. A continental breakfast comes with the rates. ~ 491 South Main Street, Tooele; 435-882-6100, 800-228-5150. MODERATE.

DINING

Being so close to Salt Lake City, it's not surprising that Tooele doesn't have much in the way of dining, but if you don't want to make the drive to the capital you surely won't go hungry. Don't, however, expect dazzling settings.

Even some native Utahns have trouble pronouncing Tooele, which is pronounced "too-WILL-ah." The name is thought to have been derived from the name of a Goshute Indian chief.

Applebee's Neighborhood Grill and Bar arrived in Tooele early in 2001 with its menu of steaks, chicken fingers, burgers and grilled sandwiches. For reliable, affordable and quick service, it's hard to argue with this national chain's formula. ~ 1280 North 30 West, Tooele; 435-882-0064. BUDGET TO MODERATE.

Mexican cuisine, along with some steaks and ribs, is served at **La Frontera**, where you can build your dinner from an à la carte menu featuring enchiladas, tostadas, burritos and tacos. The ambience is much what you would expect in a modest small-town restaurant—colorful blankets and sombreros on the walls with diners seated at tables and in booths. ~ 494 South Main Street, Tooele; 435-882-0000. BUDGET TO MODERATE.

HIDDEN ►

Since 1970 the kitchen at **Sun Lok Yuen** has been treating locals to a wide variety of Chinese entrées as well as burgers, sandwiches, steaks and chops. Among the specials is Four Treasures, a combination of chicken, scallops, shrimp and vegetables served in a hash-brown basket with rice. You'll also find Peking spare-

ribs, Hong Kong steak and seafood, chicken and vegetable platters. Inside, Chinese artworks adorn the walls while the seating
ranges from booths and tables with Chinese motifs to a banquet
area. ~ 615 North Main Street, Tooele; 435-882-3003. BUDGET.

FISH SPRINGS NATIONAL WILDLIFE REFUGE 🚶 🚲 Established **PARKS**
in 1959, this 18,000-acre refuge is centered around a remote
wetland that lures birds from miles around. Ten millennia pass   ◀ *HIDDEN*
between the time rain/snow falls in the area, seeps underground
and resurfaces through the springs—making the water here some
of the purest you'll find. The refuge attracts the most birds during the fall, but in the spring and summer there's a greater variety
of species; during the winter bald eagles call the wetlands home.
Young birds begin hatching in early summer, with ducklings and
goslings easily viewed from dike roads. Common species certain
to be seen in spring and early summer include pied-bill grebes,
Canada goose, snowy egrets (which nest on the refuge) and red-
head ducks. Also present are a variety of mammals, reptiles and
amphibians, including long-tailed weasels, antelope, collared lizards, Great Basin sagebrush lizards and striped whipsnakes. A
small kiosk contains brochures and interpretive panels describing the refuge and the birds you might see. While there is a small
picnic ground, no camping is allowed on the refuge. There is, however, primitive (no facilities) camping permitted on public lands
a quarter-mile away. ~ Take Route 36 25 miles south of Tooele
and then head west on the Old Pony Express and Stage Route
for 63 miles; 435-831-5353.

Salt Lake City is a recreationalist's nirvana.
With seven ski resorts and six wilderness areas   **Outdoor Adventures**
within an hour of downtown, one never has to
travel far to find something to do in the out-of-doors.

Despite its incredible size, the Great Salt Lake is barren of fish   **FISHING**
due to its salinity. But there are plenty of other streams, lakes and
reservoirs to try your luck. For information on fishing seasons,
fees and hot spots, contact the **Utah Division of Wildlife Resources**.
~ 1596 West North Temple, Salt Lake City; 801-538-4700; www.
nr.state.ut.us.

Near Salt Lake City, **Big and Little Cottonwood** creeks as well
as **Mill Creek** have been known to produce trout. The **Jordan
River**, meanwhile, carries trout, catfish, walleye and bass. West
of Salt Lake City are a few reservoirs near Tooele, Grantsville
and Vernon that have been productive trout fisheries. Located
about 40 miles northeast of Salt Lake City via Routes 80 and 65,
East Canyon Reservoir offers rainbow and brown trout as well
as kokanee salmon.

Outfitters   The **Four Seasons Flyfisher** can lead you to some of
the Wasatch Range's streams. ~ 6591 South 1460 West, Murray;
801-288-1028, 800-498-5440; www.utahflyfish.com. Fly-fishing
is the specialty at **Western Rivers Flyfishers**. Not only can they
outfit you with the right gear, but they can lead you to fish in the
Provo and Green rivers as well as in the streams along the south
slope of the Uinta Mountains. ~ 1071 East 900 South, Salt Lake
City; 801-521-6424, 800-545-4312; www.wrflyfisher.com. Guiding trips to the Provo River, as well as Strawberry Reservoir with
its renowned trout fishery, is **Wilderness Trout Expeditions**. ~
P.O. Box 17382, Salt Lake City, UT 84117; 800-939-2680; www.
wildernesstrout.com. Along with guiding trips to the Provo River,
the folks at **Spinner Fall Fly Shop** can take you on a float trip on
the Green River in northeastern Utah. ~ 2645 East Parleys Way, Salt
Lake City; 801-466-5801, 800-959-3474; www.spinnerfall.com.

CANOEING   With paddling possible on the Great Salt Lake, Utah Lake, Echo
& KAYAKING Reservoir, the Jordan, Provo and Weber rivers, there are plenty
of canoeing and kayaking options in the area. Wildlife watchers
will get their fill of birds at these areas, particularly the Great Salt
Lake, which is a major migratory stop for shorebirds and waterfowl that winter along the Gulf Coast and farther south while
heading north to Canada for the summers. Great blue herons are
easily spotted at Echo Reservoir, while the Provo and Weber rivers,
both stellar fisheries, attract bald eagles and moose.

At **Wasatch Touring** they can sell you a canoe or rent you a
one- or two-person kayak. ~ 702 East 100 South, Salt Lake City;
801-359-9361; www.xmission.com/~wtouring.

In search of a new canoe, kayak or whitewater raft? Or do
you just need some paddling equipment? Whatever your needs,
stop by **Sidsports**, which also carries sailing equipment. ~ 265 East
3900 South, Salt Lake City; 801-261-0300.

CLIMBING   With the Wasatch Range so close, climbing opportunities abound
in the Salt Lake area. There are climbing schools to instruct you
on the finer points of scaling mountains, boulder fields near the
bottom of Little Cottonwood Canyon where you can practice
bouldering, and even indoor climbing centers.

Scale 45-foot-tall walls and practice your belays and free
climbing at the **Rockreation Sport Climbing Center**. Lessons are
available. ~ 2074 East 3900 South, Salt Lake City; 801-278-7473.

Exum Utah Mountain Adventures, which is affiliated with the
Exum Mountain Guides that lead climbs to the top of the Grand
Teton in Wyoming, takes climbing, ice climbing and mountaineer-
ing classes into the Wasatch Range. ~ 2070 East 3900 South, Salt
Lake City; 801-550-3986; www.exum.ofutah.com.

Not to be overlooked is the **Cliff Lodge** at the Snowbird Resort. One wall of this ten-story hotel has been turned into a climbing wall for would-be speed climbers. ~ Little Cottonwood Canyon, Snowbird; 801-933-2147.

Outfitters   Climbing shoes for excursions into canyons or at Cliff Lodge can be rented at **Wasatch Touring**. ~ 702 East 100 South, Salt Lake City; 801-359-9361; www.xmission.com/~wtouring.

The folks at **International Mountain Equipment** can outfit you and direct you to the best climbing in the area. They also offer rentals. ~ 3265 East 3300 South, Salt Lake City; 801-484-8073; www.imeutah.com.

SKIING & SNOW-BOARDING

Although there are 14 alpine ski resorts scattered about Utah, the heart of the state's ski country lies in the Wasatch Range that runs along Salt Lake City's eastern border. Two of the canyons found here—Big and Little Cottonwood—together claim four resorts, not to mention countless acres of backcountry terrain open to skiers and snowboarders if they've got the leg muscle and lung capacity to reach them, or the fat wallets to join a heli-skiing trek. If the roads are clear, any of the four can be reached within 40 minutes from downtown Salt Lake City.

The skiing at **Alta Ski Lifts Company** is arguably Utah's best, but it's had since 1938 to perfect its dizzying powder chutes, steep, powder-choked bowls, and rolling intermediate terrain. Eight lifts serve 2200 skiable acres and a vertical drop of 2020 feet. More than 40 marked runs and steep bowls are graced with 500 inches of snow, on average, each winter. Snowboarders are not allowed on the slopes here. ~ Route 210, Alta; 801-359-1078; www.altaskiarea.com.

Next door to Alta Ski Lifts Company, **Snowbird** is a relative newcomer on the block. Renowned for steep pitches and chutes that rim Peruvian Gulch, Snowbird contains more than 2500 ski-

AUTHOR FAVORITE

The dazzling white vision of a mid-winter snowstorm always makes me think of zipping down the slopes at **Alta Ski Lifts Company**, cradled at the head of Little Cottonwood Canyon; it dates to 1938, when a group of Salt Lake City businessmen paid for the first ski lift. These days the resort retains much of its early-day charm: snowboards are banned, lift prices are far below those charged at most of the state's other resorts, and the snow continues to pile up deeper than anywhere else in Utah. See above for more information on the resort.

able acres for skiers and 'boarders, and a vertical drop of 3240 feet that is reached via a 125-passenger tram and nine chairlifts; it also has natural as well as manmade halfpipes. In summer the resort lures hikers, mountain bikers, and climbers who assault the world-class climbing route that runs up the side of the ten-story Cliff Lodge. ~ Route 210, Snowbird; 801-933-2222, fax 801-933-2298; www.snowbird.com.

Over the granitic ridge to the north lies Big Cottonwood Canyon with its two resorts. **Brighton**, long a favorite with snowboarders, offers about 500 inches of snow each winter and a variety of terrain across its 850 skiable acres found near the canyon's headwall. Seven lifts move skiers and 'boarders around the 64 marked trails on two mountains. Got kids? Those under 10 ski or 'board free with adults, and if you're over 70, you can ski free, too. ~ Star Route, Brighton; 801-532-4731, 800-873-5512, fax 435-649-1787; www.skibrighton.com.

When the Alta ski resort opened on January 15, 1938, skiers paid a quarter for one lift ride and $1.50 for an all-day pass.

Solitude, next door to Brighton, long has matched the definition of its name, but a growing base village and marketing are changing that. Along with 1200 skiable acres, a vertical drop of 2047 feet, 450 inches of snow annually and seven lifts, the resort has some of the most striking scenery in the Wasatch cut by 63 designated trails and three broad bowls shared by skiers and 'boarders. Though craggy Honeycomb Canyon lacks interior lifts that would eliminate the tedious roundtrip down a narrow, winding trail and multiple lift rides necessary to return to the top of the canyon, the wide bowls and tree runs hidden in the canyon make the effort worthwhile. ~ 12000 Big Cottonwood Canyon, Salt Lake City; 801-534-1400, 800-748-4754, fax 435-649-5276; www.skisolitude.com.

Skinny ski fanatics have a few options in the Wasatch Range. The **Solitude Nordic Center** offers 20 kilometers of groomed track right next door to its downhill cousin, and they're some of the toughest trails in the state. Accessories, rentals and lessons are available. ~ 12000 Big Cottonwood Canyon, Salt Lake City; 801-536-5774; www.skisolitude.com/nordicctr.htm.

East of Salt Lake City via Route 80 lies **Mountain Dell**, a golf course that doubles as a Nordic ski center when snow covers the fairways. ~ 3287 Cummings Road, Salt Lake City; 801-582-3812.

Those who detest lift lines can charter a ride with **Wasatch Powderbird Guides**, a helicopter-oriented ski and snowbird experience that flies to backcountry slopes in the Wasatch Range. ~ P.O. Box 920057, Snowbird, UT 84092; 801-742-2800; www.heliskiwasatch.com.

Ski Rentals   While you can rent your gear at any of the resorts, there are numerous rental shops in Salt Lake City. **Utah Ski & Golf** has a handful of outlets in the Salt Lake area, ranging from two valley locations (134 West 600 South, 801-355-9088; 2432 East Fort Union, 801-942-1522; www.utahskigolf.com) to two shops at the Salt Lake City International Airport (Terminals 1 & 2; 801-539-8660). Another shop with multiple outlets is **Ski-N-See** (135 West 500 South, Bountiful, 801-295-1428; 1339 East Fort Union, 801-733-4477; 2420 East 7000 South, 801-943-1970; 2125 East 9400 South, 801-942-1780; 772 East 9400 South, Sandy, 801-571-2031; 800-722-3685, www.skinsee.com), which rents skis and snowboards. Yet another possibility is **Breeze Ski Rentals**. ~ 2354 South Foothill Drive; 801-485-4850.

If you need gear for Nordic skiing or snowshoeing during your visit, **Wasatch Touring** carries rentals in both areas, as well as lots of free advice on where to go. ~ 702 East 100 South, Salt Lake City; 801-259-9361; www.xmission.com/~wtouring.

Wild Rose Mountain Sports can also outfit you with Nordic skis or snowshoes, either as a purchase or a rental. ~ 702 East 3rd Avenue, Salt Lake City; 801-533-8671, 800-750-7377.

With plenty of golf courses and mild winters, it's not impossible to swing the club on any given day of the year in the Salt Lake Valley. Due to the valley's avid duffers, reservations are suggested at every course.

GOLF

The nine-hole **Jordan River Golf Course** not far from the Salt Lake airport carries a par of 27 over its 1170 yards and makes for a quick round. ~ 1200 North Redwood Road, Salt Lake City; 801-533-4527. The par-72, 18-hole **Rose Park Golf Course** is relatively flat. The course covers 6696 yards and offers a driving range. ~ 1386 North Redwood Road, Salt Lake City; 801-596-5030.

At the airport, the **Wingpointe** course stretches its 18 holes out over 7200 yards. There's also a driving range. ~ 3602 West 100 North, Salt Lake City; 801-575-2345.

A quick nine holes can be played without leaving the city at the **University of Utah**'s nine-hole course, where the par over the 2500 yards is 33. ~ Central Campus Drive and Federal Way, Salt Lake City; 801-581-6511.

The **Bonneville Golf Course**, near the mouth of Emigration Canyon where Brigham Young first saw the Salt Lake Valley, has plenty of hills and a creek that make its par-72, 6824-yard course interesting. Be forewarned, though: this is a popular course and tee times are hard to come by. Reservations can be made a week in advance. ~ 954 Connor Street, Salt Lake City; 801-583-9513, reservations 801-484-3333.

On the east side of the city, the **Forest Dale Golf Course** is the oldest golf course in the state—and possibly the Rockies—dating to 1903 when it debuted as the Salt Lake Country Club. It offers nine holes with a par of 36 over the 2970 yards. ~ 2375 South 900 East, Salt Lake City; 801-483-5420.

The **Fore Lakes Golf Course** is dotted by many lakes. Its 18 holes are broken into two nine-hole courses, one an executive nine hole. There is a driving range. ~ 1285 West 4700 South, Salt Lake City; 801-266-8621.

Ups and downs, lots of them, make the **Old Mill Golf Course** one of the area's tougher courses. The 6731-yard course is a par 71. ~ 6080 South Wasatch Boulevard, Salt Lake City; 801-424-1302.

To escape the valley's heat, the **Mountain Dell** course is roughly ten minutes east of Salt Lake City via Route 80. The 36-hole course rises and falls across a scenic mountain setting and overlooks the Mountain Dell Reservoir. ~ Parley's Canyon, Salt Lake City; 801-582-3812.

Just a little south of Salt Lake City, the **Murray Parkway** course is user-friendly with wide fairways and spacious greens over the 18-hole, 6800-yard course, which includes a driving range. ~ 6345 Murray Parkway Avenue, Murray; 801-262-4653.

The 18 holes at **Riverbend Golf Course** are split in half—nine holes run along a bluff overlooking the Jordan River, nine at the bottom of the bluff. Water hazards are frequent both top and bottom. ~ 12800 South 1040 West, Riverton; 801-253-3673.

RIDING STABLES

Despite Utah being part of the West and with mountains nearby, horses are not the preferred mode of recreational travel in the Salt Lake Valley. Still, you can find a place to ride if need be.

At **Sunrise Riding Stables** south of Salt Lake City you can rent a steed, or sign up for Western riding lessons. ~ Route 15, roughly 16 miles south of Salt Lake City; 17000 South 1300 West, Bluffdale; 801-254-1081.

Trail rides are offered throughout the summer months at the **Deer Valley** (800-558-3337), **Park City** (435-645-7256), **The Canyons** (435-615-3412) and **Sundance** (801-225-4107) resorts.

BIKING

While the Wasatch Range is renowned for its hiking possibilities, mountain bikers know there are more than a few good paths to take into the mountains.

SALT LAKE CITY City Creek Canyon is popular with hikers and bikers. The six-mile paved trail runs out of the city and into the foothills of the Wasatch Range. To balance foot and pedal traffic in the canyon, cyclists are only allowed on odd-numbered days and never on holidays.

In Bountiful, five miles north of Salt Lake City, the 13.5-mile **Mueller Park Trail** runs from the Mueller Park Picnic Grounds on the east side of Bountiful up into the Wasatch to Rudy's Flat. Most of the trail can be handled by beginners and intermediates, though there are a few steep and rocky stretches that might turn some riders into walkers.

EAST BENCH   Along the East Bench, the **Emigration Canyon Road** that runs east from the Hogle Zoo and This Is the Place Heritage Park offers a scenic, eight-mile-long ride up into the hills. The road is narrow and curvy, though, which can make for some interesting moments when traffic passes. Near Little Mountain Pass there are views of Lookout Peak and the Mountain Dell Reservoir.

For an easier ride, the **Bonneville Shoreline Trail** runs along the benches on the east side of Salt Lake City and offers a more moderate pedaling experience. The route, which provides nice views of the Great Salt Lake, Antelope Island and downtown Salt Lake City, can be accessed via City Creek Canyon as well as just east of This Is the Place Heritage Park. Since the trail is popular with hikers and joggers, it can get congested, and Salt Lake City's diehard riders can close quickly, and quietly, upon more leisurely cyclists.

On the southeastern edge of Salt Lake City, the **Millcreek Pipeline Trail** runs six and a half miles one way along an old water pipeline right-of-way up to the head of Millcreek Canyon. The ride, which starts at Rattlesnake Gulch just past the fee station at the mouth of the canyon, rolls through thick forest and across open slopes; a steep uphill welcomes riders. To avoid this drive to the end of the canyon and access the trail at the Elbow Fork trailhead and pedal downhill through the canyon, although without a shuttle car a return uphill trip will be required. Millcreek Canyon is reached by taking Wasatch Boulevard to 3800 South and then heading east.

> The salt contained in the Great Salt Lake is not totally worthless. Several companies, including Morton, take salt from the lake to make table salt and water softeners.

SOUTH VALLEY AND MOUNTAIN RESORTS   In Big Cottonwood Canyon, the **Solitude Mountain Resort** offers lift-served mountain biking and rents mountain bikes. A five-and-a-half-mile loop trail provides access to both Lake Solitude and Silver Lake.

Across the ridge in Little Cottonwood Canyon, beginners, or flatlanders unaccustomed to Utah's elevation, should consider the **Albion Basin Summer Road** as a good starting point for a cool summer ride. Starting at an elevation of roughly 9000 feet, the two-mile-long road runs from the base of the Alta Ski Area up into the wildflower-dappled Albion Basin inside the Wasatch-Cache National Forest.

In the winter months **Grizzly Gulch** is popular with backcountry skiers and snowboarders, but come summertime the mostly uphill, four-and-a-quarter-mile trail that runs into it is preferred by mountain bikers. The trailhead is found between the Shallow Shaft and Our Lady of the Snows Center in Alta.

The **Snowbird Ski and Summer Resort** turns many of its mountain maintenance roads into mountain bike trails once the snow has melted. While you can pedal uphill for an incredible workout, it's also possible to ride with your bike to the top of Hidden Peak on the resort's tram and cycle downhill. Stop at the Activity Center located off Entry Level 2 for a trail map.

The **Wasatch Crest Trail**, part of the Great Western Trail that runs from Canada to Mexico, cuts north and south through the mountains just east of Salt Lake City. Hikers and bikers know it as a quick retreat from suburbia. Experienced cyclists in search of a strenuous workout, and intermediates looking to improve their ability, pedal a 20-mile out-and-back section accessed from the end of Millcreek Canyon. The single-track route follows the Big Water Trail to its junction with the Great Western Trail, which in turn leads to the Wasatch Crest Trail. Along the way to the turnaround point near the head of Big Cottonwood Canyon, the narrow path provides sweeping views of the Park City side of the Wasatch. Due to high demand from hikers and bikers, cyclists can only access the trail from Mill Creek Canyon on even-numbered days.

TOOELE AND THE GREAT SALT LAKE DESERT In the Tooele area, the **Copper Pit Overlook** is a 19-mile out-and-back mountain bike ride that gains nearly 4000 feet in elevation as it climbs into the Oquirrh Mountains on the way to a great view down into the Bingham Canyon Mine. The strenuous nature of the ride's first leg quickly weeds out novice cyclists. The trail, which starts with four miles of asphalt before turning to dirt and gravel, begins at the Tooele County Museum (Broadway and Vine Street).

A shorter, not-as-steep ride runs 12 miles roundtrip from the junction of Route 73 and the Ophir Canyon Road south of Tooele to **Ophir Canyon** and the site of this one-time boomtown. Along the route are old mining-car rail beds and some mine-related ruins.

The **Jacob City Trail** that starts in Stockton runs eight miles one way to the ghost town of Jacob City. As with the Copper Pit Overlook and Ophir Canyon rides, the hardest part of this ride is on the way out to Jacob City, as you gain 3140 feet in elevation. But the ruins of Jacob City, the views of Rush Valley and the Deseret Peak Wilderness Area to the west, as well as the ex-

GOOPY WHEN WET

Tempting as they are for off-road driving in the spirit of those land-speed racers, the Salt Flats are to be avoided. Ruts along Route 80 testify to the many cars and pickups that get mired in the mud beneath the salty surface crust that gets goopy when wet. When wet, the salty surface solution can short-out your rig's electrical system.

hilarating downhill return trip, make this a fun ride. The ride starts at Bryan's Service Store in Stockton at 29 North Conner Avenue.

The **Butterfield Canyon-Middle Canyon Road** runs across the Oquirrh Mountains between Salt Lake City and Tooele and offers a great view of the Bingham Copper Mine.

Mountain biking is possible on **Stansbury Island**, just north of Tooele in the Great Salt Lake. A nine-mile loop starts from a parking lot almost seven miles up Stansbury Island Road (stay left at the first junction three and a half miles up the road, then straight past a stop sign located two miles past the junction; another mile will bring you to the parking area). The ride starts with a series of steep switchbacks, but it levels out somewhat as it navigates the slopes above Tabby's Canyon before throwing several downhill stretches at riders. Summer can be an unbearably hot time for this ride.

Bike Rentals For trail information, bike sales or repairs, try **Canyon Sports**. ~ 1844 East 7000 South, Salt Lake City; 801-942-3100. **Guthrie's Bicycle** has been selling bikes for nearly a century and also carries a wide range of books and guides. ~ 731 East 2100 South, Salt Lake City; 801-484-0404, 888-480-0404.

Another source of information and repairs is **Golsan Cycles**. ~ 4678 South Highland Drive, Salt Lake City; 801-278-6820. **Bingham Cyclery**, on Salt Lake's east side, also sells, repairs and informs. ~ 1370 South 2100 East, Salt Lake City; 801-583-1940; www.binghamcyclery.com. **Wild Rose Mountain Sports** can outfit you, repair your bike or sell you a mountain bike. ~ 702 East 3rd Avenue, Salt Lake City; 801-533-8671.

Bingham Cyclery also has a shop in Midvale, south of Salt Lake City, and Sandy. ~ 707 East For Union Boulevard, Midvale, 801-561-2453; 1300 East 10510 South, Sandy, 801-571-4480.

Mountain bikes can be rented, purchased and repaired at **Wasatch Touring**. ~ 702 East 100 South, Salt Lake City; 801-359-9361; www.wasatchtouring.com.

HIKING

With canyons riddling the Wasatch Range, it doesn't take long to find a trailhead. Many of the ski resorts have excellent hiking trails within their boundaries, and some offer lift-served hiking, too. Flatlanders need to keep in mind the quickly rising elevation, which runs from 4330 feet in downtown Salt Lake City to above 11,000 feet on some of the peaks just outside the city. Rattlesnakes can be common along the trails during hot summer months, too. Any questions that might arise over hiking in the Wasatch probably can be answered by the folks at the **Public Lands Information Center**. ~ REI outlet, 3285 East 3300 South; 801-466-6411.

All distances listed for hiking trails are one way unless otherwise noted.

SALT LAKE CITY   Not to be overlooked is Antelope Island, with its handful of hikes. One of the island's longer hikes runs from **White Rock Bay to Split Rock Bay** (6.5 miles), weaving together a leg of the White Rock Bay Loop and the Split Rock Loop. Not far from the trailhead the well-worn trail crosses a grassy basin before clambering along the western flanks of Frary Peak and then dropping to the beach. While bison and antelope can occasionally be spotted in the basin, chukars, a game bird, flutter across the rocks. A short spur runs to the point of **Elephant Head** (1 mile). Not only does the hike give spectacular views of the Great Salt Lake, it passes horse corrals ranchers formed out of rock walls in the 1870s. In summer, heat and insects conspire against hikers, making this trek better done in spring or fall.

Grandeur Peak (3 miles), located 3.2 miles up Millcreek Canyon just minutes from downtown, is an unassuming summit but one that gives panoramic views of the Salt Lake Valley and the Great Salt Lake. Located on the southeastern edge of the city, the trail runs not quite three miles from the Church Fork picnic area parking lot to the summit, climbing through old-growth forest, aspen groves and wildflower meadows before topping out on a rocky outcrop at 8299 feet.

At 9026 feet, **Mount Olympus** (3 miles) is not the tallest peak fronting Salt Lake City, but its imposing presence over the city makes it a desirable hike for many. It also happens to be one of the more grueling hikes, thanks to the steady diet of switchbacks that swing the trail back and forth up the mountain. The trailhead can be found at a parking lot just above Wasatch Boulevard.

While most above-treeline trails involve scrambles across talus slopes, that's not the case with the hike to **Lookout Peak** (3.5 miles). This hike, which starts in Affleck Park, a Salt Lake County park found five miles up Route 65 from Route 80 Exit 134, runs a short way through forest before cruising through scattered scrub oak stands and then breaking completely out into the clear. The summit, reached 3.5 miles from the trailhead, offers good views of downtown Salt Lake City and the Great Salt Lake.

SOUTH VALLEY AND MOUNTAIN RESORTS   Little Cottonwood Canyon, along with being home to the Alta and Snowbird ski resorts, is chockfull of hikes that lead into the Twin Peaks and Lone Peak wilderness areas. The walk to **Red Pine Lakes** (3 miles) quickly leaves the canyon floor from the White Pine Trailhead on its way to the 30,088-acre Lone Peak Wilderness. Climbing up through a narrow side canyon, the trail runs through dense stands of conifer with aspen sprinkled liberally throughout before the trees give way near the trail's end to rugged boulder fields and two lakes puddled beneath glacial cirques. Towering above and just west of the boulder fields is the 11,326-foot Pfeifferhorn, a triangular-shaped peak that hardy hikers can reach via a ridge-line scramble.

TOOELE AND THE GREAT SALT LAKE DESERT   About 43 miles west of Salt Lake City lie the Stansbury Mountains and the Deseret Peak Wilderness, which sprawls below 11,031-foot **Deseret Peak** (6 miles). The trail is reached via the South Willow Canyon road south of Grantsville. Along the way it crosses a stream and throws a spur to Willow Lakes. From the summit there are sweeping views of the Salt Flats to the west and the Wasatch Range to the east.

A view into Nevada is offered from the summit of King Top, an 8350-foot mountain top in the Confusion Range of Utah's West Desert. Getting to the trailhead is half the job, as it lies roughly 62 miles west of Delta via Route 6. The **King Top Trail** (6 miles) hike through Cat Canyon is not particularly tough since the elevation gain is just 2100 feet. But there's no water out there and in the summer this place gets hot. Quiet, watchful hikers just might see some of the region's wild horses.

Transportation

CAR

Salt Lake City is like the center of a wheel, with two major interstate highways and numerous state routes running like spokes through Utah's capital. While **Route 80** runs east and west through the state, passing through Salt Lake City, **Route 15** runs north and south, also passing through the city. **Route 215** is the belt route that encircles the city and ties into spur **Route 190** and **Route 210** that lead into the Cotton-wood Canyons southeast of Salt Lake City as well as **Route 201**, which runs west of the capital to Magna.

AIR

Nearly a dozen airlines—American West, American, Continental, Delta, Frontier, Northwest, Skywest, Southwest, TWA and United—fly into **Salt Lake City International Airport**, which is located seven miles west of the capital. ~ 776 North Terminal Drive, Salt Lake City; 801-575-2400, fax 801-575-2679; www.ci.slc.ut.us/airport.

NO COMPASS REQUIRED

When Brigham Young and his followers laid out Salt Lake City, they made Temple Square the city's geographic center. From the square the streets are laid out in a crisscross fashion in a numerical sequence. While the southeast corner of the square is located at "0 East 0 West, 0 North and 0 South," one block north is known as "100 North," while two blocks north would be "200 North." One block south is "100 South," while two blocks south is "200 South," and so on, moving in all compass directions.

BUS   Greyhound Bus Lines makes regular stops in Salt Lake. ~ 160 West South Temple, Salt Lake City; 801-355-9579, 800-231-2222.

TRAIN   Amtrak stops in Salt Lake City to and from the West Coast. ~ 801-531-0188, 800-872-7245.

CAR RENTALS   Car-rental companies that have offices nearby or at the Salt Lake City International Airport include **Avis Rent A Car** (801-575-2847), **Budget Rent A Car** (801-363-1500), **Dollar Rent A Car** (801-575-2580), **Enterprise Rent a Car** (801-537-7433), **Hertz Rent a Car** (801-575-2683), **National Car Rental** (801-575-2277) and **Thrifty Car Rental** (801-595-6677).

There are also a number of shuttle companies that run vans or buses to and from the airport. For information, contact one of the airport's two transportation desks, located in the terminals near the baggage carousels. ~ 801-575-2477.

PUBLIC TRANSIT   The **Utah Transit Authority** operates dozens of routes through Salt Lake City and the surrounding communities. A Free Ride Zone exists in the heart of the downtown commercial district. ~ 801-287-4636.

The core of the Salt Lake Valley is cut by the TRAX **Light Rail** system, which is operated by the Utah Transit Authority and runs from the downtown area south into Sandy. ~ 801-287-4636.

The **Pioneer Trolley** runs during the summer months in the heart of Salt Lake City surrounding Temple Square. The trolley, which is guided and makes a 15-minute loop of the area, is free. If you can't spot one of the "Pioneer Trolley Stop" signs near the Joseph Smith Memorial Building, call for stop locations. ~ 801-240-6279.

TAXIS   Taxi service is available throughout the Salt Lake Valley. In Salt Lake City is the **City Cab Company**. ~ 801-363-5550. Also operating in the capital is **Yellow Cab**. ~ 801-521-2100. There's also **Ute Cab**. ~ 801-359-7788. The **Murray Cab Company** also serves the valley. ~ 801-328-5704. So does the **South Salt Lake Cab Company**. ~ 801-328-5704.

THREE

Northern Utah

Northern Utah has long been a Western crossroads, serving as both a meeting place and a thoroughfare. Long before settlers arrived, the Blackfoot, Shoshone, Paiute and Ute tribes regularly passed through the mountainous area that marks the eastern edge of the Great Basin. They came no doubt to enjoy the warm waters of the many hot springs that bubble up along the Wasatch Fault, which runs north and south through the region, and to stalk the plentiful game that roamed the forests. So revered was the Cache Valley to the Shoshone that they referred to it as "the house of the great spirit."

Spanish explorers had little more than a passing interest in the area, arriving in the 1770s from southern Utah in search of routes to the West Coast. While they made some maps, they didn't stay for long.

It was the arrival of the mountain men in the early 1800s, however, that made a lasting impact on the region; they left their names behind in settlements that slowly grew and tamed the wilderness. A young Jim Bridger, at the time just 20 years old, was one of the first mountain men to reach the Cache Valley. While chasing beaver pelts along the Bear River the trapper, working for the Rocky Mountain Fur Company, made it all the way to the Great Salt Lake, which, upon tasting, he decided must be the Pacific Ocean. The practice of trappers such as Bridger to hide, or "cache," their pelts until they could be sold at rendezvous inspired the naming of the Cache Valley and Cache County.

The region literally became a crossroads on May 10, 1869, when two steam-belching locomotives, the Central Pacific Railroad's "Jupiter" and the Union Pacific's "No. 119," met cattle guard to cattle guard at Promontory Summit not far from the northern shore of the Great Salt Lake, marking the completion of the nation's first transcontinental railroad and the beginning of the end of the "wild West."

These days the region, which remains more rural than urban, continues as a crossroads, both literally and figuratively. Interstate highways that shuttle travelers north and south through Utah and Idaho cut through the region, while smaller routes meander east and west along the contours of the landscape to Wyoming and Nevada. More figuratively, the region stands at something of an economic and societal crossroads. While Cache Valley communities like Logan, Brigham City, Wellsville and Garden City continue to tightly embrace their agricultural heritage, Ogden has been transformed into a diverse metropolitan area with its business fingers dipped into the aerospace, industrial and financial sectors.

With much of the sparsely populated region either under the waters of the Great Salt Lake or preserved by the Wasatch-Cache National Forest, it's not surprising that tourism and outdoor recreation are integral parts of the economy. Just look across the landscape. Where the fresh waters of the Bear River spill into the Great Salt Lake on the northern shores of Willard Bay they nourish a sprawling bird refuge that teems with millions of birds during their spring and fall migrations. Northeast of Brigham City, Wellsville Mountain rises nearly 5000 feet straight up to create the country's steepest range while buttressing behind it a pocket of wilderness reminiscent of that which confronted Bridger.

Liberally sprinkled across the region are state parks, bejeweled high-country lakes and sprawling valley lakes and reservoirs that conspire with the forests and mountains to create a year-round outdoor lover's dream.

▼▼▼▼▼▼▼▼▼▼

Ogden Area

Overshadowed by the prominence of Salt Lake City 35 miles to the south, but certainly not lost in that shadow, Ogden has a long, colorful history dating to the mountain men who roamed the West in the mid-19th century. Trappers regularly held rendezvous in the area; in fact, the city took its name from Peter Skene Ogden, a brigade leader for the Hudson Bay Fur Company. The valley went on to claim Utah's first white settlement, which arose in 1846 when trapper Miles Goodyear, deciding life would be easier as a merchant, built a fort and trading post near the confluence of the Weber and Ogden rivers.

Some 80 years later, it's said that gangster Al Capone found Ogden a bit too rough for his liking and boarded a train back to Chicago, where his chosen career flourished. Boxer Jack Dempsey apparently didn't mind the street life, which was colored by the city's thriving red-light district, and pummeled quite a few opponents on his climb up the heavyweight ladder.

These days Ogden is a more sophisticated city with strong industrial and financial centers. Home to Weber State University and Hill Air Force Base, the city also claims a share of the 2002 Olympic Winter Games with its ice sheet for curling and the nearby Snowbasin Ski Resort for downhill, Super-G and combined ski races, as well as the alpine events for the 2002 Paralympic Winter Games.

SIGHTS

Stretching along the western foothills of the Wasatch Range, Ogden holds an envious position among the state's metropolitan communities. It's not as big or crowded as Salt Lake City, nor does it have to share the limelight with an adjoining city, as do Provo

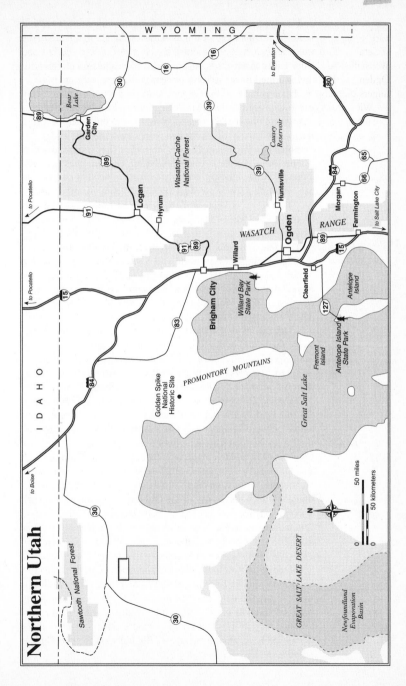

Northern Utah

and Orem. No, Ogden enjoys a modest population of 65,000 and beautiful surroundings of mountainous national forest lands to the east and the Great Salt Lake to the west. A farming and railroad community in its youth, today Ogden blends historical sites with a vibrant industrial sector and nearby recreational outlets.

For a glimpse of the Ogden's colorful past as a 19th-century rail town, head to **Historic 25th Street**, a two-block stretch of downtown that has been partially restored to the luster it enjoyed during the heyday of the United States' railroad era. Today this National Historic District boasts interesting shops, antique stores, restaurants and hotels in beautifully restored buildings scattered among private clubs and weary structures in need of restoration. See "Historic 25th Street Walking Tour" below for more details.

The anchor of Historic 25th Street is **Union Station**, a cavernous railroad depot that dates to the 1920s. You'll find a clutch of interesting museums that let you peek into northern Utah's past. While trains no longer stop here, the building also houses the **Ogden/Weber Convention and Visitors Bureau** information center, a great place to learn about the valley's history and stock up on brochures and maps as well as souvenirs and Olympic merchandise. ~ 2501 Wall Avenue, Ogden; 801-629-8444, 800-255-8824; www.ogden-ut.com.

Utah claims two theaters tied to the Egyptian revival that swept the nation in the 1920s. One is in Park City, the other here in Ogden. The fully restored 1924 **Peery's Egyptian Theater** continues to host plays and films. ~ Historic 25th Street and Washington Boulevard, Ogden; 801-395-3227, 800-337-2690.

Historic 25th Street isn't the only unique part of downtown Ogden. In the early 1900s a number of wealthy families who would prove prominent in Utah history settled in what is now **HIDDEN** ► the **Eccles Historic District**. Among the houses here is one that Leroy and Myrtle Eccles built at 2509 Eccles Avenue for more than $100,000 in 1917. A lavish home reflecting Italian Renaissance architecture, today it serves as a backdrop for weddings and receptions. A stucco home built in the Old English Cottage style, with a steeply pitched roof broken by dormers, can be found at 2580 Eccles Avenue. A brochure guiding you through this district is available at the visitors center in Union Station. ~ Bordered by 25th and 26th streets and Van Buren and Jackson avenues.

Some of the best local, regional and national art in Ogden can be found at **Eccles Community Art Center**. The center itself is a work of art, housed in a handsome 1893 Victorian sandstone mansion and now listed on the national and state registers of historic places. The adjacent Carriage House Gallery displays more works and has a small gift shop. ~ 2508 Jefferson Avenue, Ogden; 801-392-6935.

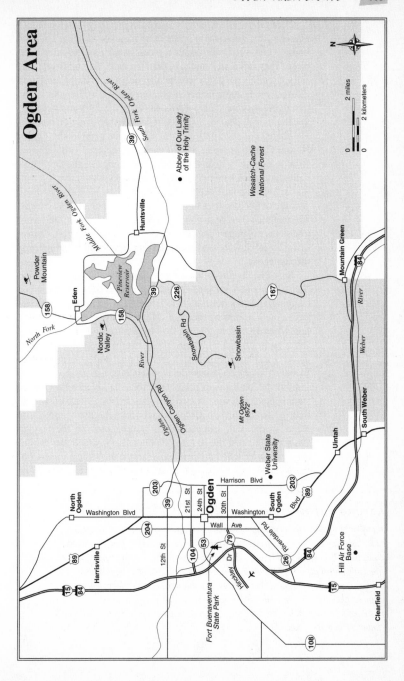

Ogden Area

N

Ogden River

South Fork Ogden River

39

Abbey of Our Lady
of the Holy Trinity •

Wasatch-Cache
National Forest

Huntsville

Middle Fork Ogden River

Powder
Mountain

Eden

Pineview
Reservoir

39

158

226

167

Mountain Green

84

Weber River

158

Nordic
Valley

River

North Fork

Snowbasin Rd

Snowbasin

South Weber

Ogden Canyon Rd

Ogden River

Mt Ogden
9572

Weber State
University

Uintah

203

Harrison Blvd

203

89

North
Ogden

Washington Blvd

203

21st St

24th St

30th St

Washington

Ogden

South
Ogden

Blvd

89

39

204

Wall Ave

Riverdale Rd

84

89

Harrisville

12th St

104

53

79

26

Hill Air
Force
Base

15

84

Hinckley Dr

Fort Buenaventura
State Park

15

Clearfield

108

0   2 miles

0   2 kilometers

Youngsters can't avoid having fun in the **Treehouse Children's Museum**, an interactive museum that focuses on reading. The treehouse is crammed with things for kids ages 2 to 12 to do and explore. They can read a book, be read to, roam through Storybook Village with its props for storytelling, or perform in the museum's theater, which stages its presentations on the last Thursday of the month. Admission. ~ 2255-B Ogden City Mall, 24th and Washington Boulevard, Ogden; 801-394-9663; www.relia.net/~treehouse.

There's no need to leave town to enjoy nature—the **Ogden Nature Center** provides a wild touch to the city. This 127-acre wildlife sanctuary near the northwestern edge of the city offers nature trails for summer strolls or winter cross-country ski outings as well as ponds, wetlands and more than 10,000 trees. Each year the center also tries to rehabilitate injured or orphaned birds. The treehouse is sure to delight the kids. Closed Sunday and from Christmas to January 2. Admission. ~ 966 West 12th Street, Ogden; 801-621-7595; www.ogdennaturecenter.org, e-mail info@ogdennaturecenter.org.

Fort Buenaventura State Park, found on 88 acres along the Weber River in West Ogden, recalls the days of the 1840s when trapping and mountain men were on their way out and settlers were slowly colonizing the West. Miles Goodyear built his trading post here in 1846, and while the original structure no longer exists, a replica based on historical records was erected on 32 acres in 1980 and includes cabins, a trading post and a visitors center. Just like the original stockade, wooden pegs, not nails, were used to hold the log walls in place. Goodyear had high hopes for his trading post, as it was located along the Hasting's Cutoff, a route that led to California. Unfortunately for Goodyear, one of the wagon trains that stopped at his trading post on the way to California carried the ill-fated Donner Party, which met an untimely disaster when it became marooned in the heavy snows of the Sierra Nevada Range. ~ 2450 A Avenue, Ogden; 801-621-4808.

ARMING THE NATION

Many of the 19th-century firearms that were used to tame the West (and hold up stagecoaches and passenger trains, for that matter) can be traced to John M. Browning, the father of the Browning Arms Company. Browning lived and worked in Ogden, where he and his employees designed and built many of the weapons that carried the Winchester, Remington and Colt labels. The company remains in business today. The Browning Firearms Museum in Union Station displays various models built by the company over the years.

With two rivers coursing through town, the three-mile-long **Ogden River Parkway** should come as no surprise. The parkway runs along the Ogden River from the mouth of Ogden Canyon into the heart of downtown. The prehistoric past rises out of the parkway in the form of the **Ogden Eccles Dinosaur Park**, which features more than 100 life-size dinosaur models such as archaeopteryx (a reptilian bird), tyrannosaurus rex and triceratops. There's also a hands-on fossil display and a paleontological laboratory. While the parkway is open year-round, the dinosaur park is only open April through October, weather permitting, so call ahead. Admission. ~ 1544 East Park Boulevard, Ogden; 801-393-3466; www.dinosaurpark.org, e-mail dinopark@ci.ogden.ut.us.

One of the town's claims to fame isn't within Ogden's borders, but rather towers over it. A knock-off of **Ben Lomond Peak**, which rises 9717 feet high on Ogden's eastern skyline, is flashed daily across television and movie screens throughout the world as the logo for Paramount Pictures.

Although you might need to enlist to stroll through the heart of Hill Air Force Base, ordinary civilians can tour the vintage aircraft and missiles on display at the **Hill Aerospace Museum**. Sprawling across 50 acres near the northwest corner of the airbase, the museum displays a wide array of jet- and propeller-driven warplanes, among them an F-15 fighter, a B-52 bomber, a Soviet MIG and an SR-71C "Blackbird" spy plane. Air Force uniforms are also among the exhibits. ~ 7961 Wardleigh Road, Hill Air Force Base; 801-777-6868; www.hill.af.mil/museum/info/museum.htm.

One of America's oldest amusement parks, **Lagoon** dates to 1886, when it was known as Lakeside Park, a popular swimming resort then located on the shore of the Great Salt Lake. Its colorful history includes a period in the 1960s when rock-and-roll stars such as the Beach Boys and Rolling Stones performed at the park. Today Lagoon is known as the largest amusement park between Kansas City and the Pacific Ocean, with more than 40 rides and four roller coasters, including "Colossus the Fire Dragon," which shuttles screaming riders through 65-foot diameter loops at speeds up to 55 mph. Nearby is "Lagoon A Beach," six acres of watery fun, ranging from waterfalls and fountains to towering "hydrotubes" and a meandering manmade river. The park also has a 15-acre re-creation of a frontier village, complete with gun shooters and live entertainment. Open daily Memorial Day through Labor Day, and weekends in April, May and September. Admission. ~ Route 15 Exit 327, 17 miles south of Ogden; 801-451-8000, 800-748-5246; www.lagoonpark.com, e-mail info@lagoonpark.com.

Got a hankering for some creamed honey with a dollop of spirituality? Then visit the **Abbey of Our Lady of the Holy Trinity,**   ◄ *HIDDEN*

Text continued on page 108.

Historic 25th Street

In late-19th-century Ogden, the railroad was the city's lifeblood. From Union Station, today the undisputed hallmark of Historic 25th Street, prosperity swept through the front doors and rolled like a wave up 25th Street. Hotels, saloons and shops in tasteful architectures quickly arose to capture the attention, and business, of those who got off the trains.

Many of those buildings remain, in many cases housing unique businesses that continue, as did their forefathers, to try to attract shoppers. A free self-guiding brochure available at the visitors center in Union Station traces the history of not just the street, but also the city.

UNION STATION   Union Station, a sprawling, Mediterranean Colonial–style depot reminiscent of America's early-20th-century love affair with railroads, is the third to stand in this location. The first depot, a small, unassuming facility, arose just after the golden spike was driven at Promontory Summit. In 1889 a more lavish, Victorian-style building replaced it. However, it burned to the ground in 1923 and was succeeded by the present building. Although trains no longer stop here, today the building retains a grand, cavernous lobby with sprawling **murals** at each end of the lobby depicting the completion of the transcontinental railroad. Outside, a cobblestone courtyard surrounds a water fountain while locomotive displays bookend the building. Kids particularly enjoy clambering over steam locomotive 4436 on the north end and peering inside its caboose. Union Station is also home to the Utah State Railroad Museum and The Natural History Museum, as well as a gift shop and the Union Grill. The **Myra Powell Gallery** displays both local and nationally known artists. One hallway displays artworks honoring Utah's railroad legacy in the form of paintings depicting locomotives at work in various settings around the state. Admission for museums. ~ 2501 Wall Avenue; 801-629-8444, 800-255-8824, museums 801-629-8535; www.ogden-ut.com/attractions/unionstation.html.

UTAH STATE RAILROAD MUSEUM   The state railroad museum sprawls both inside and outside of Union Station. Outside in the station's yards you can inspect a handful of retired locomotives and their cars and clamber inside a caboose. Inside the depot, tour the Wattis-Dumke Model Railroad Exhibit with its HO-scale model railroad. Eight different HO layouts depict how turn-of-the-20th-century crews cut through mountains as they laid tracks through the Wasatch Range, around the Great Salt Lake, and into the Sierra Mountains.

BROWNING LEGACY   Upstairs, more than a century of firearms history is on display at the **Browning Firearms Museum**, which stores the legacy of John M. Browning, an Ogden resident. The first edition of the Browning Automatic Rifle, which served the U.S. military well for 80 years, is on display, as are an assortment of machine guns. Back downstairs at the **Browning/Kimball Car Museum** you can marvel over horseless carriages from the early 1900s. Among the favorites is a 1931 Pierce Arrow once owned by Chicago mobsters who had it fitted with gun holsters.

MURPHY BLOCK   Back on Historic 25th Street, a series of shops stand on the spot where George Murphy, a Civil War veteran, developed the "Murphy Block" in 1887. Initially, Murphy ran a tobacco and cigar shop on the first floor of the "Murphy Building," while the second floor housed the Windsor Hotel. Over the years the structure fronted businesses ranging from a grocery and confectionery to a curio shop. During World War II troops were entertained by the USO here.

SENATE SALOON   Next door to the "Murphy Building" George Murphy erected the Senate Saloon in 1889, a grandiose structure festooned with elaborate cornices and moldings that are hallmarks of Italianate architecture. Today it houses a variety of shops. ~ 105–111 Historic 25th Street.

ASPEN STUDIO   Across the street stands the Aspen Studio, a two-story structure built around 1903 to house a saloon and grocery on the main floor and rented rooms on the second. The Grand Saloon took over the main floor in 1913 and was frequented by the region's sheepherders. Prohibition transformed the saloon into a billiard hall. Today the building, which has a corbeled upper cornice and a panel inscribed with "Aspen Studio," is home to a taxidermy and fine-arts shop. ~ 136 Historic 25th Street; 801-399-9052.

LONDON ICE CREAM PARLOR   One of the oldest buildings on Historic 25th Street, and perhaps one of the most architecturally significant, is the London Ice Cream Parlor. The two-story brick building carries a Greek Revival facade with pediment roof and pilasters, as well as some Italianate influences in its Roman-arched windows and bracketed cornice. Today it's home to The Athenian, a Greek-American restaurant. During its highly colorful past it had a second-floor boarding house that evolved into the "K.C. Rooms," a lively bordello. ~ 252–254 Historic 25th Street.

KANSAS CITY LIQUOR HOUSE   Directly across the street stands the Kansas City Liquor House, a two-story building built around 1890. Less decorative than others on the street, the building has square windows and no ornate stone- or brick-work. Although the location housed businesses that sold Chinese goods and furniture over the years, today it is home to a business more fitting to the building's name—Rooster's, a brewpub. ~ 253 Historic 25th Street; 801-627-6171.

a trappist monastery nestled on 1800 acres of rich farmland. After a stop in the gift shop, where you'll find 14 flavors of creamed honey prepared by the white-robed monks, attend one of their prayer sessions or listen to their Gregorian chants. ~ About 15 miles east of Ogden in Huntsville via Route 39.

LODGING

A modest variety of lodging possibilities is available in Ogden, ranging from highway chains and historic hotels to thematic bed and breakfasts.

HIDDEN ►

It might seem hokey to some, but others will find the ruggedness of the **Alaskan Inn** a wonderful escape from standard motel and hotel rooms. Located four miles up Ogden Canyon, the lodge offers 12 rooms and 11 cabins; each, through their furnishings and decor, evokes a particular flavor of Alaska, such as the Northern Lights, the Iditarod or the Mother Lode. ~ 435 Ogden Canyon Road, Ogden; 801-621-8600, 888-707-8600; www.alaskaninn. com, e-mail mail@alaskaninn.com. DELUXE.

If you don't mind settling into a nondescript, generic lodging, Ogden offers quite a few in the budget to moderate range. A bit pricier but located in the heart of downtown and close to Ogden's corporate, government and aerospace centers as well as Historic 25th Street and shopping centers is the **Ogden Marriott**, which has nearly 300 rooms. The rooms are designed to suit business travelers, complete with dataport phones, irons and coffee makers. Also within the complex is a restaurant, a sports bar, a pool and a workout room. ~ 247 24th Street, Ogden; 801-627-1190, 888-825-3163, fax 801-394-6312; www.marriott.com. MODERATE TO DELUXE.

Not far south of Historic 25th Street, the **Days Inn Ogden** provides reliable lodging and a free continental breakfast along with a swimming pool, a hot tub and an exercise room. You'll also find a restaurant and lounge on the grounds. ~ 3306 Washington Boulevard, Ogden; 801-399-5671. BUDGET TO MODERATE.

AUTHOR FAVORITE

You can sense the elegance early-20th-century railroad travel brought to Ogden by staying in the **Ben Lomond Historic Suite Hotel**. Located a short walk from the historic Union Station that once ushered thousands of travelers into northern Utah, the hotel retains some of that romantic period's elegance with the cherrywood furniture, wing chairs and four-poster beds that grace its 122 suites and 22 rooms. Of course, if you're traveling with kids they'll focus on the video-game machines and two TVs in each suite. ~ 2510 Washington Boulevard, Ogden; 801-627-1900, 888-627-8897, fax 801-394-5342; www.benlomondhotel.com. MODERATE TO DELUXE.

The **Best Rest Inn** and its 101 standard roadside-motel rooms can be found on the west side of Ogden just off Route 15 Exit 346. Close by you'll find not only the Ogden Nature Center but also the Ogden Raptors baseball stadium. ~ 1206 West 2100 South, Ogden; 801-393-8644, 800-343-8644. BUDGET.

Work and relaxation can be accommodated at the **Comfort Suites** motel just off the 21st Street exit along Route 15. While the rooms provide dual data ports to connect your laptop to, you'll also find an indoor pool and hot tub to relax in or, come summer, an outdoor basketball court and volleyball pit where you can work up a sweat. The rooms, nicely done in soft pastels and desert hues, are accompanied by a complimentary hot breakfast buffet. ~ 1200 West 2250 South, Ogden; 801-621-2545, 800-462-9925, fax 801-627-4782; www.ogdencomfortsuites.com. MODERATE.

Another quick, reliable option is the **Holiday Inn Express**, across from Comfort Suites. Along with 75 rooms and an indoor pool, hot tub and fitness center, the motel offers a business center where you can finish that report or fax a letter. ~ 1200 West 2245 South, Ogden; 801-392-5000, 800-465-4329. MODERATE.

At the **High Country Inn**, a Best Western property, the 111 rooms are supported by a heated outdoor pool, an exercise facility, rooms equipped with Nintendo machines to keep the kids happy, and Jeremiah's Restaurant (see "Dining" below), which many argue serves up the best breakfast in northern Utah. ~ 1335 West 12th Street, Ogden; 801-394-9474, 800-594-8979, fax 801-392-6589; www.bestwestern.com/highcountryinn. MODERATE TO DELUXE.

Themes run through **Wright's Getaway Lodge**, a bed-and-breakfast establishment 15 miles northeast of Ogden near Eden. Located on four acres of heavily treed land in a canyon above the Nordic Valley ski resort, the lodge has three suites equipped with surround-sound, jetted tubs, gas fireplaces, two-headed marble shower stalls and hand-painted murals. You can choose from the Aloha Suite, with a waterfall jacuzzi and 250-gallon salt-water aquarium; the Moonlight Rendezvous, with its black lights and 60-inch TV screen; and the Wild Kingdom, with its steam shower and "under bed" sound system. ~ P.O. Box 247, Eden, UT 84310; 801-745-4848; www.getawaylodge.com. DELUXE.

◀ HIDDEN

If you're simply passing through the Ogden area but wouldn't mind zipping into town for an afternoon, **Red Roof Inn** is just west of town along Route 15. No frills—just clean, predictable rooms. Outside you'll find a heated pool. ~ 1500 Riverside Road, Riverdale; 801-627-2880, 800-466-8356. BUDGET.

Ogden's various heritages come to bloom in the wide array of eateries. Along with Mexican and hearty American fares you can find Italian, traditional German dishes and even Louisiana 'gator served up regularly in town.

DINING

The **Club Deli** puts its own unique spin on Ogden's gangster history with sandwiches such as the "Al Capone," which features prosciutto ham, feta cheese, a sun-dried tomato/basil spread, lettuce tomato, balsamic vinegar and olive oil, and the Bootlegger's Best, which comes with turkey, provolone cheese, mayo, mustard, lettuce and tomato. The New York–style deli, which can throw together a box lunch for you, also offers vegetarian sandwiches and grilled creations. No dinner. Closed Saturday and Sunday. ~ 126 Historic 25th Street, Ogden; 801-395-0166, fax 801-395-0825. BUDGET.

An open doorway separates the deli from **Grounds for Coffee**, a coffee bar where you can sate your caffeine addiction six days a week. You can relax here with an espresso or iced coffee, or non-coffee drinks such as teas, juices or Italian sodas, and some pastries. Closed Sunday. ~ 126 Historic 25th Street, Ogden; 801-392-7370. BUDGET.

The **La Ferrovia Ristorante** is a mom-and-pop Italian eatery that dates to 1988, when Giuseppina and Rita Iodice arrived from Naples, Italy, and moved into a space at Union Station; in fact, the restaurant's name is a result of that original location, as it translates roughly to "the iron road." Today located in a storefront on Historic 25th Street, the restaurant features *cannellone, cotoletta alla bolognese* and *bistecca all capricciosa,* a ribeye steak in a special marinade served with freshly marinated tomatoes. Of course, you'll also find spaghetti, lasagna, pizza and calzones. During warm weather ask for a table on the back patio. Closed Sunday and Monday. ~ 234 Historic 25th Street, Ogden; 801-394-8628. BUDGET TO MODERATE.

Locals often crowd **Karen's Café** for the breakfast and lunch specials that are rolled out each week. Just about everything is homemade, even the hamburger buns. While the lunch menu often features roast beef and chicken-fried steak, the breakfast burrito is usually a hit. No dinner. ~ 242 Historic 25th Street, Ogden; 801-392-0345. BUDGET.

Not far up the street is **Rooster's**, a brew pub that operates out of the historic Kansas City Liquor House. Pizzas aren't run of the mill here, carrying everything from rock shrimp and asparagus to smoked salmon. The menu also includes portobello mushroom and chicken-breast sandwiches, as well as jambalaya, beer-battered fish-and-chips, and Alaskan king salmon. Among the house brews are Golden Spike Ale, Two-bit Amber, Junction City Chocolate Stout and Bee's Knees Honey Wheat. ~ 253 Historic 25th Street, Ogden; 801-627-6171, fax 435-627-1353. BUDGET TO MODERATE.

HIDDEN ►

Four blocks north of Historic 25th Street is **Farr's Ice Cream**, a longstanding testament to Utahns' love affair with ice cream. Standing in the same location since the 1920s, the ice cream company has been in the same family for four generations. Enter the tiny ice cream shop and you'll be overwhelmed first by the lime-green walls and then by the many ice cream, sherbet and sorbet selections, not to mention the fresh fudge churned out daily. If you can't make up your mind, go with the Willard Bay Blackberry, which features locally grown berries. ~ 274 21st Street, Ogden; 801-393-8629. BUDGET.

An authentic taste of Louisiana's bayou country can be found at the **Cajun Skillet**, where chef Thomas Jackson flies his alligator and crawdads—and just about all his ingredients—in fresh from his home state. How your alligator is prepared depends on how you want it: fried, stewed, blackened. The 26-item menu also features seafood and steaks if you're not up for 'gator. ~ 2550 Washington Boulevard, Ogden; 801-393-7702. BUDGET TO MODERATE.

◄ HIDDEN

Jeremiah's consistently serves up one of the best breakfasts in town, both from a taste and price vantage point. The "Break of Dawn" special is an all-you-can-eat feast with eggs and bacon, French toast, pancakes and more. Lunch and dinner, meanwhile, revolve around burgers, sandwiches, fajitas and fish. During your meal you can check out the area's trail network, which is laid out on the place mats. ~ 1307 West 1200 South, Ogden; 801-394-3273. BUDGET.

Mexican, not Southwestern, cuisine is served up at **El Matador**, which is famous for its "Vera Cruz Combination." Featuring two cheese enchiladas, two jumbo shrimp and one beef taco, the combo isn't likely to leave you hungry. ~ 2564 Ogden Avenue, Ogden; 801-393-3151. BUDGET.

The poodle dress–clad waitresses have a giggle in their talk and a wiggle in their walk at the **Galaxy Diner**, a shrine to the Big Bopper, Buddy Holly, Elvis and other 1950s rock-and-roll stars. The food's straight out of the '50s, too, with breakfast served all day, burgers and sandwiches on the lunch menu, and turkey, pot roast and meatloaf gracing dinner plates. ~ 4250 South Harrison Boulevard, Ogden; 801-621-2161. BUDGET.

AUTHOR FAVORITE

To me, atmosphere is as important as an outstanding menu, and **Bistro 258** on Historic 25th Street combines the two perfectly with its crisp table linens, warm wood floors, historic brick walls, smartly dressed waiters and creative menus. The only problem is choosing an entrée—the *linguini alla bucaniera* is a wonderful dish of shrimp, scallops, clams and salmon drizzled with a saffron cream, but it's hard to pass up hand-cut filet mignon served with a creamed stoneground mustard demi sauce. Closed Sunday. ~ 258 Historic 25th Street, Ogden; 801-394-1595. MODERATE.

Rich Teutonic dishes crowd the menu at the **Bavarian Chalet**, a traditional German restaurant where the wiener schnitzel comes in veal, pork or turkey. You'll also find sauerbraten, beef *rouladen* and *schlachtplate*. If you're uncertain, try the King Ludwig Sampler, which includes wiener schnitzel, *jaeger schnitzel*, sausages and vegetables. If that's too hearty, Chef Wolfgang Stadelmann also offers steaks, fish and vegetarian dinners. Dinner only. Closed Sunday and Monday. ~ 4387 South Harrison Boulevard, Ogden; 801-479-7561; www.bavarian-chalet.com. MODERATE.

HIDDEN ►

Off the beaten path near the junction of Valley Drive and Canyon Road lies **The Greenery**, a long-time Ogden favorite that's part of Rainbow Gardens (see "Shopping" below). The menu is diverse, finding room for clam chowder and vegetable soup next to crab salad and turkey sandwiches as well as halibut steaks. The setting is airy and the service prompt. ~ 1851 Valley Drive, Ogden; 801-392-1777. BUDGET.

HIDDEN ►

Thematic businesses aren't restricted to lodgings in the Ogden area. The **Timbermine** offers dining in the surroundings of an old underground mine, complete with well-worn timbers and ore cars. Steak and prime rib are the motherlode here, although the menu also includes lobster, shrimp, halibut and salmon. Dinner only. ~ 1701 Park Boulevard, Ogden; 801-393-2155; www.timbermine.com. MODERATE TO DELUXE.

Ogden early on was known as "Junction City," a reference to its railroading fame.

Not to be outdone by some creaky mine, the **Prairie Schooner** is a steakhouse that circles the wagons for dinner. Meals are served inside covered wagons reminiscent of Oregon Trail days. Along with steaks, the menu features prime rib, seafood and chicken. Lunch is also served, but not in the wagons. ~ 445 Park Boulevard, Ogden; 801-392-2712. MODERATE TO DELUXE.

There are a number of restaurants to be found outside Ogden's limits that are good places to stop when hunger strikes.

Although it started out in 1912 as a summer home, the **Gray-Cliff Lodge Restaurant** has been feeding folks since 1945. Tables can be found throughout the house in what used to be the family room as well as on a long covered porch that offers beautiful views of Ogden Canyon's forests and an airy meal during the summer months. Located five miles up Ogden Canyon, the restaurant specializes in lamb, steak, poultry and local trout. Dinner only; brunch is served Sunday. Closed Monday. ~ 508 Ogden Canyon, Ogden; 801-392-6775, 800-879-6775; www.graycliff lodge.com. MODERATE TO DELUXE.

HIDDEN ►

Some say the country's best hamburger, the Star Burger, can be found in **The Shooting Star Saloon** in tiny Huntsville, just eight miles east of the Snowbasin resort. Along with the usual hamburger patty, this burger boasts a piece of bratwurst. This hole-in-the-wall watering hole also happens to be Utah's oldest continually operating bar, dating to 1879 when it was known as "Hoken's Hole" after its proprietor, Hoken Olsen. Of particular note besides the hamburgers is the stuffed bust of a 300-pound St. Bernard. ~ 7350 East 200 South, Huntsville; 801-745-2002. BUDGET.

At **Eats of Eden,** nine miles northeast of Ogden in a gap within the Wasatch Range, you'll find sandwiches built upon home-baked breads, hand-crafted pizzas, pastas, soups and burgers. Located unobtrusively in a small storefront shop along Route 162 next to Eden's post office, this café lures in locals with its manicotti (made with three-cheese crêpes instead of pasta) and bread pudding. ~ 2595 North Route 162, Eden; 801-745-8618. BUDGET.

◄ HIDDEN

Along with charming architecture, **Historic 25th Street** offers intriguing shopping in the form of many antique and pawn shops.

SHOPPING

Young's General Store carries an incredible potpourri of items, ranging from fine and costume jewelry to silverware, antique bottles and toys, watches, guns and oak furniture. ~ 109 Historic 25th Street, Ogden; 801-392-1473.

Aaron Lily, an antique shop, focuses on jewelry, custom clothes, furniture and artworks. ~ 111 Historic 25th Street, Ogden; 801-392-8023.

Next door, the **Painted Lady** proffers Victorian furnishings, china, clocks and lamps among the crowded stock within its walls. ~ 115 Historic 25th Street, Ogden; 801-393-4445.

Artworks and stuffed animals share the space at **Aspen Studio and Gallery,** which is housed in the historic Aspen Studio. Inside are bronze works, sculptures, oils, watercolors, photographs and mounted wildlife. ~ 136 Historic 25th Street, Ogden; 801-399-9052.

At **Needlepoint Joint** you can find Beatrix Potter, Danforth Pewter and Winnie the Pooh collections as well as all your yarn and needlepoint thread needs. Closed Sunday. ~ 241 Historic 25th Street, Ogden; 801-394-4355.

Looking for that hard-to-get kitchen gadget? Try **Pan Handlers,** where kitchenware and crockery are king. In fact, they claim to have everything the cook needs. ~ 260 Historic 25th Street, Ogden; 801-392-6510.

At the **Cowboy Tradin' Post** you'll not only find a narrow shop overflowing with Western antiques but an old-fashioned barber shop chair near the rear of the store. Sit down in the chair and for $10 you can get a haircut. ~ 268 Historic 25th Street, Ogden; 801-399-9511.

Book lovers head to **The Bookshelf,** which stocks the latest titles as well as comic books, Japanese magazines and unusual journals. ~ 2432 Washington Boulevard, Ogden; 801-621-4752.

The **Ogden City Mall** in the heart of downtown doesn't offer scores of outlets, but you can find jewelry, sunglasses, clothing, souvenirs, music and a quick bite to eat. Plus, children can occupy themselves in the Treehouse Children's Museum while you shop. ~ 24th and Washington Boulevard, Ogden; 801-399-1314.

The **Newgate Mall** likewise offers dozens or stores offering everything from toys and kids' clothes to sporting goods and jewelry. In addition to the food court with its resident outlets, you'll find an entertainment center where the kids can work off extra energy. ~ 36th Street and Wall Avenue, Ogden; 801-621-1161.

HIDDEN ▶

What started out as a spa at the mouth of Ogden Canyon is now self-described as "Western America's Largest Gift Emporium." **Rainbow Gardens** offers more than 20 departments packed with such items as scented soaps and candles, baskets, picture frames, silk flowers, greeting cards and children's games. The operation dates to 1890, when a real estate developer made plans to turn the existing hot springs into the Ogden Canyon Sanitarium. A hotel and bathhouse finally arrived in 1903, and by 1906 trolley cars were ferrying folks from downtown Ogden to the spa. While the spa went out of business in 1972, the operation saw its first gift shop open in 1970 and the owners have never looked back. When you descend into the "Gift Garden" you are actually stepping down into one of the old spa's bathing pools. ~ 1851 Valley Drive, Ogden; 801-621-1606.

NIGHTLIFE   An early-20th-century classic, **Peery's Egyptian Theater** has hosted a dozen Utah premiers, one U.S. premier, and even a world premier. Weber State University's Department of Performing Arts frequently stages its plays here. ~ Historic 25th Street and Washington Boulevard, Ogden; 801-395-3227.

Concerts, ballet and dramatic presentations are often offered in the Ogden area. The **Utah Musical Theater**, which stages its performances in Peery's Egyptian Theater, offers a mix of Broadway classics such as *The Unsinkable Molly Brown* and *1776*. ~ 2415 Washington Boulevard, Ogden; box office 801-626-8500.

The **Ogden Symphony Ballet Association** brings the Utah Symphony, Ballet West and the Utah Opera Company to town and holds its performances in the Browning Center at Weber State

◆◆

GETTING PHYSICAL

In town and looking for a workout? Head over to the **Mount Ogden Exercise Trail**. The loop actually consists of two paths—one paved for bicycles, the other covered with bark chips for joggers and walkers. The two follow a flat route around Mount Ogden park and golf course and offer access to the Bonneville Shoreline Trail, Waterfall Canyon and Taylor's Canyon.

University as well as the Egyptian Theater. ~ 638 East 26th Street, Ogden; 801-399-9214.

For a ten-week run each summer local musicians show off their skills at **Talent in the Park** shows held Wednesday nights in MTC Park on the Ogden River Parkway. ~ 1750 Monroe Boulevard, Ogden; 801-629-8242.

A spectrum of live music—rock, bluegrass and ska—can often be heard at **Jackson Street Junction**. Cover. ~ 2280 Jackson Avenue, Ogden; 801-627-3988. **Teaser's Sports Bar & Grill** is a private club that books live rock bands on weekends and offers other entertainment mid-week. ~ 366 36th Street, Ogden; 801-395-1517.

For a few chuckles, check out **Laughs**, which schedules stand-up comics Thursday through Saturday. Cover. ~ 208 25th Street, Ogden; 801-622-5588.

Billiards, darts, pizza and rock-and-roll share the scene at **Brewski's**, one of three private clubs owned by the same management. What's the advantage of joint ownership? Well, one membership fee gets you into all three. ~ 244 Historic 25th Street, Ogden; 801-394-1713.

Practically next door is **Beatnik's**, which features live music and poetry slams Tuesday through Sunday. ~ 240 Historic 25th Street, Ogden; 801-395-2859.

If neither of those nightclubs feels right, try the **City Club**, where you'll find cocktails, chit-chat and Beatles paraphernalia. ~ 264 Historic 25th Street, Ogden; 801-392-4447.

FORT BUENAVENTURA STATE PARK Located on the site of the first permanent white settlement in the Great Basin, the focal point of this 88-acre park is a replica of the 1846 fort mountain man Miles Goodyear built with hopes of drumming up business with the wagon trains heading West. Today guides in period dress recount the fort's history, while exhibits delve into the lives of the mountain men and American Indians who lived in the region. While no individual campsites are within the park, group sites are available. There also are picnic grounds, canoe rentals, restrooms and fishing along the Weber River. Day-use fee, $4. ~ 2450 A Avenue, Ogden; 801-621-4808; www.nr.state.ut.us/parks/www1/fort.htm.

PARKS

OGDEN WHITEWATER PARK The careful placement of rock created this kayak "rodeo arena" on a short stretch of the Weber River that flows past Ogden. Running along 200 yards of river that streams under the Wilson Lane Bridge at 24th Street, the free whitewater park challenges kayakers with waves they can surf and play in. ~ Wilson Lane and 24th Street, Ogden.

◀ HIDDEN

WASATCH-CACHE NATIONAL FOREST The Ogden District, the northern tier of the 1.2-million-acre Wasatch-Cache National Forest cuts north to south through northern Utah. Squeezed between the Great Salt Lake and the Wyoming border, this section of forest offers Ogden residents and visitors a quick escape from the urban landscape into the mountains' dense forests, hiking trails and ski areas. The forest is home to the Snowbasin Ski Resort, the host of the downhill and Super-G races of the 2002 Olympic Winter Games, as well as seemingly endless hiking, biking and equestrian trails. ~ Many trails in the national forest have trailheads in Ogden, while Route 39 eastbound runs six miles through Ogden River Canyon to numerous access points around Pineview Reservoir, as well as continuing 16 miles farther east to the Monte Cristo Range; Ogden Ranger District, 507 25th Street, Suite 103, Ogden; 801-625-5112; www.fs.fed.us/wcnf.

▲ The Ogden District of the Wasatch-Cache National Forest contains 326 campsites in 14 developed campgrounds; $5 to $12 per night; 7-day maximum stay at developed campgrounds, 14 days at undeveloped sites.

Brigham City Area

The transcontinental railroad put Brigham City on the map when the rails were joined at nearby Promontory Summit, but the rich agricultural lands that surround the community keep it going. Members of the LDS Church arrived in the area late in 1851 and quickly laid out their farms the following spring. Despite attacks by the Shoshone tribes that lived in the area, Brigham Young was determined to see a community hacked out of the wilderness. In 1854 he sent out 50 Salt Lake City families with hopes they could get the job done. Their arrival gave what had been a small, rustic settlement the makings of a more formal community—one named Brigham City in honor of the church leader.

Agriculture was the wellspring of Brigham City's economy. In 1855 a settler returned from Salt Lake City with 100 peach stones and planted them around town. The resulting harvests were so bountiful that in 1904 the town started its annual harvest festival, Peach Days.

While the area held onto its agrarian roots for more than a century, in 1957 Brigham City's economy got a decided boost when Thiokol Chemical Corporation, in search of a somewhat remote yet easily accessible area, selected Box Elder County for the home of its solid fuel rocket propellant plant. Located 27 miles west of Brigham City, the Thiokol plant not only became the biggest employer in the country but nearly doubled Brigham City's population with its employees.

While Thiokol continues to be a major cog in the local economy due to its work with NASA's shuttle program, Brigham City and surrounding Box Elder County continue to rely on the agricultural sector, which produces crops such as corn, tomatoes, alfalfa, potatoes, onions and fruit as well as cattle and sheep. If you drive on Route 89 between Brigham City and Ogden, you'll find numerous opportunities to buy fresh fruit and produce during the growing season.

Also dear to Brigham City's heart is the Bear River Migratory Bird Refuge. Proof of this endearment is the archway that frames Main Street and proclaims to all: "Brigham, Gateway—World's Greatest Game Bird Refuge."

On the way from Ogden to Brigham City (a distance of 21 miles) you'll come upon **Willard,** and if you bypass this tiny town you'll overlook one of the most unique collections of stone houses in Utah. Willard's dozen or so stone houses date to the late 19th century and reflect the fine craftsmanship, as well as the professions, of some of the Mormon missionaries who settled here near the edge of the Great Salt Lake. One, for instance, was the home of a composer, who personalized his home by having wooden notes carved into the eaves. These structures were built by Welshman Shadrach Jones, who designed them after those in his native Wales. So architecturally and historically significant are the homes that in the 1970s a 12-block swath of Willard was listed in the national and state historic registers. For information on a walking tour, call 435-734-2634. ~ Route 15 Exit 360, 12 miles south of Ogden.

SIGHTS

◄ *HIDDEN*

Just across Route 15 from the town of Willard is **Willard Bay State Park,** a popular swimming, boating and waterskiing spot during the summer months, a reliable fishing hole year-round, and a favorite with eagles during the winter months. The freshwater bay, created by an impoundment that separates the bay from the salty lake, covers 9900 acres on the eastern edge of the Great Salt Lake. ~ Take Route 15 and get off on Exit 360, 900 West 650 North #A, Willard; 435-734-9494, 800-822-3770.

Once you reach Brigham City, you'll discover that the blending of history, rocketry, agriculture and natural resources have left the area blessed with a wide range of attractions. For a taste of that history and a primer on the area, stop by the **Chamber of**

ALL ALONG THE FRUITWAY

Northern Utah is known for its fresh fruits, so much so that the stretch of Route 89 between Willard and Brigham City is referred to as "the Fruitway." The highway winds through orchards that have long provided produce for northern Utah. During the harvest season roadside hawkers sell just-picked apples, peaches, pears, pumpkins, corn and other produce from their stands.

Commerce offices inside the **Old City Hall and Fire Station**. The two-story building was erected in 1909; the fire department took up the ground floor, city offices the second. A jail cell was fitted into the building's southeastern corner, while a "hobo apartment" was situated in the basement. The fire department eventually moved into its own building in 1935, the police department left in 1966, and the rest of the city offices in 1973. ~ 6 North Main Street, Brigham City; 435-723-3931.

The **Brigham City Pioneer Co-op** across the street from the chamber opened for business in 1891. However, it didn't stay open for long. A fire damaged the building in late 1894 and the business never recovered. Down through the years the restored building has housed a bank, a furniture store, a post office, a mortuary and a variety of other businesses. In 1990 the structure was placed on the National Register of Historic Places. These days a bank occupies the building, which sports beautiful brickwork on the wall facing the street and a north-facing wall of rock. ~ 5 North Main Street, Brigham City.

One of Utah's oldest manufacturing businesses exists in the form of the **Baron Woolen Mill**, which first produced wool products in 1870 when it was part of the Brigham City Mercantile Cooperative. The building housing the mill is actually the fourth to bear the company's name: the first burned down in 1877, the second in 1907, and the third in 1949. While the mill's looms were idle from 1990 to 1993, it reopened in 1995 for a few years to produce Virgin American Wool and cotton blankets with its century-old equipment. Though the operation shut down early in 1999, the community is working to restore the mill and open it as a museum. ~ 56 North 500 East, Brigham City.

Just a bit east of Main Street is the **Grist Mill**, which dates to 1856 and was intended to serve as the northeastern corner of a rock wall that would encircle Brigham City for defense against Indians. For a while the mill actually functioned as a guardhouse of sorts, with men stationed on the upper floors to watch for trouble. A monument company took over the flour mill around 1890 and it continues operations there today. ~ 327 East 200 North, Brigham City.

Brigham City's love for the nearby bird refuge is reflected by the **Welcome to Brigham City Arch** erected over Main Street in 1928 shortly after the refuge was designated. The original arch, which was replicated in 1984 with the archway now spanning the street, stood nine feet high and 33 feet wide. Foot-high letters spelled out "Welcome to" while 30-inch letters added "Brigham." Sprawled across the bottom of the original sign were the words, "Gateway to the World's Greatest Game Bird Sanctuary." Images of flying ducks topped the sign, which carried more than 350

lights to illuminate it at night. ~ Spanning Main Street between
Forest Street and 100 South.

Most Utah communities in the late 1800s featured tithing offices, where LDS Church members would contribute one-tenth of
their annual earnings to the church. In many cases the contribu-
tions were in the form of goods and produce if cash wasn't available. Brigham City's two-story **Tithing Office** dates to 1877. The
basement contained storage rooms for dairy products and meat,

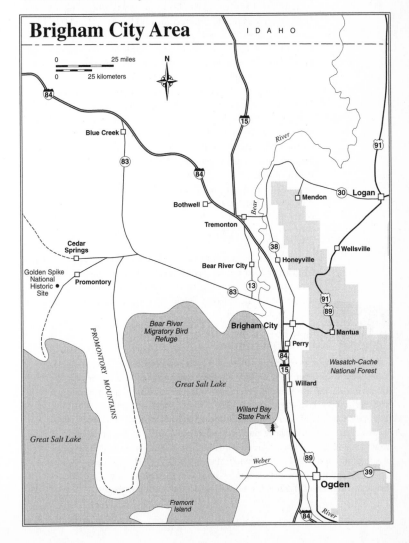

while outside a rock wall, long-since removed, surrounded the building to corral livestock tithed to the church. These days the building contains rental apartments. ~ 66 South 100 West, Brigham City.

When Brigham Young visited Brigham City in the 1860s he selected "Sagebrush Hill," the highest spot on Main Street, as the site for the **Box Elder LDS Tabernacle**. Although construction began in 1868, the limestone and sandstone building wasn't completed until October 1890. A fire gutted the building six years later, but it was rebuilt and rededicated in 1897. The LDS Church closed the tabernacle, which was placed on the National Register of Historical Places in 1971, from 1986 to 1987 to restore it. Guided tours are available in the summer months. ~ 251 South Main Street, Brigham City; 435-723-5376.

Although the **Brigham City Train Depot** is not open for rail business, Amtrak trains shoot by the historic building twice a day, and town officials hope someday a short-line railroad will chug between the depot and Promontory Summit. When it was opened by the Union Pacific Railroad in 1906, freight trains arrived with coal shipments from central Utah's coal mines while outgoing trains carried fresh and canned fruit and vegetables. In 1994 the railroad turned over the depot to Box Elder County, which immediately deeded it to the Golden Spike Association. Restoration of the depot is still in progress. Closed Wednesday and Sunday; shortened hours in winter. ~ 833 West Forest Street, Brigham City; 435-723-2989.

Fifteen miles west of town via Forest Street lies the **Bear River Migratory Bird Refuge**, which has been luring hundreds of feathered species for centuries to the marshlands created around the mouth of the Bear River. When explorer John C. Fremont came

AUTHOR FAVORITE

East met West, as the saying goes, at Promontory Summit 32 miles west of Brigham City on May 10, 1869, when the locomotives from the Union Pacific and the Central Pacific railroads met head-on. Being a model railroad addict, I take every chance I get to watch vintage steam locomotives belch clouds of smoke at the **Golden Spike National Historic Site**. Visitors can learn about the laying of the rails that tied the country together and view vintage railroad films. Also on location are replicas of the "Jupiter" and the "119," the two trains involved. See "The Golden Spike" spread for more information. ~ Route 83, 32 miles west of Brigham City; 435-471-2209, fax 435-471-2341; www.nps.gov/gosp.

upon the area in 1843 he wrote that "the waterfowl made such a noise like thunder . . . as the whole scene was animated with waterfowl." Encompassing 74,000 acres, the watery refuge regularly lures more than 200 bird species, including tundra swans, white-faced ibis and Western grebe. White pelicans can be seen most of the year. ~ Bird Refuge Road, 15 miles west of Brigham City; 435-723-5887, fax 435-723-8873.

Fragments of America's aerospace history can be glimpsed at the **Thiokol Rocket Display**, just five miles north of the Golden Spike National Historic Site. Thiokol, which is headquartered in Ogden, bought 11,000 acres in northern Utah in 1956 with visions of a sprawling rocket plant. In 1958 the U.S. Air Force hired the company to build the first stage of their Minuteman intercontinental ballistic missile. Since that first project Thiokol has worked on "Poseidon" and "Trident" missiles for the Navy as well as the Air Force's "Peacekeeper" nuclear missile. The display, located on the west side of the plant, includes some of the solid rocket motors used by NASA. ~ Route 83, 26 miles west of Brigham City.

One of the best known examples of "earthwork," a late-1960s art genre in which artists used the landscape as their palettes, can be found just beneath the surface of the Great Salt Lake not far from Promontory Point. The **Spiral Jetty** was created by Robert ◄ HIDDEN Smithson in 1970 using earth and black basalt to form a 1500-foot-long coil that runs counterclockwise out into Rozel Bay. Unfortunately, the Great Salt Lake was at a very low level when Smithson, who died in 1973, built the jetty. Since then the lake has risen and submerged the jetty, which is very difficult to find. Stop at the visitors center at Golden Spike Historic Site for a detailed map to the jetty since the route crosses unmarked roads and private lands.

If you head 15 miles north of Brigham City on Route 38, you'll find that the area is more than just birds, trains and rockets. For centuries the region's hot springs were a source of rejuvenation for weary travelers. Long used by Shoshone and Bannock Indians who wintered in northern Utah, **Crystal Springs** has been soothing bathers' muscles commercially since 1901 when an Ogden entrepreneur opened the hot springs to the public. During World War II the operation flourished; bands even played in the evening. Today the resort offers hot tubs, an Olympic-sized pool, water slides and a lap pool. The adjoining campground offers 130 campsites with full hookups. Admission. ~ 8215 North Route 38, Honeyville; 435-279-8104.

Marble Park is an intriguing slice of Americana. Located ◄ HIDDEN about 25 miles north of Brigham City in Bothwell via Route 15, the park was once a weed-choked gravel pit. From the wasteland

Text continued on page 124.

The Golden
Spike

"We have got done praying. The spike is about to be presented."

That message raced across the nation's telegraph lines on May 10, 1869, just before the final, golden spike was used to bind together America's first transcontinental rail line at Promontory Summit, 32 miles west of Brigham City. The joining of the rails laid by the Central Pacific and Union Pacific railroads brought the "Jupiter" and the "119," the respective railroads' locomotives, nose to nose and kicked off a heady celebration. Although a golden spike, engraved with the names of the CP's directors and the notation, "the last spike," on its head, was briefly dropped into a hole bored into a finely polished tie hewn from California laurel to symbolize the joining of the rails, an ordinary iron spike was driven into the tie with powerful strokes that reverberated across the country via the telegraph wires attached to it.

With the line complete, emigrants would no longer need to follow dusty wagon trails that meandered across the Western landscape to reach the fabled lands of California and Oregon. Trains had conquered the prairie and would turn what had been months'-long treks into comparatively short journeys.

Today you can stand at Golden Spike National Historic Site on the rolling ground near Promontory and gaze across a landscape that has hardly changed since the rails were joined. While ramshackle collections of saloons, hotels and bordellos sprang up along the line east and west of Promontory as the rail workers brought the two lines towards each other, they just as quickly evaporated after the lines were joined and the workers moved on. Not even the "Jupiter" and "119" enjoyed their fleeting fame; the "Jupiter" was scrapped for its iron in 1901, and the "119" met a similar fate in 1903.

Sadly, trains don't clickity-clack past the summit anymore. In 1904 the 123-mile-long Promontory Branch was lost to obscurity when the Lucin Cutoff, a 12-mile-long route built on trestles across the Great Salt Lake, diverted train traffic away from Promontory. In 1942 most of the iron rails were removed from the area to help fuel America's efforts in

World War II. As for the golden "last spike," it resides at Stanford University, California.

For a hint of the excitement that spread out from Promontory Summit on May 10, 1869, try to visit the historic site on May 10 to take in a re-enactment of the joining of the rails. The first re-enactment of the driving of the last spike was held in 1948, and in 1957 the 2735-acre historic site was created by Congress.

Start your visit by checking the activities board in the visitors center to see if any talks are scheduled. During summer months, living-history presentations are often on tap. Also, the "Jupiter" and "No. 199" replicas come out several times a day between mid-April and mid-October to blow their stacks while chugging back and forth on nearly two miles of track that were relaid in the 1960s by the National Park Service. Youngsters between 8 and 12 should sign up for the Junior Engineer Program, which uses a workbook to help them learn more about America's rail history.

A self-guided tour leads you by foot along the "Big Fill Walk," which covers a mile and a half of the original Central Pacific and Union Pacific grade, while the "Promontory Trail" is a nine-mile-long auto tour that retraces part of the historic railroad grade.

More ambitious visitors strike out along the Transcontinental Railroad National Back Country Byway, a 90-mile route that follows the original railroad grade. There are no services along the route, so be sure to fill up your gas tank, pack water, and see that your spare tire is inflated (old spikes occasionally surface on the route and puncture tires).

The visitors center is open daily, offering a glimpse of the past through slide shows, films and exhibits. While the annual Railroader's Festival is held the second Saturday in August, during the last week in December the locomotives chug out into the cold winter air for steam demonstrations. Visitors can also tour the engine house. Admission. ~ From Brigham City, drive 32 miles west on Route 83 to reach Golden Spike Historic Site, P.O. Box 897, Brigham City, UT 84302; 435-471-2209; www.nps.gov/gosp.

Boyd Marble has created sculptures from old wagon-wheel rims, milk cans, tractor seats and whatever other scraps of farm equipment he could lay his hands on. While some of the exhibits reflect historic farm implements, other sculptures honor American Indians, mountain men, cowboys and even the Mormon Temple in Salt Lake City. Away from the sculptures, the park has room for picnics and family reunions. ~ 11150 West 11200 North, Bothwell; 435-854-3740.

HIDDEN ▶ Minutes away from Marble Park along Route 102 is the largest private collection of horse-drawn wagons in the West. **Eli Anderson's Wagons** range from handcarts and Conestoga wagons to stagecoaches, horse-drawn hearses and hook-and-ladder trucks. Showings are by appointment only. ~ 8790 West Route 102, Bothwell; 435-854-3760.

LODGING Lodging possibilities are few and modest in Brigham City, although with Ogden just 21 miles away you shouldn't have trouble finding a bed if the local options are sold out.

The most rooms in Brigham City can be found at the **Crystal Inn**, which offers 52 as well as a swimming pool and a continental breakfast. The rooms are comfortable, a bit larger than most motel units, with TVs, phones, microwaves and small refrigerators. ~ 480 Westland Drive, Brigham City; 435-723-0440, 800-408-0440; www.crystalinns.com. MODERATE.

If all you need is a warm, dry place to lay your head, then try out the **Galaxie Motel**. There are 29 rooms here but no pool. ~ 740 South Main Street, Brigham City; 435-723-3439, 800-577-4315. BUDGET.

For "chain reliability," head to the **Howard Johnson Inn** in the heart of town. Not only is the motel a half hour from Golden Spike National Historic Site and 15 minutes from the Bear River Migratory Bird Refuge, there's an indoor pool and jacuzzi on site and a golf course across the street. ~ 1167 South Main Street, Brigham City; 435-723-8511, 800-446-4656. BUDGET TO MODERATE.

DINING Hearty and plentiful menus are the hallmark in the Brigham City area, and considering the agricultural heritage of the area, that should come as no surprise.

HIDDEN ▶ Just eight miles south of Brigham City lies Perry and the **Maddox Ranch House**, one of the best steak houses in all of Utah. The restaurant dates to World War II, when Irv Maddox opened a seven-stool counter café on Main Street in Brigham City. In 1949 Maddox and his wife Wilma bought a small piece of property in Perry, which at the time was in the middle of nowhere. The Maddoxes realized the remoteness of the location at the time and therefore built a small log restaurant that was mounted on skids— easily moved if business dictated. Today the restaurant remains in the exact location and continues to feature family-style dinners. Closed Sunday and Monday. ~ 1900 South Route 89, Perry; 435-723-8545, 800-544-5474. BUDGET TO MODERATE.

Locals long have driven up to **Peach City Ice Cream** for sweet   ◄ HIDDEN
desserts as well as hamburgers, sandwiches and one of the 30 flavors of milkshakes. Good luck downing the Walt Mann Special, a confectionary delight that swells with six scoops of ice cream and your choice of toppings. ~ 306 North Main Street, Brigham City; 435-723-3923. BUDGET.

Lunch and dinner at **Ricardo's Restaurant**, which is housed in a rustic-style café that blends Mexico with the American West, revolve around Mexican dishes like enchiladas, tostadas, burritos and tacos. Closed Sunday and Monday. ~ 131 South Main Street, Brigham City; 435-723-1811. BUDGET.

Surrounded by a festive atmosphere of dangling piñatas, pottery and bright pastel colors, regular diners at **Melina's Mexican Restaurant** have made favorites out of the fish tacos and beef, chicken and shrimp fajitas. Closed Sunday. ~ 40 West 700 South, Brigham City; 435-723-6000. BUDGET.

Located in the heart of downtown, **The Idle Isle Café** has been   ◄ HIDDEN
feeding souls since May 1, 1921, when P. C. Knudson and his wife Verabel opened an ice cream and candy store. With its classic marble soda fountain counter and wooden booth tables, the café has weathered good times and bad with consistent, reliable service, a home-style menu and prices that have developed a strong local following. The café's name was the result of a local contest. ~ 24 South Main Street, Brigham City; 435-734-2468. BUDGET.

Another Main Street stalwart is **Bert's Café**, which opened for business a decade after the Idle Isle. Not a place to watch your cholesterol, this eatery is known for its meaty breakfasts, ranging from bone-in ham and chicken-fried steaks to omelettes—all of which come with eggs and homemade hash browns. While the sign says the café doesn't open until 6 a.m., caffeine fiends can get a mug of joe by 5:30 a.m. ~ 89 South Main Street, Brigham City; 435-734-9544. BUDGET.

BOBBING FOR LOBSTERS

Live lobsters in Utah? You'll find them at **Belmont Hot Springs**, 31 miles north of Brigham City. The crustaceans are raised along with tropical fish in the 95° water churned out by Belmont Hot Springs. If you're not in the mood for lobster, you can still swim, golf and even scuba dive at the resort. ~ 435-458-3200.

SHOPPING Shopping options are meager in Brigham City. Main Street stays busy with office-supply stores, copy centers, insurance offices, real-estate office and not much more. As a result, most locals drive to Ogden for serious shopping binges.

There are, however, souvenirs and curios to be found at the **Brigham City Train Depot**. ~ 833 West Forest Street, Brigham City; 435-723-2989.

NIGHTLIFE Aside from the movie theater on Main Street and the playhouse south of town, there's not a heckuva lot to do in Brigham City when the sun sets. The **Capitol Theatre** has two screens. It's open Monday through Friday at 6:30 p.m., and Saturday at noon with matinees. Closed Sunday. ~ 53 South Main Street, Brigham City; 435-723-3113.

For a cold beer mixed with some local color, head to **B&B Billiards**, a half-block south of Main Street on Forest Street. Just be forewarned that the atmosphere can be smoky and the juke-box loud. ~ 21 West Forest Street, Brigham City; 435-734-2673.

At the **Heritage Theater** near Perry, local troupes offer some touch-notch productions, with actors coming from Utah State University's theatrical department as well as surrounding communities. Performances are on Friday, Saturday and Monday. ~ 2505 South Route 89, Perry; 435-723-8392.

PARKS **WILLARD BAY STATE PARK** A 9900-acre freshwater lake separated from the Great Salt Lake by dikes, Willard Bay offers year-round fishing for walleye, crappie, wiper and catfish, as well as a playground for waterskiers. The state park is divided into a north and a south marina. The north marina has restrooms, showers, boat slips and rentals, and sandy beaches. The south marina features restrooms, showers and boat ramps. Day-use fee, $6. ~ 900 West 650 North #A, take Route 15 to Exit 354 for the south marina or 15 miles north to Exit 360 for the north marina; 435-734-9494; parks.state.ut.us/parks/www1/will.htm.

▲ The north marina has 62 campsites; $12 per night; 14-day maximum stay; open year-round. The south marina has 30 campsites; $12 per night; 14-day maximum stay; open April through October. For reservations, call 800-322-3770.

WASATCH-CACHE NATIONAL FOREST The Logan District of the 1.2-million-acre Wasatch-Cache National Forest lies less than five miles east of Brigham City, providing a quick getaway for outdoors lovers. A dozen miles northeast of the city lies the **Wellsville Mountains Wilderness Area**, which covers 23,750 acres of incredibly rugged land. The western edge of the wilderness area is shored up by Wellsville Mountain, which, due to its narrow base and 5000-

foot rise from the valley floor, is considered the steepest mountain in the country. Once heavily logged, the wilderness area is returning to what it was when 19th-century trappers made their way through the Rocky Mountain West—dense forests cut by streams and broken by wildflower-dappled meadows and small alpine lakes. Moose, mountain lion and occasionally bighorn sheep can be seen here. ~ From Brigham City, Routes 38 and 89/91 offer quick access to the wilderness area; Logan Ranger District, 1500 East Route 89, Logan; 435-755-3620; www.fs.fed.us/wcnf.

Among the species that rely on the Bear River Migratory Bird Refuge are tundra swans, white pelicans, great blue herons, black-crowned night herons, snowy egrets and black-necked stilts.

▲ The Logan District of the Wasatch-Cache National Forest contains 139 campsites in 14 developed campgrounds; $5 to $7 per night; campgrounds have a 14-day maximum stay.

SAWTOOTH NATIONAL FOREST 🚶 🚲 🐎 ⛺ ⟶ A tiny slice of the 2.1-million-acre, Idaho-based Sawtooth National Forest extends into Utah just to the northwest of the Great Salt Lake and about 90 miles west of Brigham City. Known as the **Raft River Division**, the forest's peaks rise to 9600 feet and, on clear days, offer sprawling views of the Great Salt Lake to the south, the Snake River Plain and the Sawtooth Mountains to the north, and Nevada to the west. Much of this section of forest is sparsely wooded, although there are some heavy stands of piñon and juniper. ~ From Brigham City, take Route 84 49 miles north to Snowville, then follow Route 30 west 41 miles to the forest. The Raft River Division is managed by the Burley Ranger District of the Sawtooth National Forest, 3650 South Overland Avenue, Burley, ID 83318; 208-678-0430; www.northrim.net/sawtoothnf/genmess.html.

▲ The Raft River Division has one campground with 14 campsites; no fee; 14-day maximum stay. Closed November through May.

BEAR RIVER MIGRATORY BIRD REFUGE 🚲 ⟶ Dating to 1928, this bird sanctuary was nearly wiped out in 1983 when heavy snows and rainfall raised the level of the Great Salt Lake and inundated the freshwater marshlands near the mouth of the Bear River. The lake's encroaching saline waters killed many of the refuge's trees and pond vegetation that waterfowl had relied upon and destroyed all of the refuge buildings. Although the refuge had attracted as many as 60,000 tundra swans to its waters prior to the flood, after the flood those numbers dropped to 259 in 1984 and just three the following year. By 1989 the lake's level receded to the point where the refuge's dikes could be rebuilt. As the lake's level dropped the marshlands regained their health.

Today they once again attract millions of birds during the spring and fall migrations. Visitors can take a 12-mile auto tour along the dikes that wind through the marshes. ~ From Brigham City, head west 15 miles on the Bear River Refuge Road; 435-723-5887, fax 435-723-8873; www.r6.fws.gov/refuges/bear/bear.htm.

Logan Area

Twenty-five miles northeast of Brigham City via Route 89/91 lie Logan and the Cache Valley, which have long lured explorers. Early in the 19th century mountain men such as Jim Bridger and Jedediah Smith traversed the length of Logan Canyon in search of beaver, trapping their way to the Great Salt Lake where they wondered whether they had reached the Pacific Ocean. And it was a trapper, Ephraim Logan, whose name stuck on the town that was founded in 1859. Settlers dispatched to the region by the LDS Church arrived at the 15-mile-wide-by-60-mile-long valley in 1855 and soon appreciated the rich soils and long growing season that would turn the Cache Valley into Utah's fruit basket. The valley's agricultural heritage made it the logical site for Utah State University, which in 1888 was established in Logan as Utah's land-grant university. While agriculture remains king in the Logan area, the university has diversified its curriculum, offering classes from agriculture to space technology for its 20,000 students.

Although it lies 40 miles northeast of Logan, Bear Lake has long been linked to the Cache Valley, harkening back at least to the gregarious lakeside rendezvous staged in the late 1820s by the Rocky Mountain Fur Company for trappers and Indians alike. These gatherings offered the trappers a time to come down out of the mountains, renew old acquaintances, swap goods and, frankly, wash away months of solitude with whiskey and carrying on.

Modern-day explorers continue to head to Bear Lake, northern Utah's premier watery vacation spot, where they can camp on the shores and boat on the lake. In August, the Raspberry Festival draws thousands to the lake and surrounding raspberry patches. The ride from Logan to the lake runs through spectacular Logan

TAKEN FOR A RIDE

Capitalists built this country, and proof can be found in the annals of the transcontinental railroad. While the Central Pacific and Union Pacific railroads were hired by Congress to build the line, they took some liberties with the contract, which paid them according to the amount of rail they laid. With hopes of squeezing a few extra dollars out of the federal government, the two railroads actually laid two parallel grades alongside each other for more than 200 miles.

Canyon, where the canyon's mile-high variegated limestone walls are covered with lush vegetation.

After leaving Brigham City, but before you get to Logan, is the turnoff to Route 101 and the **Hardware Ranch**, which has been around since 1945 when it was established to provide critical winter habitat for wildlife and to serve as a feeding ground for elk. Each winter the ranch is home to more than 700 elk. Wagon rides are popular during the summer months; in winter, when weather allows, sleighs pulled by Clydesdale horses haul visitors through the refuge for an up-close look at the elk. On winter weekends you can sign on for both a sleigh ride and an all-you-can-eat chicken or rib barbecue dinner at the ranch headquarters. ~ Located 25 miles southeast of Logan and 18 miles east of Hyrum at the head of Blacksmith Fork Canyon on Route 101; 435-753-6168; www.hardwareranch.com, e-mail hardwareranch@sisna.com.

SIGHTS

Back on Route 89/91 north on the way to Logan lies Wellsville and the **American West Heritage Center**. The American West has long been glamorized and continues to be heralded for its wide open spaces, frontier life and rugged mountains. At this 160-acre Western heritage center you can come to grips with the West between the years 1820–1920. A small pioneer village, with two "dugouts" and two log cabins, is in place, as is a general mercantile, an opera house and a livery stable. During the Festival of the American West, held each summer in late July and early August, a mountain man rendezvous site, an American Indian village, and a military encampment come to life. ~ Six miles south of Logan, 4025 South Route 89/91, Wellsville; 435-245-6050, box office 800-225-3378, fax 435-245-6052; www.americanwestcenter.org, e-mail awhc@cc.usu.edu.

Under the auspices of the American West Heritage Center, the 127-acre **Jensen Historical Farm** captures a slice of early-20th-century life. At the living-history museum the long days of 1917 farm life are recounted throughout the summer by Utah State University students, from barn raising to sheep shearing and even the re-enactment of a turn-of-the-20th-century wedding. Visitors can take part in churning butter, gathering eggs and harvesting apples, or watch demonstrations on candlemaking, spinning, quilting and blacksmithing. In the fall a corn maze is open to the public, while sleigh rides are offered around Christmas time. Closed Sunday. Admission. ~ 4025 South Route 89, Wellsville; 435-245-6050 or 435-245-4064.

From Wellsville, **Logan** is just six miles to the north in the sprawling Cache Valley, which is nestled between the Wellsville Mountains to the west and the Bear River Range to the east. A college town, Logan has much more going on than Brigham City.

If you're traveling with children, or just love animals, stop by Logan's **Willow Park Zoo**, where you'll see monkeys and eagles, coyotes, kangaroos and more. While you set up your picnic the youngsters can feed the ducks and geese. ~ 419 West 700 South, Logan; 435-750-9893.

Logan still has that small-town feel, thanks to preservation efforts that have kept many of the town's old buildings in shape. The **Dansante Building**, which holds the administrative offices and box office of the Utah Festival Opera Company, has long ties to entertainment. Built in 1900, the building early on housed a roller skating rink. It was later converted into a dancehall that stayed in business for nearly 30 years, drawing upwards of 3000 revelers on major holidays. Although two clothing companies occupied the building for a time, in the mid-1990s the opera company bought the building, restored it and expanded it for the festival. Today it harbors a 124-seat recital hall, rehearsal halls and prop, costume and scenery shops. ~ 59 South 100 West, Logan; 435-750-0300.

Theatrical renovations are a habit in Logan. The Capitol Theater, Logan's fourth opera house when it opened for business in 1923, arose on the spot where the Thatcher Opera House had stood until it burned down on April 17, 1912. The Capitol Theater dominated the Cache Valley's performing-arts circle for 30 years before performances were halted in the 1950s and the theater fell into disrepair. But a multimillion-dollar restoration project allowed the neoclassical-style theater to reopen in 1993 as the **Ellen Eccles Theater**. Inside you'll find not only a state-of-the-art theatrical system, but plush red seats, a grand foyer, sweeping balconies and impeccable acoustics that serve touring Broadway productions, musicals, ballet and symphonies. ~ 43 South Main Street, Logan; 435-752-0026 or 435-753-6518.

The **Bluebird Restaurant** is one of the oldest and busiest historical sites in Logan. Operating as a restaurant since 1914, the Bluebird boasts a marble soda fountain where you can still get an ice cream float. ~ 19 North Main Street, Logan; 435-752-3155.

Another Logan theater has been restored to its original elegance—the 1913 **Lyric Theater**, now the home of the Old Lyric Repertory Theater and, thespians swear, to a ghost clothed in Elizabethan garb topped by a fool's hat. Charm exudes from this Victorian-style proscenium-arch playhouse that can seat 388. During the summer months a mix of professional and aspiring actors join forces to stage comedies, musicals and dramas. ~ 28 West Center Street, Logan; 435-797-1500.

If genealogy sparks your interest, be sure to stop at the **Logan Tabernacle** before leaving town. Opened in 1891 after 25 years of volunteer laboring, the tabernacle is recognized as home to the second largest genealogy library in Utah, just behind the Family

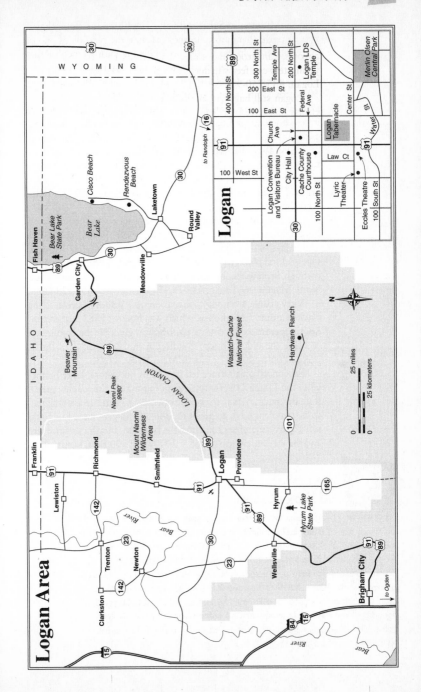

Logan Area

Logan

Labels on map (Logan inset):
- 300 North St
- Temple Ave
- 200 North St
- 89
- 400 North St
- 300 North St
- Logan LDS Temple
- 200 East St
- Center St
- 100 East St
- Federal Ave
- Water St
- 91
- Merlin Olsen Central Park
- Church Ave
- Logan Tabernacle
- 91
- Logan Convention and Visitors Bureau
- City Hall
- Cache County Courthouse
- Law Ct
- 100 West St
- 100 North St
- 30
- Lyric Theater
- Eccles Theatre
- 100 South St

Labels on map (Logan Area):
- 30
- WYOMING
- 30
- 16
- to Randolph
- Cisco Beach
- Rendezvous Beach
- Laketown
- 30
- Round Valley
- Bear Lake State Park
- Fish Haven
- 89
- Bear Lake
- Garden City
- 30
- Meadowville
- IDAHO
- Beaver Mountain
- 89
- Naomi Peak 9980'
- Mount Naomi Wilderness Area
- LOGAN CANYON
- Wasatch-Cache National Forest
- Hardware Ranch
- N
- 25 miles
- 25 kilometers
- 101
- 89
- Franklin
- 91
- Lewiston
- Richmond
- Smithfield
- 142
- Logan
- Providence
- 89
- 91
- 165
- Hyrum
- Bear River
- 23
- Trenton
- Newton
- 142
- Clarkston
- 30
- 91
- Hyrum Lake State Park
- Wellsville
- 23
- 91
- 89
- Brigham City
- to Ogden
- 84
- 15
- Bear River
- 15

History Museum in Salt Lake City. The librarians claim that if you can give them an hour, they'll locate the records of one of your ancestors. In the 1870s and 1880s the local women's Relief Society used the tabernacle to make hats, baskets, brooms and sewing projects. Tours are scheduled throughout the summer. ~ 50 North Main Street, Logan; 435-755-5594.

One of Logan's earliest federal buildings, the **Hall of Justice** is now home to the **Logan Convention and Visitors Bureau** as well as the Bridgerland Travel Region offices. These offices can answer questions about the Cache Valley and load you up on brochures, maps and ideas. Also available is a pamphlet that lays out a 45-minute walking tour of historic Main Street. ~ 160 North Main Street, Logan; 435-752-2161, 800-882-4433, fax 435-753-5825; www.bridgerland.com, e-mail btr@sunrem.com.

The **Daughters of Utah Pioneers** have squeezed their museum into what used to be the building's courtroom. Inside are displays of the days of the mountain men as well as early pioneer artifacts. Open Monday afternoon and Tuesday through Friday from June through September; by appointment the rest of the year. ~ 160 North Main Street, Logan; 435-752-5139 (summer), 435-753-1635.

Kitty-corner from the Convention and Visitors Bureau is the **Cache County Courthouse**, which was built in 1883 and continues to operate as the county courthouse, giving it the distinction of being the oldest county building in the state still used for its original purpose. ~ 179 North Main Street, Logan.

Ensconced on a terrace left behind by prehistoric Lake Bonneville, the **Logan LDS Temple** looks out across the Cache Valley. Built during a seven-year-period between 1877 and 1884, the limestone temple is an example of modified Gothic architecture. Only LDS Church members can enter the building, but the architecture and the view are worth a visit. ~ 200 North 200 East, Logan; 435-752-3611.

AUTHOR FAVORITE

I can't think of a better way to spend a late summer day than on the shore of **Bear Lake**, munching on locally grown berries in-between swims in the 28,000-year-old lake. Located 40 miles northeast of Logan on Route 89, this 112-square-mile body of water straddles the Utah–Idaho border. Donald Mackenzie, an explorer for the North West Fur Company, discovered the lake in 1819 and named it Black Bear Lake, although years later the "black" was dropped. Formed by an earthquake 28,000 years ago, Bear Lake has a unique aquamarine color created by the sunlight refracting off limestone particles suspended in the water. ~ Route 89, 41 miles east of Logan; 435-946-3343.

Logan is home to Utah's land-grant college, **Utah State University**. Huddled on the northeastern edge of town, the university sits atop a hill overlooking town. Founded in 1888, the university boasts eight colleges and more than 20,000 students. Although its roots are in agriculture, the school has a rich array of degree programs, ranging from agronomy to rocketry. ~ Utah State University, Logan; 435-797-1000; www.usu.edu.

As one of the largest cheese-producing regions of the country, the Cache Valley has more than its share of dairy product outlets. Much of the valley's cheese finds its way onto the hamburgers churned out by Burger King and McDonald's. Beyond cheese, Utah State University played a role in pioneering the production of ice cream. You can sample the product—**Aggie Ice Cream**—at the university's Nutrition and Food Science Building. Closed Sunday. ~ 750 North 1200 East, Logan; 435-797-2109.

Despite the rolling agricultural land and forests that surround Utah State University, not all the work done there revolves around agriculture. The university's **Space Dynamics Laboratory** has played a research and development role in the U.S. space program since the early 1960s and currently is recognized as a leader in space instrumentation and research. As a result, the university has placed more experiments on space shuttles than any other university. To learn about the lab's involvement in U.S. exploration of Mars, call ahead to arrange a tour of the facility. ~ 1695 North Research Park Way, Logan; 435-797-4600.

It's not often that animals get historical markers, but when you're reputed to be the biggest grizzly ever killed in the continental United States, well, you deserve more than just a hole in the ground. Be forewarned, however: it's a five-and-a-half-mile hike to **Old Ephraim's Grave**. For the curious, Old Ephraim, who roamed the mountains east of Logan, stood nine feet, eleven inches tall. Killed in 1923, the grizzly's skull was displayed for a while at the Smithsonian Institution. ~ The trailhead is located 9.2 miles up Logan Canyon at the end of Right Hand Fork Road.

Not far from the trail to Old Ephraim's resting place is the **Jardine Juniper**, which, at an estimated 1500 years old, is believed by some to be the world's oldest juniper tree. A four-and-a-half-mile hike takes you to the old gnarled tree, which is sadly slipping away, a victim of age and disease. ~ The trailhead is found at the Wood Camp turnoff a dozen miles up Route 89 from Logan.

The popular **Rendezvous Beach,** part of Bear Lake State Park, carries its name from the gatherings fur trappers and Indians held there in 1827 and 1828 to trade goods. These days sailboats and powerboats play on the water's surface, while swimmers splash along its beaches and scuba divers explore the eastern shoreline.

A stone's throw from the western shore of Bear Lake, **Garden City** is a small outpost along Route 89 that dates to 1864. One of the lake's more fertile spots, the town of less than 300 is home to several raspberry farms, motels and Bear Lake State Park and marina. Each August is overrun by berry lovers in town for the annual Bear Lake Raspberry Days Festival.

LODGING   Between Logan and Bear Lake, there are quite a few lodging possibilities. Look hard enough and you can find bed-and-breakfast operations in wonderfully historic homes, or you can settle for a shoreside resort setting at Bear Lake.

HIDDEN ►   Two miles south of Logan, history and comfort cross paths at the **Providence Inn Bed & Breakfast**, which is part of the "Old Rock Church" built between 1869 and 1871. Stones for the original building were carved from a nearby quarry. In 1926 a much larger wing was added to the church and it evolved into the bed and breakfast; the entire building is listed on the National Register of Historic Places. Within the walls you'll find a sweeping staircase, vaulted ceilings and Palladian windows. The 17 rooms are decorated in either Early American, Georgian or Victorian style. While the parlor sports a roaring fireplace, each room has a private bath and TV. ~ 10 South Main, Providence; 435-752-3432, 800-480-4943; www.providenceinn.com, e-mail provinn@providenceinn.com. MODERATE TO ULTRA-DELUXE.

Among Logan's stately Victorian homes is the **Logan House Inn**, a historic mansion that boasts its own ballroom and fine "Arts and Craft" workmanship, such as the stained-glass window over the grand staircase. A private residence for many years, today the turn-of-the-20th-century Greek Revival/Georgian Manor home serves as a bed and breakfast. Most of the six guest rooms feature fireplaces as well as jetted tubs. A favorite is The Library, which holds more than 500 books in its cherrywood cabinets. Breakfasts range from pancakes or French toast stuffed with almond cream filling and almond raspberry sauce to simple continental fare. ~ 168 North 100 East, Logan; 435-752-7727, 800-478-7459, fax 435-752-0092; www.loganhouseinn.com, e-mail loganinn@loganhouseinn.com. MODERATE TO DELUXE.

The **Best Western Weston Inn** in downtown Logan offers convenience (it's within walking distance of dining, shopping and entertainment) as well as reliability. Eighty-nine rooms with microwaves, refrigerators and jetted tubs are available. Other amenities include an indoor pool and fitness center on the premises. ~ 250 North Main Street, Logan; 435-752-5700, 800-532-5055, fax 435-752-9719. BUDGET TO MODERATE.

Not far from the Logan River golf course lies the **Crystal Inn**, an independently owned motel where the rooms come with microwaves, refrigerators and free local calls. You'll also find an indoor pool, a hot tub and an exercise room. Suites are available. Continental breakfast included. ~ 853 South Route 89, Logan; 435-752-0707, 800-280-0707, fax 435-787-2207; www.crystal inns.com/logan.html. MODERATE.

While most of the options at Bear Lake revolve around resort accommodations, the **Eagle Feather Inn** lets you get away from the crowds in a modest clapboard home where you can rent a room or the entire building. The inn, just across the street from the lake, offers three bedrooms with private baths, as well as a hot tub in the garden. Two-night minimums are required in summer, and three-night minimums are required during Memorial Day and Pioneer Day weekends. ~ 135 South Bear Lake Boulevard, Garden City; 435-946-2846, 877-977-2846; www.go-utah.com/eagle featherinn, e-mail slonek@dcdi.net. BUDGET TO MODERATE.

At the **Bear Lake Motor Lodge** your pets can join you on vacation. Half of the 20 rooms have kitchenettes, although there is a restaurant on the grounds if you don't want to bother with cooking. The lodge also comes with a beachfront perfect for after-dinner strolls or a mid-day swim. ~ 50 South Bear Lake Boulevard, Garden City; 435-946-3271. BUDGET TO MODERATE.

There are 14 beachfront cabins and eight condo units at the **Blue Water Beach Resort** just down the street. Although the cabins are on the rustic side, you'd be hard-pressed to beat the location. The resort also has an RV park, pitch-and-putt golf, an outdoor swimming pool and a hot tub. ~ 2126 South Bear Lake Boulevard, Garden City; 435-946-3333, 800-756-0795. MODERATE TO DELUXE.

Not only is the **Canyon Cove Inn** a short walk from the lake shore, it's surrounded by some of the raspberry patches that provide the crucial ingredients for the raspberry shakes that are famous in Garden City. This two-story motel offers five varieties of rooms, ranging from budget-oriented one-bedroom units to suites with a private bedroom and a living area with a couch, refrigerator and microwave. If it's too cold for a swim in the lake,

AUTHOR FAVORITE

You can lick up some history at **Aggie's Ice Cream Shop** on the campus of Utah State University, which pioneered modern-day ice cream production. I find that stopping here after an outing in Logan Canyon is a great way to cool down with some of the best ice cream in northern Utah. The ice cream is made at the university's Dairy Science Building and delivered right to Aggie's. ~ 750 North 1200 East, Logan; 435-797-2109. BUDGET.

the motel has an indoor pool. ~ 315 West Logan Highway, Garden City; 435-946-3565, 877-232-7525; www.canyoncove.com, e-mail info@canyoncove.com. BUDGET TO DELUXE.

Overlooking Bear Lake from a spot just north of Garden City, the **Harbor Village Resort** offers one of the most complete lodging packages at the lake. The 40 modest but comfortable guest rooms are supported by an on-site restaurant, exercise facilities, a spa, laundry facilities and an indoor/outdoor pool. ~ 900 North Bear Lake Boulevard, Garden City; 435-946-3448. MODERATE TO ULTRA-DELUXE.

DINING

Logan hardly bursts with culinary treasures, but there are a few.

If you want to eat where the locals do, head to the **Copper Mill Restaurant**, where meals come with fresh-baked rolls and homemade raspberry jam. Closed Sunday. ~ 55 North Main Street, Logan; 435-752-0647. BUDGET TO MODERATE.

HIDDEN ►

Most towns have a hidden, yet renowned, restaurant, and in Logan that would be **The Grapevine**. Situated in a modest house with just two dining rooms holding 16 tables, the restaurant's menu has chicken and pasta dishes joining unexpected dishes such as "Cache Valley Rabbit," pork tamales and lamb shank Tangier. Closed Sunday through Tuesday. ~ 129 North 100 East, Logan; 435-752-1977. MODERATE.

Italian dishes, steaks and chicken dominate the menu at **Gia's Restaurant**, where Utah State University students head to meet friends in the basement pizzeria, while the upstairs dining room offers more formal table service. ~ 119 South Main Street, Logan; 435-752-8384. BUDGET TO MODERATE.

For that old-time, soda fountain feeling, try the **Bluebird Restaurant**, a landmark since 1914. You can still sit at the marble soda fountain bar and gorge yourself on a banana split. Dinners run the gamut, from prime rib and steak to the restaurant's signature "Bluebird Chicken," which has an Asian flavor. ~ 19 North Main Street, Logan; 435-752-3155. BUDGET TO MODERATE.

Pierre Micheli had a sure-hit recipe when he decided to open **Le Nonne** in Logan. Pierre, who hails from Tuscany, borrowed many of the recipes his grandmother used in Italy for the family's

THE BEES' KNEES

For something sweet, visit **Cox Honeyland and Gifts**. Owned by a family whose honey production goes back five generations, the shop offers pure honey as well as creamed honey spreads containing fresh fruit such as raspberries, oranges and apricots. ~ 1780 South Route 91, Logan; 435-752-3234.

restaurants there. Not surprisingly, he named his restaurant for his grandmother, as Le Nonne translates to "The grandmother's." Enter his café-style eatery and you'll find hearty northern Italian flavors in the homemade pastas such as spinach and ricotta ravioli or chicken ravioli and seafood dishes such as salmon with lemon capers or charbroiled swordfish topped with fresh diced tomatoes, garlic and basil. No lunch on Saturday or Sunday. ~ 132 North Main Street, Logan; 435-752-9577. BUDGET TO MODERATE.

When visiting Bear Lake, fresh raspberry shakes are served up at **LaBeau's** (69 North Bear Lake Boulevard, Garden City, 435-946-8821), the **Hometown Drive-In** (105 North Bear Lake Boulevard, 435-946-2727) and a few other places in Garden City. BUDGET.

For a sit-down meal with a romantic view, the **Harbor Village Restaurant** overlooks the lake. ~ 785 North Bear Lake Boulevard, Garden City; 435-946-3448. MODERATE.

Being a college town as well as the only major outpost in extreme northern Utah, Logan offers an eclectic and diverse shopping experience. In downtown, Federal and Church streets harbor antique and craft shops while 100 East is popular for bicycles as well as collectibles and gardening supplies.

SHOPPING

Earthly Awakening is the kind of bohemian shop you'd expect to find in a college town, with its herbal remedies, potpourris and crystals. ~ 21 Federal Avenue, Logan; 435-755-8657.

Down the street at **On the Avenue** are local crafts such as painted furniture, whimsical dolls, candles, garden sculptures and stained-glass items. ~ 34 Federal Avenue, Logan; 435-753-1150.

Browse through shelf after shelf of contemporary fiction and children's books at **Chapter Two Books**, which is housed in an elegant Victorian house. ~ 130 North 100 East, Logan; 435-752-9089.

Smiling Moon is a toy store that believes that toys should be powered by kids, not batteries. Located in a nicely restored Victorian, the house offers wooden blocks, wooden trains and, naturally, wooden Lincoln Logs. You'll also find wooden puzzles, kites, hand and finger puppets and, for the older folks, brain puzzlers. ~ 146 North 100 East, Logan; 435-752-0055.

To focus your shopping in one contained area, visit the **Cache Valley Mall** on the north end of town. Here more than 40 shops, including a few chain department stores, are clustered together under one roof. Surrounding the mall are restaurants and theaters. ~ 1300 North Main Street, Logan; 435-753-5400.

Not far from downtown is **Gossner Foods**, a family-owned company where you can stop by and sample and purchase cheeses, ice cream and gourmet milks, such as root beer–flavored milk. If that's not to your liking, they also have chocolate, strawberry,

◄ HIDDEN

mocha and banana. Closed Sunday. ~ 1000 West 1051 North, Logan; 435-752-9365.

They recycle trees at the **Urban Forest Woodworks**, which stocks hand-crafted jewelry boxes and candle holders from downed trees that normally would end up in landfill. Closed Sunday. ~ 1065 West 600 North, Logan; 435-752-7268.

NIGHTLIFE During the summer, warm, dry evenings come alive at the **Sherwood Hills Summer Theater**, where actors bring melodramas to life on an outdoor stage. A bonus for guests is the chuckwagon suppers that precede the shows. Closed Sunday through Wednesday. ~ Route 89/91, Wellsville; 435-245-5054, 800-532-5066; www.sherwoodhills.com.

Looking for a burger or sandwich paired with a beer or refreshing drink amid a younger crowd? The **White Owl** is the college hangout in Logan. ~ 36 West Center Street, Logan; 435-753-9165.

Opera is not out of the question in Logan during the summer, when the **Utah Festival Opera Company** stages a four-week season in the Ellen Eccles Theatre, an 1100-seat playhouse built in 1923. Since the productions, which might include *Carmen, Julius Caesar* or *The Mikado*, are performed in a revolving repertory, several shows can be seen over the course of three days. ~ 59 South 100 West, Logan; 800-262-0074; www.ufoc.org, e-mail opera@ufoc.org.

The Eccles Theatre is also the backdrop for touring Broadway shows and concerts throughout the year.

Open during summer months is the **Old Lyric Repertory Theatre**, which stages dramas, comedies and even musical revues. ~ 28 West Center Street, Logan; 435-752-1500.

For those staying at Bear Lake, the **Pickleville Playhouse** stages musical melodramas during the summer. ~ South Bear Lake Boulevard, Garden City; 435-946-2918 or 435-755-0961.

PARKS   **WASATCH-CACHE NATIONAL FOREST** 🏃 🚴 🧗 🏊
East of Logan lies the northern tip of the Wasatch-Cache National Forest and the 44,964-acre **Mount Naomi Wilderness Area**. Within its boundaries, moose, elk and beaver, in addition to five species of flowers unique to the area, thrive. Also found in the national forest is the "Jardine Juniper" (at an estimated 1500 years old it's one of the oldest juniper trees in the world) and countless miles of hiking trails. ~ Trailheads to Wind Cave and the Jardine Juniper are located off Route 89 heading east through Logan Canyon. Logan Ranger District, 1500 East Route 89, Logan; 435-755-3620; www.fs.fed.us/wcnf.

▲ Within this section of the forest's Logan District are 256 campsites in 22 developed campgrounds; free to $14 per night; most have a 14-day maximum stay. For reservations, call 877-444-6777; www.reserveusa.com.

BEAR LAKE STATE PARK 🚶 🚲 ⛵ 🎣 🏊 🛶 🛥 🚤

Thanks to its shimmering turquoise waters, Bear Lake is often referred to as the Caribbean of the Rockies. Stretching 20 miles north to south and eight miles east to west, the lake and its sandy beaches are a popular summer retreat for boaters, sailors, scuba divers, anglers, cyclists and campers. You'll find a 45-mile cycling loop that wraps the lake, state-owned beaches, campgrounds and ma- rina, and seven boat ramps located along its shores. Bear Lake State Park is broken into three units: the marina on the west shore with its 305 boat slips and a five-lane boat ramp, Rendezvous Beach on the south shore, and Eastside/Cisco Beach on the east side. Day-use fee, $5. ~ Route 89, 41 miles east of Logan; 435-946-3343; parks.state.ut.us/parks/www1/bear.htm.

> Wind Cave, a series of grottos cut by erosion, is one of the highlights in the Logan District of Wasatch-Cache National Forest.

▲ There are 136 lakeside sites at Rendezvous Beach, 25 sites at Bear Lake Eastside, and 13 sites at the marina; $15 to $19 per night; 14-day maximum stay. For reservations, call 800-322-3770.

Among private campgrounds, **Bear Lake KOA Campground**, located one mile north of Garden City, has 140 sites, some with full hookups; $18 to $27 per night. There's also a heated swim- ming pool, tennis courts and bike rentals. ~ 485 North Bear Lake Boulevard, Garden City; 435-946-3454, 800-562-3442.

HYRUM LAKE STATE PARK 🚲 ⛵ 🎣 🛶 🛥 🚤

Southeast of Logan along Route 101, this tiny state park is wrapped around a 450-acre lake that provides fishing and small boating oppor- tunities. There are restrooms and showers. Sixteen miles farther east on Route 101 lies the **Hardware Ranch** (see "Logan Sights" above), which is a winter feeding ground for elk. Day-use fee, $5. ~ Route 165, eight miles south of Logan, 405 West 300 South, Hyrum; 435-245-6866; parks.state.ut.us/parks/www1/hyru.htm.

▲ There are 40 campsites; $12 per night; 14-day maximum stay. For reservations, call 800-322-3770.

Although you won't catch any fish in the Great Salt Lake, there are endless miles of streams and a good number of reservoirs and high- country lakes in the mountains of northern Utah to keep anglers occupied throughout the fishing season.

Outdoor Adventures

FISHING

OGDEN AREA   Streams rushing out of the mountains east of Ogden are full of fish. While the **Ogden, Weber** and **South Fork** streams are reliable trout fisheries, Rocky Mountain whitefish occasionally can be hooked in the South Fork. Smallmouth bass are stocked in the lower Weber River on the west side of Route 15.

Young anglers are often found at the **21st Street Pond** in Ogden. Found just off the Route 15 freeway ramp at 21st Street, the pond is popular with families and productive in spring and winter.

Just ten miles east of Ogden via Route 39 shimmers **Pineview Reservoir**, a warm-water fishery rich in bass, catfish, crappie, bluegill, yellow perch and tiger musky. Not even winter slows the fishing since the reservoir freezes over and draws ice fishermen.

Trout anglers head to **Causey Reservoir**, a deep, narrow reservoir about 30 miles east of Ogden on the South Fork of the Ogden River. Cutthroat, rainbow, brook and brown trout have been pulled from the reservoir, which sees the best action in spring and fall.

HIDDEN ▶ **BRIGHAM CITY AREA**   Bluegill anglers should head to **Mantua Reservoir** along Route 89/91 in Wellsville Canyon. Along with bluegill, it is stocked with bass and trout.

Some of northern Utah's best dry fly-fishing can be had along Route 101 in Blacksmith Fork Canyon east of Hyrum. While stone fly and salmonfly hatch between mid-May and June, from July through September grasshoppers are the bait of choice.

LOGAN AREA   What would fishing be without tall tales of the one that got away? Well, they say a 40-pound trout was once pulled from the **Logan River** in Logan Canyon. The river's fishing is at its best from June into August. Farther up Logan Canyon lies **Tony Grove Lake**, which is stocked with rainbow trout. To get there, head 19 miles up the canyon on Route 89, then take the turnoff seven miles to the lake.

Bear Lake is a vibrant trout fishery, renowned for its cutthroat stock. The Idaho record cutthroat, weighing 19 pounds, was pulled from this lake. Also found in the waters are lake trout and Bonneville whitefish, which can be hooked from shore in the late fall. Trolling and jigging are most productive in the winter and spring months. Bonneville cisco, thought to exist only in the lake, are a member of the whitefish family. These seven-inch-long fish run at the end of January and early February, drawing hundreds to the lake shores with dipping nets.

MOUNTAIN MEN MEETINGS

Northern Utah was a popular place for rendezvous in the early 1800s. In 1826 the mountain men gathered near the mouth of Blacksmith's Fork Canyon, near Hyrum. In 1827 and again in 1828 the gathering was moved to the south end of Bear Lake. After two years in Wyoming, the annual rendezvous was moved back to the Cache Valley in 1831. Late each May, the Cache Valley Renaissance Rendezvous is held near Hyrum and recalls the heady days of trappers.

Tackle, but no guides, can be found at **Al's Sporting Goods** in Logan. ~ 1617 North Main Street, Logan; 435-752-5151. **Bear River Basin Outfitters** can lead you to fish in extreme northern Utah and southeastern Idaho. They guide along the Bear River system, Bear Lake and in some private lakes in the mountains above Laketown. ~ 2123 South Bear Lake Boulevard, Garden City; 435-946-2876.

WATER SPORTS Where there are mountains in Utah, there usually are lakes are reservoirs that capture the spring runoff and provide places to fish or swim during the summer months.

OGDEN AREA With 2879 surface acres, **Pineview Reservoir**, ten miles east of Ogden via Route 39 (Ogden Scenic Byway), is a popular retreat for boaters, windsurfers and waterskiers.

Diamond Peak rents sit-on-top kayaks, inflatable kayaks and canoes for use on the reservoir. ~ 2429 North Route 162, Eden; 801-745-0101.

BRIGHAM CITY AREA Although it covers just 554 acres, waterskiers still manage to enjoy themselves on **Mantua Reservoir**, ◄ HIDDEN
located on Route 89 east of Brigham City. Possibly due to its small size, the reservoir is often overlooked. As a result, boaters sometimes find that they have Mantua to themselves, even on summer weekends.

LOGAN AREA Snug in the mountains eight miles south of Logan, **Hyrum State Park** offers a 450-acre reservoir perfect for canoeing and swimming. ~ 405 West 300 South, Hyrum; 801-245-6866.

The 160-square-mile **Bear Lake**, the state's second largest freshwater lake, is *the* destination for water-sports enthusiasts in northern Utah. Power boaters, sailors, windsurfers, scuba divers and plain old swimmers are also lured by the water and the white-sand beaches that rim the lake.

There are plenty of boat ramps to go around, although they fill up quickly during the summer. Bear Lake State Park has a 305-slip marina and boat rentals, while several other businesses in the area rent watercraft. **Bear Lake Sails** rents sailboats, power boats, canoes and more. ~ 2141 South Bear Lake Boulevard, Garden City; 435-946-2994. Rentals are also available at **Bear Lake Funtime**. ~ 1217 South Bear Lake Boulevard, Garden City; 435-946-3200.

CLIMBING Nearly 300 climbing routes, ranging in difficulty, have been blazed up the limestone and quartzite cliffs in Logan Canyon east of Logan, and roughly 230 of these are bolt-protected. Check with the Logan District Ranger Office to see which climbs have been closed to protect threatened or endangered plant species. Available in many Logan bookstores, *Logan Canyon Climbs* by Tim Monsell details the canyon's climbs.

Aspiring climbers can work on their techniques at **Bitter Sweet**, an indoor facility perfect for getting used to hanging onto rocks with your fingers and moving across rock faces. ~ 51 South Main Street, Logan; 435-752-8152; www.bittersweetgear.com.

DOWNHILL SKIING & SNOW-BOARDING

Although northern Utah can't claim as many alpine resorts as the Salt Lake City and Park City areas, this doesn't mean that those you will find are any less worthy. In fact, if you want to avoid crowds, this just might be the part of Utah to consider.

OGDEN AREA   Nordic Valley doesn't pretend to be one of Utah's big boys when it comes to skiing, instead offering a low-key family experience. With just 85 skiable acres, a vertical drop of but 960 feet and only two lifts, this tucked-away area 15 miles east of Ogden is open nightly for night skiing, and Friday through Sunday for day skiing. ~ Located 15 miles east of Ogden off Route 158, 3567 Nordic Valley Way, Eden; 801-745-3511 (seasonal).

Overlooked when compared to Wasatch Range resorts, **Powder Mountain** offers access to 5500 acres of skiing, of which 2800 acres are lift-served and the rest accessed by Snowcat or return shuttle. Nineteen miles east of Ogden, the resort offers four lifts and three surface tows that haul skiers and boarders around the 70-plus runs. ~ Located 19 miles east of Ogden and just past Nordic Valley via Route 158; 801-745-3772; www.powdermountain.net.

The 2002 Olympic Winter Games pumped badly needed life into **Snowbasin**, which faced a "mom-and-pop" existence until the Salt Lake Organizing Committee decided the resort should host the Games' downhill and Super-G ski races. Skiers and snowboarders alike use the resort's nine lifts to get around the 3200 skiable acres. The base reformation is a work in progress, but once done expect an upscale ski-and-golf resort in the mold of Sun Valley. ~ Routes 39 and 167, 17 miles east of Ogden, Huntsville; 801-399-1135; www.snowbasin.com.

Diamond Peaks Heli-Ski Adventures uses helicopters, not lifts, to reach the slopes. The company has access to 12,000 acres of backcountry skiing and snowboarding with a vertical drop of

AUTHOR FAVORITE

The consummate mom-and-pop resort, operated by the same family since 1939, **Beaver Mountain** is a diamond in the rough—this is one of my favorite resorts for a low-key day spent in an incredibly beautiful area. No mega-seat high-speed lifts here, no ritzy restaurants, no trophy homes littering the mountain—just 464 acres of some of the best powder skiing and boarding in northern Utah. Tucked away near the head of Logan Canyon, the resort has a 1600-foot vertical drop and five lifts. ~ Route 89, 27 miles east of Logan, Logan Canyon; 435-753-0921.

2800 feet. ~ P.O. Box 12302, Ogden, UT 84412; 801-745-4631; www.diamondpeaks.com.

Most of the cross-country ski opportunities in northern Utah require you to work a little harder at the sport as you'll more than likely have to break trail, although there is a resort in the Logan area that offers groomed trails.

CROSS-COUNTRY SKIING

OGDEN AREA   No need to leave Ogden to get a decent cross-country workout: the 127-acre **Ogden Nature Center** found on the city's west side off of 12th Street has hiking trails that skiers can use in the winter.

Out of town, the **Maples Campground** at the Snowbasin Ski Area features a five-kilometer-long ski trail with only a moderate elevation gain of 6360 feet to 6500 feet. ~ Head 17 miles east of Ogden via Route 39 and 167 to the Snowbasin Ski Area and the campground.

Going nearly 30 miles east of Ogden via Route 39, the trail leading from the **South Fork Campgrounds** runs four kilometers and has a negligible elevation rise. ~ Route 39.

Another popular area with cross-country skiers is **North Fork Park** along **Avon-Liberty Road**. To get there, from Ogden head 15 miles toward the Nordic Valley ski area and take the left fork onto North Ogden Divide Road. How far you ski down the road is up to you.

LOGAN AREA   Not far from Logan, **Sherwood Hills** offers 20 kilometers of groomed trails that wind through the forests in the Wellsville Mountains. Lessons, rentals and even night skiing are also available. ~ Located on the south end of Wellsville along Route 89/91, Wellsville; 435-245-5054, 800-532-5066.

The awarding of the 2002 Olympic Winter Games brought a bevy of winter sports facilities to Utah's Wasatch Range. In Ogden, the **Ice Sheet**, next to the Dee Events Center, is used by ice hockey leagues as well as the city's curling and figure skating clubs. Learn-to-curl classes are held weekly at the facility. Time is also set aside for the general public to skate on the rink. ~ 4390 Harrison Boulevard, Ogden; 801-399-8750.

OTHER WINTER SPORTS

The **21st Street Pond** usually freezes over during the winter months and is popular with ice skaters. If you go, check the ice before heading out across the pond. ~ East of Route 15 on 21st Street, Ogden.

Golf is more popular than skiing in Utah, which explains the countless courses. During mild winters, golf can be a year-round sport.

GOLF

OGDEN AREA   **The Barn**, a 6000-yard, 18-hole public golf course named after a white barn that is now used for the course lounge, is nestled on farmland in Ogden's northern foothills. A relatively flat, tree-lined course, three duck-filled ponds add to the natural hazards. ~ 305 West Pleasant View Drive, Ogden; 801-782-7320.

The **Ben Lomond** golf course spreads its 18 holes over 6200 yards. Like The Barn, this par-72 course is also fairly flat, but the holes are longer. Its relatively low elevation enables this course to be one of the first to open in the spring. ~ 1800 North Route 89, Ogden; 801-782-7754.

El Monte Golf Course has nine holes cradled in the mouth of Ogden Canyon and features rolling hills and water that occasionally lure moose. Located across from the Eccles Dinosaur Park, this course can be demanding when the dinosaurs roar as you're getting ready to tee off. ~ 1300 Valley Drive, Ogden; 801-629-8333.

The **Mount Ogden** course on Ogden's East Bench is one of the more challenging 18-hole courses in the region thanks to its dramatic elevation changes and narrow, heavily treed fairways. Several dog-leg holes make it impossible to see the pin from the tee. ~ 1787 Constitution Way, Ogden; 801-629-8700.

Mulligan's Golf & Games offers a short 9-hole course, a lighted driving range, and two 18-hole miniature courses. ~ 1690 West 400 North, Ogden; 801-392-4653.

The **Pleasant Valley Golf Center** boasts an 18-hole natural grass putting course as well as a driving range. ~ 5600 South 500 East, Ogden; 801-475-4787.

Views of the Great Salt Lake and Antelope Island might distract you when you're putting around the 18-hole, 6800-yard public course at **Schneiter's Bluff.** ~ 300 North 3500 West, West Point; 801-773-0731.

The **Wolf Creek Resort** offers an 18-hole, 7000-yard public course that is hilly and very challenging due to its sand and water traps, roughs and long holes. This is one of the state's most scenic mountain courses, thanks to the nearby ski resorts and Pineview Reservoir; wildlife in the form of moose, elk and fox often crop up. ~ 3900 North Wolf Creek Drive, Eden; 801-745-3365.

ALL IN FUN

Based 30 minutes east of Ogden in Huntsville, **Red Rock Ranch and Outfitters** mixes work with fun. The century-old working ranch still offers livestock for sale and entertains tourists with a taste of the Old (and the new) West. While snowmobile tours and sleigh rides are offered during the winter months, come summer wagon rides, hay rides, Dutch-oven dinners, guided horseback rides and even overnight pack trips are the way of life. ~ Huntsville; 801-745-4305, 800-352-5193; www.redrock ranchandoutfitters.com.

The **Valley View Golf Course** is often the backdrop of amateur tournaments. Its 18-hole, 6800-yard course is par 72. ~
2501 East Gentile, Layton; 801-546-1630.

BRIGHAM CITY AREA   The 18-hole, 6769-yard **Eagle Mountain
Golf Course** in Brigham City is supported by a driving range, a
putting green and a chipping area. Built onto the side of a moun-
tain, this par-71 course, which provides sweeping views of the
Great Salt Lake, requires precise drives. ~ 960 East 700 South,
Brigham City; 435-723-3212.

Brigham City's other course is **Brigham Willow Golf Course**,
a 3300-yard, par-37, nine-hole course that can challenge beginning players while giving more experienced duffers someplace to
work on their shots. ~ Junction of Routes 89 and 30, Brigham
City; 435-723-5301.

LOGAN AREA   In Smithfield four miles north of Logan, the 18-
hole, 6770-yard **Birch Creek Golf Course** is set on the side of the
Bear River Range, offering sweeping views of the Cache Valley
and providing challenging greens. ~ 600 East Center Street,
Smithfield; 435-563-6825.

Located in Sardine Canyon just a dozen miles southwest of
Logan on Route 89/91 is the **Sherwood Hills Golf Course**, a modest nine-hole course that spans 3315 yards and features narrow,
heavily treed fairways. ~ Located on the south end of Wellsville
along Route 89/91, Wellsville; 435-245-6055, 800-532-5066.

Thanks to its tight fairways and scenery the 18-hole, 6502-
yard **Logan River Golf Course** is viewed not only as one of Utah's
top ten courses but as one of the top 500 in the country. Built in
1993, the par-71 course flows in and out of groves of trees along
the Logan River. ~ 550 West 1000 South, Logan; 435-750-0123.

It's not as challenging as the courses on the west side of the
mountains, but the **Bear Lake Golf Course** offers a nice respite
from boating on Bear Lake. The nine holes cover 3126 yards and
overlook the lake. ~ 2176 South Bear Lake Boulevard, Garden
City; 435-946-8742.

The Wasatch Range that dominates northern Utah offers countless areas for riding horseback.

Logan Canyon is great to ramble through on horseback, with
its gorgeous canyons and forests. **Beaver Creek Trail Rides** can
get you into the mountains east of Logan with one-hour, three-
hour or custom rides. ~ Route 89, 12 miles west of Garden City
near Beaver Mountain, P.O. Box 139, Millville, UT 84326; 435-
946-3400.

During the summer months horseback rides can be arranged
through the **Sherwood Hills Resort**. These rides, which run one
and two hours and are suitable for beginners, head off into the
Wellsville Mountains. ~ Located on the south end of Wellsville

**RIDING
STABLES**

on Route 89/91, Wellsville; 435-245-5054, 800-532-5066; www. sherwoodhills.com.

BIKING   There's no lack of riding terrain in northern Utah, although, as with other parts of the state, you will be expected to earn the mileage as the mountains result in a lot of elevation in most rides.

OGDEN AREA   In the Ogden area, mountain bikers looking for a full day's ride like the **Skyline Trail**, which starts from the west side of Pineview Reservoir one and a half miles from the dam, from the Willard Basin or from North Ogden Divide. The trail, which ranges from 6184 feet to 8100 feet, runs for 22 miles and is also used by horseback riders, motorbikes and hikers.

Beus Canyon offers a shorter ride, one covering seven miles. Access can be found at the Snowbasin Ski Area. It, too, is part of the Great Western Trail and also is used by horseback riders and hikers.

A more level ride is along the **Running Water Jeep Loop**, which runs 9.2 miles along forest roads. Access is via Forest Road 192 or Forest Road 144 from the Curtis Creek Road. While no hikers or horseback riders use this loop, which begins at an elevation of 8200 feet and ends at 8600 feet, you may be sharing it with ATVs.

BRIGHAM CITY AREA   Hard-core mountain bikers will enjoy pedaling down **Willard Peak Road**. Running 12 miles one way, this out and back route begins at the LDS Church on the south side of Mantua and climbs 4200 feet on the way to Inspiration Point near Willard Peak. Wildlife such as deer, moose and elk are often seen. From Inspiration Point are great views of both the Wasatch Mountains and Great Salt Lake.

A longer but less grueling ride in terms of elevation is the 32-mile route between **Brigham City** and **Golden Spike National Historic Site**. Traversing paved state and county roads, the jaunt is pretty flat, outside of the short climb to Promontory Summit. Along the way to the historic site the path winds through irrigated farmland, wetlands and the Thiokol Rocket Manufacturing Plant. Access in Brigham City is at the Willows Golf Course parking lot at the junction of Routes 38 and 13. In the summer this can be a long, hot ride, with temperatures near 100° possible.

LOGAN AREA   Bird lovers will appreciate the **Bear River Bird Refuge Road**. The 12-mile-long refuge loop runs along dikes built to create ponds for waterfowl. In the spring this ride provides views of dozens of bird species, and possibly a fox or two. You can pick up a bird checklist at a kiosk near the refuge entrance.

Mountain bikers in the Bear Lake area often frequent **Hodge's Canyon Road**, which runs from the western shores of Bear Lake at Pickelville to a 10-mile loop that winds through aspen groves and past the South Sinks area, where the landside is indented by sinks caused by water eroding the limestone beneath the earth's surface. Another popular ride—one that's a bit easier and suitable for beginners—involves a 15-mile loop that runs from Meadowville to Route 30 on the western shore of Bear Lake, south to Laketown and then back west into Round Valley before returning to Meadowville. Along the way you'll pass a pioneer cemetery as well as a ghost town.

One of the most popular rides along Bear Lake is on the 4.3-mile **Garden City Bicycle and Pedestrian Trail**. The 10-foot-wide asphalt strip lures, hikers, joggers, rollerbladers and skateboarders, too. The 45-mile **Bear Lake Loop Bicycle Trail** offers not only a more strenuous workout but a geology primer on the lake and surrounding landscape through interpretive signs.

Bikers like the 4.5-mile **Swan Creek** loop trail, accessed off Route 89 near Lakota north of Garden City. A more grueling ride goes 15.5 miles from the Bear Lake Summit to Meadowville. **Bike Rentals** In Ogden, **Kent's Sports Store** sells bikes and services all brands of bikes. ~ 307 Washington Boulevard, Ogden; 801-394-8487. Another repair shop can be found at **Miller's Ski & Cycle Haus**, which also sells bikes. ~ 834 Washington Boulevard, Ogden; 801-392-3911, 801-392-8666. **Diamond Peak** rents bikes for cycling around Pineview Reservoir. ~ 2429 North Route 162, Eden; 801-745-0101; www.diamondpeak-sport.com. If you need bike rentals or repairs in Brigham City, try **Loveland's Cycle**. ~ 352 North Main, Brigham City; 435-734-2666. In Logan, you can find repairs and sales at **Sunrise Cyclery**. ~ 138 North 100 East, Logan; 435-753-3294.

HIKING

With national forests blanketing the mountains due east of Logan, Brigham City and Ogden, hiking opportunities in the area overflow. From short morning or afternoon treks to multiday excursions into the mountains, the options are many. All distances listed for hiking trails are one way unless otherwise noted.

HELPFUL HIKING HINTS

Looking for cascading waterfalls or dense groves of juniper and cedar? Searching for panoramic views or a quiet alpine lake for a few hours of fishing? All these possibilities and more can be found in northern Utah's forests. Although you will come across streams in the mountains, it's best to pack your own water or carry a good water filter to avoid slurping down bacterial parasites that could make your life miserable once you return to civilization. Also, realistically judge your ability before setting out. Not only are many of the trails steep and strenuous, many trailheads are found at an elevation of 5000 feet, which means surprisingly thin air for those coming from near sea level.

OGDEN AREA The **Bonneville Shoreline Trail** is a nearly complete route that runs north and south along the Wasatch Front. In the Ogden area, it is a major artery that provides access to all the trails climbing up Mount Ogden. Trailheads can be found at 22nd Street and 46th Street. Between 22nd Street and 46th Street, which crosses the mouth of Beus Canyon, the trail crosses Taylor's, Waterfall and Strong's canyons.

The **Indian Trail** (4.3 miles) begins near the east end of Ogden's 22nd Street and runs to the mouth of Ogden Canyon, quickly rising from 5000 feet to 6000 feet and offering nice, if at times precipitous, views. Its name relates to the American Indians who used the route when high water made Ogden Canyon impassable. A spur located a half mile up the Indian Trail wends two miles to **Hidden Valley**.

Families with youngsters not ready for the rigors of mountain hiking will enjoy the **North Arm Wildlife Viewing Trail** (1 mile) that runs along the north side of Pineview Reservoir east of Ogden. The trailhead can be found along Route 162 on the north side of the reservoir.

The **Beus Canyon Trail** (6 miles) climbs more than 4000 feet from 46th Street towards the 9572-foot summit of Mount Ogden. It's popular with hikers, mountain bikers and equestrians, but is highly challenging due to the grade. Cresting at a saddle just below the summit, the route continues down the eastern flanks of Mount Ogden towards Snowbasin.

For a quick, moderate hike, the **Strong's Canyon Trail** (.5 mile) offers a short trek through trees along Strong's Creek. The trailhead is found at 36th Street and follows the Mount Ogden Exercise Trail for a short distance veering upstream.

The short, steep **Waterfall Canyon Trail** (1 mile) begins at 29th Street and climbs 1000 feet to Malans Falls. Along the way to the falls, the trail parallels a cascading stream and offers nice views of Ogden and Great Salt Lake. The trail passes through a mix of scrub oak, aspen and conifer forest.

BRIGHAM CITY AREA You won't find as many hiking options in the immediate vicinity of Brigham City as you will around Logan and even Ogden, mainly because of the in-your-face steepness of the Wellsville Mountains, but if you look, there are some possibilities. If you take Route 91/89 around to the eastern side of the mountains and then head roughly seven miles north on Route 23 to Mendon you'll find two trails that climb up into the mountains. The **Deep Canyon to Wellsville Ridge and Stewart Pass** (5 miles), thanks to the pitch of the Wellsville Mountains, can be strenuous; in summer this hike takes you through nice wildflower meadows. The trailhead is along the north end of 300 North in Mendon.

Another route to Stewart Pass can be reached via the **Maple Bench Trail** (7 miles). This out-and-back course is another tough uphill climb into the Wellsville Mountain Wilderness Area. It runs two miles up to Stewart Pass, and then continues for another one and a half miles to Stewart Peak. The trailhead can be found at the end of Forest Service Road 86 located south of Mendon.

LOGAN AREA   Around Logan, hikers almost instinctively head up Logan Canyon and its many jumping off points to get away from it all. The trailhead to **Old Ephraim's Grave** (5.5 miles) can be found off Right Hand Fork Road found 9.2 miles up Logan Canyon. The hike is a good one, and the elevation rises only 1600 feet along the way. At the gravesite stands an 11-foot-tall stone, which some say represents the bear's height, although others put him closer to 10 feet.

Wind Cave Trail (1.3 miles) is another popular destination for hikers, although it's steep and can be brutally hot in the summer because there's little shade along the way. A relatively short hike, the trail leads to the cave, which is actually a series of small caverns and arches sculpted by ice and wind. Watch for snakes in summer. The trailhead is located across from the Guinavah-Malibu Campground 5.3 miles up Logan Canyon from Logan.

A relatively quick jaunt that gets you to the highest point in the Bear River Range is the **Naomi Peak Trail** (2.9 miles), which starts at the Tony Grove Lake Parking Area. The trail is rocky and steep in places on the way to the summit of 9980-foot Naomi Peak. The turnoff from Route 89 in Logan Canyon to the parking area is located 19 miles from Logan. Once you turn off the highway, it's another seven miles to the parking area.

A wonderful path near the mouth of Logan Canyon is the **Riverside Trail** (4.2 miles), which, as its name implies, follows the Logan River. Moose frequent the river corridor, so watch out for them when hiking. There are six areas where you can jump onto the trail: near the canyon mouth across Route 89 from the national forest boundary sign; at the Red Bridge turnoff on the right side of the road about a mile up the canyon; at the Bridger Campground; at the Gus Lind Dispersed Campground; at the Spring Hollow Campground; and at the Guinavah Campground.

Transportation

CAR

Interstate **Route 15** is the major thoroughfare through northern Utah, passing right by Ogden and Brigham City. Logan is a bit off the beaten path, requiring a jaunt up **Route 89** from Brigham City.

Other key roads in the region include **Route 39**, which heads east from Ogden and works its way into Wyoming, and interstate **Route 84**, which leads west from Wyoming to Ogden. At Ogden, Route 84 overlaps Route 15 north to Tremonton, where the two part ways, with 84 continuing northwest towards Twin Falls, Idaho, and 15 continuing north towards Pocatello, Idaho.

AIR

See Chapter Two for information about **Salt Lake City International Airport**, the closest airport serving these parts.

In Ogden, **Mountain Valley Transportation** offers shuttles from area hotels to Salt Lake City International Airport as well as to Powder Mountain and Snowbasin. ~ 877-834-3456.

In Logan, **Cache Valley Limo Airport Shuttle** (435-563-6400, 800-658-8526) provides rides to Salt Lake International, as does CVC **Shuttle** (435-752-4555).

BUS

Greyhound Bus Lines (800-231-2222) has regular service through northern Utah. In Ogden the bus stops at 2501 Grant Avenue, 801-394-5573; in Logan at 754 West 600 North, 435-752-2877; and in Brigham City at the Trailside General Store at 38 East 100 South.

**CAR
RENTALS**

Many of the major car-rental agencies have offices in Ogden, including **Avis Rent A Car** (3110 Wall Avenue; 801-621-2980) and **Enterprise Rent A Car** (36th and Riverdale; 801-399-5555). **Hertz Rent A Car** is located in the heart of downtown Ogden. ~ 2805 Washington Boulevard, Ogden; 801-621-6500.

Hertz Rent A Car can also be found in Brigham City. ~ 816 North Main Street, Brigham City; 435-723-5255.

Rental cars can be obtained at a number of Logan locations. **Hertz Rent A Car** has an office in the Comfort Inn. ~ 447 North Main Street, Logan; 435-752-9141. **Enterprise Rent A Car** has its own offices on Main Street. ~ 1849 North Main Street, Logan; 435-755-6111. A third is **Discount Rent A Car**. ~ 1180 West 200 North, Logan; 435-755-9234.

**PUBLIC
TRANSIT**

Travel around Ogden is made easy by **Utah Transit Authority**, which makes countless stops around town. ~ 801-621-4636.

In Brigham City, **Utah Transit Authority** offers service within the city as well as a route to Ogden. ~ 435-734-2901

Within Logan, LTD **Bus Service** provides free transportation between 6:15 a.m. and 9:45 p.m. Monday through Friday; on Saturday, service runs from 9 a.m. to 9:45 p.m. No service on Sunday. ~ 435-752-2877.

TAXIS

Both Ogden and Logan have taxi services; Brigham City does not.

For getting around town, try **Yellow Cab Company**. ~ 1450 Washington Boulevard, #52, Ogden; 801-394-9411.

CVC **Shuttle** (435-752-4555) offers taxi service in Logan, as does **Logan Taxi** (435-753-3663).

FOUR

Northeastern Utah

From world-class ski resorts to sandstone cliffs rife with dinosaur fossils, no part of Utah is as diverse—in appearance, in economics, in lay of the land—as the state's northeastern corner. The region defines diversity, from the tony ski resort community of Park City with its multimillion-dollar homes, chic restaurants and crisp mountain air to the sleepy and bucolic feel of Heber Valley with its ranches and slower pace to blue-collar Vernal with its tidy neighborhoods, fast-food eateries and dusty landscape.

Just as diverse as the communities' walks of life are their backgrounds. Park City, ever the epitome of nonconformity in generally strait-laced Utah, gained foothold as a boomtown in the mid-1800s when silver was plucked from its mountains by Union soldiers on a mission to lure outsiders into the dominion of the Church of Jesus Christ of Latter-day Saints. They succeeded grandly—Irish, Chinese, Scandinavians, English, Swedes and others poured into Park City to feast upon silver's succor.

Most mining booms, however, tend to bust, and Park City's was no exception. At one time arguably the richest mining camp in the world, by the early 1900s the town's economy was in a state of collapse. It was a condition that wasn't really righted until the ski industry arrived for good in the 1960s and brought with it a certain cachet that enticed the rich. By the 20th century's end, this mountain playground had lured not only the rich but also lower classes who work in Park City's service industry and middle-class commuters who head daily to the Salt Lake Valley to work. An offshoot of the town's gentrification—some might call it snobbishness—and the resulting division between the haves and have-nots is the ongoing clash over the town's future. How much growth is enough? How much is too much? Is the community in truth merely a commodity available to the highest bidder? These are questions that continue to spur debate.

The same can't be said of the communities found farther east, in the eye-blink towns of Heber City, Duchesne, Roosevelt and Vernal and within the 3.3-million-acre Uintah and Ouray Indian Reservation. Heber City tries to snare its share of

Park City's winter market, although with rolling cross-country courses and hot springs instead of alpine resorts. In summer the town caters to anglers, hikers and campers heading to nearby state parks or into the high country of the Uinta Mountains or the Wasatch Range.

In Vernal and the Uintah and Ouray Indian Reservation, without ski slopes running to their doorsteps, most residents eke a gritty living from the landscape, toiling on ranches, farms, mines and oil and gas wells. Some have also turned to the natural resources for a living, guiding customers down the rivers, into the mountains and across the riddled landscape in search of pictures, history and wildlife.

If there's one thing that knits this far-flung region together, it would be the rumpled mountains and their playgrounds. From the Wasatch Range that cradles three ski resorts in and around Park City to the towering Uinta Range that attracts backcountry skiers, hikers, anglers and campers to its canyons and high-country lakes, northeastern Utah's geography lends itself to human exploration and recreation.

Major John Wesley Powell left his mark on the land in 1869 when he and a small, gritty band of men pushed their wooden dories into the Green River in southwestern Wyoming and rode the river south through today's Flaming Gorge and Dinosaur National Monument to its confluence with the Colorado River outside Moab and farther south through the Grand Canyon. A predecessor of today's whitewater cowboys who ply the bucking rivers for a living, Powell marveled at the fantastic scenery time had cut into the land, a scenery that remains just as amazing and breathtaking today.

▼▼▼▼▼▼▼▼▼▼▼
Park City Area

Park City, nestled in a small, north–south running valley on the backside of the Wasatch Range 31 miles east of Salt Lake City on Route 80, is Utah's only true ski town. Nowhere else in the state, which boasts 14 alpine resorts, will you find such a vibrant, pulsating town curled up right at the bottom of the slopes.

It wasn't always so. The town stumbled into life as a rough-and-tumble outcast, a place decidedly out of step with the rest of the pious state. Union troops, stationed in Salt Lake City during the Civil War to ensure that Brigham Young and his Latter-day Saints didn't try to wrest the territory from the United States, were encouraged to prospect in the Park City area with hopes that a strike would lure hundreds of non-LDS prospectors into the territory. Silver was finally found in the thickly timbered mountains above town in 1868 and the boom was on, drawing thousands of Irish, Swedish, Finnish, Cornish, Chinese, Scottish and Yugoslavian miners, who in turn gladly patronized the 27 saloons and a notoriously popular red-light district. The prevalence of alcohol in the town was a strong pull even in pious Salt Lake City, which from time to time would see its thirsty citizens head east to Park City for a little libation.

During Park City's mining heyday, its ore beds produced 23 millionaires, including George Hearst, grandfather of newspaper-

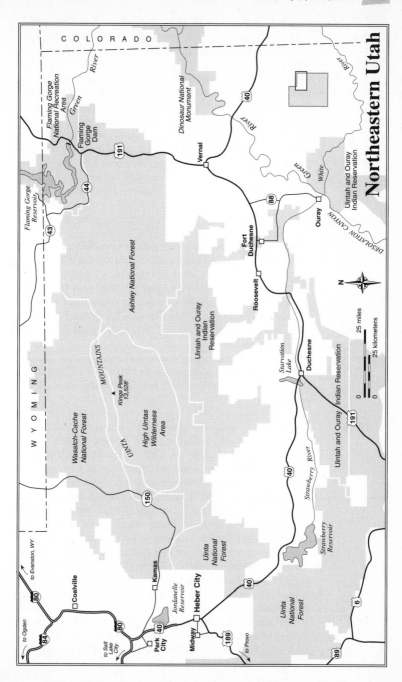

Northeastern Utah

man William Randolph Hearst. All told, more than $400 million in silver was hauled from the mountains. Today memories of the miners drift through more than 1200 miles of tunnels that remain within the mountains. At one point the boom made Park City the country's richest mining camp, with silver, lead, gold and zinc reserves boasting a gross value of $2.5 billion. Still, the boom was relatively short-lived. The town's mines were wallowing by 1907 when a recession shuddered through the country.

While Prohibition left most towns across the country dry, the good times continued to roll in Park City, where officials looked the other way. However, when Prohibition ended, the town's economy, already struggling with the slumping mining industry, plummeted further. And while Park City dabbled with skiing from the 1920s onward, it wasn't until the 1960s when the town truly realized the figurative gold mine buried in the heavy snows that often inundated Park City.

In 1962, in a bid to mine that potential windfall, a delegation from the Utah Press Association, during lunch at the White House with President Kennedy, broached the topic of a ski resort and boldly inquired about federal funding for the project. The following year Park City qualified for a federal loan through the Area Redevelopment Agency and the Treasure Mountain Resort was born, opening on December 31, 1963, with a gondola, chairlift and two J-bars.

Since that small step, the town's ski industry has steadily grown. So reliable is the skiing that the "White Circus," the World Cup ski tour, stops here each fall to race at the Park City Mountain Resort.

SIGHTS   Does Park City today evoke the quaint, yesteryear mining town image that city tourism officials would have you believe? Not entirely. Outside of Main Street, a half-mile-long stretch of pavement buttressed by shops and restaurants housed in an architectural amalgamation of 19th-century and present-day motifs, the town appears much like any other resort community chasing the almighty dollar. Although locals hate comparisons with Aspen, their town is rife with developers studding the hillsides with "starter castles"; real estate prices rocket ever upward.

On the way to Main Street, visit the **Park City Chamber Bureau Visitors Center** on the corner of Kearns Boulevard and Route 224 at the north end of town. Inside are maps of both the immediate area and the region as well as reams of brochures detailing everything from restaurants and lodgings to activities and local history. There's also a brief description—in words, pictures and memorabilia—of Park City's mining and skiing heritage. ~ 750 Kearns Boulevard, Park City; 435-658-4541, 800-453-1360, fax 435-649-4132; www.parkcityinfo.com.

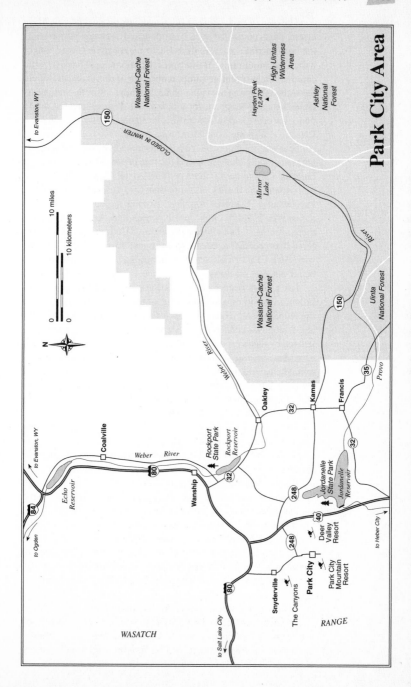

Park City Area

The soul of Park City's "**Old Town**," or original core, is **Main Street**, particularly the stretch sandwiched between 9th Street at the bottom and Daly Avenue at the top. This is the town's tourist hub, with restaurants, bars, art galleries and shops. An afternoon could easily be spent drifting up one side of the street and down the other, browsing in shops, admiring the early-20th-century architecture, and stopping for a bite to eat. Plaques erected on 45 buildings provide detail on historic structures. Please see "Historic Park City Walking Tour" for more details.

Few original buildings remain from the town that was incorporated in 1884, though, since a fire that broke out in the American Hotel in the pre-dawn hours of June 19, 1898, crackled through Old Town. The flames left more than 200 businesses and homes in ashes and 500 folks homeless. Among the buildings lost was the town's $30,000 opera house, which had been open for just three months. A call to arms throughout Utah produced a workforce that reconstructed the town in just 18 months; in keeping with Park City's ribald reputation, among the first businesses to be rebuilt was a saloon.

For a quick primer on historic Park City, and to pick up a $1 brochure outlining a walking tour of the historic district, stop at the old **City Hall**. Today this two-story brick and masonry building, which was erected in 1895 and rebuilt after being mostly destroyed by the fire, houses a small visitors center as well as the **Park City Museum and Territorial Jail**. There are exhibits on Park City's mining past and, in the basement, four dank cells that constituted the Utah Territorial Prison. One of the exhibits explains how Utah's "Silver Queen," Susanna Bradford, made her millions. ~ 528 Main Street, Park City; 435-649-6104.

Towering over the southern end of Main Street—and town—for that matter, is **Deer Valley Resort**, one of three ski resorts that call Park City home. The resort is renowned for its magnificent lodgings, expensive second homes, and delectable menus. The skiing's not bad, either. In summer the resort is a haven for mountain bikers and outdoor-concert enthusiasts. ~ From Main Street, head south one mile on Deer Valley Drive to the resort; 435-649-1000, fax 435-645-6939; www.deervalley.com.

Near the bottom, or north end, of Main Street you can find an expansive collection of local and regional art at the **Kimball Art Center**, which is housed in a restored, 1940s-era, service station. ~ 638 Park Avenue, Park City; 435-649-8882; www.kimball-art.org.

On the north side of Heber Avenue just a block east of Main Street extends an arm of Park City's trails system. The paved pathway runs along Poison Creek to **City Park**, which is constantly in motion during the warm-weather months with a wide variety of sports. There's also a pavilion there for barbecues, picnic areas and a playground for younger children. A focal point in the park is the **Old Miner's Hospital**, a charming brick building that was once a hospital for Park City's silver miners and a home for the town's library. These days it contains city offices and public meeting rooms. Just south of the old hospital is a sprawling skateboard park. ~ Vehicle access to City Park can be made off Park Avenue between 13th and 14th Streets.

Large Spring Camp, a quarter-mile beyond Mormon Flat along East Canyon Road, was used by emigrants as an overnight stop.

Just northwest of Main Street sprawls the **Park City Mountain Resort**, the granddaddy of the city's ski scene. One of Utah's largest ski areas in winter, in summer the hills are open to hikers and mountain bikers; kids love the alpine slide. ~ From Park Avenue, take Lowell Drive a half-mile to the resort base; 1310 Lowell Avenue, Park City; 435-649-8111, 800-222-7275; www.parkcitymountain.com.

Beginning (or ending, depending on your direction of travel) in Park City, the **Historic Union Pacific Rail Trail State Park** winds for 28 miles along a narrow railroad corridor between Park City and Echo Reservoir to the east. Rail service along the corridor began in 1880, when Park City's burgeoning silver mines brought freight trains into town. During the mid-1970s passenger service was offered with hopes that skiers would provide steady winter business, but it never caught on. In the mid-1980s freight service to Park City also ended. When the Union Pacific Railroad abandoned the line in 1989, the Utah Division of Parks and Recreation moved to convert it into a recreational trail. On Oct. 3, 1992, the rail trail was dedicated and became the first non-motorized trail in the state. ~ The trailhead is located on the east side of Park City and can be accessed from the parking lot on the south side of Prospector Avenue; Prospector Square, Park City. (See "Parks" below for more information.)

◄ HIDDEN

Find a hilltop near Park City's eastern boundary and you can almost see **Jordanelle State Park**, where a shimmering 3300-acre reservoir dances with some two million trout and bass. With Deer Valley Resort providing an alpine backdrop to the west and groves of scrub oak, juniper, pine and aspen studding the surrounding rolling hillsides, the state park that opened in 1995 is nestled in a valley that was homesteaded for ranching in 1864. ~ Route 40, four miles east of Park City.

Just beyond Park City's northern boundary lies **The Canyons**, a burgeoning all-season recreational empire. With more than 6000 skiable acres in the resort's future, this property stands to become one of the largest ski resorts in North America. As with Park City's other two resorts, hiking and mountain biking are big here in the summer, while a small amphitheater at the base of the resort occasionally offers concerts. The folks at NBC were so smitten with The Canyons' setting that they'll broadcast *The Today Show*

Historic Park City

Park City arose as the antithesis of Salt Lake City. Union soldiers were encouraged by their officers to look for silver in the mountains surrounding the town with hopes a strike would lure thousands of non-LDS miners into the state. The strike made in 1872 not only put Park City on the nation's map as arguably the richest silver camp around, it also saw Park City become one of the few Utah communities founded by non-Mormons. The richness of the boom brought prosperity to town, as well as 27 saloons, a number of bordellos, and some magnificent buildings that you can admire during an hour or so walk up and down Main Street.

THE IMPERIAL HOTEL   By starting in front of this building at the top, or south end, of Main Street, your tour will be downhill. Located on the west side of Main Street, the hotel arose in 1904 as the Bogan Boarding House and remains as one of just four historic boarding houses for miners that exist in the Park City area today. When it first opened, the boarding house's steam-heated rooms were rented by the day, week or month. In 1918, when a flu epidemic swept the area, the building became an emergency hospital. After a fire gutted the structure in 1940, it languished until 1987, when it was restored as the Imperial Hotel. Today it does business as the "1904 Imperial Hotel." ~ 221 Main Street; 435-649-1904, 800-669-8824; www.1904imperial.com.

THE EGYPTIAN THEATER   Head a block south and onto the east side of the street and you'll find that Park City's hankering for the arts is not a come-lately desire. After the 1898 fire the Dewey Theater was built on the site of a livery stable and equipped with 600 wooden opera chairs and a floor that could be tilted toward the stage during shows or laid flat for parties and dances. When heavy snows collapsed the theater's roof in 1916, just hours after a show, the Egyptian Theater arose like the proverbial phoenix from the rubble a decade later. Architecturally reflective of the "Egyptian Revival" style that swept the country in the

during the Olympics from the Grand Summit Resort Hotel at the resort's base complex. ~ The Canyons is located five miles north of Park City off Route 224, 4000 The Canyons Resort Drive, Park City; 435-649-5400, 888-226-9667; www.thecanyons.com.

HIDDEN ▶   For peace and quiet, visit the **Swaner Nature Preserve** about seven miles north of Park City along Route 80. In the spring and late summer or early fall you'll share the open meadows with sandhill cranes that arrive during their migrations. A privately owned

1920s, the 400-seat theater offered Park City's first "talkies," as well as vaudeville acts. Since 1981 the theater has been the home of Egyptian Theater Company. ~ 328 Main Street; 435-649-9371.

350 MAIN   A few doors below the Egyptian Theater is a landmark of America's department store history. In the early 1900s when J.C. Penney opened his first department store in western Wyoming, it was known as the Golden Rule Mercantile Co. In 1909 the chain arrived in Park City on Main Street and remained a mainstay until the 1930s, when the store moved out and a pharmacy moved in. Through the decades the building's evolution continued and went on to house a grocery, a popular bar and restaurant and, today, the 350 Main Seafood & Oyster Co. ~ 350 Main Street; 435-649-3140.

BELL TOWER   Not quite two blocks south, on the same side of the street, stands the remains of not only Park City's first city hall but also its first fire alarm. After the 1898 fire, city officials realized they needed more than a constable discharging his revolver to alert residents to a fire, so they erected a three-story wooden bell tower that ran up the south wall of City Hall and remains there today. Though a 1500-pound bell initially was used as the alarm, in 1905 it was replaced by an electric siren that doubled, until 1980, as a 10 p.m. curfew signal for minors. ~ 518 Main Street.

PARK CITY MORTUARY   A half-block farther south on the street is the site of one of the town's shrewdest merchants. From his two-story building on Main Street that was rebuilt after the 1898 fire, Bill Fennemore operated a small grocery as well as Park City's first mortuary, which he promoted with a small casket-shaped sign. A more enterprising mortician, George Archer, assumed the business in 1921 and supplemented his income in alcohol-dry Utah by driving his hearse 52 miles to Evanston, Wyoming, where he loaded it with bootleg liquor that he would sell to Park City bar owners. Today a Japanese restaurant, Kampai, occupies the main floor. ~ 586 Main Street; 435-649-0655.

nature preserve that's open to the public, Swaner's 938 acres offer a growing trail network for hiking, cross-country skiing and snowshoeing as well as birding. A nature center similar to the one found at Rock Cliff in Jordanelle State Park is planned for the park. ~ Route 80, seven miles north of Park City; 801-363-4811.

About ten miles north and west of Park City lies **East Canyon**, which was a popular route for mid-19th-century travelers heading West. Through the canyon passed the ill-fated Donner-

Reed Party in 1846, and in July 1847 Mormon pioneers led by Brigham Young came through on what became the Mormon Trail. **HIDDEN ▶** **Mormon Flat** is the spot where Young and his followers rested and prepared for the final push into the Salt Lake Valley. For the next 22 years an estimated 200,000 travelers—trappers, Mormons, '49ers, freight wagons, stagecoaches and even Pony Express riders —came down the east side of the canyon and exited over Big Mountain Pass. The pass was the steepest sustained climb on the 1300-mile-long Mormon Trail, rising 1400 feet in just four miles. ~ To visit the site and adjacent Large Spring Camp, head west from Park City on Route 80 and take Exit 143 to the Jeremy Ranch subdivision. At the bottom of the exit ramp, turn right, then left at the four-way stop. Take the first right, Jeremy Road, which leads about a mile through the subdivision to the mouth of East Canyon. From here, East Canyon Road, a dirt road that is not maintained during the winter, runs five miles to Mormon Flat.

Above the left side of the road just before you reach Mormon Flat you can make out two rock **"breastworks"** built into the hill-side. These were erected by the Utah Militia in the fall of 1857 to guard Salt Lake City against U.S. troops summoned to squelch the so-called Mormon Rebellion that never arose.

Tales of Spanish gold, dense forests of conifer and aspen, and rugged mountains dotted with sparkling lakes lie just 13 miles east of Park City on Route 150 in the **Wasatch-Cache National Forest**. The forest's western gateway is in **Kamas**, a small ranching town that launches the Mirror Lake Highway (Route 150) up into the Uinta Mountains, which is the only major range in the country that runs east–west instead of north–south.

The Uintas are Utah's tallest range of mountains, rising above 13,000 feet, stretching 100 miles between Kamas and Flaming Gorge, and covering 3500 square miles. While summer is the bus-

AUTHOR FAVORITE

The royal blood in me relishes a night at the **Stein Eriksen Lodge**, with 50 suites and 81 deluxe rooms. Named in honor of the great Norwegian skier of the 1950s, the lodge lies mid-mountain at the Deer Valley Resort and features elegant restaurants, a spa and a rustic atmosphere that evokes Scandinavia. In the main lobby, a display case glows with Stein's many medals and trophies. The plush suites have wood-burning fireplaces, balconies overlooking the slopes, and full kitchens. Of course, you'll pay dearly for them. ~ To reach the lodge, head about three-quarter-mile south on Deer Valley Drive to Royal Street and follow it to 7700 Stein Way, Deer Valley; 435-649-3700, 800-453-1302, fax 435-649-5825; www.steinlodge.com, e-mail info@steinlodge.com. ULTRA-DELUXE.

iest season in the national forest, when thousands engage in fishing, camping and hiking, in winter snowmobiles, cross-country skiers and even dogsleds skim through the snow-covered parcel. In the very heart of the national forest is the **High Uintas Wilderness Area**, a 456,705-acre swath of wild, rugged backcountry that appears today much as it always has.

Perhaps more intriguing than the forest's recreational possibilities is the legend of lost gold that dates to the mid-1800s. As the story goes, Spanish explorers who some think first reached the Uintas in the mid-1600s spent much of their time mining for gold as well as looking for caches of gold that they believed were hauled there and hidden by Aztecs. When Brigham Young and his Mormon followers arrived in Utah in 1847, they were virtually penniless. However, a Ute Indian chief offered to supply Young with gold. Supposedly, the gold the chief gave the Mormons came from mines left behind by the Spaniards, and some believe many caches remain today.

Although far less crowded than the Wasatch Range closer to the Salt Lake Valley, the Uintas seduce more and more people each year and summer weekends often mean crowded campgrounds; if you head down one of the backcountry trails you'll escape most of the hordes. ~ Wasatch-Cache National Forest, Kamas Ranger District, 50 East Center Street, Kamas; 435-783-4338.

LODGING

With nearly 18,000 rentable beds in Park City, finding a place to stay isn't a terribly hard task. However, it can be an expensive one if you wait until the last minute during the middle of the ski season. Conversely, during the shoulder seasons of May and June and September and October bargains are easily found. Depending on your taste, during the high season you can pay less than $100 a night for a clean and comfortable motel room, or as much as $4000 for space in one of the sumptuous lodges at Deer Valley.

There is a small handful of bed-and-breakfast establishments in town and they're much in demand. The historical **Old Miner's Lodge** was built in 1889 as a boarding house for miners. Originally, much of the lumber that went into the lodge was salvaged from area mines. Today the lodge's dozen rooms and suites have been restored to their late-1800s best, and furnished with antiques and down comforters and pillows. Downstairs in the cozy living room is a large fireplace. There's also an outdoor hot tub. Full breakfast is included. Gay-friendly. ~ 615 Woodside Avenue, Park City; 435-645-8068, 800-648-8068, fax 435-645-7420; www. oldminerslodge.com, e-mail stay@oldminerslodge.com. MODERATE TO ULTRA-DELUXE.

Less than two blocks away is the frilly **Angel House Inn**, which takes its name from archangels who, if you believe in such things, play a role in romance or pleasures of the natural world. Some of their names grace the Victorian inn's nine guest rooms. Follow a day on the slopes (one of which runs adjacent to the inn) or knocking about town with a plate of hors d'oeuvres and a book in front of the parlor's fireplace. ~ 713 Norfolk Avenue, Park City; 435-647-0338, 800-264-3501; www.angelhouseinn.com, e-mail jrush@parkcityus.com. MODERATE TO ULTRA-DELUXE.

The 1904 **Imperial Hotel**, like the Old Miner's Lodge, has history on its side, but a decidedly more colorful history. Like the lodge, the Imperial Hotel started out as a boarding house for miners. Over the years, though, it also logged time as a brothel. The ten guest rooms bear the names of historic area mines and include phones and color televisions. Downstairs, the hot tub sits in a room used for wine-making during Prohibition. ~ 221 Main Street, Park City; 435-649-1904, 800-669-8824, fax 435-645-7421; www. 1904imperial.com, e-mail stay@1904imperial.com. MODERATE TO ULTRA-DELUXE.

HIDDEN ►

Perhaps the town's most unobtrusive abode, yet one with turn-of-the-20th-century elegance and charm, is the **Mary E. Sullivan House**, located high up on Main Street. A reclaimed mining shack dating to 1892, today the two-story Victorian home features three bedrooms, a kitchen and sitting room, a family room and game room, and a formal parlor. The hand-stenciled borders, clawfoot tubs and artworks dating to the late 19th century harken to a simpler time, while the outdoor hot tub makes you glad to be alive in the 21st century. Closed mid-April to mid-November. ~ 146 Main Street, Park City; 800-803-9589; www.thistlesprings.com. ULTRA-DELUXE.

The **Blue Church Lodge** started out in 1897 as a Mormon church. Today the lodge, which is on the National Register of Historic Places, and its associated townhouses are a short walk from both Main Street and the Town Lift that provides access to the Park City Mountain Resort. Ambience in the rooms and condos ranges from country elegant to rustic mountain lodge, and you'll find full kitchens, fireplaces and spas. Closed mid-April to mid-November. ~ 424 Park Avenue, Park City; 435-649-8009,

---

STILL IN SESSION

The **Washington School Inn**, with its limestone block walls, withstood the fire of 1898. Once laid out with three large classrooms, the school later served as a social hall for the Veterans of Foreign Wars before becoming an inn in 1984. Inside are a dozen rooms and three suites, while outside the original carved-wood bell tower still caps the building. ~ 543 Park Avenue, Park City; 435-649-3800, 800-824-1672. MODERATE TO ULTRA-DELUXE.

800-626-5467, fax 435-649-0686; e-mail bcl@ditell.com. DELUXE TO ULTRA-DELUXE.

A good number of hotels are scattered throughout Park City. Many countries' ski teams call **The Yarrow** home during the annual World Cup ski races at the Park City Mountain Resort due to its handy location. Situated on the northern end of town, the 181-room hotel is located next to a grocery store, ski shops and movie theater; inside the hotel is a cozy lounge with a fireplace, outside there's a bus stop for Park City's free shuttle buses. ~ 1800 Park Avenue, Park City; 435-649-7000, 800-327-2332; www.hart hotels.com/yarrow1.htm. DELUXE TO ULTRA-DELUXE.

The **Park City Marriott** opened in summer 1999 after investing millions in a makeover of the former Olympic Park Hotel. Along with 199 standard rooms the upgrade added a fitness center to go along with the indoor pool. ~ 1895 Sidewinder Drive, Park City; 435-649-2900, 800-234-9003; www.parkcityutah.com. DELUXE TO ULTRA-DELUXE.

DINING

With just 6400 residents, Park City easily has the most culinary options per capita in Utah. Heck, the town even boasts that it has more chefs per capita than Paris! Not surprisingly, the more than 100 restaurants and bars that are shoe-horned into town guarantee that your toughest choice come meal time is not *what* to eat, but *where*.

Caution: During the height of ski season, reservations are mandatory at most restaurants. That said, tables could be particularly hard to find during the Olympics, as many restaurants began taking reservations midway through 2001 while others were rented out entirely for the Games by corporate sponsors. Also take note that during the shoulder seasons—late spring and early fall—some restaurants close to give their staffs a rest, refresh their menus, and occasionally spruce up their interiors, so call ahead.

While the skiing at Deer Valley is among the West's best, a strong argument can be made that food is the resort's forte, and **The Glitretind** in the Stein Eriksen Lodge buttresses that argument. Nestled amid evergreens and aspens, the restaurant treats eating as a celebration of life. Choosing an entrée at the restaurant, which is named after the "Shining Peak," Norway's highest mountain, requires that you first decide whether to eat "Western," with the broiled T-bone of lamb, or be a bit more adventurous with the Yukon Gold potato lasagna with pan-seared ahi tuna or the seafood ravioli. ~ 7700 Royal Street East, Stein Eriksen Lodge, Deer Valley; 435-649-3700 ext. 83, 435-645-6455; www.steinlodge.com. DELUXE.

Across the street within the the Chateaux Hotel lies **Bistro Toujours**, an elegant French-influenced retreat perfect for a romantic après-ski evening. From a wood-burning oven chefs pull chickens roasted in herbs alongside seasonal vegetables and beef tenderloin served with Roquefort creamed spinach and cabbage. Too heavy? Try a plate of wood-oven roasted vegetables or the whole-roasted fish of the day. If the dozens of wines the restaurant stocks are overwhelming, the on-staff sommelier will help make your choice easier. ~ 7815 Royal Street East, Deer Valley; 435-940-2200. MODERATE TO DELUXE.

Perhaps the most intimate dining experience at the Deer Valley Resort is at the **Mariposa**, a 22-table restaurant that only serves dinner. Meals before a flickering fireplace might include baked Sea Bass Mariposa with honey-soy glaze and fresh ginger sauce, or the Mariposa mixed grill that includes lamb chop, venison medallion and seared pheasant sausage with caramelized shallot, shiraz wine and crack-grain mustard, portobello mushrooms and mashed potatoes. Heading into the 2000–2001 ski season the restaurant was honored by the *Wine Spectator* with its Award of Excellence. Dinner only. ~ Silver Lake Lodge, Deer Valley; 435-645-6716. DELUXE.

Back in Park City proper, top-notch restaurants line Main Street. Deciding which to try could depend entirely on how far up the street (there's a steady uphill grade as you head south) you want to walk.

At the top of Main Street, when you enter the **Grappa Italian Restaurant** it's almost as if you've walked into a Tuscan farmhouse. Underfoot are heavy tiles, while the walls are a combination of plaster and heavy beams. Garlic-rich aromas waft steadily from the kitchen. The center of the two-story building is open, allowing diners on the second-floor to gaze down on those on the first, and in summer you can dine on the patio. Depending on the chef's whims, you could start with wild-mushroom-and-brie ravioli before an entrée of crispy pan-fried game hen with spinach

AUTHOR FAVORITE

Growing up on the East Coast, fresh seafood was an integral part of my diet. Fortunately, living in the Rockies doesn't mean I have to go without. The Seafood Buffet the Deer Valley Resort serves up in its **Snow Park Lodge** during the ski season allows me an opportunity to gorge myself on shellfish, Dungeness crab, New Zealand clams and other seafood flown in fresh on a daily basis. Of course, the prime rib and barbecued babyback ribs make sure I don't forget I'm in beef country. Sadly, this restaurant will close to the public February 2 and remain closed throughout the month because of the 2002 Olympics. ~ Snow Park Lodge, Deer Valley; 435-645-6632. DELUXE.

tortellini and honey brandy carrots. ~ 151 Main Street, Park City; 435-645-0636. DELUXE.

Across from Grappa is the **Wasatch Brew Pub,** which, dating to 1986, owns the distinction of being the state's first modern-day microbrewery. Largely a sports bar in appearance that draws its share of ski bums and resort employees once the slopes close, the pub serves up surprisingly good rack of lamb on occasion, tasty Utah trout served with roasted garlic herb butter, among other dishes, and an array of microbrews. ~ 250 Main Street, Park City; 435-649-0900; www.wasatchbeers.com. MODERATE TO DELUXE.

A few doors down from the pub, on the same side of the street, is the **Morning Ray Café and Bakery,** which is renowned for its breakfasts of wonderfully baked breads and pastries, pancakes, waffles and egg dishes. Once upon a time this relaxing restaurant only served breakfast, but now you can stay all day and long into the night and enjoy meals built on bagels flown in daily from New York City. Open until midnight Sunday through Wednesday and until 2 a.m. Thursday through Saturday, this café also offers a modest selection of beers. ~ 268 Main Street, Park City; 435-649-5686. BUDGET.

At **Chimayo,** the Southwestern/Spanish flavor of the food extends into the decor with heavy wooden beams and tables, thick floor tiles, and leather-wrapped menus. Try the steamed "rope-grown" mussels, which are served in a slightly spicy chipotle garlic sea broth for a starter, and then settle down to the baked sea bass served with a crispy baked spinach gratin topped with a sweet corn butter sauce, or maybe the grilled top sirloin of lamb cooked on a willow branch and basted with roasted garlic and rosemary. ~ 368 Main Street, Park City; 435-649-6222. DELUXE.

350 Main Street offers the only oyster bar in town, and with seafood flown in daily, the kitchen starts out with some of the freshest ingredients when the chefs mix their bouillabaisse and sear their peppered ahi loin. The steamed clams, although listed as an appetizer, could qualify as a meal with support from a salad and loaf of bread. The building, which began life in the early 1900s as a department store, has a marvelous copper ceiling as well as an airy deck out back for warm summer evenings. ~ 350 Main Street, Park City; 435-649-3140. MODERATE TO DELUXE.

Utah is one of the leading states when it comes to ice cream consumption, so it shouldn't be surprising that you can find a scoop or two of ice cream on Main Street. Stop by **Cow's** and marvel at their numerous flavors. You'll also be able to grab a cup of coffee from Starbucks, which occupies one side of the store. ~ 402 Main Street, Park City; 435-647-7711. BUDGET.

HIDDEN ▶   **Mileti's** has long been a townie's favorite, in part because of
its bar that gets hopping on weekends. The food isn't quite as
good as Grappa's, but the prices are definitely friendlier. Entrées
are pretty much what you'd expect from an Italian restaurant—
fettuccine and linguine dishes, lasagnas, eggplant parmesan and
spaghetti. The menu also offers beef and seafood dishes for those
not in the mood for pasta. ~ 412 Main Street, Park City; 435-
649-8211. BUDGET TO MODERATE.

Café Terigo, with its outdoor patio fronting Main Street, is a
great place for a leisurely lunch or dinner during the warmer
months. When cooler weather arrives, diners move indoors to the
café's cozy dining room. Creative pizzas—such as the BLT or the
grilled chicken caesar—make lunch a mouth-watering adventure,
while dinner might feature sautéed Utah trout with citrus herb
butter, wild rice cakes and asparagus or oven-roasted pork tenderloin accompanied by maple whipped sweet potatoes. ~ 424
Main Street, Park City; 435-645-9555. MODERATE TO DELUXE.

You normally wouldn't confuse Irish and Mexicans unless you
stumbled upon the oddly named **The Irish Camel**. This long, narrow eatery dishes up some of the best Mexican food on Main Street
amidst an atmosphere of ski memorabilia and other antiques,
not to mention a plastic camel's head, hanging from the walls. ~
434 Main Street, Park City; 435-649-6645. BUDGET TO MODERATE.

Long ago Park City had a significant Chinese population due
to the laborers who catered to the mine companies. Today their
cuisine is doled out at **Szechwan Chinese**, an eatery with a tastefully subdued setting. The Mandarin and Szechwan dishes are
served up quickly, tastefully and inexpensively. ~ 438 Main Street,
Park City; 435-649-0957. BUDGET TO MODERATE.

Zona Rosa serves "nuevo Latino" cuisine that melds traditional Southwestern dishes with a splash of the ocean deep. Entrées
might include barbecued prawns glazed with honey and served
with seared greens and rice as well as marinated Caribbean yel-
lowtail tuna served with roasted peppers, cucumbers and wasabi

---

MAMA'S MUNCHIES, MARGARITAS AND MORE

Where do Park City locals go for a casual dinner? Well, if they like Southwestern cuisine they head to **Nacho Mama's**, which can be found in a
nondescript building about a five-minute drive from Main Street. Traditional
Mexican favorites are available, as are less traditional entrées such as
green-chile burgers and grilled chicken topped with pecans and pineapple
salsa. Also known for its margaritas, the eatery has a pool table, foosball,
a bar and TVs to stay on top of Sunday afternoon's (or Monday night's)
game. ~ 1821 Sidewinder Drive, Park City; 435-645-8226; www.nacho
mamas.com. MODERATE.

guacamole. ~ 501 Main Street, Park City; 435-645-0700. MOD-
ERATE TO DELUXE.

During his two visits to Park City, former President Bill Clin-
ton would regularly turn up at the **Main Street Deli** for a cup of
coffee and something to munch on. Thankfully, you don't need
a Secret Service detail to get into this Main Street mainstay that
serves up budget-priced breakfasts, lunches and dinners. ~ 525
Main Street, Park City; 435-649-1110. BUDGET.

Looking for a budget-conscious meal for the hordes? Then
head below street level at the **Main Street Pizza and Noodle**, where
you can build a pizza from scratch, order a calzone or go simple
with a pile of pasta. Stirfries and hot sandwiches also are on the
menu, as are local beers. ~ 530 Main Street, Park City; 435-645-
8878. BUDGET TO MODERATE.

For reliably good food, a somewhat eclectic atmosphere, and
a sample of Park City's musical talents, there's no better place
than the **Riverhorse Café**. Housed in the old Masonic Hall, this
second-floor restaurant offers a Main Street balcony for watching
the comings and goings during warm-weather dinners, a local pianist or guitarist to supply background music, and everything from
chops and steaks to seafood and vegetarian creations. Dinner
only. ~ 540 Main Street, Park City; 435-649-3536. MODERATE TO
DELUXE.

Park City restaurants come and go with unsettling frequency,
but one that hopefully will become a mainstay is **Wahso**, a 2000
arrival that strives to recreate the elegance and pampering of the
1930s Orient with crisp, white linen tablecloths, china settings,
elegant teapots and warmed finger towels. The menu spans the
Pacific Rim, with dishes from Malaysia, Vietnam and China. Come
summer, the second-floor restaurant opens its doors to a balcony
set with tables that overlook Main Street. ~ 577 Main Street,
Park City; 435-615-0300.DELUXE.

The expected backdrop of Japanese artworks and decorations
is found at **Kampai**, where you can sit back and watch as the chefs
whip together sashimi, sushi, sukiyaki and teriyaki dishes. The
restaurant is tiny, so show up early or late during the height of
the ski season to assure a seat. ~ 586 Main Street, Park City; 435-
649-0655.

Zoom, Robert Redford's "roadhouse grill," lies on the northeastern corner of Main and Heber inside an old train depot. This
two-story restaurant, a reliable spotting ground for celebrities
during the Sundance Film Festival, features a relaxed roadhouse-
style dining room and bar on the lower level, while the upper floor
contains a much more comfortable and spacious dining room.
During the summer months, a sunken patio wrapped with flower
gardens just off the main floor offers the best al fresco dining in
Park City. With a menu offering ribs with cornbread and coleslaw,

Black Angus steaks with french fries, and grilled Calypso tri-tip steak with mango salsa, this is not the place to count calories. ~ 660 Main Street, Park City; 435-649-9108. MODERATE TO DELUXE.

Across the street to the southwest is the **Mediterraneo**. As its name implies, the menu here is stacked with Mediterranean dishes such as citrus and semolina coast calamari served with a spicy tomato sauce; yellow pepper and basil soup; wood-oven baked sea bass with Moroccan *chermoulah*; and paella, a traditional dish of rice, calamari, chicken, clams, mussels and shrimp. ~ 628 Park Avenue, Park City; 435-647-0030. MODERATE TO DELUXE.

Don't confine your epicurean excursions to Old Town, as there are a handful of worthy restaurants located off Main to sample.

HIDDEN ► Tough to find if you're not looking for it, but definitely worth the search, is **Chez Betty**, which occupies a floor in the Copper Bottom Inn just off Park Avenue. Consistently hailed for its service, the menu is one of the best in Park City. Appetizers range from sautéed Pacific curry oysters to smoked salmon crêpes, and entrées might include grilled beef tenderloin on a crispy potato pancake and grilled giant mushroom served with sap sago risotto. A fireside table is an elegant way to wind down the day. ~ 1637 Short Line Road, Park City; 435-649-8181. MODERATE TO DELUXE.

HIDDEN ► North of Park City by about eight miles is the **Sage Grill**. Easy to overlook in a commercial complex salted with banks, department stores, groceries and shops, the restaurant offers Park City cuisine at a reduced price and without the downtown parking hassles. Entrées range from house-made linguine topped with clams (still in their steamed-open shells) swimming in a garlic butter and white wine sauce to grilled buffalo ribs with a side of rattlesnake baked beans, coleslaw and fries. ~ 6300 North Sagewood Drive, Park City; 435-658-2267, fax 435-658-2270. MODERATE TO DELUXE.

East of Park City by 13 miles lies Kamas, and in this tiny cow town is a great little restaurant that's been resurrected by a chef who once worked at the Deer Valley Resort. Once upon a time the

HIDDEN ► **Gateway Grill** would have worn the "greasy spoon" moniker, but Sean Wharton has introduced the locals to butternut squash soup, enoki mushrooms, succulent steaks and fresh seafood, not to mention a modest wine list. Burgers and fries are still possible, too. ~ 215 South Main Street, Kamas; 435-783-2867. MODERATE.

Across the street from the Gateway Grill stands **Pasillas Restaurant**, a relaxing Southwestern-flavored eatery where you can challenge your taste buds with the rellenos, play it safe with the steak fajitas, or feast on the grilled ahi tuna steak. ~ 185 South Main Street, Kamas; 435-783-6982. BUDGET TO MODERATE.

SHOPPING   **Main Street**, with its interesting and unique locally owned shops squeezed into clapboard- and brick-fronted buildings—some historic, some replicas—is shopping central in Park City. While many resort towns these days are being overrun by national chains, Park City has, so far, dug its heels in against this move.

Rock and Silver, one of the oldest Main Street businesses, offers insight into the minerals and gems to be found inside both Utah's mountains and mountains the world over with its collections of gemstones and mineral deposits. ~ 312 Main Street, Park City; 435-649-5427.

Southwestern-influenced jewelry can be found, along with clothing and home furnishings, at **Nativo**, which shares its address with Rock and Silver. ~ 312 Main Street, Park City; 435-645-8088.

> The "Friday Night Strolls" of Main Street's art galleries, held on the first Friday of every month from 6 p.m. to 9 p.m., begin at the Kimball Art Center.

Photographer Thomas Mangelsen perhaps is best known for his picture of an Alaskan brown bear snatching a fish out of mid-air, but he's taken quite a few other incredible wildlife pictures during his lengthy career. You can find many of them at **Images of Nature**. ~ 364 Main Street, Park City; 435-649-7598.

Just down and across the street is **La Niche Gourmet & Gifts**, which doubles as a gift shop and source for gourmet kitchen utensils and knickknacks. On a hot summer day you'll also find refreshing frozen coffee drinks and ice cream. ~ 401 Main Street, Park City; 435-649-2372.

At the **Expanding Heart** you'll find an eclectic and metaphysical collection of books, aromatherapy products, massage oils, bath salts, crystals, candles, incense, jewelry and CDs. ~ 505 Main Street, Park City; 435-649-1255.

Dolly's Book Store is the town's best when you're in search of regional books and guides as well as national bestsellers and contemporary music selections. It shares its building with the **Rocky Mountain Chocolate Factory**, so you can feed your sweet tooth and your literary soul at the same time. ~ 510 Main Street, Park City; 435-649-8062.

Local artworks and organic teas can be found at the **Queen of Arts Tea Room and Gallery**. Take time to order a cup of steaming tea while you study the paintings, potteries and other creations. ~ 515 Main Street, Park City; 435-647-9311.

Don't have enough warm clothing to enjoy Utah's winter? Stop by **Jan's Mountain Outfitters**, where you can pick up a fleece jacket and other warm items, as well as souvenirs of your visit to Park City. ~ 518 Main Street, Park City; 435-655-3032.

Need a roll or two of film or looking to get your film developed overnight? Then duck in **The Main Street Photographer**, where you also can find unique picture frames. ~ 523 Main Street, Park City; 435-649-6465.

What could be Park City's largest collection of wooden skis and snowshoes can be found at **Southwest Indian Traders**, where

there's also a wide variety of turquoise jewelry and Western antiques. ~ 550 Main Street, Park City; 435-645-9177.

Stroll into **Mountain Body** for an intoxicating selection of
herbal skin-care products ranging from massage oils and bath salts
to body rubs made with herbs like rosemary and lavender, citrus
and salt from the Great Salt Lake. ~ 608 Main Street, Park City;
435-655-9342; www.mountainbody.com.

Are you an eclectic decorator? If so, visit **Bedlam**, where you'll
stumble across home furnishings few other stores dare to carry.
~ 613 Main Street, Park City; 435-647-9800.

A strong representation of some of the West's best artworks
can be found at the **Rich Haines Gallery**. Oils, pastels, watercolors,
acrylics, bronze sculptures and other mediums are on display. ~
625 Main Street, Park City; 435-647-3881.

Some of the best deals in Park City are actually found about
eight miles north of town in the **Factory Stores at Park City** complex. This strip mall harbors about 50 outlet shops ranging from
Eddie Bauer and Bose to Nike and OshKosh B'Gosh. ~ 6699
North Landmark Drive, Park City; 435-645-7078; www.charter-
oak.com/parkcity.

White Pine Touring, near the bottom of Main Street, is the best
in-town source for Nordic equipment, and also runs Park City's
20-kilometer Nordic track. The shop also offers hiking and backpacking gear as well as mountain bikes. ~ 201 Heber Avenue,
Park City; 435-659-8710.

HIDDEN ▶ North of town near Route 80 in the Kimball Plaza you'll find
Nordic Equipment, which carries a complete line of Nordic gear
and clothing in addition to snowshoes, mountain bikes and
kayaks. ~ 1612 Ute Boulevard, Park City; 435-655-7225.

NIGHTLIFE Park City has a refreshing dose of year-round activity. When the
snow finally runs off and the mud dries (usually by mid-June),
the mountains come alive with outdoor concerts, an international
jazz festival and a "Concerts in the Park" series. Many summer
weekends find local musicians performing on the Town Lift
square on lower Main Street. Early August delivers a three-day

LIGHTS, CAMERA, FAME

Park City is overrun each January when Robert Redford brings his **Sundance Film Festival**, the country's most prestigious independent film
festival, to Park City for ten usually snowy days of premieres, competitions
and haggling between Hollywood studios and, in many cases, young and
upcoming directors. Among the productions that gained fame at Sundance were *The Blair Witch Project*, *sex, lies and videotape* and *The
Brothers McMullen*. ~ 801-328-3456.

arts festival, which overruns Main Street with dozens of booths offering everything from oil paintings and bronze sculptures to pottery and wooden crafts. Throughout the year you can usually find performances at both the Eccles Center for the Performing Arts or the community-run Egyptian Theater.

The **Deer Valley Resort** on the south end of town brings music to the mountains with the likes of Lyle Lovett, Kenny Loggins, B. B. King and Doc Severinsen. ~ 2250 Deer Valley Drive South, Park City; 435-649-1000, 800-424-3337.

The **Eccles Center for the Performing Arts** presents concerts, ballet, modern dance, comedy and avant-garde theater. In mid-January the center is given over to the Sundance Film Festival for screenings. ~ 1750 Kearns Boulevard, Park City; 435-655-3114.

Local thespians tromp the stage at the refurbished **Egyptian Theater** on Main Street, and during the Sundance Film Festival you'll find films screened here as well. ~ 328 Main Street, Park City; 435-649-9371.

Along with being a popular restaurant, **Mileti's** also lures lo- ◄ *HIDDEN*
cals and visitors to its bar, particularly on weekends. ~ 412 Main Street, Park City; 435-649-8211.

Harry O's is where the frisky twenty-something crowd rocks on weekends, sometimes to live acts, sometimes to deejays. ~ 427 Main Street, Park City; 435-647-9494.

One of Main Street's oldest buildings today houses the **No Name Saloon**, a private club that jumps through the night and early into the next morning. ~ 447 Main Street, Park City; 435-649-6667.

Mother Urban's Ratskeller takes its name from one of Park City's infamous madams. Housed in the basement of a Main Street building, this bar draws a lively crowd. Beware: the smoke can get thick. ~ 625 Main Street, Park City; 435-615-7200.

Renee's Bar and Café is a delightfully refreshing oddity in Utah —a private club that bans smoking! Just a block away from Main Street, this welcome addition to Park City's nightlife offers a lengthy wine list, local beers on tap, light fare, and live entertainment that attracts young and old. ~ 136 Heber Avenue #107, Park City; 435-615-8357.

Many restaurants and bars have some form of entertainment during the ski season, whether it's in the form of a pianist or gui-tarist. On occasion live jazz can be found in some establishments. To see who's playing where, check *The Park Record*, Park City's local newspaper, or, if you're computer-capable, log onto www.parkcityinfo.com to see who's playing where and when.

CITY PARK 椶 Naturally, there's a park in Park City. City Park   **PARKS**
occupies one of the few stretches of flat ground in town. With soccer fields, a softball diamond, a playground, basketball courts

and sand volleyball courts, the park is constantly busy during the warm-weather months. A quarter-mile bike path runs the length of the park alongside Poison Creek. ~ Accessed via Sullivan Lane between 13th and 14th streets along Park Avenue.

WASATCH-CACHE NATIONAL FOREST 🏃 🚴 🐎 🏕 ⛵ 🛶

Drawing its name from both American Indians and mountain men, the Wasatch-Cache National Forest stretches across 1.2 million Utah acres, from the northeastern corner through the northern end of the state all the way to the Idaho border. While "Wasatch" is a Ute word meaning "high mountain pass," "cache" comes from the mountain men who would "cache," or store, their pelts in pits or caves until they could be traded at a rendezvous. One of the most heavily utilized forests in the country, the Wasatch-Cache sees most of its recreational pressures centered around the craggy granite peaks that harbor four alpine resorts southeast of Salt Lake City and along the northern and western slopes of the Uinta Range east of Park City and northeast of Heber City. Summer brings anglers, hikers, backpackers, biking, boating and horseback riding to the Kamas, Mountain View and Evanston districts; winter sees skiers, snowshoers and snowmobilers. Forest highlights include the **High Uintas Wilderness**, a 456,705-acre tract east of Park City and north of Vernal. Day-use fee, $3 per vehicle. ~ Route 150 runs through the forest from Kamas, Utah, to Evanston, Wyoming; Kamas Ranger District, 50 East Center Street, Kamas, UT 84036; 435-783-4338. Winter users can call 801-364-1581 for information on avalanche conditions in the forest.

> Winter definitely, and rightly so, receives top billing in Park City. The U.S. Ski and Snowboard Association (435-649-9090; www. usskiteam.com) calls Park City home.

🔺 In the forest's Kamas, Mountain View and Evanston ranger districts northeast of Park City there are 38 campgrounds with 904 designated campsites (no hookups); free to $14; most have a 14-day maximum stay. For reservations, call 877-444-6777.

JORDANELLE STATE PARK 🏃 🚴 🐎 🏕 🎣 🛶 ⛵ 🚤

Jordanelle State Park's 3300-acre reservoir and its close proximity to the Wasatch Front make this park one of the state's busiest, particularly in the summer when the mercury tops 100 degrees in Salt Lake City. While boaters, anglers and swimmers converge on the water, the park's perimeter trail attracts hikers, mountain bikers, horseback riders and even Nordic skiers. The mixture of water, woodlands and sage meadows is a favorite with birders. Finches, sparrows, hawks, owls, kestrels, woodpeckers and golden eagles frequent the **Rock Cliff area**, while waterfowl such as grebes, pelicans and loons enjoy the marshlands and open waters. The **Hailstone area** often attracts mountain bluebirds, western meadowlarks and northern flickers; since Hailstone lies along a major raptor migration route, in the spring turkey vul-

Skiing at
Your Doorstep

Park City arguably offers the most accessible skiing in the United States, thanks to the proximity of Salt Lake City International Airport just 36 miles away. Travelers on either coast can board a morning flight and be skiing by early afternoon. Between them the Deer Valley Resort, Park City Mountain Resort and The Canyons offer nearly 50 lifts and, at last count, 8350 skiable acres cut by 309 designated trails.

The terrain varies greatly, from easy, almost melancholy runs to steep chutes down precipitous cliffs. There are thickly treed mountainsides for skiers and boarders to weave through, wide-open bowls to see how many turns you can link through knee-deep powder without stopping, and long cruisers for testing your stability at high speeds.

Accessibility aside, what makes the skiing so heady is the snow. Each year, on average, more than 29 feet of snow bury the Park City resorts. It's snow with a ridiculously low moisture content thanks to the atmospheric "wringing" that takes place as storms born in the Pacific cross the Sierra Nevada and Great Basin before slamming into the Wasatch Front. While resorts in other parts of the country generally see snow with an 11 or 12 percent moisture content, Utah's snow typically has a water content of just 4 percent.

Although they're competitors, the three resorts realized that if one brings customers to town, those customers will likely try out the other two resorts. This thinking resulted in the "Silver Passport," which allows the holder to ski all three resorts with an interchangeable lift ticket.

The passport, which can only be purchased in conjunction with a lodging package, comes in four varieties: one version is good for four days of skiing over a five-day period, another for five days out of six, a third good for six days of skiing in seven days, and a fourth for seven days of skiing in a nine-day period.

However, Deer Valley still does not allow snowboarders, and this pass won't get shredders onto that mountain.

tures, golden eagles and a variety of hawks often can be seen drifting overhead. Fishing is excellent for rainbow trout, cutthroat trout and smallmouth bass, while the Provo River that fills the reservoir is a brown trout fishery. Facilities include two developed recreation sites, picnic grounds, beaches, restrooms, showers, boat launches, day-use cabanas, laundry facilities, a marina and a restaurant. The park also has a 12-mile-long trail that circles the reservoir and draws hikers, bikers, equestrians and Nordic skiers. The trail ties into the Historic Union Pacific Rail Trail State Park, making it possible to ride, hike or jog from Park City to Jordanelle. In the future, officials hope to develop a trail system that will connect Jordanelle to the nearby Deer Creek, Rockport and Wasatch Mountain state parks. Day-use fee, $6 per vehicle. ~ The Hailstone entrance is located off Exit 8 of Route 40, just four miles from the Park City exit, while the Rock Cliff entrance is eight miles from Route 40 on Route 32; Hailstone visitors center, 435-649-9540; Rock Cliff, 435-783-3030; parks.state.ut.us/parks/www1/jord.htm.

▲ Four campgrounds have 236 sites, 103 equipped with RV hookups; $12 to $17 per night; 14-day maximum stay. For reservations, call 800-322-3770.

ROCKPORT STATE PARK 🏃 🏕 ⛵ 🎣 🚤 🚣 🛶 One of the most overlooked of Utah's parks, possibly due to its dearth of shade, Rockport State Park lies 27 miles east of Park City. The park revolves around a manmade reservoir created by damming the mouth of a canyon. The surrounding hillsides are covered mostly with scrub oak and brush, although the campgrounds have some trees to provide a modicum of shade. Rockport is popular with boaters, anglers, waterskiers and swimmers. In winter months cross-country skiers skim across the reservoir's frozen surface. Facilities include campgrounds, picnic areas, restrooms and showers. Day-use fee, $5 per vehicle. ~ 9040 North Route 302, Peoa; 435-336-2241; parks.state.ut.us/parks/www1/rock.htm.

▲ Eight campgrounds have 200 tent sites and 36 RV sites with hookups; $8 to $15 per night. For reservations, call 800-322-3770.

HIDDEN ►   **HISTORIC UNION PACIFIC RAIL TRAIL STATE PARK** 🏃 🚵 🏇
🏕 Hikers, mountain bikers, equestrians, joggers and, in winter, cross-country skiers all work out at the Historic Union Pacific Rail Trail State Park, which is nothing more than a 28-mile-long, 125-foot-wide corridor. Early morning or early evening treks might produce sightings of mule deer, elk or even moose. The trail runs through lands with significant geological, archaeological and paleontological significance. In the 1960s an excavation not far from the trail corridor unearthed fossilized remains of both mastodons and sabertooth cats. No facilities. ~ Trail access in Park City is

along either Prospector Avenue or Cochise Court; 435-649-6839; parks.state.ut.us/parks/www1/hist.htm.

Heber City is one of those towns we all want to move to. In stark contrast to the bustling, increasingly high-tech 21st-century personality of the Wasatch Front communities of Ogden, Salt Lake City, Provo and Orem, Heber City and its namesake valley on the Wasatch Back reflect the state's less hectic, bucolic demeanor. Eastbound Route 40, which divides the town of 7500 in half, shuttles you past sheep, cattle, llamas and, on occasion, some bison grazing alongside the highway. Overhead, golden eagles and redtail hawks wheel on the air currents.

Heber City Area

The Provo River, Utah's best-known blue-ribbon trout fishery, meanders through the valley, luring both anglers and raptors, while deer, elk, moose and black bear roam the rimming mountains. Sandhill cranes browse the fields bordering the river during their migrations, and rare whooping cranes have occasionally been spotted there, too.

Although intent on retaining its rural roots, Heber City is not bashful about keeping in step with the economic times. Just 40 miles east of Salt Lake City via Route 80 and Route 40, and 24 miles from Provo by way of Route 189, Heber City is a growing bedroom community for those cities.

It doesn't take long to negotiate this four-stoplight town. While there's talk of rerouting Route 40 around the heart of town,

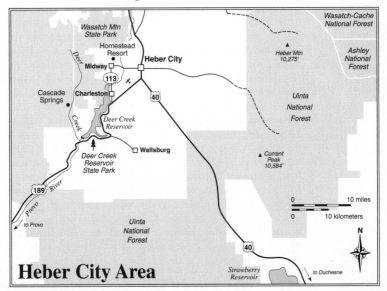

Heber City Area

for now it still doubles as Heber City's Main Street, cutting straight through the business district.

Farming and ranching remain integral parts of the Heber Valley's lifeblood, although tourism and recreation are gaining prominence. Cradled in the valley's western corner is Soldier Hollow, a portion of Wasatch State Park where the biathlon and Nordic events of the 2002 Winter Olympic Games will be staged. Headquartered on the western edge of town, the steam-powered Heber Valley Historic Railroad stands ready to haul you back to a simpler time, if for only a few hours.

SIGHTS
If you arrive in Heber City from the north via Route 40, stop first at the **Heber Valley Chamber of Commerce Visitors Center**. Not only can you bone up on the valley's—and city's—history here, the center is a gold mine of information on Heber City's lodgings and eateries, as well as area attractions. ~ 475 North Main Street, Heber City; 435-654-3666; www.hebervalleycc.org, e-mail hebercc@shadowlink.net.

One of the oldest buildings in town is the **Wasatch Stake Tabernacle**, which the LDS Church built in 1889. Today this structure, built from red sandstone quarried just east of Heber City, houses the city offices. A small museum on the first floor recounts some of the history of Wasatch County. Hanging on one wall is a quilt made in 1996 by the Daughters of Utah Pioneers that depicts some of the county's barns in fine stitchwork. ~ 75 North Main Street, Heber City; 435-654-0757.

Departing Heber City on a regular basis throughout the year is the **Heber Valley Historic Railroad**, which uses steam locomotives and an occasional diesel to haul passengers across the valley and past Deer Creek Reservoir into Provo Canyon. These 17-mile trips, featured daily through the summer and mid-fall, run three and a half hours roundtrip. Shorter trips to Soldier Hollow or the Deer Creek Dam are offered on winter weekends as well as throughout the warmer months. Special rides involving evening barbecues, murder mystery plays and even fiddlers are available throughout the year. During the Christmas season the railroad offers a trip that revolves around narration of Chris Van Allsburg's *The Polar Express*, as well as a visit by Santa Claus. Reservations for all trips are highly recommended. ~ 450 South 600 West, Heber City; 435-654-5601, fax 435-654-3709; www.hebervalleyrr.org, e-mail hebervalleyrr@shadowlink.net.

Heber City can't be discussed without mention of its neighbor, **Midway**, located just three miles to the west. This lilliputian town in the afternoon shadow of the Wasatch Range is even more rustic than Heber City, with its homes and few businesses landlocked by ranches, farms and mountains.

In this Swiss-flavored hamlet lies **The Homestead Resort,** a stately, turn-of-the-20th-century retreat built up around a massive hot spring that soothed the weary muscles of miners who toiled all week in the silver mines of Park City. There aren't many places in the country where you can spend the morning skiing and the afternoon scuba diving, but Midway is one thanks to the 65-foot-deep hot spring at The Homestead. Entombed in a towering, 55-foot mound of minerals deposited over the millennia by the hot spring's mineral-laden waters, the inside of the crater with its watery pool is perfect for learning how to scuba dive, spending some time snorkeling, or simply swimming. Instruction and equipment rentals are available on site. ~ 700 North Homestead Drive, Midway; 435-654-1102, 800-327-7220; www.homesteadresort.com, e-mail info @homesteadresort.com.

Cascade Springs pump out seven million gallons of water each day.

◀ *HIDDEN*

Memorial Hill rises abruptly from the pastureland on the eastern edge of Midway. A road that corkscrews its way to the hilltop leads to a memorial dedicated to the county's war veterans, though brass plaques honoring them were stolen from the rock memorial atop the hill. Still, the ride to the top is worth it—the 360-degree view of Midway, Heber City, the Heber Valley and Mount Timpanogos is outstanding. ~ About 300 North on River Road, Midway.

◀ *HIDDEN*

Set in the afternoon shadow of Mount Timpanogos is **Sundance Farms,** which Robert Redford started in 1988 to raise organically grown produce, flowers and herbs for his resort's restaurants and guest rooms. Back then the garden took up about a half-acre at his resort located 20 minutes away in Sundance. Today the operation covers 30 acres near the hamlet of **Charleston,** located on the western edge of the Heber Valley. During the growing season you can roam the gardens, learn to make herbal potpourri or vinegar, or buy seed mixes or some of the other products that go into the resort's rooms. ~ 3303 West 2400 South, Charleston; 435-654-2721, fax 435-654-4026; www.sundancefarms.citysearch.com.

◀ *HIDDEN*

The best way to leave the valley and get into the mountains, at least during the warmer months of the year, is to visit **Cascade Springs** via a spur of the Alpine Loop Scenic Backway. Cascade Springs is actually a series of springs that spill down the mountainside through a string of limestone pools and terraces, only to disappear back into the mountain. The U.S. Forest Service has installed boardwalks around the springs. In the summer, lush patches of vegetation surround the springs. Look closely for trout in the springs. Fishing is not allowed here, though. ~ The 24-mile loop runs from near Timpanogos Cave National Monument, up through a mountain pass on the end of the Mount Timpanogos Wilderness

Area, past the Sundance Resort and down the Provo River Canyon to Orem and then back north to the monument. Coming from Heber City, take Route 113 west to Midway, where it bends to the south. After about three miles on 113 you'll come to Tate Lane, where you turn to the west. Another quarter-mile or so brings you to Cascade Springs Road (a dirt lane that may be impassable in muddy weather), which runs for seven miles to the springs.

Within 15 minutes of Heber City's Main Street you'll find three state parks. Which to visit depends on whether you want to fish or play golf during the warmer months or ice-fish or cross-country ski during the winter months. **Jordanelle State Park** (see "Park City Area") north of Heber City is primarily a boater's paradise since the main feature is a 3300-acre reservoir, but there are hiking trails and campgrounds to enjoy, too. **Wasatch Mountain State Park** to the west offers something for most outdoors lovers, with a sprawling golf course, hiking trails, campgrounds and cross-country skiing come winter. **Deer Creek State Park** southwest of Heber City makes its living entertaining anglers with its fishing and boaters who flock here for skiing and windsurfing. (See "Parks" below for more information.)

LODGING   Quaint and removed from the bustling Salt Lake Valley, the Heber Valley has a small collection of accommodations for travelers.

For local color, the **Swiss Alps Inn** on Main Street features a working, life-size glockenspiel clock atop the main building. Inside you'll find clean and unassuming rooms. There's also an indoor spa and outdoor heated pool. ~ 167 South Main Street, Heber City; 435-654-0722; www.swissalpsinn.com, e-mail alps@swiss alpsinn.com. BUDGET TO MODERATE.

The ubiquitous **Holiday Inn Express** has standard rooms. ~ 1268 South Main Street, Heber City; 435-654-9990. MODERATE.

Drifting asleep to the sound of splashing water is possible at the **Johnson Mill Bed & Breakfast**, along the eastern boundary of Midway. Occupying a century-old flour mill, the five-room inn sits on 25 acres next to the Provo River. You can walk from your room onto the covered wraparound porch and then down to spring-fed ponds and streams crowded with German brown, and rainbow trout and a family of swans. There's even a gazebo in one pond accessed by a wooden pier. And, of course, the natural waterfall that once powered the grist mill remains. ~ 100 North Johnson Mill Road, Midway; 435-654-4466, 888-272-0030, fax 435-657-1454; www.johnsonmill.com. MODERATE TO DELUXE.

The **Inn on the Creek** reflects the valley's Swiss heritage by recreating the feel of a small mountain village. In the spring colorful bursts of wildflowers erupt around the 50-room inn's main building, which functions as a bed and breakfast. Outlying chalets feature kitchens for when you don't feel like heading to the inn for your meals. There's also a heated pool for recouping after a hard ski or day on the links, or you can relax before your room's fireplace. ~ 375 Rainbow Lane, Midway; 435-654-0892, 800-654-0892, fax 435-654-5971; www.innoncreek.com. DELUXE TO ULTRA-DELUXE.

Directly across from Wasatch Mountain State Park and just two miles from Soldier Hollow, site of the Salt Lake Games' cross-country, biathlon and Nordic combined events, the **Blue Boar Inn** holds just 14 rooms, but they come with fireplaces, full bathrooms and televisions if you can't find enough to do outdoors. Meals—breakfast is included in your room charge—is served downstairs in the dining room. ~ 1235 Warm Springs Road, Midway; 435-654-1400, 888-650-1400, fax 435-654-6459; www.theblueboar inn.com. ULTRA-DELUXE.

For pure indulgence in the Heber Valley, stay at **The Homestead Resort**. After a day of hiking or skiing in Wasatch Mountain State Park or the surrounding mountains, or perhaps sailing or wind-surfing on either Deer Creek or Jordanelle reservoirs, you can squirrel yourself away in one of the executive cottages, a family-style room, or even the Virginia House, a Victorian-style structure that operates like a B&B. While relaxing in your room you can even sate your sweet tooth with the complimentary fudge. ~ 700 North Homestead Drive, Midway; 435-654-1102, 800-327-7220; www.homesteadresort.com, e-mail info@homesteadresort.com. DELUXE TO ULTRA-DELUXE.

Daniels Summit Lodge, 16 miles southeast of Heber City   ◄ HIDDEN
along Route 40, is the gateway to more than 200 miles of snow-mobile trails, which in the summer turn into mountain bike routes. The log and stone lodge offers 42 lodge rooms and eight cabins, most equipped with fireplaces and jetted tubs. You'll also find an indoor pool and spa, a restaurant, a general store and a gift shop, as well as snowmobile rentals and guided tours in winter and guided horseback rides in summer. ~ P.O. Box 490, Heber City, UT 84032; 800-519-9969, fax 435-548-2982; www.danielssum mit.com. DELUXE TO ULTRA-DELUXE.

AUTHOR FAVORITE

If you're just passing through Heber City on the way to some-where else and it's hot out, the incredibly thick and rich milkshakes at **Granny's** will cool you down and fill you up at the same time. Choosing one of the 44 flavors could take some time. ~ 511 South Main Street, Heber City; 435-654-3097. BUDGET.

DINING

Unlike Park City, Heber City is not exactly a culinary hotbed, but you can find some surprisingly good meals in the area.

You can find Mexican dishes in both Midway and Heber City at **Don Pedro's**, a locally owned eatery featuring the usual Mexican fare. ~ 1050 South Main Street, Heber City, 435-657-0600; 42 West Main Street, Midway, 435-654-0805. BUDGET TO MODERATE.

HIDDEN ►

Not far from Main Street in Heber City is the **Snake Creek Grill**, a locals' favorite where the meals are on par with those served in Park City but at roughly two-thirds the cost. The grill is housed in a clapboard building right out of the Old West. Inside you'll find a truly eclectic dinner menu that includes entrées such as blue cornmeal–crusted trout, ten-spice salmon with red curry–Japanese noodle stirfry, and zucchini-tomato risotto with spice-grilled white shrimp. Reservations suggested. ~ 650 West 100 South, Heber City; 435-654-2133. MODERATE.

The Homestead Resort offers the formal **Simon's Restaurant** for dinner and Sunday brunch throughout the year, and **Fanny's Grill**, which serves three meals a day in a more casual atmosphere. Housed inside the main building, the restaurants carry a country atmosphere befitting the resort's location. Simon's is decidedly the more expensive of the two, although the Sunday brunch is well worth it, with multiple stations offering made-to-order omelets, French toast, pastries, cereals, meats and desserts. Fanny's menus offer somewhat more traditional—and heartier—country fare, such as ribs, chops and fried chicken dishes for dinner and burgers and steak sandwiches, as well as pastas, for lunch. ~ 700 North Homestead Drive, Midway; 435-654-1102, 800-327-7220; www.homesteadresort.com. MODERATE TO DELUXE.

Virtually next door to The Homestead Resort lies the **Inn on the Creek**, a laid-out European resort whose restaurant is dominated by a large fireplace. Dinner entrées might include grilled veal Paillarde, rack of pork marinated with regional apples, or Utah trout sautéed with honey mustard. ~ 375 Rainbow Lane, Midway; 435-654-0892, fax 435-654-5871; www.innoncreek.com. MODERATE TO DELUXE.

SHOPPING

When it comes time for serious shopping in Heber City, most locals head to nearby Park City or even Provo. But this doesn't mean the town and nearby Midway are entirely devoid of intriguing shops. At **Old Heber Town**, a small cluster of shops housed in buildings out of the Old West, you'll find restaurants, antique shops, craft stores and even an art gallery. ~ 650 West 100 South, Heber City.

Just minutes away is **Water From the Moon**, an eclectic shop with clothing, sterling silver items, and gifts for the home. ~ 118 South 500 West, Heber City; 435-654-2267.

In Midway, **Books and Beyond** is housed in a century-old, two-story Gothic Revival home where each room hosts a specific literary genre. ~ 103 East Main Street, Midway; 435-657-2665.

At **Sundance Farms** in Charleston, located west of Heber City, you can buy many of the organically produced and handmade items that turn up in the rooms at the Sundance Resort. ~ 3303 West 2400 South, Charleston; 435-654-2721.

They don't roll up the streets in Heber City come nightfall, but it can certainly seem like it. If you don't mind smoke and are only looking for a cold beer and possibly a game of pool, head to **The Other End** at the northern edge of town. ~ 1223 North Route 40, Heber City; no phone.   **NIGHTLIFE**

For a movie, try **Reel Theatres**. ~ 94 South Main Street, Heber City; 435-654-1181.

Or, you can roll a game or two at **Holiday Lanes**. ~ 515 North Main Street, Heber City; 435-654-0372.

UINTA NATIONAL FOREST 🚶 🚴 🐎 🏕 🛶 🚤 ⛴ Within its 958,258 acres the Uinta National Forest claims high desert, rugged canyons and lofty peaks reaching to 11,877 feet. It also contains three wilderness areas and the Mount Timpanogos Cave National Monument, which is administered by the National Park Service. Also in the forest and not far from Heber City are the **Strawberry Reservoir Recreation Area** (23 miles south of Heber City via Route 40) and the **Currant Creek Reservoir Recreation Area** (head 40 miles south of Heber City on Route 40 to Currant Creek Road, a dirt road that runs 17 miles to the reservoir). Elk, black bear, cougar, moose, mountain goats, bighorn sheep and mule deer are often spotted in the forest. The Provo River that runs between the Jordanelle and Deer Creek reservoirs and then on through Provo Canyon west of Heber City to Provo is an outstanding trout fishery. Facilities include picnic areas, restrooms, a ski resort and cross-country ski trails. Two major highways, Route 189 between Provo and Heber City and Route 40 between Heber City and Fruitland, bisect portions of the forest. ~ Heber Ranger District, 2460 South Route 40, Heber; 435-654-0470.   **PARKS**

In Soldier Hollow, at the southern end of Wasatch Mountain State Park, you can kick-and-glide or skate-ski along the same routes Olympic athletes will follow in 2002.

▲ Throughout the forest, there are 26 campgrounds in the three ranger districts with 1314 RV/tent sites, some with hook-ups; the bulk of the sites are in the Heber Ranger District; free to $12 for individual sites; most have a 14-day maximum stay. For reservations, call 877-444-6777.

WASATCH MOUNTAIN STATE PARK 🚶 🚴 🐎 🏕 Cradled in the nook of the eponymous mountain range, the 22,000-acre

Wasatch Mountain State Park offers both finely manicured fairways of a USGA-sanctioned golf course and rugged mountains for hiking and mountain biking. The golf course boasts 27 holes and ten lakes waiting to swallow your drives. Beyond golf, you'll find wonderful hiking opportunities and plenty of campsites complete with picnic tables and grills. In the fall, which usually begins to show its colorful hand in early September, the park's forests ignite in a blaze of crimson, orange, yellow and brown leaves of maples, aspen, scrub oaks and serviceberry. Things don't slow down in the winter, when storms bury the golf course and surrounding hillsides and meadows under snows perfect for cross-country skiing. Facilities at the park include a visitors center, restrooms and showers, and a group picnic pavilion as well as a ranch-style building (complete with kitchen) known as the "chalet" that groups can rent summer and winter. Day-use fee, $4. ~ Routes 113 and 224, about six miles northwest of Heber City; 435-654-1791 (visitors center), 435-654-3961 (campground); parks.state.ut.us/parks/www1/wasa.htm.

▲ There are two campgrounds with 139 sites; $10 to $16 per night; 14-day maximum stay. For reservations, call 800-322-3770.

DEER CREEK STATE PARK
Created by the damming of the Provo River at the head of Provo Canyon, Deer Creek State Park is built around a sprawling reservoir designed to quench Wasatch Front water needs. Within its 3260 acres, you'll find tremendous fishing and reliable breezes for windsurfing and sailing. Facilities include a concrete boat launch, fish-cleaning stations, a restaurant and marina (which rents boats and sells gas), restrooms, showers and a group picnic pavilion. Day-use fee, $5. ~ Route 189, about five miles southwest of Heber City; 435-654-0171; parks.state.ut.us/parks/www1/dear.htm.

▲ There are 35 campsites, 22 for RVs and 10 for tents; $12 per night; 14-day maximum stay. For reservations, call 800-322-3770 (May through September).

Vernal Area

Connecting Park City, Heber City and Vernal likes dots on a connect-the-dots puzzle is Route 40. This sturdy, two-lane highway that climbs through mountains and races across the plains is the key artery across northeastern Utah. From Heber City it runs 128 miles to Vernal, passing through majestic, pine-covered mountains as well as tedious scrublands along the way.

At first glance, Vernal seems little more than a drab waystation between Salt Lake City and Denver. Indeed, cruising down Route 40 from point A to B, Vernal materializes through the windshield as little more than a humdrum rural community that somehow ekes out a living from a barren, custard-colored landscape. Pause for a moment, though, and take note of your surroundings. Northeast of town lies the rugged sandstone maze that is Dinosaur National Monument; to the north rise the snow-capped Uinta Mountains, the Rocky Mountains' only range that runs east to west; while to the south sprawls the roughly 3.3 million-acre Uintah and Ouray Indian Reservation.

These "playgrounds" make Vernal a perfect jumping-off point for a diverse array of recreational options: hiking, fishing or cross-country skiing in the Ashley National Forest that drapes across the canyon-riddled flanks of the Uintas, floating down the nearby Green or Yampa rivers, wading through the geologic wonderland known as Fantasy Canyon, tracing prehistoric history in Dinosaur National Monument. You'll also find museums that recall the days of Butch Cassidy and the Sundance Kid as well as the towering dinosaurs that once trod across the land here.

So smitten, in fact, is Vernal with its proximity to Dinosaur National Monument that it's known as the heart of "Dinosaur-land," a common moniker for this corner of Utah. Enter town from the west on Route 40 and you'll be greeted by a towering replica of a tyrannosaurus rex, while from the town's eastern

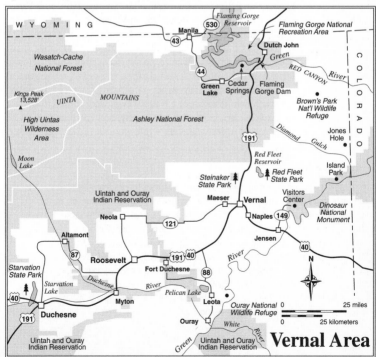

Vernal Area

gateway you'll encounter "Dinah," an outrageously pink Barney lookalike.

SIGHTS

Water is a precious resource in northeastern Utah's high-desert landscape. The U.S. Bureau of Land Management realized just how important water in the Uintah Basin was to wildlife in the early 1970s when the agency spotted waterfowl living in Pariette Draw, which is 48 miles southwest of Vernal. BLM biologists realized they could multiply the benefit of the draw's water by developing 20 ponds and other waterways along the draw. Since its completion

HIDDEN ►

in 1975, the **Pariette Wetlands** have become a waterfowl magnet as well as the BLM's largest waterfowl management area in Utah. Each year nearly 2000 ducks are born and reared in the wetlands, which also attract geese and shorebirds such as avocets and black-necked stilts as well as white pelicans and herons during the summer months. ~ To reach the 9033-acre preserve, just west of Myton turn south off Route 40 and onto the Sand Wash–Green River access road. After 1.7 miles of paved road you'll come to Nine Mile–Sand Wash Junction, where you turn left and follow the wetlands signs for 23 miles. For more information, call the BLM's Vernal office at 435-781-4400.

Back on Route 40, about 130 miles east of Heber City is **Vernal**, a town of about 7100 people. Once in Vernal, you'll find the town's most handsome building in the form of the **Vernal Temple**. Built by the LDS Church between 1900 and 1907 as the Uintah Tabernacle, the temple's architecture is a simpler version of the Georgian New England Church design. During the nearly eight years of construction, financially strapped officials shrewdly assembled the tabernacle at a cost of $37,000. Logs were hauled from nearby canyons, bricks were made locally, and the pine woodwork was painted to resemble oak while wooden pillars were painted

BRICK BY BRICK

In 1916 it cost quite a bit in freight to haul textured bricks from Salt Lake City into the Uintah Basin by rail. While the bricks sold for only seven cents apiece, hauling them to Vernal ran 28 cents each, a price banker William Colthart couldn't stomach. Being an ingenious sort, though, Colthart realized that the U.S. Postal Service only charged 52 cents to send a 50-pound parcel from Salt Lake to Vernal. So, he had the 80,000 bricks packed in 50-pound bundles and mailed to Vernal. You can see the result of his craftiness—the so-called "**Parcel Post Bank**"—on the southwest corner of Vernal Avenue and Main Street in the form of the Zion National Bank. ~ 3 West Main Street, Vernal.

to resemble marble. In 1992 the building was closed to the public because of structural concerns. Three years later the LDS Church embarked on a $7 million renovation and transformed the tabernacle into a temple. Though non-church members can't enter the temple, they can stroll the tidy grounds and admire the exterior of the building. ~ 170 South 400 West, Vernal.

Across the street from the tabernacle is the **Pioneer Museum**, which is open during the summer months and run by the local chapter of Daughters of the Utah Pioneers. The museum is housed in the original **Vernal Tithing Building**, a rock building erected in 1887 and used to collect farm products members of the LDS Church donated to the church. Inside are historic artifacts and photographs of the Uinta Basin from the mid-1800s that impart a taste of life in the West. Closed Labor Day through May. ~ 200 South 500 West, Vernal; no phone.

A must-stop on your way to Dinosaur National Monument (see "Dinosaur National Monument" in this chapter), which lies 20 miles east of town, is the **Utah Field House of Natural History State Park**. Located on Main Street two blocks from the center of Vernal, this facility is a catalog of eastern Utah's geologic past and natural history. Outside on the park grounds you'll find a kid-pleasing "dinosaur garden" stocked with 18 life-sized replicas of prehistoric nasties such as tyrannosaurus rex and utahraptor, a voracious carnivore whose fossilized remains were discovered not too long ago in central Utah's outback. The replicas depict a wide slice of dino life, coming from periods ranging from 65 million to 150 million years ago. Kids can experience their own fossil "dig" in a sandbox containing casts of actual bones. Inside, the field house exhibits more recent history—artifacts from the Fremont and Ute cultures that once roamed the region as well as geology displays that chronicle 600 million years of life. Before you leave the museum, stop in the adjoining travel information center to pick up a free Dinosaur Hunting License. Admission. ~ 235 East Main Street, Vernal; 435-789-3799; parks.state.ut.us/parks/www1/utah.htm.

Next door to the field house in a corner of the Uintah County Library is the **Ladies of the White House Doll Collection**, a doll-lover's display of First Ladies in their inaugural ball gowns. Done in conjunction with the country's bicentennial celebration, the exhibit includes pictures of the Vernal-area women who made the dresses as well as short histories on the First Ladies. The library is closed Sunday. ~ 155 East Main Street, Vernal; 435-789-0091.

◀ HIDDEN

Bits and pieces of Uintah County's outlaw past are on display at the county-owned **Western Heritage Museum**, which not only touches on Butch and Sundance's Wild Bunch Gang but also has extensive exhibits on the Old West and American Indians. A mock-

Text continued on page 188.

Dinosaur National Monument

Twenty miles east of Vernal via Routes 40 and 149, Dinosaur National Monument would rightly be a national park if it weren't so remote. Within its 210,000 acres you can retreat into prehistory while studying the world's largest Jurassic period fossil quarry, lose yourself on a float down the Green or Yampa rivers, or stand atop a sandstone cliff overlooking a deep river gorge.

Standing amid the monument's serrated sandstone and sage landscape, it's hard to, in your mind's eye, superimpose a broad expanse of savannah, one with a shallow, nourishing ribbon of river running through it. Such a setting did exist here, though it was hundreds of millions of years ago when dinosaurs stalked the earth, when today's sandstone was only sand. The sand not only evolved into the rich sandstone ridges and cliffs that today define the region's geography, but it also preserved in rock a veritable Jurassic Park of fossilized dinosaurs.

For this maze of land, left rumpled when the Earth's occasional upheavals tilted the ancient savannah on its side, it's probably best that the landscape lies within a monument, not a national park. Without the more prestigious "park" distinction, the preserve enjoys a largely obscure existence, one that ensures visitors solitude throughout most of the year, aside from the high season of June through August.

Whether it's your first or last stop during a trip to Dinosaur, the fossil quarry is definitely a must-see. Although paleontologists no longer chip away at the famous hillside Earl Douglass, a paleontologist sent fossil-hunting by Pittsburgh's Carnegie Museum, discovered in 1909 when he spied eight tail vertebrae of an Apatosaurus sticking out of the ground, exhibits and life-sized models in the quarry's visitors center recount the prehistoric history. Between 1909 and 1924 more than 350 tons of fossils—plants, crocodiles, clams, dinosaurs—and their surrounding rock were plucked from the ridge.

Today at the visitors center, which was built over the fossil-rich ridge Douglass uncovered, more than 2000 fossilized bones remain embedded in the 200-foot-long wall. Leg bones, back bones, ribs and even toothy skulls can be seen on the rock face from the visitors center's walkway. While the skulls can be difficult to spot, peer through the small length of pipe mounted on the railing and you'll easily make out the skull of a Camarasaurus.

Most of the bones were from vegetarian sauropods—better known to most of us as brontosaurs—although some meat-eating theropods are also represented in the quarry.

While paleontologists halted work on the rock face in 1991, these days they are busy at work on digs elsewhere in the monument. From time to time you can find them cleaning specimens in the visitors center's paleontology lab, which you can peer into through large windows on the lower level of the visitors center.

Although it's known as the "dinosaur" national monument, the landscape has more to offer than just a dinosaur graveyard. The Green and Yampa rivers flow through the monument, of which almost two-thirds lies in Colorado, and carry hundreds of paddlers downstream during the summer months. Through most of the year self-guided auto tours can take you away from the dinosaur quarry and the monument head-quarters in Dinosaur, Colorado, and deeper into the monument, past jagged ridges of sandstone stained orange, yellow, red, brown and grey from various mineral deposits, to the cabins of early homesteaders and to pictographs and petroglyphs ancient American Indians left behind.

The 22-mile-long "Tour of the Tilted Rocks" auto tour starts near the quarry's visitors center. It winds past petroglyphs, hiking trails and the historic Josie Morris homestead, all the while revealing the monument's twisted geology. If you enter the monument in Colorado, the 62-mile-long "Journey through Time" leads across the Blue Mountain Plateau, offering spectacular overlooks of the Green and Yampa rivers. Booklets detailing these drives can be purchased at both the dinosaur quarry visitors center and the monument headquarters at Deerlodge, Colorado.

Though there are few established long-distance hiking trails in Dinosaur, with a good map and compass skills you can venture off the beaten path. There are six campgrounds within the monument, including two near the quarry. Admission. ~ The monument's dinosaur quarry is located seven miles north of Jensen via Route 149; monument headquarters is located two miles east of Dinosaur, Colorado, along Route 40; 970-374-3000; www.nps.gov/dino.

up of a general store stands in one corner of the museum, while elsewhere in the hall you'll find hammers, pliers, nails and horse-shoes from a blacksmith's shop, saddle and rifle collections, Fre-mont Indian arrowheads and woven baskets, and even the 25 pounds of medical tools and drugs that one of Vernal's first doc-tors toted about in his black bag. Closed Sunday. ~ 300 East 200 South, Vernal; 435-789-7399.

As evidenced by Dinosaur National Monument, the Uintah Basin is a treasure trove of dinosaur fossils. You can also find **di-nosaur tracks**, if you know where to look. One good area is **Red Fleet State Park** found ten miles north of Vernal. More than 200 three-toed tracks belonging to a bipedal dinosaur are frozen in stone on the shore of Red Fleet Reservoir across from the boat ramp. ~ Route 191, ten miles north of Vernal, Vernal; 435-789-4432.

HIDDEN ► The **Dry Fork Petroglyphs** ten miles north of town via 3500 West and the Dry Fork Canyon Road are a dazzling display of the Fremont Culture's artistry. The 1200-to-1600-year-old rock art, most of which is composed of trapezoidal figures, covers a 200-foot-high Navajo sandstone cliff. Some of the pictures are nine feet tall. Next to the parking area is a replica of a saloon as well as a general store. ~ 3500 West, located ten miles north of Vernal.

While the bizarre rock formations of southern Utah are well-known and preserved in the form of national parks, there's a can-yon about 27 miles south of downtown Vernal that also bears otherworldly rock configurations worth visiting. Although the

HIDDEN ► area is not actually a canyon, it's known as **Fantasy Canyon** due to its fragile sandstone formations. These formations, between 38 million and 50 million years old, were created by sediments that filled the prehistoric Lake Uintah that once inundated the region.

One of the more unusual minerals found in Fan-tasy Canyon is gilsonite. This shiny black mineral exists in a one-inch wide vertical vein. Thicker, com-mercially mined veins of gilsonite are found near Bon-anza and Ouray. A fossilized turtle shell can also be seen in the canyon. ~ To reach Fantasy Canyon, head south of Vernal on Route 45 for 21 miles, then turn right onto Glen Bench Road and take it 18 miles to the canyon. For a map, stop at the BLM office at 170 South 500 East; 435-781-4400.

Fantasy Canyon's strange, delicate compositions have inspired another nickname for this natu-ral wonder: "Nature's China Shop."

Thirty-six miles north of Vernal lies **Flaming Gorge National Recreation Area,** a 207,363-acre playground for boating, hiking, camping and some of the world's best lake-trout fishing. The gorge was named in 1869 by Major John Wesley Powell, who was enchanted by the way the setting sun reflected off the can-yon's red-rock cliffs. Part of the landscape was submerged, though, in 1964 when the Flaming Gorge Dam was completed. A close-up look at the area's twisted and folded rock formations can be had on the 11-mile **Sheep Creek Geologic Loop**, a scenic drive that most vehicles can handle. In the fall, kokanee salmon enter Sheep Creek from the reservoir to spawn. The "Drive through the Ages" runs from Vernal to the national recreation area, using a series of interpretive signs to highlight 80 million years of geology. From Vernal, the drive along Route 191 to the visitors center at Dutch John takes about an hour as the highway darts and jogs up and over the Uinta Mountains before reaching the **Flaming Gorge Dam**. Erected in 1964, the 502-foot-high hydroelectric dam created a reservoir that runs 91 miles north into Wyoming. See "Parks" for more information about Flaming Gorge National Recreation Area.

Although it's roughly 40 miles northeast of Vernal by a questionable road in the best of weather or 77 miles via a roundabout way on better roads, the **John Jarvie Ranch Historic Site** next to   ◀ HIDDEN **Brown's Park National Wildlife Refuge** lets you step back into the late 1800s. The area in general was a favorite with the Blackfoot, Sioux, Cheyenne, Arapaho and Navajo nations, who enjoyed the area's relatively mild winters. Later, notorious outlaws like Butch Cassidy and the Sundance Kid would hole up in the park between robberies. For them, the coming together of the states of Wyoming, Colorado and Utah made it easy to flee law officers whose jurisdiction ended at the state line. The 35-acre ranch itself is in Utah, although the wildlife refuge is in Colorado.

Jarvie, a Scot, settled here in 1880 to run a ferry across the Green River. He later added a general store and post office. Today four of the original structures, each more than a century old, remain in place. Although the general store is a replica of the one built in 1881, inside you'll find many of the artifacts from Jarvie's life, as well as a safe that was robbed on the night Jarvie was murdered. Tours of the property are offered daily from May through October. ~ If the weather is good and dry, head east from Vernal on Brown's Park Road for 25 miles to a signed turnoff to the north. This 16-mile-long dirt road passes through some spectacular country. If the weather is questionable, take Route 191 north for 55 miles to the Wyoming border, then east 22 miles along Clay Basin Road, a maintained gravel road; 435-885-3307; www-a. blm.gov/utah/vernal/rec/john.html.

The remote setting of the 13,455-acre wildlife refuge, which straddles the Colorado–Utah border just downstream of the Flaming Gorge Dam, provides lush habitat for mule deer, elk, pronghorn antelope, marsh hawks, American kestrels and about 12,000 waterfowl during peak migrations. The fishing in the Green River is pretty good, too.

Southwest of Vernal by 32 miles via Routes 191/40 and 88 is one of three wildlife refuges nurtured by the Green River. As with the other two—Seedskadee in Wyoming and Brown's Park along the Colorado–Utah border—**Ouray National Wildlife Refuge** is a nesting ground for waterfowl. It also plays a special role in efforts by the U.S. Fish and Wildlife Service to recover dwindling populations of the Colorado pike minnow and the razorback sucker. It's roughly a 90-minute drive from Vernal to this 9033-acre preserve. ~ To reach the refuge, head 15 miles west of Vernal on Route 191/40 and then south 17 miles on Route 88; 435-545-2522 or 435-789-0351; www.r6.fws.gov/ouray.

LODGING   Cruise Vernal's Main Street and you'll quickly be surrounded by familiar names: Weston, Best Western, Days Inn, Econo Lodge. For reliable accommodations, you can't really go wrong with one of these outfits, but if you look a bit farther afield you'll find comfortable establishments that offer a more personalized touch.

The **Landmark Inn** blends a part of Vernal's past with a taste of the countryside. Originally the setting for the Landmark Missionary Baptist Church, the two-story building was converted in the fall of 1996 into a bed and breakfast by two brothers from North Carolina who brought the flavor of a country inn west with them. Each of the three suites and eight bedrooms carry their own character; some have four-poster beds, others rough-hewn log bed frames. The suites offer jetted tubs, large-screen TVs and fireplaces. Not far from the heart of downtown, the Landmark Inn is just a block south of the Utah Fieldhouse. ~ 288 East 100 South, Vernal; 435-781-1800, 888-738-1800; www.landmark-inn.com, e-mail landmark@easilink.com. MODERATE TO ULTRA-DELUXE.

If you're planning to split your time between Dinosaur National Monument and the Flaming Gorge National Recreation Area, there are two lodges not far from Flaming Gorge that offer quieter, prettier mountain settings than you can find in Vernal.

Located 39 miles north of Vernal on the shores of a 20-acre lake in the Ashley National Forest just ten miles from Flaming Gorge Reservoir, the **Red Canyon Lodge** has been catering to

FIT FOR A KING

The sport of kings—falconry—continues to be practiced in Utah at **Falcon's Ledge**, a unique lodge hidden away in Altamont, a small town 15 miles north of Duchesne. The lodge's reputation stems largely from its fly-fishing opportunities, but from September through March falconry comes to roost. Birding also fills the lodge's time during those months, while fly-fishing dominates the schedule from April through October, with time for gold panning tossed in. ~ At Duchesne, turn north off Route 40 and onto Route 87 for 15 miles; Box 67, Altamont, UT 84001; 435-454-3737, 877-879-3737, fax 435-454-3392; www.falconsledge.com. ULTRA-DELUXE.

tourists since 1930 with a variety of cabins. Surrounded by thick forest, the lodge is a great base of operations for hiking, biking, fishing or boating. There's a range of cabins to meet most budgets, from simple units offering just beds with a central shower house and restroom a short walk away all the way up to luxury cabins that can sleep four, boast two queen beds, kitchenettes and full bathrooms. All cabins have free-standing wood stoves. Kids have their own trout pond at the lodge. Along with accommodations, the lodge offers boat rentals for East Greens Lake, mountain bike and cross-country ski rentals, horseback riding, fly-fishing lessons and its own tackle shop. Open April to early October, and weekends only during the winter. ~ 790 Red Canyon Road, Dutch John; 435-889-3759, fax 435-889-5106; www. redcanyonlodge.com, e-mail info@redcanyonlodge.com. BUDGET TO DELUXE.

Just seven miles from Red Canyon Lodge and 38 from Vernal is the **Flaming Gorge Lodge**. There are no charming log cabins here, but rather a variety of motel and condominium units. However, unlike the cabins at Red Canyon, the rooms have televisions, VCRs and telephones just in case you don't want to stray too far from civilization. The 24 one-bedroom condos can sleep four and come with kitchens. The 21 motel rooms feature two double beds. There's a dining room and café on the property, as well as a general store and gas station, a tackle shop, a liquor store, and raft and bike rentals. Winter days at the lodge revolve around snowmobiling and cross-country skiing. ~ 155 Greendale Road, Route 191, Dutch John; 435-889-3773, fax 435-889-3788; www. fglodge.com, e-mail lodge@fglodge.com. MODERATE TO DELUXE.

DINING

Vernal is chockfull of eateries, but most are of the fast-food genre. Cruise Main Street and Route 40 on either end of town and you'll find plenty of burger, Mexican and pizza joints, as well as rib restaurants and an occasional Chinese diner.

The **Curry Manor**, however, offers fine dining in a two-story brick home built in 1910. Meals are served in five (3 upstairs, 2 down) elegant dining rooms draped with lace curtains and filled with antiques. Chicken, pasta, beef and seafood can be found on the lunch and dinner menus, which might include three-cheese tortellini, king crab legs and Maine lobster. ~ 189 South Vernal Avenue, Vernal; 435-789-2289. MODERATE TO DELUXE.

At **La Cabana** the menu is dominated by Mexican fare—burritos, tacos and fajitas, as well as 22 combination platters—but you also can find hamburgers and steaks. Closed Sunday. ~ 56 West Main Street, Vernal, 435-789-3151. BUDGET.

Need a quick dose of caffeine, looking for a book, or just want to check your e-mail? Then drop by **Reader's Roost**, where you'll be able to order a cup of coffee, read a novel or cruise cyberspace via the internet stations. Oh yeah, if hunger strikes you can order from their deli menu. Closed Sunday. ~ 27 West Main Street, Vernal; 435-789-8400.

SHOPPING The state of shopping in Vernal is about what you'd expect from a ranching and mining community: you can find lots of overalls and work boots, but beyond that the pickings are pretty slim.

A seasonal business, but one definitely worth a stop if you pass through in summer, is **Remains To Be Seen**, a rock and fossil shop on Main Street. Closed October through May. ~ 177 West Main Street, Vernal.

If you're in a need of a pair of cowboy boots or a saddle, stop by the **Bull Ring**. ~ 1801 West Route 40, Vernal; 435-789-9474.

NIGHTLIFE When the sun goes down in Vernal, about the best thing to do in this sleepy town is head for your lodging's pool or hot tub, find a good book to read or turn on the television.

At the **Gateway Saloon and Social Club** you can find a game of darts if you don't mind the country-and-western tunes chugging out of the jukebox or the smoky atmosphere. ~ 773 East Main Street, Vernal; 435-789-9842.

During summer months, local soft-rock bands play occasionally at **Jule's Java**, where espressos, coffees and Italian sodas help wash down cheesecake and other desserts. ~ 67 East Main Street, Vernal; 435-789-5933.

PARKS **ASHLEY NATIONAL FOREST** 🚶 🚲 🐎 🏕 ⛵ Visible from Vernal but requiring a short drive to reach is the Ashley National Forest. Draped across the southern half of the Uinta Mountains and dipping south of Vernal, the national forest shelters alpine high country that offers a cool respite from the dry, dusty summers that descend on most of northeastern Utah. The forest shelters the headwaters of a vast watershed that flows all the way down through Nevada and into California via the Green and Colorado rivers. Within its 1.4 million acres (of which 1.3 million lie in Utah) are thick stands of forest dotted by high-country lakes, Utah's highest point (13,528-foot Kings Peak), more than half of the 456,705-acre High Uintas Wilderness Area and the Flaming Gorge National Recreation Area. Mountain goats, elk, moose and black bears can be found in the forest, which draws more than 2.5 million visitors a year for boating, fishing, camping, hiking, backpacking, horseback riding, cross-country skiing and snowmobiling. ~ From Vernal, Route 191 runs north into Ashley National Forest; along the way it provides numerous access routes to the forest. Access can also be gained via 2500 West and 3500 West out of Vernal; 435-789-1181; www.fs.fed.us/r4/ashley.

▲ The forest, which also spills into southwestern Wyoming, has 46 campgrounds with 1216 sites, most of which are in the immediate area of Flaming Gorge National Recreation Area; free to $14; 14-day maximum stay. For reservations, call 877-444-6777.

FLAMING GORGE NATIONAL RECREATION AREA 🏃🚴🐎🎣
🛶⛵⛴🚣⛵ Straddling the Utah–Wyoming border, the Flaming Gorge National Recreation Area is centered around a 91-mile-long reservoir but offers a wide range of activities, from boating and fishing to hiking, camping and cross-country skiing. There are two designated swimming areas—the Sunny Cove beach is near the Mustang Ridge campground just north of the dam, while the Lucerne beach is one mile west of the Lucerne campground; no lifeguards. Day-use fee, $2 per vehicle. ~ Off Route 191, 41 miles north of Vernal; P.O. Box 279, Manila, UT 84046; 435-784-3445; www.fs.fed.us/r4/ashley/fg_html_aw.html.

▲ There are 20 campgrounds, including 4 boat-in sites; $6 to $18 per night; 16-day maximum stay. For reservations, call 877-444-6777.

RED FLEET STATE PARK 🏃🛶⛵🚣⛵ Three towering
fins of Navajo sandstone that jut up from the Red Fleet Reservoir inspired the name for Red Fleet State Park, since from the air they look like a fleet at sail. The 650-acre reservoir is a favorite of local boaters, in large part due to its sandstone cliffs and remote sandy beaches hidden in side canyons. Along with water sports, the park offers a fishery noteworthy for rainbow and brown trout as well as bluegill and bass. The park's campground sprawls across a hillside that provides great views of the reservoir. The park gained fame in 1987 when a dinosaur trackway with more than 200 tracks was discovered on the shore directly across from the boat launch. Facilities include modern restrooms, fish-cleaning stations, barbecue grills and picnic tables. Day-use fee, $4 per vehicle. ~ Route 191, ten miles north of Vernal; 435-789-4432; parks.state.ut.us/parks/www1/redf.htm.

Many of the wildlife and avian species, such as mule deer, ring-necked pheasant, cinnamon teal ducks and great blue herons, that you can spy at Ouray were present when John Wesley Powell explored the Colorado River Basin in the late 1800s.

▲ There are 38 sites, 29 for RVs; $10 per night; 14-day maximum stay.

STEINAKER STATE PARK 🏃🛶⛵🚣⛵ Just five and a
half miles north of Vernal via Route 191 is Steinaker State Park, which is wrapped around a reservoir. In the middle of summer the waters warm to 70 degrees, making the park popular with water lovers. Off-highway-vehicle areas are nearby; one can be accessed from the park grounds, while another is just two miles away. Facilities include restrooms, picnic grounds and a boat ramp. Anglers like the reservoir for its rainbow trout and largemouth

bass fisheries. Day-use fee, $4. ~ 4335 North Route 191, five and a half miles north of Vernal off Route 191; 435-789-4432; parks. state.ut.us/parks/www1/stei.htm.

▲ There are 31 tent/RV sites; $10 per night; 14-day maximum stay.

OURAY NATIONAL WILDLIFE REFUGE Thirty-one miles southwest of Vernal lies the 12,000-acre Ouray National Wildlife Refuge, a squat tract of land that started out in 1960 as a waterfowl breeding grounds. Today it lures hundreds of mule deer, elk, bald eagles in addition to more than 200 species of birds. It's also the backdrop for the Ouray National Fish Hatchery that works to help the endangered Colorado pike minnow and the razorback sucker rebound from the brink of extinction. These two unusual residents are hard to spot, for they live in the Green River's murky waters; they were doomed by the dams that sprang up throughout the Colorado River Basin in the 1960s and created a cooler, clearer river flow than the fish prefer. Now, efforts to bolster their numbers have resulted in increasing seasonal flows from the dams to replicate spring floods, allowing the flooding of some bottomlands to provide spawning grounds for the fish, and controlling winter flows from the dams so they don't scour the river bottoms or break up any ice caps that form. ~ To reach the refuge, head 15 miles west of Vernal on Route 191/40 and then south 17 miles on Route 88; 435-789-0351.

▼▼▼▼▼▼▼▼▼▼▼▼▼▼
Outdoor Adventures

Chockfull as northeastern Utah is with mountains, national forests and state parks, you don't need to look far for something to do in the outdoors no matter what season you visit.

FISHING

Park City and Heber City's best fishing arguably can be found in the **Provo River**, both in the sections above and below **Jordanelle Dam** and farther south below **Deer Creek Dam**. Brown and rainbow trout are plentiful in both areas. Most anglers tend to overlook the stretch of the river that flows into the Jordanelle Reservoir near the state park's Rock Cliff area, so you can often find a more solitary, yet just as productive, fishing experience.

If you prefer lake fishing, both Jordanelle and Deer Creek reservoirs near Heber City feature boat ramps, fish-cleaning stations and sizeable populations of rainbow and cutthroat trout as well as smallmouth bass. Just off Route 40, 26 miles southeast of Heber City is **Strawberry Reservoir**, another popular fishing spot in summer and winter.

The **Green River** below Flaming Gorge Dam is an outstanding trout fishery, where as many as 22,000 trout per mile have been counted.

While the Wyoming portion of the **Flaming Gorge National Recreation Area** is predominately high desert, the Utah section offers pristine mountain scenery covered by thick forests of piñon pines and junipers and cut by steep canyons. While the reservoir holds bass and catfish, most anglers come for the lake trout, which can top 50 pounds. German trout weighing more than 30 pounds have also been pulled from the reservoir, as have rainbow trout over 25 pounds.

Other reliable reservoirs in the region include **Starvation Reservoir** west of Duchesne and **Steinaker** and **Red Fleet reservoirs** north of Vernal. **Pelican Lake**, off Route 88 south of Vernal, is a popular bluegill and bass fishery. Many of the trails in the Uinta, Wasatch-Cache and Ashley national forests lead to pristine mountain lakes stocked with trout, including rare Colorado cutthroats.

Outfitters & Guides   A few Park City–based guide services can lead you to fish. **Jan's Mountain Outfitters** offers free fly-casting lessons in the summer and guides trips to the Provo, Green and Weber rivers, as well as to lakes in the Uinta Mountains. ~ 1600 Park Avenue, Park City; 435-649-4949, 800-745-1020; www.jans. com. The **Park City Fly Shop** offers year-round guide service, fishing the Provo and Upper Green rivers. ~ 2065 Sidewinder Drive, Park City; 435-645-8382, 800-324-6778; www.pcflyshop.com. **Trout Bum 2** stalks the Provo, Green and Weber rivers, as well as high-country lakes. ~ 4343 North Route 224, Suite 101, Park City; 435-658-1166, 877-878-2862; www.troutbum2.com.

Flaming Gorge National Refuge Area outfitters include **Green River Outfitters**, which leads guided fishing trips on the Green River and the reservoir. ~ P.O. Box 368, Dutch John, UT 84023; 435-885-3338. **Conquest Expeditions** also guides on the Green and Flaming Gorge Reservoir. ~ P.O. Box 487, Manila, UT 84046; 435-784-3370. **Trout Creek Flies** also serves the area. ~ P.O. Box 247, Dutch John, UT 84023; 435-885-3355, 800-835-4551.

BOATING

While both Deer Creek and Jordanelle state parks revolve around their respective reservoirs, Jordanelle is the bigger of the two and therefore offers more play space on the water. Muscle-powered boats usually enter the reservoir in the long, watery arm near Rock Cliff, while power boats and other fuel-powered water toys and

HOT-AIR BALLOONING

Winter is the busy time for drifting above Park City's mountains in a colorful hot air balloon, although trips are possible throughout the year. Try **ABC Hot Air Balloons**. ~ 514 Main Street, Park City; 435-649-2223, 800-820-2223. Also offering trips above Park City is **Park City Balloon Adventures**. ~ P.O. Box 1344, Park City, UT 84060; 435-645-8787, 800-396-8787.

sailboats enter at Hailstone on the western shore of Jordanelle. The marinas at both state parks have rentals.

In Park City, try **Peak Experience,** which rents kayaks. ~ 875 Iron Horse Drive, Park City; 435-645-5366. Canoes, kayaks and fishing boats can be rented in Heber City from **Daytrips Outfitters.** ~ 625 North Main Street, Heber City; 435-654-8294, 888-654-8294.

At Flaming Gorge, boat rentals can be found at two local marinas. **Lucerne Marina,** which also rents fishing equipment and houseboats, is roughly 63 miles north of Vernal and seven miles east of Manila via Routes 191, 44 and 43. ~ P.O. Box 10, Manila, UT 84046; 435-784-3483, 888-820-9225. **Cedar Springs Marina,** about 45 miles north of Vernal and two miles west of Flaming Gorge Dam on Route 191, rents boats and offers guided tours. ~ P.O. Box 337, Dutch John, UT 84023; 435-889-3795.

CANOEING, KAYAKING & RIVER RUNNING

Most of the lakes in the Uinta Range are either too small or too hard to reach for paddling, although **Washington Lake, Trial Lake** and **Mirror Lake** along Route 150 east of Kamas and the **Smith and Morehouse Reservoir,** reached via State Route 213 north of Kamas, are all large enough and easily accessible for hours of canoeing fun.

Most of northeastern Utah's rivers are too small for paddling anything other than kayaks, and then only early in the floating season, although the Green, Yampa and White rivers to the north, east and south of Vernal have outstanding reputations with paddlers of kayaks, canoes and rafts. How experienced you are dictates which river you can handle on your own; you'd be best advised to sign on with one of the region's commercial outfitters.

The seven-mile stretch of **Green River** between the Flaming Gorge Dam and Little Hole makes a great day for an unguided trip and does not require permits. The rapids are timid, the views fantastic, and fishing incredible. Experienced paddlers can con-

BACK ON THE LOOSE

Until 1981 the black-footed ferret, a small, weasel-like animal, was thought to be extinct. But then a ranch dog near Meeteetse, Wyoming, lugged one home. Wyoming wildlife officials, in a bid to boost the numbers of what then was considered to be the rarest mammal in North America, embarked on a captive-breeding program that has since produced more than 2000 ferrets. As part of the effort to return the mammals to their historic habitat, about 70 ferrets were released into the Coyote Basin about 30 miles southwest of Vernal in fall 1999. Spotting them can be tricky, though, as the ferrets are largely nocturnal creatures.

tinue all the way to the Colorado border, stopping at campsites along the way. While the eight miles between Little Hole and Indian Crossing may contain Class III rapids, the 11-mile stretch between Indian Crossing and the Colorado border is gentle. For more information, contact the Flaming Gorge Ranger District. ~ Ashley National Forest, P.O. Box 279, Manila, UT 84046; 435-784-3445.

The Green and Yampa rivers through Dinosaur National Monument are popular with whitewater enthusiasts and are plied by a number of commercial companies. At high water, a Class IV rapid occasionally can be found on the Green River near the Gates of Lodore, although for the most part these two rivers feature Class III and lesser rapids through Dinosaur. For paddlers who aren't interested in commercial trips but are experienced with Class III waters, a nice daytrip through the monument begins at Rainbow Park and concludes about nine miles downstream at the Split Mountain Campground. Permits from the National Park Service are required for both commercial and private trips; applications can be obtained either from Dinosaur National Monument's river office or from the agency's website. ~ 970-374-2468; www.nps.gov.dino/river/riverdoc/appl.htm.

Outfitters   Paddlers can obtain river flow information by calling 800-277-7571. For a booklet outlining Utah's river outfitters, call the **Utah Travel Council**. ~ Council Hall, Salt Lake City, UT 84114; 801-538-1030, 800-200-1160; www.utah.com.

There are a number of raft companies that run these rivers.

Adrift Adventures plies the waters of the Green and Colorado rivers. ~ P.O. Box 192, Jensen, UT 84035; 435-789-3600, 800-824-0150; www.adrift.com.

Chapoose Canyon Adventures, owned by a member of the Ute Tribe, floats sections of the Green River and provides American Indian narration to areas considered sacred by the tribe. ~ P.O. Box 766, Fort Duchesne, UT 84026; 435-722-4072, 877-722-4001; www.chapoose.com.

Dinosaur River Expeditions navigates the Green and Yampa rivers through Dinosaur National Monument. ~ P.O. Box 3387, Park City, UT 84060; 435-649-8092, 800-247-6197; www.dino adv.com.

Trips down the Colorado, Green and Yampa rivers can be arranged through **Sheri Griffith Expeditions**. ~ 2231 South Route 191, Moab; 435-259-8229, 800-332-2439; www.griffithexp.com.

Sections of the Colorado, Green and Yampa rivers are run by **Hatch River Expeditions**. ~ P.O. Box 1150, Vernal, UT 84078; 435-789-4316, 800-342-8243; www.hatchriver.com.

Holiday Expeditions can arrange trips down the Colorado, Green, San Juan and Yampa rivers. ~ 544 East 3900 South, Salt Lake City; 801-266-2087, 800-624-6323; www.bikeraft.com.

Since 1985 **Centennial Canoe Outfitters** has offered a variety of multiday canoe trips down the Green and Colorado rivers. ~ P.O. Box 3365, Centennial, CO 80161; 303-755-3501, 877-353-1850; www.centennialcanoe.com.

DOWNHILL SKIING & SNOW-BOARDING Much of Utah's skiing credit goes to the resorts in the Park City area. A testament to the Park City resorts' challenging terrain are the 2002 Winter Olympic Games, which turned to the resorts for some of the Games' venues.

Salt Lake City gave its name to the 2002 Winter Olympic Games, but Park City lends its ambience, not to mention some pretty darn good skiing. From the middle of Main Street you can gaze south and see the manicured slopes of Deer Valley, the host for the slalom, mogul and aerial events during the Games, while to the west the runs of the Park City Mountain Resort, the host of the giant slalom and snowboarding events.

The **Park City Mountain Resort**, with 750 acres of bowls and 100 trails snaking down 3300 acres of skiable terrain, offers more uphill capacity than any other in the state with 14 lifts, four of which can haul six skiers or snowboarders at a time. You won't find the steepest terrain or the deepest powder in Utah here, but there is something for everyone, from first-time skiers to long-toothed experts and shredders. ~ 1310 Lowell Avenue, Park City; 435-649-8111, 800-222-7275; www.parkcitymountain.com.

Separated from the Park City Mountain Resort by just a narrow ridgeline of trees, the **Deer Valley Resort** epitomizes the elegance of alpine skiing. Green-clad hosts stand ready to unload your skis when you drive up to Snow Park Lodge at the base of the Bald Eagle Mountain or to take them from you at Silver Lake when you stop for a bite of lunch, and 35 to 50 percent of the terrain is manicured, seemingly with a fine-tooth comb, every night during the season. Nineteen lifts service 87 trails and six bowls spread across 1750 acres. While the resort, which bans snowboards, has long been frowned upon for lacking heart, that reputation is overcooked. Daly Chutes, Daly Bowl and Anchor Trees in Empire Canyon challenge the most experienced skier. ~ 2250 Deer Valley Drive South, Park City; 435-649-1000, 800-424-3337; www.deervalley.com.

Five miles north of Park City off Route 224 lies the area's other downhill ski and snowboarding area, **The Canyons**, which is blossoming into a year-round destination resort. Encompassing seven mountains, the resort spans 3300 heavily treed acres with 130 trails and a number of bowls reached via 13 lifts. ~ 4000 The Canyons Resort Drive, Park City; 435-649-5400, 888-226-9667; www.thecanyons.com.

Powder skiing without lifts? Hitch a ride—albeit an expensive one—with **Park City Powder Cats** and spend a day on 20,000 acres in the Uinta Mountains, knee-deep or higher in some of Utah's famously dry snow. After each run a comfy Snowcat hauls you back to the top of the mountain. ~ 1647 Short Line Road, Park City; 435-649-6596, 800-635-4719; www.pccats.com.

Ski Rentals Park City is home to a great number of ski shops in town for rentals, purchases and accessories. Two of the best, and Park City's oldest, are **ColeSport** and **Jan's Mountain Outfitters**. Both have a half-dozen or so shops scattered about town and area ski resorts. Their flagship stores face each other on Park Avenue. ~ ColeSport is at 1615 Park Avenue, 435-649-4806; Jan's is at 1600 Park Avenue, 435-649-4949, www.jans.com.

CROSS-COUNTRY SKIING

Skinny-ski fanatics have long used the meadows and mountains found throughout northeastern Utah for their exercise. While there's not an abundance of groomed cross-country resorts, the ones that exist are wonderful. The region's mountains offer mile after mile of ungroomed terrain for Nordic skiers.

PARK CITY AREA Cross-country-ski fans in the Park City area have only one choice for groomed trails—the **White Pine Touring Center**, which takes over the Park City Municipal Golf Course once the snow flies. There are 20 kilometers of groomed track for both classic and skate skiers; the ski shop handles rentals, sales and accessories. ~ Park Avenue, Park City; 435-615-5858.

For the adventurous, the **Norwegian Outdoor Exploration Center** can arrange an ambitious cross-country nature tour into the Uinta Mountains. A less strenuous guided twilight snowshoe tour in the mountains surrounding Park City is also available. ~ 333 Main Street, Park City; 435-649-5322, 800-649-5322.

HEBER CITY AREA The **Soldier Hollow** area of Wasatch Mountain State Park offers about 24 kilometers of trails for a wide variety of abilities. Most of the terrain is designed to test world-class athletes, however, so expect a tough workout. ~ Routes 113 and 224, Heber City; 435-654-1791.

The U.S. Forest Service also maintains ski trails in the Wasatch-Cache and Uinta forests. The **Beaver Creek Trail**, found along the Mirror Lake Highway east of Kamas in the Wasatch-Cache Forest,

RESORT CONNECTION

Five resorts, one day, one pass. It's possible with the **Ski Utah Interconnect Tour**, which leads higher-level skiers through the backcountry from the Park City Mountain Resort to Solitude, Brighton, Alta and Snowbird before calling it a day. If five different slopes in a day is just a tad bit too much, a four-resort excursion is also available. Reservations recommended. ~ 801-534-1907; www.skiutah.com.

is an easy, mostly flat trail ideal for beginners or a quick workout, while the **Little South Fork Trail** in the Uinta forest southeast of Heber along Route 35 is more demanding with rolling terrain.

VERNAL AREA In the Vernal area there are no groomed courses such as those in the Park City or Heber City areas, although there are eight defined backcountry routes that range in length from 2.5 miles to 12.5 miles. The **Canyon Rim Trail**, although lengthy at 12.5 miles round-trip, is relatively level and can be handled by novices and provides fantastic views of Red Canyon and the Uinta Mountains as well as the chance to spot moose and elk. More experienced skiers will like the **Dowd Mountain Trail**, a ten-mile loop that mixes flat and steep terrain and offers breathtaking vistas of Flaming Gorge, Red Canyon and the Uintas. Brochures describing these routes and providing directions to them can be obtained from the Dinosaurland Travel Board. ~ 25 East Main Street, Vernal; 435-789-6932, 800-477-5558; www.dinoland.com.

Utah is the second top ski state in the U.S. (Colorado ranks first).

GOLF Ski in the winter, golf in the summer. What better way to exercise in northeastern Utah? Obviously, more than a few souls share this sentiment, as evidenced by the many golf courses that can be found in the region.

PARK CITY AREA Already well-known for its skiing and snowboarding, Park City is building a reputation as a duffer's paradise. The thin air at the relatively high elevation of 7000 feet adds distance to drives and summer days never get unbearably hot.

The 18-hole **Park City Municipal Golf Course** is popular with locals who didn't splurge on the pricy memberships required at the Jeremy Ranch Golf Course or the Park Meadows Country Club. The par-72 municipal course is located near the base of the Park City Mountain Resort and has 6400 yards of rolling terrain dotted with small lakes, aspens and firs. ~ 1451 Thaynes Canyon Drive, Park City; 435-615-5800.

A 20-minute drive northwest of Park City via Routes 224 and 80 lies **Mountain Dell**, a rolling, 18-hole, 6150-yard course that's nestled in Parley's Canyon. ~ 3287 Cummings Road, Salt Lake City; 801-484-3333.

HEBER CITY AREA The Heber City–Midway area has two golf courses. The **Homestead** offers an 18-hole, par-72, 7000-yard course with a sweeping view of the Heber Valley. ~ 700 North Homestead Drive, Midway; 435-654-1102, 800-327-7220. **Wasatch Mountain State Park**'s 27 holes are laid out in a fashion that allows duffers to play mountain, valley or lake courses. ~ Routes 113 and 224, Heber City; golf course 435-654-0532.

VERNAL AREA The 6780-yard, par-72 **Dinaland Golf Course** features 18 holes against a backdrop of the Uinta Mountains. ~

675 South 2000 East, Vernal; 435-781-1428. In Roosevelt, the 18-hole **Roosevelt Golf Course** offers an array of land and water hazards, and features one hole where the green is on an island. ~ 1155 Clubhouse Drive, Roosevelt; 435-722-9644.

Through winter and summer, on designated trails and across mountain meadows, riding on the back of a horse is a great way to get to know a place.

RIDING STABLES

Experienced riders can gallop through the mountains surrounding Park City with **Wind in Your Hair Riding**. ~ 2565 South State Road 32, Wanship; 435-649-4795, 435-655-1190; www.windinyourhair.com.

Horse rides can also be arranged through the **Rocking "R" Ranch** on its 2000-acre spread, or at the Deer Valley Resort or Park City Mountain Resort. ~ 435-645-7256, 800-303-7256; www.rockymtnrec.com.

In the Vernal area, **All 'Round Ranch** offers multiday horse trips into the surrounding mountains. ~ P.O. Box 153, Jensen, UT 84035; 435-789-7626, 800-603-8069; www.allround.com.

Horseback trips into the Uinta Mountains, either for fishing or just to enjoy the scenery, are available through a number of outfitters. For a thorough directory of those who lead trips into the Uintas, contact the **Utah Travel Council**. ~ Council Hall, Salt Lake City; 801-538-1030, 800-200-1160; www.utah.com.

PACK TRIPS & LLAMA TREKS

The folks at **All 'Round Ranch** can take you on multiday trips that mix riding across the Blue Mountain Plateau near Dinosaur National Monument with helping wranglers keep track of cattle. You'll learn how to round up strays, use a branding iron, and even move herds around. ~ P.O. Box 153, Jensen, UT 84035; 435-789-7626, 800-603-8069; www.allroundranch.com.

While you'll find a few road-bike fanatics pedaling across northeastern Utah when warm weather arrives, far and away mountain bikes are the preferred mode of travel for those who like to ride. With ski resorts turning into mountain biking resorts in the summer, and the endless miles of trail in national forests, this comes as no surprise.

BIKING

PARK CITY AREA   In the Park City area, mountain bikes replace skis on the tops of locals' cars when the snow melts, and for good reason. Each of the three Park City resorts has miles and miles of lift-served bike trails, and the surrounding national forests offer single-track trails as well as forest roads that are perfect for exploring on bike. Maps of the biking possibilities in the Park City area can be found at the town's bike shops.

A popular, 20-mile, out-and-back trail with locals (and one of the most picturesque in the area), is the **Ridge Trail**, aka the

Wasatch Crest Trail. This breathtaking—both due to the views as well as the uphills—single-track route follows the ridgeline from the Deer Valley Resort, across the top of the Park City Mountain Resort and past The Canyons.

The **Deer Valley Resort** boasts one of the best mountain bike schools in the state, and has miles of trails to support it. Cyclists can either ride a chairlift to the top of Bald Mountain and follow one of numerous single- or double-track trails that wind their way back to the base, or slog it uphill from the bottom to the top and then back down.

The **Historic Union Pacific Rail Trail** runs 26 miles from Park City to Echo Junction and makes for a fun ride, although it tilts downhill a bit heading to Echo, making the return trip something of a grunt if the day is hot.

During late summer, wild currants, chokecherries and service berries ripen along the Historic Union Pacific Rail Trail, making it easy to stop for a while and munch.

Round Valley offers a six-mile-long route on the east side of Park City that is easy enough for beginners yet challenging enough to keep more experienced riders happy. Starting near the National Ability Center's equestrian center on Route 248, the trail follows a relatively level path to Trailside Park.

Advanced bikers gut their way up the **Sweeney Switchbacks**, a two-mile-long series of switchbacks that cuts back and forth through aspens and evergreens as it climbs uphill. The trail, which starts near the south end of Lowell Avenue in Park City, connects to the Park City Mountain Resort trail system.

VERNAL AREA   In the Vernal area, numerous hiking/biking trails wind through the Ashley National Forest. In Dinosaur National Monument, a 20-mile loop stitches together paved roads, dirt roads and even a section of slickrock for mountain bikers.

A 21.5-mile route through **Dry Fork Canyon** ten miles north of Vernal via the Dry Fork Canyon Road is perfect for road bikers and leads to dramatic displays of petroglyphs. The gentle grade makes this a good family ride.

Views of Flaming Gorge Reservoir and the Uinta Range are blended with Western history at the historic **Swett Ranch**. A six-mile mountain bike loop that follows graded roads around the ranch property, which contains a collection of old farm implements and offers some insight into pioneer life, winds through aspen groves and crosses streams.

Bike Rentals   In the Park City area, bike rentals, repairs and sales can be found at **ColeSport** (1615 Park Avenue; 435-649-4806), **Jan's Mountain Outfitters** (1600 Park Avenue; 435-649-4949) and **White Pine Touring** (201 Heber Avenue; 435-659-8710).

Sacred Bear Adventures, a cycling outfitter, can put together one-day and multiday trips not only in northeastern Utah but also in the southern half of the state. ~ 33 Racquet Club Drive, Park City; 435-655-7250, 888-842-3274; www.sacredbear.com.

More trail information and rentals in the Vernal area can be found at **Altitude Cycle**. ~ 510 East Main Street, Suite 8, Vernal; 435-781-2595. Or try **Basin Saw and Cycle**. ~ 450 North Vernal Avenue, Vernal; 435-781-1226.

The Wasatch-Cache, Uinta and Ashley national forests all offer incredible backcountry trails that quickly lead you into the aspen and conifer forests that blanket the mountains. All distances listed for hiking trails are one way unless otherwise noted.

HIKING

The Mirror Lake Highway (Route 150), that runs 80 miles between Kamas and Evanston, Wyoming, is the quickest way to get into the Uinta Mountains. Shared by the three forests, the Uintas offer everything from developed campgrounds that are over-run just about every summer weekend to primeval forest.

Close to Kamas, the **Yellow Pine Trail** (4 miles) starts off Route 150 six miles east of Kamas and runs to Yellow Pine Lakes; it's a steep trail in places that quickly tests your stamina. The reward is a wonderful subalpine setting bursting with wildflowers in midsummer.

Across the road from the Yellow Pine parking area is the **Beaver Creek Trail** that parallels its namesake creek. Offering a wonderful, not-too-strenuous hike for youngsters, during the winter months this trail is perfect for classic skiing, leading skiers through aspen groves and thick pockets of conifers. How far you ski is up to you, although a 4-mile out-and-back ski is perfect for a half-day outing.

The **Shingle Creek Trail** (5 miles) is found only about three miles east of the Yellow Pine trailhead and follows its namesake creek north towards Shingle Creek Lake. While it starts out some-what rugged in terms of steepness and rocks, the trail soon be-gins to parallel the creek while climbing gently through thick for-est. In winter, this is a wonderful place to retreat with snowshoes.

Kids like the **Mirror Lake Shoreline Trail** (1.5 miles), found 31 miles east of Kamas along Route 150. Circling the lake, it offers countless opportunities for tossing stones into the water or fishing; adults like the views of Bald Mountain and Hayden Peak.

Thirty-four miles east of Kamas is the **Highline Trail** (60 miles), which runs along the roof of the Uintas, crossing the headwaters of many drainages along the way. From the trailhead along Route 150 it takes just a mile to reach the High Uintas Wilderness bound-ary. Seven and a half miles from the trailhead you reach Rocky Sea Pass, a rocky, above-treeline pass cluttered with huge boulders that inspired the area's name. The trail is for the most part a nice hike, rising only 1200 feet and passing several small lakes along the way, although the final push to the pass is over steep, rocky terrain.

Forty-six miles east of Kamas along Route 150 lies the trail to **Christmas Meadows** (2.5 miles), passing willow thickets that are favorites with moose and aspen forest before climbing uphill along a cascading creek. Six miles from the trailhead lies **Amethyst Lake**, a shimmering high-country lake with several prime campsites.

Kings Peak, the highest point in Utah at 13,528 feet, can be reached from the **Henry's Fork Trailhead**, which is reached by taking the Route 80 business loop that runs through Evanston, Wyoming, and then heading south to Mountain View, where you need to take Route 410 to the trailhead. The hike to Kings Peak through Gunsight Pass runs 12 miles one way and gains 4200 feet.

In the Uinta National Forest, the 11,788-foot summit of **Mountain Timpanogos Trail** (6 miles) starts from either the North Fork in Provo Canyon or the Timpooneke Campground in American Fork Canyon.

In the Ashley National Forest, one of the best routes into the High Uintas Wilderness is via the **Uinta Canyon Trailhead**, also known as the Uinta River Trailhead, found near the U-Bar Ranch 18 miles north of Neola via Route 121. Three miles down the trail lies the wilderness area's boundary; 12 miles in lies Lake Atwood, a sprawling lake scooped out of the landscape by long-gone glaciers.

Two popular hikes in Dinosaur National Monument are the treks to Jones Hole and Harper's Corner. The short **Harper's Corner Trail** (1 mile) provides great geology lessons and fantastic views into the canyons created by the Green and Yampa rivers. The hike into **Jones Hole Trail** (4 miles) starts at the Jones Hole National Fish Hatchery, located about an hour's drive from the dinosaur quarry via the Brush Creek Road and Diamond Mountain Road. This trail passes by various faults and formations and mixes in prehistoric rock art. About 1.8 miles down the trail lies the **Island Park Trail**. Just a quarter-mile up this trail is a nice waterfall surrounded by Douglas fir and birch trees, something you wouldn't expect from the more desert-like surroundings in the rest of the monument. A third of a mile past the waterfall is a fork in the trail—the left fork runs 7.5 miles to the historic Ruple Ranch in Island Park, the right-hand fork runs another two or three miles into a series of box canyons known as the Labyrinths.

AUTHOR FAVORITE

The one-mile **Stewart Falls Trail** is an enjoyable, kid-friendly hike in the Uinta National Forest that starts at the Sundance Resort and roams through the forests below Mount Timpanogos to a gorgeous waterfall that's most furious in the early summer as snowmelt spills off the mountain. The trail follows a gentle grade through aspen and evergreens before reaching the moss-covered base of the 40-foot-tall waterfall.

Routes 80 and 40 are the main travel corridors through northeastern Utah. While 80, an interstate freeway, heads east past Park City before entering western Wyoming near Evanston, 40 dips south near Park City and then veers east through Duchesne, Roosevelt and Vernal before entering Colorado.

Transportation

CAR

Route 191 runs north from Vernal, past Flaming Gorge National Recreation Area and on to Rock Springs, Wyoming, and south to Price, Green River and eventually Moab. Route 150 runs northeast from Kamas through the Wasatch-Cache National Forest to Evanston, Wyoming.

For road and travel information, call 801-964-6000.

AIR

The Salt Lake International Airport is 36 miles west of Park City off Route 80. See Chapter Two for more information.

Commuter service via Skywest (800-453-9417) is available from Salt Lake International to Vernal Municipal Airport.

BUS

Greyhound Bus Lines (800-231-2222) serves northeastern Utah from Salt Lake City. It operates on a flag stop basis through Park City, Heber City and Duchesne, with a station stop in Vernal.

Lewis Brothers Stages serves Park City from Salt Lake City. ~ 549 West 500 South, Salt Lake City; 801-359-8677, 800-826-5844; www.lewisbros.com.

CAR RENTALS

Rentals in Park City can be arranged through All-Resort Car Rental (435-649-3999), Budget Rent A Car (435-645-7555, 800-237-7251), Mountain Car Rental (435-649-7626) and Park City Car Rentals (435-658-0403, 800-724-7767).

In Heber City, Daytrips Outfitters can line you up with a car or four-wheel-drive vehicle. ~ 675 North Main Street, Heber City; 435-654-8294, 888-654-8294. Avis Rent A Car (800-331-1212) has a desk at the municipal airport in Vernal.

PUBLIC TRANSIT

Park City has a free shuttle bus system that operates within the city limits. Between Memorial Day and Labor Day the buses run daily between 7:30 a.m. until 10:30 p.m. During the ski season the schedule shifts slightly to 7 a.m. to 1 a.m.

TAXIS

Among the taxi companies serving Park City are Park City Taxi (435-649-8515), Powder for the People (435-649-6648) and Ace Cab Company (435-649-8294). In Heber City, you can catch a ride from Daytrips Transportation. ~ 675 North Main Street, Heber City; 435-654-8294, 888-654-8294. When in Vernal, Vernal Cab can move you about town. ~ 44 West Main Street, Vernal; 435-790-1212.

FIVE

2002
Olympic Winter Games

More than three decades in the making, the Salt Lake Games are as much a celebration of winter sports as well as a proclamation to the rest of the world that Utah has some pretty incredible mountains and snow to go with them. Since the 1960s Utah's capital has chased the Games, not only to play host to the world's athletes but also to showcase the Wasatch Range as a world-class winter destination.

Twice the city's Olympic bids finished second to Japanese cities: in 1966, when Sapporo was selected to host the 1972 Winter Olympics, and again in 1991, when the 1998 Games were handed to Nagano. The disappointment of losing fueled the tenacity of the Salt Lake Bid Committee's 2002 bid. With nearly $7 million in private funds, committee members traveled the world to court International Olympic Committee members and brought many to Utah to see first-hand the venues that either already were in place or where under construction. Additionally, the committee enlisted the help of the U.S. State Department, which had its embassies invite IOC delegates to dinner. Determined not to miss any lobbying opportunities, in 1994, when Lillehammer, Norway, played host to the Winter Games, the Salt Lake Bid Committee rented a 260-year-old Norwegian farmhouse and had a Salt Lake City restaurant corporation fly its chefs, culinary equipment and food to the Games so IOC members could be courted over dinner. Among the IOC guests who came to dinner were Prince Albert of Monaco and Norway's King Harald. Among the hosts was NFL great Steve Young, a descendant of Brigham Young.

Not surprisingly, when it came time in June 1995 to select a site for the 2002 Olympic Winter Games, IOC members meeting in Budapest could not overlook Salt Lake City's technological advantages—many of its venues were already in place while other bid cities had theirs on drawing boards. The resulting vote was a landslide for Salt Lake City, which defeated Sion, Switzerland; Ostersund, Sweden; and Quebec, Canada, on the IOC's first ballot; not in 30 years had a city won the right to host a Games on the first ballot involving more than two cities.

Although a bid scandal, based on accusations that the bid committee used bribes ranging from free medical care to free tuition at Utah universities to curry favor with some IOC members, later raised doubts about Salt Lake City's win, the bottom line that can't be refuted is that the city's bid was superior to the others.

The infrastructure Utahns erected in anticipation of some day hosting an Olympics—the Utah Olympic Park with its bobsleigh, luge, and skeleton track and ski-jumping hills, the Utah Olympic Oval and the Soldier Hollow cross-country complex, not to mention the state's existing alpine resorts—has convinced quite a few of America's top athletes to move to Utah for training. Downhill speed queen Picabo Street is the director of skiing at the Park City Mountain Resort, top freestyle skiers Eric Bergoust and Joe Pack both live in Park City, as does 2001 World Cup skeleton champion Lincoln DeWitt, and Jean Racine and Jen Davidson, the world's best female bobsledders heading into the Olympic winter of 2002, also call Utah home.

Although he doesn't compete any more, the dean of Utah's winter Olympic athletes is Stein Eriksen, a Norwegian who in the 1950s dominated international ski racing. The gold medalist in the giant slalom at the VI Winter Games in Oslo in 1952, in 1954 this golden Norseman crushed the competition at the World Championships to become the first alpine skier ever to win the giant slalom, slalom and combined events at one competition. Today Eriksen is director of skiing at the Deer Valley Resort, where he spends most winter days making turns despite his 70-plus years.

▼ ▼ ▼ ▼ ▼ ▼ ▼ ▼ ▼ ▼ ▼ ▼ ▼

Survival Strategies

Surviving the XIX Olympic Winter Games is more than merely landing some tickets (although that's a necessary start), finding a place to stay, and making sure you have dinner reservations long before you arrive. Here are a few tips you might find useful when preparing for your Olympic trip.

CLIMATE

Face it, the bulk of these Games is being contested outdoors in the middle of a Rocky Mountain winter. How much cold should you be prepared to endure? The Utah Olympic Park, home to the bobsleigh, luge, skeleton, ski jumping and Nordic combined events, just might be the Games' coldest venue. In mid-February the temperature there can be in the single digits (or below) early in the morning and head there in the early evening, when some events will be getting under way. The Deer Valley, Park City, Soldier Hollow and Snowbasin venues can also have brutal conditions.

Another concern is Utah's altitude. If you're coming from sea level, the thinner air at 4000 feet and above will very likely leave you exhausted the first day or two. A telltale sign that the altitude is troublesome is a headache. The best way to deal with this is to take it easy the first few days and drink plenty of water.

Another climate-related problem is a bloody nose brought on by the dry air. Compared to coastal states, Utah has no natural humidity. At least it feels that way. Lip balm helps your lips cope with this, while hand and body lotion will relieve the rest of your body. Many lodgings near the alpine venues often have humidifiers available so don't hesitate to ask for one to make sleeping easier and to help your nostrils combat the dryness.

PACKING   Since you need to be just as prepared for blizzard conditions as for a gorgeous spring-like day courtesy of warm chinook winds, you'd be wise to dress warmly in layers. Try a synthetic turtleneck covered by a thick wool sweater and topped off with a weather-resistant shell jacket that offers either a synthetic or down layer of insulation. Then, cover your legs in a good pair of water-resistant or waterproof shell pants that you can wear over a nice warm pair of fleece pants.

Night or day, a good pair of warm, comfortable hiking boots will be invaluable since you'll spend part of your time walking to the venues and part of it milling about the venues. Most spectators will also spend all their time on their feet during the events, although there will be some reserved seating. For daytime events, a wide-brimmed hat shades your face from the bright sun (for which you'd be wise to also invest in sunglasses)—even though it's winter, at Utah's relatively high elevation the radiation is more intense than at sea level. Don't forget to slather on some quality sunscreen, too, for while the hat might block the sunshine from above, snow-covered ground does a great job of reflecting the rays back up at you! Come nightfall, be sure to have a good warm hat, one that you can pull down over your ears.

Don't forget gloves or mittens, and bring a daypack to stow items. It also wouldn't hurt to toss a bottle or two of water into your pack each day. Standing outside for hours can be dehydrating, and quaffing your own beverage is a lot cheaper than buying something on-site.

LAST-MINUTE PLANNING   **LODGING**   No Olympic Games, summer or winter, has ever been sold out. Although room reservations might have seemed impossible to find before the Games opened, rooms often become more available the closer the opening ceremonies approach, as sponsors who previously locked up large blocks of rooms begin to release those they don't need. To track down these available rooms, log on to the following websites and click on the links to lodging. ~ www.saltlake2002.com, www.saltlakeinfo.org. Or, you can call the Visitor Information Services Coalition of Utah (VIS). ~ 888-222-5562.

DINING   Many northern Utah restaurants began taking reservations months ago, so get on the phone now. You can expect reservations to be hard to obtain, as some establishments are being

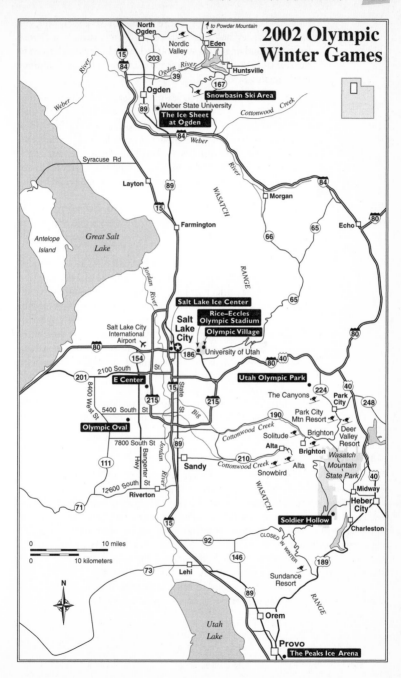

2002 Olympic Winter Games

to Powder Mountain

North Ogden

Nordic Valley

Eden

Huntsville

167

Snowbasin Ski Area

203

84
15

Ogden River

39

Ogden

89

Weber State University

Cottonwood Creek

The Ice Sheet at Ogden

84 Weber

Weber River

Syracuse Rd

Layton

89

Morgan

84

15

65

Echo

80

Farmington

66

WASATCH

Antelope Island

Great Salt Lake

Jordan River

RANGE

65

80

Salt Lake Ice Center

Rice-Eccles Olympic Stadium

Olympic Village

Salt Lake City International Airport

Salt Lake City

186

University of Utah

80 40

2100 South

154 St

201

E Center

8400 West St

Utah Olympic Park

40

The Canyons

224

Park City

248

215

15

State St

215

Big

190

Park City Mtn Resort

Deer Valley Resort

5400 South St

Olympic Oval

Cottonwood Creek

Solitude

Brighton

Brighton

7800 South St

89

Alta

Wasatch Mountain State Park

40

111

Jordan River

Bangerter Hwy

210

Cottonwood Creek

Alta

Snowbird

Midway

Sandy

12600 South St

Heber City

Riverton

71

15

Soldier Hollow

Charleston

0   10 miles

92

CLOSED IN WINTER

0   10 kilometers

146

189

73

Lehi

N

Sundance Resort

89

RANGE

Orem

Utah Lake

Provo

The Peaks Ice Arena

booked exclusively for the entire Games by sponsors. Still, the Salt Lake Valley has a wide spectrum of fine eateries to choose from, and outlying areas such as the Heber Valley and Kamas to the east of Park City have some good restaurants that might not book up so quickly.

TICKETS Believe it or not, scalping is legal in Utah. To accommodate ticketholders who can't attend their events, the Organizing Committee plans to have specially designated areas where those tickets can be sold to the highest bidder. Additionally, the committee plans to have officials on hand to authenticate the tickets. You also can check the Organizing Committee's website to see which events have tickets remaining. ~ www.saltlake2002.com.

GETTING AROUND

CAR RENTALS If you're renting a car, front-wheel drive should be sufficient. Utah's highway department does a pretty good job clearing snowstorms off the pavement, so a four-wheel-drive really isn't necessary.

Whether you've got tickets for an outdoor or indoor event, plan on getting an early start to the venue. Traffic jams *will* occur and parking *will* be difficult at best. The Salt Lake Organizing Committee started to worry about Games-time transportation months ago. Its solutions will, in some cases, inconvenience visitors as well as add to their expenses. Though the organizing committee has arranged for sprawling parking lots near some alpine venues, many of those require you to then ride a bus to the venue. With some lots holding upwards of 7000 vehicles, those bus lines could be substantial.

Many fans, no doubt, would find such lines welcome at the Utah Olympic Park, where ticket holders will be expected to walk

CREAM OF THE CROP

Who will be competing for the U.S. at the Salt Lake Games? That's hard to say: the entire Team U.S. won't be decided until late January since some U.S. Olympic Trials events don't conclude until January 27th. Many of the teams will be selected during competitions in late December and early January. For instance, the men's and women's bobsleigh teams will be selected during year-end competitions at the Utah Olympic Park, the skeleton teams on January 2, also at the park, and the biathlon teams during competitions stretching between December 26th to January 8th at Soldier Hollow. The U.S. Ski Team isn't scheduled to name its Olympic delegation until January 27th—its athletes will be chosen based on their performance at World Cup races.

uphill nearly a mile to the venue, a stroll that could leave low-landers gasping for breath. Add bitter cold or a snowstorm and that walk will be particularly nasty. The organizing committee does plan to have some buses available to assist those who really can't make that march, but it expects most ticket holders to walk.

Whether you'll be charged to park in the lots was uncertain at press time; the organizing committee was considering not only a parking fee but also a surcharge for those who don't carpool.

BUS SERVICE   The organizing committee plans to offer bus service from downtown Salt Lake City to the mountain venues. Transport from Salt Lake City to Snowbasin, Utah Olympic Park, Deer Valley Resort, Park City Mountain Resort and Soldier Hollow may cost as much as $30 per person roundtrip. Additionally, there will be service from Weber State University Football Stadium in Ogden to Snowbasin and from Utah Valley State College in Provo to Soldier Hollow for $20 roundtrip. Contact SLOC (866-566-4428; www.saltlake2002.com) for details. This might be a nice option if you don't want the hassle of driving into the mountains, but if you want to linger in Park City after an event you'll have to find your own way back to Salt Lake City, as the buses are scheduled to return to the capital approximately two hours after an event.

Perhaps the most beautiful of the 2002 Olympic Winter Games venues is Bear Hollow, a tree-flanked bowl nestled in a finger of the Wasatch

Utah Olympic Park

Range just north of Park City along Route 224. Officially known as the Utah Olympic Park, this 389-acre setting is the crown jewel of Utah's Olympic movement, combining the natural beauty of the surrounding mountains and their elk, deer and moose herds with engineering masterpieces needed for the Winter Games' sliding and jumping events.

Sprung from a dream that Salt Lake City might one day host an Olympic Winter Games, the park began to take form in 1991—four years before Salt Lake City was awarded the 2002 Winter Games. Paid for through a voter-endorsed tax diversion, the facility partially opened in 1993 when its ski-jumping facilities were finished.

Four years later the bobsleigh, luge and skeleton track was completed—a 4400-foot-long icy labyrinth that, while not an overly technical course, is one of the world's fastest due to the relatively thin air at Bear Hollow's high elevation. Situated at 7226 feet above sea level, the track is the world's highest.

More than 14,000 spectators are expected to check out each of the ten days of bobsleigh, luge and skeleton competition. In bobsleigh, men will race in both two-man and four-man events, while

Text continued on page 214.

There's More to an
Olympics than Athletics

Attending the Olympics goes beyond watching athletic competitions. After all, the Games are a cultural melting pot: athletes from roughly 80 countries, many with fan bases in tow, come in search of gold, silver and bronze.

Salt Lake City and Utah will enhance that backdrop with its rich and varied landscapes and Old West rituals and mannerisms. Beyond that, the Salt Lake Organizing Committee has procured a diverse lineup of entertainment that reflects America's eclectic cultural tastes, from the classic vibrato of violinist Itzhak Perlman and the sultry riffs of the Billy Taylor Trio and other jazz outfits to the cowboy wit of Waddie Mitchell.

These artists and many others are part of the Cultural Olympiad that will run throughout the Games as the Olympics' official arts festival, a celebration that places art and athletics side by side. Stray from the Games' field of play and you'll be able to choose from among 49 major events, 6 major art exhibitions, and countless community celebrations.

For those who want to come away from the Games with a taste of the American West, the Olympic Command Performance Rodeo slated for the Games' opening weekend pits the greatest U.S. cowboys against a likewise remarkable team from Canada at the Davis County Legacy Center in Farmington. Waddie Mitchell, one of America's greatest cowboy poets, will put his homespun twist on the West as he tries to explain and describe cowboy life through humor and songs during a performance at the Capitol Theatre in the heart of Salt Lake City. The cowboy with the heavy handlebar mustache was even commissioned by the organizing committee to script a poem reflecting the Olympic spirit and produced one aptly named, "That No Quit Attitude."

"I believe, like dogs and horses, we're all born with resolution and, like muscles and good habits, it needs use and exercise," reads part of Mitchell's work. "If left dormant it's in jeopardy of loss to evolution, for eventually it shrivels up in atrophy and dies. But when flexed it blossoms heroes and a source of inspiration, for we recognize the virtues of that 'no quit' attitude. And it proves its attributes in competition and vocation, which evokes appreciation and a show of gratitude."

While Itzhak Perlman's Abravanel Hall performance with the Utah Symphony sold out almost immediately after tickets went on sale last

February, a handful of other concerts can be found during and even after the Olympics. Elaine Paige, recognized as the "first lady" of British musical theater, will be backed by the symphony while performing a number of Andrew Lloyd Webber's works in mid-February. Jazz pianist Billy Taylor and other renowned jazz artists will perform in the hall February 10th; four days later Taylor's trio will move over to the Capitol Theatre and attempt to answer the question, "What is jazz?"

Kids have hope of being entertained at the Cultural Olympiad, too: Peter Seeger and the Children's Dance Theater will perform a selection of time-honored American folk music and children's dance at the Capitol Theatre on February 11th.

Adults who love dance will have many choices. The Jose Limon Dance Company will premiere "Limon and Jazz" during the Cultural Olympiad at the Browning Center for Performing Arts in Ogden; the Ririe-Woodbury Dance Company will showcase a work commissioned for the Games at the Capitol Theatre on February 13th; and the Pilobolus Dance Theatre, also commissioned by the organizing committee, will perform at the Capitol Theatre on February 16th and 17th and at the George S. and Dolores Dore Eccles Center for the Performing Arts on the 19th. The Repertory Dance Theatre will look back on the rich history of modern dance on February 21, when, for the first time in seven decades, Martha Graham's Diversion of Angels, Doris Humphrey's With My Red Fires and Helen Tamaris' Dance for Walt Whitman are performed together. Productions by the American Folk Ballet, Ballet West, the Axis Dance Company and Savion Glover, a Tony Award–winning tap dancer, will also be featured by the Cultural Olympiad.

No visit to Salt Lake City would be complete without taking in a performance by the Mormon Tabernacle Choir. Through February and into March the choir will perform with a number of guest artists ranging from Frederica Von Stade and Evelyn Glennie to the King's Singers.

Exhibits are also part of the Cultural Olympiad, and one allows you to appreciate the works of one of America's greatest glass smiths. Dale Chihuly, who has displayed his glass artworks throughout the world, will have a series of glass pieces commissioned by the Salt Lake Organizing Committee on display at the Salt Lake Art Center from late January into mid-March. American Indian artists weren't overlooked when the Cultural Olympiad's schedule was compiled. Sixteen sculptures by the late Allan Houser, considered one of the country's most influential and respected American Indian artists, will be on display at the Salt Lake City and County Building from fall 2001 to mid-March 2002.

women will be featured in a two-woman race. Luge will feature men's and women's singles as well as mixed doubles, an event that typically involves two men, while skeleton features men's and women's singles.

These sliding sports are some of the most spectator-friendly of the Games, allowing fans close proximity to the athletes and the track as well as the adrenaline that speed can generate in both competitors and spectators. They're also some of the most technically demanding sports—not only are bobsleigh, luge and skeleton sleds built to exacting specifications, they're closely policed for weight and even runner temperatures.

A short walk from the bobsleigh/luge/skeleton track rise the three jumping hills that will be used during three days of ski-jumping competition and three days of Nordic combined, a competition that blends ski jumping with cross-country skiing. There are three ski-jumping competitions (two individual events and one team event) and three Nordic combined events (two individual and one team event). Room exists for roughly 20,000 spectators to watch these events.

GETTING THERE
The Utah Olympic Park is located 25.4 miles southeast from the Olympic Village in Salt Lake City. From the capital, head southeast on Route 80 to Exit 145. At the light turn south onto Route 224 and proceed less than a half-mile to the park's parking area. Large parking lots exist near the park, although during the Games spectators will be expected to walk nearly a mile uphill to the bobsleigh track and jumping hills. ~ 3000 Bear Hollow Drive, Park City; 435-658-4200.

SIGHT LINES
Where's the best spot to watch Bear Hollow's sliding events? If you're interested in the poetry-in-motion of bobsleigh and skeleton starts, elbow your way into a spot along the top 50 meters

ROYAL COMPETITION

Although he's never finished better than 19th in Olympic competition, the Prince of Monaco—Albert Alexandre Louis Pierre Grimaldi—hopes to be in the starting field once again when the four-man bobsleigh competition opens at the Utah Olympic Park. Perhaps the prince, who competed at the Calgary Games in 1988, the Albertville Games in 1992, the Lillehammer Games in 1994, and the Nagano Games in 1998, could enhance his medal prospects by switching sports and seasons. His grandfather, Jack Kelly, Sr., won three gold medals in rowing while competing in the 1920 and 1924 Summer Games. His son, Jack Kelly, Jr., won bronze in rowing in 1956.

of the track near the start. Like turns? Head for turn 6, nick-named "Snowy," where racers whip through a 180-degree turn, or the inside of turn 12, the Olympic curve where the Salt Lake 2002 emblem is painted onto the course. Turns are also the best places to watch luge. Just be sure not to let your eyes stray from the track once the lugers are on their way down, as they whip by incredibly fast and are gone.

Prefer mayhem? If there's going to be a crash in either the bob-sleigh or luge events, it most likely will occur coming out of turn 13 or somewhere in turn 14, aptly named "Sling Shot," and there's plenty of room along this section of track to watch. Under luge rules, athletes cannot cross the finish line without their sled, so if an athlete crashes in one of these turns and is determined to fin-ish, you'll be well-positioned here to watch as they struggle along the icy track while holding onto their sled.

There are two main areas to watch ski jumpers and Nordic combined competitors—in a sprawling area just beyond the land-ing zone at the base of the jumps and on terraces along the sides of the ski jumps. At the base, bleachers will be able to handle 11,000 spectators, who will pay slightly higher ticket prices for this option; another 10,000 will encounter standing-room-only views. If you're standing, head to the terraces for a unique per-spective on this sport.

Concession food is good for tiding you over during an event, but for a real meal in a relaxing and warm atmosphere following the races, head over to **Sage Grill** (page 168).

DINING TIPS

UTAH OLYMPIC PARK EVENTS

Bobsleigh

One of the original Olympic Winter Games sports, bobsleigh (bobsled to us Yanks) pits powerful sprinters in a con-test of speed measured in hundredths of seconds. Although the sled has progressed through a variety of evolutions through the decades, the basics remain intact: Get the sled going with a burst of speed from the athletes, who then synchronize graceful leaps into the sled, and have the driver deftly yet ever-so-slightly steer the sled by pulling on two ropes, much as you would a Flexible Flyer. Speed is built through the powerful start and by whipping through curves along perfect "lines"; it can be lost by bouncing the sled off the icy walls along the way to the finish.

At Bear Hollow, 15 curves and speeds approaching 90 mph confront the men's and women's teams that are scheduled to compete over a ten-day period. Men's competition features both two-person and four-person sleds; women compete only in the two-person category.

The men's competition is held over two days, with teams making two runs each day. The winner is determined on the combined time of those four runs. The women's competition involves two runs made on one day, with the lowest combined time dictating the gold medalist.

On the men's side, the Germans are powerful. Christoph Langen, who drove to victory in the four-man race at the Nagano Games in 1998, should be back to defend his Olympic title. Although slowed last season by leg injuries, Langen was also more focused on testing equipment than winning. Nevertheless, he drove to victory in the 2001 World Championships four-man race.

Fellow German Andre Lange was second at the World Championships but won the 2001 overall World Cup title so can't be counted out, nor can countryman Matthias Benesch, who finished second in the World Cup standings last season.

Challenges to the Germans should come from Swiss drivers Martin Annen and Christian Reich or Latvia's Sandis Prusis. The Americans, despite racing at home, are dark horses. If one U.S. sled is to rise to the occasion, it could be that of driver Todd Hays, who won last season's final race and finished fourth in the World Cup standings.

In the two-man race, a handful of drivers in the field could medal: Switzerland's Annen, who won the overall World Cup title a year ago; Reich; Germans Rene Spies or Andre Lange, who finished second and third in the overall standings; or Canadian Pierre Lueders, the gold medalist at Nagano.

OLYMPIC VILLAGE

To accommodate the 3500 athletes, coaches and officials during the Salt Lake Games, the Salt Lake Organizing Committee built the 70-acre Olympic Village, which required U.S. Defense Department permission to center the complex around Fort Douglas, a military post that dates to the Civil War. These 21 one- to three-bedroom apartment units are decorated with artworks produced by Utah schoolchildren. Along with the housing, the Olympic Village—which is off-limits to the general public—offers athletes 24-hour dining facilities, a cyber café, a dry-cleaning outlet, a bank, a post office and retail outlets. When the Olympics are over, the accommodations, located on the University of Utah campus, will be used for student housing.

Frankly, if an American is to reach the podium in bobsleigh, it's most likely to be a woman. Women's bobsleigh makes its first Olympic appearance in 2002 and the Americans are heavy favorites to win at least one medal. Last season's World Cup finale saw the Americans sweep the medals as Jean Racine drove USA I to gold, followed by Bonny Warner in USA II and Jill Bakken in USA III. Unfortunately, only two of those teams can qualify for the Olympics so there's no chance for a red, white and blue sweep.

Who will challenge the American women? If the German women can enjoy the technological advances that their men's team enjoys, they could. Sandra Prokoff, second to Racine in the overall World Cup standings, and Susi-Lisa Erdmann, who finished fourth, both quickly adapted to the Bear Hollow track when they raced on it at the end of last season. While Prokoff recorded a win and a fourth-place finish, Erdmann was fourth and fifth in the two races.

Others to watch include Switzerland's Francoise Burdet, the tour's top driver until Racine arrived on the scene in 1998, and Canada's Christina Smith.

BOBSLEIGH COMPETITION SCHEDULE

Event	Time
SATURDAY, FEBRUARY 16 Men's two-man bobsleigh	3 pm–6:30 pm
SUNDAY, FEBRUARY 17 Men's two-man bobsleigh	3 pm–6:30 pm
TUESDAY, FEBRUARY 19 Women's bobsleigh	4:30 pm–6:30 pm
FRIDAY, FEBRUARY 22 Men's four-man bobsleigh	3:30 pm–6:30 pm
SATURDAY, FEBRUARY 23 Men's four-man bobsleigh	3:30 pm–6:30 pm

Luge

The only Olympic sport in which competitors are measured in thousandths of a second, luge is a sport of finesse, subtlety and relaxation: the key to a fast run is relaxing on the sled while making a few toe or shoulder movements to control its path.

The sport, named after the French word for "sled," pits competitors who get a start by rocking their sleds back and forth while pulling on bars set in the track. Once out of the start the athletes quickly recline on their backs and race feet-first down the course. Doubles' competition features two athletes on a sled, one atop the other once out of the start.

Utilizing a different start than bobsleigh competitors, male luge athletes encounter 17 curves on the Bear Hollow track while women and doubles teams start a bit lower and must negotiate a dozen curves on their way to the finish.

In the men's and women's individual competitions, winners are determined by the cumulative time of four runs taken over two days. In the doubles event, racers make two runs in one day, with the lowest time the winner.

In recent years the sport has been dominated by Europeans. Entering the 2001–2002 season, the German women's team had not lost a race since December 1997 and they claimed the top two spots in the overall World Cup standings last season and four of the top six. On the men's side, while the Germans couldn't claim the overall 2001 World Cup title individually, they still placed three of their competitors in the top five.

Whom to watch at the Salt Lake Games? On the women's side Germany's Silke Kraushaar and Sylke Otto finished one-two in last season's overall standings, while Sonja Wiedemann was fourth and Barbara Niedernhuber sixth. Look for at least one of these three, if not all three, to medal. Hoping for an upset? Then keep an eye on Austria's Angelika Neuner, who finished third in the World Cup standings, or Latvia's Iluta Gaile, who ended the year fifth.

The U.S. squad is young, with a quartet of young twenty-somethings: Courtney Zablocki, Becky Wilczak, Ashley Hayden and Brenna Margol. The four are equally talented, finishing ninth through twelfth in last season's standings, but shouldn't be expected to pose a great threat to the Germans.

SLIDING HISTORY 101

How old is the sport of luge? Historians tell us they've traced the use of sleds by Vikings to as far back as A.D. 800. They apparently enjoyed sledding on the countryside near the Oslo Fjord. More recently, the first international race was held in Davos, Switzerland, in 1883, with teams from Australia, England, Germany, the Netherlands, Sweden, Switzerland and the United States. Since luge became an Olympic medal sport in 1964, 88 of the 90 medals handed out went to athletes from either Germany, Austria, Italy or the former Soviet Union. The two exceptions occurred during the 1998 Nagano Games when the U.S. took silver and bronze in the doubles competition.

Germany is also the team to beat in the men's competition, with heavily decorated Olympic veteran Georg Hackl leading the way. Hackl, who finished second in the overall World Cup standings a year ago, is vying to become the first luge athlete to win a gold medal in four different Olympic Games. He struck gold at Albertville in 1992, Lillehammer in 1994 and Nagano in 1998. Teammates Albert Karsten and Jens Mueller also are within range of a medal at Bear Hollow.

Hackl should also be threatened by Italy's Armin Zoeggeler, who won both the World Championship and the overall World Cup title last season, and, if he returns for the Games, Austria's Markus Prock, who finished second to Hackl at Albertville and Lillehammer.

In the doubles competition, the Germans again are the ones to beat, although the U.S. team of Mark Grimmette and Brian Martin won bronze in Nagano and were the 1998–99 overall World Cup champions and could produce an upset on their home track.

If you can't fit the Olympics into your schedule but want to see luge at its best, mark your calendar for February 2005 when the World Luge Championships will be held at the Utah Olympic Park.

LUGE COMPETITION SCHEDULE

Event	Time
SUNDAY, FEBRUARY 10	
Men's singles luge	4 pm–7 pm
MONDAY, FEBRUARY 11	
Men's singles luge	9 am–12:30 pm
TUESDAY, FEBRUARY 12	
Women's singles luge	4 pm–7 pm
WEDNESDAY, FEBRUARY 13	
Women's singles luge	4 pm–7 pm
FRIDAY, FEBRUARY 15	
Doubles luge	9 am–11:30 am

Skeleton

Skeleton, a sport in which athletes race head-first down a bobsleigh track on a sled barely larger than a cafeteria tray, has had an off-and-on relationship with the Olympics. The sport, which dates to 1892 when an Englishman concocted it during a winter vacation in Switzerland, appeared in the 1928 Winter

Games at St. Moritz. It didn't return to the Olympics until 1948, again at St. Moritz, and then went on hiatus until the fall of 1999 when the Salt Lake Organizing Committee agreed to include skeleton in the 2002 Games.

As in bobsleigh, racers can surpass 80 mph while negotiating 15 curves along a track that drops 104 meters from top to bottom. Competitors make two runs down the track, with their combined times used to determine the champions.

In the men's competition, Lincoln DeWitt is a solid hometown favorite who could medal. Raised in Vermont, DeWitt has lived in Park City for more than a decade. Although he's only been involved with the sport for four years, last season he won the overall World Cup skeleton title. Teammate Jim Shea, Jr., also can't be ruled out of reaching the podium. A third-generation Olympian, he won the 1998–99 skeleton World Championship.

International sliders to watch include Austria's Martin Rettl, Japan's Koshi Kazuhiro, and Canada's Jeff Pain.

On the women's side Alexandra Coomber, Great Britain's best chance for a medal in the Salt Lake Games, has dominated the competition in recent years. She won the overall World Cup title the past two seasons and, if healthy, will be a heavy favorite. Challenges should come from Canada's Michelle Kelly, Germany's Steffi Hanzlik, the overall World Cup champion back in 1998–99, and Switzerland's Maya Pedersen.

If Ekaterina Mironova spent the summer figuring out how to follow up her blistering starts with solid driving, the Russian with a sprinter's background could be a serious threat.

SKELETON COMPETITION SCHEDULE	
Event	Time
WEDNESDAY, FEBRUARY 20	
Men's and women's singles	9 am–12 pm

Ski Jumping

Superman would enjoy the jumping hills at the Utah Olympic Park, for they surely translate into leaping from tall buildings. You could comfortably fit a 50-story building between the landing zones at the base of the two ski jumps and the start houses at the top of the jumps. Athletes with vertigo definitely would not make very good ski jumpers, since at the start the jumpers sit on a bar, waiting for their coach to wave them down the hill.

While you might think that the jumpers fly off an elevated lip on the jump, in reality they launch themselves from a point where the hill drops off a mere 10 degrees.

Believe it or not, judging a ski-jumping competition involves more than seeing who sails the farthest, although that obviously is a big part of it. The judges also scrutinize the jumpers' form in the air (they look for strong takeoffs and a steady aerodynamic form) as well as how they land—leaping the greatest distance is little good if you fall on your face.

In the individual jumping events, each athlete makes two jumps, while in team jumping each team has four jumpers whose cumulative score determines the standings.

The two main jumping hills that the Olympians will use are the K90 "normal" hill and the K120 "large" hill. The "90" in K90 refers to a point 90 meters downhill from the jump's take-off point, whereas in the "120" in K120 refers to a point 120 meters downhill from the takeoff point. On the normal hill, jumpers who land 90 meters from takeoff receive 60 points; those who go farther receive higher scores, those who fall short of that point receive lower scores. On the large hill, a jumper who lands 120 meters from takeoff also receives 60 points; those who go farther receive higher scores, those who fall short receive lower scores.

For the jumpers' safety, "forerunners," jumpers not in the competition, jump from the hills before the official competition begins. If they go too far past the "K point," which can occur with a strong backwind, the starting bar can be lowered a bit down the jump. Conversely, if the forerunners don't reach the K point, the starting bar can be moved up the hill to give the competitors more speed on their approach.

INDEPENDENCE ON DISPLAY

Anyone curious about the founding of the United States will be interested in glimpsing one of the last surviving copies of the Declaration of Independence. The document will be on display at the Utah State Capitol rotunda February 1 through March 15, 2002, from 9 a.m. through 4 p.m. Admission to the exhibit is free. The document is believed to be one of only four in private hands. In June 2000, Norman and Lyn Lear and David and Storey Hayden purchased the document for $8.14 million. The document is in near-mint condition and is thought to be one of the three best-preserved of the 25 original surviving copies.

Although the Americans have been training on the Bear Hollow jumps for several years, they're not the favorites heading into the Olympics. Rather, Martin Schmitt of Germany, Norway's Tommy Ingebrigtsen and Poland's Adam Malysz—if they're healthy and competing—should contend for gold, silver and bronze. Schmitt, known at home as the "Black Forest eagle," is a two-time world champion, Malysz was the overall World Cup champion last season and Ingebrigtsen is a former world junior champion.

Schmitt, who turns 24 on January 29, 2002, was 14th on the large hill and 19th on the normal hill at the Nagano Games in 1998. However, with teammates Sven Hannawald, Hansjoerg Jaekle and Dieter Thoma he won silver in the team-jumping competition. By the 1998–99 season Schmitt had developed into a superstar, winning the overall World Cup title, a title he successfully defended during the 1999–2000 campaign, a campaign in which he captured 11 individual World Cup events.

The slightly built Malysz (he stands just 5'5" and weighs only 135 pounds) ran a hot streak last season, at one point winning five straight competitions and ten overall by winter's end en route to the overall World Cup title. The Pole's performance has been linked to his work with a psychologist and a performance physiologist who is considered an expert in muscle contractions.

Others who could reach the podium include Finn Janne Ahonen and Japan's Masahiko Harada, a hot and cold jumper over a career that saw him crowned K90 world champion in 1993 and K120 world champion in 1997.

SKI JUMPING COMPETITION SCHEDULE

Event	Time
FRIDAY, FEBRUARY 8	
K90 individual ski-jumping qualifications	9 am–11:30 am
SUNDAY, FEBRUARY 10	
K90 individual ski-jumping finals	8:30 am–11 am
TUESDAY, FEBRUARY 12	
K120 individual ski-jumping qualifications	8:30 am–11 am
WEDNESDAY, FEBRUARY 13	
K120 individual ski-jumping finals	8:30 am–11 am
MONDAY, FEBRUARY 18	
K120 team ski-jumping finals	8:30 am–11:30 am

Nordic Combined

Also using the Utah Olympic Park's ski jumps are the Nordic combined athletes. Their event pairs a day of ski jumping followed by a day of cross-country skiing at Soldier Hollow. The ski-jumping portion of the Nordic combined event surfaced in Norwegian ski carnivals in the mid-1800s; it wasn't until the 1900s that the cross-country segment was adopted by the carnivals.

While the ski-jumping competition is scored under normal ski-jumping rules, the winner of the jumping phase is first out of the gate for a 15K cross-country race with the rest of the field following in a staggered start based on their jumping scores. There's also a team Nordic combined event in which the cross-country portion of the competition is staged like a relay race, with each athlete skiing 5 kilometers.

Austria's Felix Gottwald ran away with the 2000–2001 individual Nordic combined title, winning six times in a breakout season for him. Germany's Ronny Ackermann, who finished second to Gottwald in the World Cup rankings, is expected to challenge him at the Salt Lake Games. Norway's Bjarte Engen Vik, who finished third in the World Cup and is the defending Olympic champion, decided to hang up his skis at the end of last season.

The Nordic combined event is considered the most difficult of the Nordic sports.

Finland's Samppa Lajunen should also mount a serious challenge. The Finn, who entered his first cross-country race when he was just two years old and began ski jumping when he was nine, won silver medals in the individual Nordic combined and team event at Nagano. Lajunen won the overall Nordic combined World Cup title at the end of the 1996–97 season and again during the 1999–2000 season. Last season the Finn finished fifth in the overall standings.

America's best hope for a medal in Nordic combined is Todd Lodwick, who competed at both Lillehammer in 1994 and Nagano in 1998. Although Lodwick, who was raised and continues to live in Steamboat Springs, Colorado, struggled with the skiing portion of the event in those two Games, he's worked on his skiing and is expected to be near the front of the field at Salt Lake. The 1997–98 season proved to be Lodwick's breakout, as he won the Holmenkollen event in Oslo, the sport's most famous race, and finished the season ranked fourth in the world. Last winter Lodwick, the elder statesman of the U.S. Nordic combined squad, finished eighth in the world.

NORDIC COMBINED COMPETITION SCHEDULE

Event	Time
SATURDAY, FEBRUARY 9	
K90 individual jumps	9 am–12:15 pm
SUNDAY, FEBRUARY 10	(at Soldier Hollow)
Men's 15K cross-country	9 am–10 am
THURSDAY, FEBRUARY 14	
K90 team jumps	8:30 am–11:30 am
FRIDAY, FEBRUARY 15	(at Soldier Hollow)
Team 4 x 5K relay	9 am–2 pm
THURSDAY, FEBRUARY 21	
K120 sprint	10:30 am–12:30 pm
FRIDAY, FEBRUARY 22	(at Soldier Hollow)
Men's 7.5K cross-country sprint	10 am–11:30 am

Utah Olympic Oval

The fastest ice on Earth. That's the reputation the Utah Olympic Oval gained in March 2001 when the world single-distance speed-skating championships officially christened the indoor arena. When the oval first opened in 1995 it was an open-air rink known as the Oquirrh Park Oval. But in May 1999 renovation work began on a $28 million project to enclose the oval and provide locker rooms and offices.

The oval's speedy reputation is tied directly to its elevation— 4700 feet above sea level. At this altitude the air is thinner, so skaters face less resistance and ice makers can make particularly hard, and fast, ice. Prior to the Utah Olympic Oval, the Calgary Olympic Oval, which was used for the 1988 Winter Games, had the reputation as the world's fastest ice. During the 2001 World Championships, 5 world records, 57 national records and 127 personal records were set, clearly establishing the Utah oval as the world champion when it comes to speed-skating records. That reputation is expected to grow during the Salt Lake Games, as by then the facility's ice makers will have perfected the ingredients— air temperature, ice temperature and humidity—for perfect speed-skating ice.

During the 2002 Winter Games there will be a dozen competition days at the Utah Olympic Oval.

The Utah Olympic Oval is located 10.5 miles southwest from the
Olympic Village in Salt Lake City. From Salt Lake City, head south
on Route 15 to 2100 South and proceed west to the Bangerter
Highway. Go south on Bangerter Highway to 5400 South, then
head west to 4800 West. At 4800 West turn left and follow the signs
to the oval. ~ 5624 South 4800 West, Kearns; 801-988-8800.

**GETTING
THERE**

While neither Italian nor French skaters figure to medal in speed
skating, you can still celebrate their efforts over dinner by jumping on Route 215 for a short ride to **Tuscany** (page 78) for a
northern Italian meal or **La Caille** (page 78) for French cuisine.

**DINING
TIPS**

How much your tickets cost determines where you'll sit during the
races. The higher-priced ducats are for seats along the straight-
aways, while the cheaper seats are on either end of the oval, a
good place to be if there are to be any crashes.

**SIGHT
LINES**

UTAH OLYMPIC OVAL EVENTS

Men's Speed Skating

One of the glamour events of the Olympics, speed
skating has long enamored spectators who come to watch skaters
zipping around in circles and, occasionally, crashing into one another. Men race 500 meters, 1000 meters,
1500 meters, 5000 meters and 10,000 meters. Since the oval is 400 meters from start
to finish, not all races start and finish at the
same location. For example, the 500-meter race
entails one-and-a-quarter laps of the track, the
1500-meter race three-and-three-quarter laps, and
the 10,000-meter race 25 laps. Additionally, all but
the 500-meter races involve staggered starts so the
skaters must stay in designated lanes; the distance
covered in the outside lane is longer than that in the
inside lane.

Four-hundred ounces of gold, one
ton of sterling silver and 1100
pounds of copper were dug out
of Kennecott Utah Copper's
Bingham Canyon Mine for
O.C. Tanner, the jewelry
manufacturer that crafts
the Olympic medals.

In the long-distance events of the 5000 and 10,000 meters,
will anyone be able to match the pace set by Holland's Gianni
Romme? That will likely be the prevailing question as Romme,
who celebrates his 29th birthday on February 12, 2002, looks to
add to his gold medal collection. At the Nagano Games, he won
gold in both the 5000 and 10,000 meters. During the 2000 season, the lanky skater (6'3" and 190 pounds) won the world all-

around title, and last season he established world records in the 3000, 5000 and 10,000 meters. Romme's spectacular success is incredible when one considers that his country's Olympic coach at one time said the athlete lacked coordination.

In the sprints, look to Canada's Jeremy Wotherspoon to be the pacesetter in the 500- and 1000-meter races. A silver medalist in the 500 at Nagano, the Canadian went on to not only win three consecutive World Cup titles in the 500 and 1000 but to also set world records in those distances. Not to be overlooked, though, is Wotherspoon's teammate, Michael Ireland, who was the 2001 world sprint champion, or Japan's Hiroyasu Shimizu, the 1998 500-meter gold medalist. Over the years Wotherspoon, Ireland and Shimizu have created an exciting rivalry, one that should continue in Salt Lake.

Americans who could contend include K. C. Boutiette, Casey FitzRandolph, who won the 500-meter bronze at the 2001 World Single Distance Speedskating Championships, and Derek Parra, who won the 1500-meter silver at the championships.

MEN'S SPEED SKATING COMPETITION SCHEDULE

Event	Time
SATURDAY, FEBRUARY 9	
Men's 5000-meter speed skating	12 pm–3:30 pm
MONDAY, FEBRUARY 11	
Men's 500-meter speed skating	1 pm–2:30 pm
TUESDAY, FEBRUARY 12	
Men's 500-meter speed skating	1 pm–2:30 pm
SATURDAY, FEBRUARY 16	
Men's 1000-meter speed skating	1 pm–3 pm
TUESDAY, FEBRUARY 19	
Men's 1500-meter speed skating	1 pm–3:30 pm
FRIDAY, FEBRUARY 22	
Men's 10,000-meter speed skating	12 pm–3:15 pm

Women's Speed Skating

In the women's races, the skaters compete at 500 meters, 1000 meters, 1500 meters, 3000 meters and 5000 meters. Count on the German women to haul in the medals at the Salt Lake Games. In the long-distance events, Gunda Niemann-Stirnemann is back to defend her gold medal in the 3000-meter event and will also be a favorite at 5000 meters. Germany's most prolific medalist on ice, Niemann-Stirnemann already has eight Olympic medals—three gold, four silver, one bronze. With three more medals she will set a career record for Olympic medalists. The Salt Lake Games will mark her fifth Olympic Games. (Niemann-Stirnemann, a product of the now-defunct East German sports machine, came to speed skating in a roundabout way. She started out playing volleyball at age 12 before being moved to track and field and finally to speed skating.)

Despite Niemann-Stirnemann's legacy, at Salt Lake she can expect stern challenges from teammates Anni Friesinger, who won bronze in the 3000-meter race at Nagano, and Claudia Pechstein, who already owns five Olympic medals in the distance races, including the last two 5000-meter gold medals.

America's best hope in the distance races is Jennifer Rodriguez, who finished fourth in the 3000-meter race at Nagano. Although now known as a speed skater, Rodriguez' background includes a career as one of the world's top roller skaters. During that stage of her life she won a dozen World Championship medals. She didn't switch to speed skating until 1995. Late last season, Rodriguez set American records in both the 1500 meters (1:55.30) and 3000 meters (4:06.59) in the World Cup finale.

The shorter races could be a showcase for Canada's Catriona Le May Doan and Germany's Monique Garbrecht-Enfeldt. Doan was the 1998 gold medalist in 500 meters and the world-record holder in that event; Garbrecht-Enfeldt was the 2001 world sprint champion and the world-record holder at 1000 meters.

Chris Witty carries America's best hopes in the sprints. She was the country's only double medalist at Nagano, winning silver in the 1000 meters and bronze in the 1500-meter race. Will she choke skating before a home crowd? Witty says she struggled at Nagano, where she was the favorite in the 1000-meter race, because of high expectations.

❖❖

MEDAL METALS

Precious metals mined just southwest of Salt Lake City were used to make the medals that will be draped around the necks of the Olympians who finish first, second or third in their events during the 2002 Salt Lake Games. While each of the roughly 1600 medals contains a silver core, by decree of the International Olympic Committee each of the first-place medals must be finished with at least six grams of pure gold. The silver and bronze medals, meanwhile, are coated with a mixture of copper and zinc that produces the bronze outer covering.

WOMEN'S SPEED SKATING COMPETITION SCHEDULE

Event	Time
SUNDAY, FEBRUARY 10	
Women's 3000-meter speed skating	1 pm–3:30 pm
WEDNESDAY, FEBRUARY 13	
Women's 500-meter speed skating	5 pm–6:30 pm
THURSDAY, FEBRUARY 14	
Women's 500-meter speed skating	5 pm–6:30 pm
SUNDAY, FEBRUARY 17	
Women's 1000-meter speed skating	5:15 pm–7:15 pm
WEDNESDAY, FEBRUARY 20	
Women's 1500-meter speed skating	1 pm–3 pm
SATURDAY, FEBRUARY 23	
Women's 5000-meter speed skating	1 pm–2:45 pm

Soldier Hollow

The Salt Lake Organizing Committee's search for a parcel of rolling land that could be used for cross-country races as well as biathlon and Nordic combined competitions led them to Soldier Hollow, a gently sloped hillside at Wasatch Mountain State Park, about 45 miles southeast from Salt Lake City.

Named in all likelihood for a 19th-century company of soldiers led by Captain James Simpson, the hollow located just south of Midway will be the busiest place during the Games' 17-day run since 16 of those days feature some sort of competition at Soldier Hollow.

Although recent mild winters have brought little snow to the hollow, a snowmaking system allows course managers to lay down a sufficient bed of snow for the racers. Unlike the rest of the world's Nordic venues in which skiers vanish into the woods soon after a race's start, only to materialize shortly before the finish, Soldier Hollow's open layout lets as many as 20,000 spectators follow most of the racing.

Although cross-country skiing has a Scandinavian background, athletes from the former Soviet Union are the most decorated in Olympic competitions, with 77 total medals. Norway is second, with 73.

During the Games male athletes will compete in a 50K classic technique race, a 30K freestyle race, a 15K pursuit/freestyle race, a 10K classic race, a 1.5K sprint race, and a 4 x 10K classic/free-style relay. Women will compete in a 30K classic race, a 15K free-style race, a 10K pursuit/freestyle race, a 5K classic race, a 1.5K sprint race, and a 4 x 5K classic/freestyle race.

Biathlon events include a men's 20K, 10K, 4 x 7.5K relay and 12K pursuit as well as a women's 15K, 7.5K, 4 x 7.5K relay and 10K pursuit.

Three Nordic combined events will be staged at Soldier Hollow: a 15K individual, a 4 x 5K team relay, and a Nordic combined sprint.

Outside of winter, the 16-mile-long trail system is open to the public for hiking, roller skiing and even mountain biking. In the not-so-distant future the state plans to construct a 36-hole golf course nearby.

GETTING THERE

Soldier Hollow is located 43.4 miles from the athletes' village. From Salt Lake City, head east on Route 80 to Exit 148 and bear south onto Route 40 into Heber City. Once in Heber City, turn left onto Route 113 and proceed west to Soldier Hollow. ~ Soldier Hollow at Wasatch Mountain State Park; 435-654-1791.

SIGHT LINES

The beauty of the Soldier Hollow course is that it's out in the open, unlike any other Olympic cross-country course. In Europe, fans see the athletes only at the start and the finish of the races; in between the racers are off dashing through the woods. At Soldier Hollow, the trails loop back and forth almost entirely out in the open so spectators at the finish line can follow them nearly from start to finish. Though bleachers are set up at the start/finish area, I prefer to roam the spectator access areas, strolling from the start/finish area to nearby bridges that span the course and give you a wonderful perch to watch as the athletes pass by underneath. With a good pair of binoculars one could watch the racers as they cruise along the back stretches of the course. If you like to watch the shooting in biathlon, find a spot along the fence near the start/finish line.

WHIMSICAL MASCOTS

Powder, Copper and Coal? Sound familiar? In Utah you can relate these items to the state's famous natural resources … or you can connect them to the 2002 Olympic Winter Games, as these are the names attached to the Games' three mascots. "Powder" is a snowshoe hare, "Copper" a coyote, and "Coal" a black bear.

DINING
TIPS For Park City food at Heber Valley prices, try the **Snake Creek Grill** (page 180). For a more formal setting, visit the **Inn on the Creek** (page 180).

SOLDIER HOLLOW EVENTS

Cross-country Skiing

Through the woods and over the hills as fast as you can go—that's the bottom line to cross-country ski racing. Although Johann Muehlegg, a German who skis for Spain, stamped his signature all over the Soldier Hollow course last February when the World Cup tour came to Utah and he captured both the 30K skate race and the 15K classic event, he did so without being challenged by Sweden's Per Elofsson, who stayed home to train for the World Championships.

Elofsson's decision paid off: he was a double gold medalist at the world championships, winning the 15K classic race and the 10K individual pursuit, and he'll be a favorite to the lead the Olympic field in the events he enters. His victories at the World Championships were the first by a Swede in eight years, and at just 24 years old (he turns 25 on February 4, 2002), Elofsson should be a national hero in Sweden for years to come.

If Elofsson falters, look out for Muehlegg or Norwegian Thomas Alsgaard, the gold medalist in the 30K race at the Lillehammer Games in 1994. Four years later Alsgaard won gold again, this time in the 15K freestyle pursuit event. Italy's Pietro Piller Cottrer, who finished fourth in the World Cup standings last season, also could find himself on the podium.

On the women's side, the Russians boast a very deep team led by Julija Tchepalova, 2000's overall World Cup champion. By the end of the 2000–2001 season Russians had claimed five of the top eight spots in the World Cup rankings. In addition, at the World Championships, Tchepalova won the 5K title while teammates Elena Buruhina came in second and Larissa Lazutina third.

Among those bidding to keep the Russians off the podium during the Games are Norway's Bente Skari, who won World Championship gold in the 15K classic race as well as in the 10K classic race and finished second to Tchepalova in the overall World Cup rankings, and Italian teammates Stefania Belmondo and Gabriella Paruzzi.

For Russia's Lazutina, the Salt Lake Games will be her final Olympic competition. Skiing since she was 5 years old, the 36-

year-old has claimed five Olympic medals and 11 world titles. In 1998 she received the "Hero of Russia" award, her country's highest honor, after winning three gold medals, and five medals overall, at the Nagano Games. Belmondo also plans to make the Salt Lake Games her last Olympic competition. Ironically, it was at a Salt Lake event, a 15K freestyle race in 1989, that Belmondo won her first World Cup title. Despite her longevity on the circuit, the Italian has never won an Olympic gold medal, although she earned two World Championship gold medals in 1999.

Americans do not figure to challenge for medals in either the men's or the women's races.

CROSS-COUNTRY SKIING COMPETITION SCHEDULE

Event	Time
SATURDAY, FEBRUARY 9	
Women's 15K cross-country	9 am–10 am
Men's 30K cross-country	12:30 pm–2 pm
TUESDAY, FEBRUARY 12	
Women's 10K cross-country	9 am–10:30 am
Men's 15K cross-country	12 pm–1:30 pm
THURSDAY, FEBRUARY 14	
Men's 10K cross-country	9:15 am–10:30 am
Men's 10K cross-country pursuit	12 pm–1 pm
FRIDAY, FEBRUARY 15	
Women's 5K cross-country	9 am–10 am
Women's 5K cross-country pursuit	11:30 am–12 pm
SUNDAY, FEBRUARY 17	
Men's 4 x 10K cross-country relay	9:30 am–11:30 am
TUESDAY, FEBRUARY 19	
Men's and women's 1.5K freestyle cross-country sprint	9 am–2:30 pm
THURSDAY, FEBRUARY 21	
Women's 4 x 5K cross-country relay	12:30 pm–2 pm
SATURDAY, FEBRUARY 23	
Men's 50K classic cross-country	9:30 am–1 pm
SUNDAY, FEBRUARY 24	
Women's 30K classic cross-country	9:30 am–12 pm

Biathlon

In this sport of speed and steadiness, cross-country racers test their endurance on the ski trails and their marksmanship on the shooting range where, in between laps of the race, they shoot at small metal targets. Missing on the shooting range is costly. In the individual races, each missed target adds a minute to the racer's overall time. In the sprint and pursuit competitions, each missed target requires the racer to ski around a 150-meter penalty loop before returning to the main race course. Making things even more interesting in these races, competitors must alternate their shooting positions throughout the race, from prone positions to standing positions.

In the four-person relay races, each racer shoots twice: the first time from a prone position, the second while standing. In these races the skiers have eight shots to hit five targets. The first five rounds are in their rifle's magazine, the next three must be loaded individually. If the skier fails to hit all five targets within these eight shots, they must ski an extra 150-meter loop for each missed target.

For the men, the individual gold medals could come down to two racers who swapped the lead in the World Cup standings back and forth throughout the 2000–2001 season. In the end, France's Raphael Poiree edged Norway's Ole Einar Bjoerndalen by just 10 points, amassing 921 points over the course of the season to the Norwegian's 911, so expect these two to be at the forefront of the biathlon races. From there the competition drops off somewhat, although as a team Norway, the birthplace of biathlon, may be unbeatable, with four athletes among the top seven of last season's final World Cup rankings.

If Poiree and Bjoerndalen do falter, Norway's Frode Andresen, Russia's Pavel Rostovtsev or Germany's Sven Fischer could make runs for the gold.

On the women's side, the question likely will come down to who will win silver behind Sweden's Magdalena Forsberg, who has dominated the competition in recent years. Forsberg started her competitive career as a cross-country skier, and was on the Swedish relay team that captured a bronze medal at the 1987 World Championships. In 1993, however, she bought a rifle and learned how to shoot. Last season Forsberg crushed the competition, winning the overall World Cup biathlon title with 1021 points; Norway's Liv Grete Skjelbreid-Poiree was a distant second with 804 points.

A German could find her way onto the podium, though, as four—Andrea Henkel, Uschi Disl, Kati Wilhelm and Martina Glagow—all finished among the top nine in the final World Cup rankings, and teammate Katrin Apel was 12th.

As with the cross-country competition, no Americans are expected to finish among the top ten in this event.

BIATHLON COMPETITION SCHEDULE	
Event	*Time*
MONDAY, FEBRUARY 11	
Women's 15K individual biathlon	11 am–1 pm
Men's 20K individual biathlon	1:30 pm–3:30 pm
WEDNESDAY, FEBRUARY 13	
Men's 10K sprint biathlon	11 am–12:30 pm
Women's 7.5K sprint biathlon	1:30 pm–3 pm
SATURDAY, FEBRUARY 16	
Men's 12.5K pursuit biathlon	9 am–10 am
Women's 10K pursuit biathlon	12 pm–1 pm
MONDAY, FEBRUARY 18	
Women's 4 x 7.5K relay biathlon	11:30 am–1:30 pm
WEDNESDAY, FEBRUARY 20	
Men's 4 x 7.5K relay biathlon	11 am–1 pm

Deer Valley Resort

Although the Salt Lake Organizing Committee had to build the Utah Olympic Park and the Utah Olympic Oval in order to host the 2002 Winter Games, the alpine venues were already in place and simply needed to be rented.

The venerable Deer Valley Resort bordering the south end of Park City will host the men's and women's slalom events, as well as the men's and women's moguls and aerials competitions. Renowned for its restaurants as well as its attention to customers' needs, the resort's skiing is often overlooked. For the slalom races, spectators will become well-familiar with the "Know You Don't"

SUMMIT LODGE PROGRAM

Ticketholders for events at the Deer Valley Resort might be interested in SLOC's Summit Lodge program. For $125 a day, this program allows you to escape the elements by retreating into a heated tent with dining and beverage service—for a fee—as well as live video feeds from all ongoing events. ~ 800-361-8892. There will also be heated "comfort stations" at the outdoor venues, with restrooms equipped with changing facilities for babies.

course, while "Champion" will be used for the men's and women's mogul races and "White Owl" for the aerials events. Eighteen-thousand spectators should be able to watch the slalom races, while capacity is 14,000 for moguls and 16,000 for aerials.

GETTING THERE

Deer Valley Resort is located 27.9 miles southeast from the Olympic Village in Salt Lake City via Routes 80 and 40. From the capital, drive east on Route 80 to Exit 168 and head south on 40 to the intersection of 40 and Route 248, where ticketholders will be required to park and board shuttle buses to the ski area. Parking for the Olympics will be at a lot at the junction of Routes 40 and 248 east of Park City. ~ 2250 Deer Valley Drive, Park City; 435-649-1000.

SIGHT LINES

For the slalom and moguls, while higher-priced bleacher seats are situated near the finish line, general-admission tickets let you roam along the lower stretches of the slalom course, giving you a much better view of the racers as they negotiate the gated turns and moguls.

Since the jumps are located near the bottom of White Owl, for the best view of the aerials action you should be situated in the general-admission area just below the landing zone.

DINING TIPS

With Park City's eateries (see Chapter Four) a short ride away, you'll have plenty of choices ranging from burgers to filet mignon. Don't want to ride that mile to downtown Park City? Then seek out a table at **Bistro Toujours** (page 163) at Silver Lake Village.

DEER VALLEY RESORT EVENTS

Slalom

This event blends speed and precision—speed in going from top to bottom on a race course, precision in cleanly and quickly weaving back and forth through gates set up on the course. Austria is the powerhouse of alpine countries, and that fact will show through during the skiing events. For example, last year Austrian skiers finished first, second and third in the final men's World Cup slalom rankings, and claimed six of the top twelve spots overall.

So, who's the favorite in the men's slalom? Well, it could be Benjamin Raich, who won the overall title last season; Heinz Schilchegger, who finished second; or Mario Matt, who wound up third. But while Raich pretty much ran away with the title,

Schilchegger and Matt were closely followed by France's Pierrick Bourgeat, Norway's Hans-Petter Burass and Slovenia's Jure Kosir.

If you like sentimental dark horses, cheer on American Erik Schlopy. Although he finished 22nd in the overall slalom rankings last year, he had four top-10 finishes in the giant slalom. While he prefers the giant slalom over the slalom (he finished third overall in that event last season), don't write off Schlopy, who calls Park City home these days.

While the 2002 Olympic competitions will be spread over eight days at Deer Valley Resort, the world's attention will return to the resort in 2003 when the World Ski Freestyle Championships are staged there.

On the women's side, Croatia's Janica Kostelic was the overall World Cup slalom champion last season, but she had surgery on her left knee early in the off-season to repair her outer meniscus following an injury during glacier training and had to take the bulk of the summer off. If she struggles to get back in shape, Austria's Renate Goetschl, France's Regine Cavagnoud or Switzerland's Sonja Nef all could claim gold.

Although American Kristina Koznick has displayed the talent to be a consistent top-10 finisher in the slalom, she's been plagued by inconsistency, something that might have been tied to her decision heading into last season to leave the U.S. Ski Team and train on her own. An American who came on strong towards the end of last season was Sarah Schleper. The native of Glenwood Springs, Colorado, recorded four top-10 World Cup finishes, including a second in a slalom race and a third in a giant slalom event.

SLALOM COMPETITION SCHEDULE	
Event	Time
WEDNESDAY, FEBRUARY 20	
Women's slalom	10 am–2 pm
SATURDAY, FEBRUARY 23	
Men's slalom	10 am–2 pm

Moguls

It's hard to follow the scoring in this event because it goes by so fast. Simply put, the skiers make runs down a course lined with moguls. At certain points along the way they're required to leap into the air for maneuvers. The judges base their scores on how the racers turn (50 percent), how they perform in

Text continued on page 238.

Stein

Just as "Babe" sufficed for George Herman Ruth in baseball and "Pele" for Edson Arantes do Nascimento in soccer, so too does "Stein" suffice for Stein Eriksen in skiing. "Mr. Eriksen" is too awkward for his warm, charismatic personality and too ambiguous for one of skiing's icons. In a sport that typically gains attention in the United States only every four years when the Olympic Winter Games arrive, Stein has crafted a lasting reputation not only as a champion but as a graceful, elegant skier to be emulated. If only that were possible.

How does he make a sport famous for broken legs and shredded knee ligaments look so easy? Stein can trace his fluidity on the slopes to a boyhood filled with gymnastics. His father Marius was a gymnast on the Norwegian team at the 1912 Olympic Games and he raised his children to be gymnasts, too. While Stein diverged from his father in choice of sports, the ingrained agility he developed through his gymnastic foundation aided Stein when it came to skiing—and he demonstrated it to the world when the Olympic Winter Games came to Oslo in 1952.

Prior to the 1952 Games most skiers made wide, sweeping turns through the gates set up on slalom and giant slalom courses. Stein figured he could shave precious seconds off his races by using his hips to lead his body into lightning quick turns past the gates. As his body drew even with the gates, Stein would twist his shoulders away from the turn and immediately begin to set up for the next gate. The technique paid off at the Oslo Games, where Stein won the giant slalom race and proved that he was one of the world's best skiers. Two years later, at the World Championships in Aare, Sweden, the Norseman showed he might be the very best on the mountain by continuing his golden streak with victories in the slalom, giant slalom and combined events.

And then, at just 28 years old, Stein retired from competition. Realizing that he had reached his peak, both athletically and competitively, Stein retired from the Norwegian ski team and headed to the United States to teach skiing. His rugged good looks, exotic accent and athletic grace lured newcomers to a cold, winter sport that barely a half-million folks practiced at the time. Beyond that, his unmatched ability earned him leading roles in "extreme skiing" movies filmed by the likes of John Jay, Dick Barrymore and Warren Miller that soon had skiers wishing they could ski "just like Stein."

Stein's legacy lives on in these films as well as at the Deer Valley Resort, where the Norwegian is director of skiing. Inside the lobby of his namesake Stein Eriksen Lodge at mid-mountain, a display case holds the pins, medals, trophies and cups produced by his ski-racing career. The honors continued long after Stein abandoned racing. In 1997 the King of Norway recognized him as "Knight First Class," a designation given to a handful of Norwegian nationals who live outside Norway.

If the television networks are willing, the world likely will glimpse Stein's renowned style during the Salt Lake Games when he celebrates the 50th anniversary of his gold-medal performance at the Oslo Winter Games. And don't be surprised if the golden Norseman shows the world, during a break in action from the Games, just how he won that giant slalom medal. For though he'll be 74 years old when the Games open, Stein heads to the slopes upwards of 100 days each winter and still offers tips on how to improve your form.

"It's always the same story," Stein says when asked what the crux of his suggestions is. "It's so easy to develop bad habits and they hang on for the rest of your life. So if you are taking up skiing for the first time, I would certainly get guidance from the beginning to get the basic steps imprinted in my system, so I have something sound to build on."

That the Games will be in his backyard during the 50th anniversary of his Olympic achievement is extremely fitting, says Stein.

"It brings back all the memories of a wonderful skiing career. To be able to celebrate the 50th anniversary of a gold medal, still feeling as I do and being as actively involved as I am, it's a bonus," he says. "It's a great feeling and a great satisfaction to be able to perform to such an extent fairly well 50 years later."

the air (25 percent), and how quickly they negotiate the course (25 percent). Although Finnish men grabbed the top two spots in the World Cup mogul standings last season, the Americans weren't far behind, with Ryan Riley finishing fifth and Evan Dybvig, Toby Dawson and Travis Ramos standing seventh through ninth, respectively.

Still, Finland's Mikko Ronkainen and Janne Lahtela will have to be considered the favorites if they remain healthy and focused heading into the Games. Ronkainen was the overall freestyle World Cup champion last season as well as the circuit's moguls champion. Nevertheless, expect challenges from Canada's Pierre-Alexandre Rousseau or teammate Stephane Rochon, France's Richard Gay, or the American contingent.

An American who could come out of the pack to medal in 2002 is Jonny Moseley, the 1998 Olympic moguls champion. Following the Nagano Games Moseley took two years off and last season he entered only four World Cup competitions and still finished 19th overall out of 49 athletes.

Over on the women's side, Norway's Kari Traa, last season's overall female moguls champion; Japan's Aiko Uemura; and America's Hannah Hardaway are slightly ahead of the rest of the field, although Canada's Jennifer Heil (last year's rookie of the year), Finland's Minna Karhu or France's Katleen Allais could surprise the leaders.

MOGULS COMPETITION SCHEDULE	
Event	Time
SATURDAY, FEBRUARY 9	
Women's freestyle moguls	9 am–1 pm
TUESDAY, FEBRUARY 12	
Men's freestyle moguls	9 am–1 pm

Aerials

No Australian has ever won a gold or silver medal at a Winter Olympics, but Jacqui Cooper is poised to do so at the Salt Lake Games in an event that features skiers launching themselves off a jump and into the air to perform aerial gymnastics for which they are scored. Twenty percent of the score is based on their aerial routines, 50 percent on their overall form, and 30 percent on their landing. One of the most daring of the women aerialists, Cooper won back-to-back-to-back World Cup overall freestyle titles in 1999, 2000 and 2001, won at the 1999 World Championships, and won the 2001 Aerials World Cup title. However, she's had a bit of a problem with Olympic competitions. At Lillehammer in 1994 Cooper finished 16th, and at Nagano four years later she wound up 23rd after crashing on one jump that left her with a concussion and bed-ridden for two days.

The Salt Lake Organizing Committee used branding iron designs borrowed from Utah's cowboy roots to inspire the 19 pictograms that represent each Winter Games sport.

What happens if Jacqui Cooper chokes on the jumps? Any number of women could leap past her, from Belarus' Alla Tsuper or China's Nannan Xu to Canada's Veronika Bauer or America's Emily Cooper.

In the men's aerials competition, the U.S. is hoping to go one-two with Eric Bergoust and Joe Pack, who finished that way in the 2000 World Cup rankings, separated by a mere four points. Not to be overlooked, however, are Dmitri Dashinski, who hails from Belarus and Canadians Steve Omischl, Andy Capicik and Nicolas Fontaine.

For Bergoust, the Winter Olympics are the "Big Show." Throughout his career the 1998 Olympic gold medalist has preferred to perform at his best in big events rather than striving to win an overall World Cup title. "I'd rather stick it and win or crash and finish 10th," he says. His resumé boasts not only the highest score ever in a competition, but also the three highest-scoring aerial jumps in the sport's history. Bergoust can trace his appetite for "big air" to his childhood days in Missoula, Montana, where he would jump from the roof of his two-story house onto an assortment of mattresses and other soft items. These days Bergoust lives in Park City, where he and Pack train at the Utah Olympic Park.

AERIALS COMPETITION SCHEDULE	
Event	Time
SATURDAY, FEBRUARY 16	
Women's freestyle aerials qualifications	10 am–12 pm
Men's freestyle aerials qualifications	1:30 pm–3:30 pm
MONDAY, FEBRUARY 18	
Women's freestyle aerials finals	12 pm–1 pm
TUESDAY, FEBRUARY 19	
Men's freestyle aerials finals	12 pm–1 pm

Park City Mountain Resort

Long a regular stop on the "White Circus," as the World Cup ski tour is known, the Park City Mountain Resort has developed an international following for its dependable snow conditions and annual "America's Opening" races.

While the Salt Lake Games will give the resort an Olympic-competition reputation, it already has an Olympian on its staff—1998 gold medalist Picabo Street, who is director of skiing. Street is not expected to compete at her home resort during the Games since she's a downhill and Super-G specialist and the resort will host the men's and women's alpine giant slalom races as well as the men's and women's parallel giant slalom and halfpipe snowboard events.

The alpine and the parallel giant slalom snowboard races will be staged on C.B.'s Run, a 4700-foot, top-to-bottom run that drops 1355 vertical feet. The race course takes its name from Craig Badami, the son of one of the resort's former owners whose foresight brought World Cup ski racing to Park City. Sadly, Badami was killed in 1989, the day after the annual America's Opening race, in a helicopter accident.

Halfpipe competitions will be staged in a "Super Pipe" sculpted from the snow at the base of C.B.'s Run. This halfpipe is broader and deeper than traditional halfpipes, allowing riders to soar higher and conduct greater maneuvers.

There's room for upwards of 20,000 spectators on the slopes.

GETTING THERE

The Park City Mountain Resort is located 27.9 miles from the Olympic Village in Salt Lake City. From Salt Lake City, drive east on Route 80 to Exit 145 and head south on Route 224 to a large parking area near the Utah Olympic Park where you'll leave your car and board a shuttle bus to the ski resort. Or, continue east

KICKING AND GLIDING

Need a break from the Games? Then head to the Uinta Mountains just east of Park City for some cross-country skiing or snowshoeing. Classic-style Nordic skiers enjoy solitude along the Beaver Creek Trail, while skate skiers can head to the end of Route 150 (the Mirror Lake Highway), where they share the snow-covered road with snowmobilers. If you prefer snowshoeing, the Yellow Pine, Shingle Creek, and North Fork of the Provo River trails found on the north side of the highway are closed to snowmobiles. Skis and snowshoes can be rented in Park City. For trail information, contact the Kamas Ranger District. ~ 435-783-4338.

on Route 80 to Exit 148 and head south on Route 40 to the parking area at the junction of Routes 40 and 248, where you'll also be able to board shuttle buses to the resort. ~ 1345 Lowell Avenue, Park City; 435-649-8111.

Watching the action at the Park City Mountain Resort is akin to attending a large outdoor block party. You and thousands of your best friends line the race course and ring cow bells and other noise makers as the racers zip by. How far up the race course you go to find what you think is a good view depends on your stamina. After all, you're at an elevation of roughly 7000 feet and climbing ever upward on snow. If you buy some of the higher-priced tickets, you get to sit in bleachers at the finish line.

SIGHT LINES

For those familiar with "mosh pits," that's a fairly good description of the sight lines for snowboarding halfpipe, as thousands of fans crowd around the pipe to watch the competition.

This resort is even closer to downtown Park City than Deer Valley, so take advantage of the many restaurants in Old Town (see "Park City Dining" in Chapter Four). Try to land a table at **Chez Betty** (page 168) or **Nacho Mama's** (page 166).

DINING TIPS

PARK CITY MOUNTAIN RESORT EVENTS

Giant Slalom

In this event, a longer version of the slalom, the man to watch is Hermann Maier. The Austrian became something of a household name around the world in 1998 when he crashed spectacularly in the downhill at the Nagano Games, flying through the air for perhaps 90 feet before smashing through two safety nets. Despite the horrific appearance of the crash, the man known as "The Herminator" got up and walked away uninjured. He went on to win gold in the Super-G at those Games as well as gold in the giant slalom.

Maier has been either on top or near the top of the alpine standings ever since his dramatic performance at Nagano. Last year he won the overall World Cup title with almost twice as many points as runner-up and teammate Stephan Eberharter—and also claimed World Cup titles in the downhill, Super-G and giant slalom events. Long overlooked is that, as a youth, Maier was booted out of the

Text continued on page 244.

Uncluttered Slopes

While the Olympic Winter Games focus worldwide attention on host and venue cities, for some reason they also scare off tourists who normally would visit these communities. In the case of the Salt Lake Games, the Olympic winter of 2001–2002 is expected to be horrible for Utah's ski industry, which expects business to be down anywhere from 20 to 40 percent. Why? There's a misconception that the Salt Lake Games will lure stifling crowds to venue cities, making it challenging, at best, to get around, difficult to book a place to stay, or, if you're a skier or 'boarder, impossible to find untracked powder. Oddly, this misconception affects tourism not only during the Games' 17-day duration, but throughout the winter of 2001–2002.

While this isn't good news for Utah's ski industry, it's great news for savvy travelers. You'll be rewarded with discounted lift tickets and uncrowded slopes since only two percent of Utah's skiable terrain will be involved in the Games. About the only problem you're likely to encounter will be finding lodging in and nearby the venue cities during the Games, as most rooms were sold out long ago. Still, some rooms could miraculously open up. For tips on locating a room at the last minute, turn to page 208. Early- and late-season skiers and snowboarders, however, shouldn't have any problem finding a bed and could actually realize some out-of-pocket savings.

If Games-time lodging isn't a problem, by all means head to the slopes. Not all the runs are reserved for the Games and, if business really is down 20–40 percent, you'll never wait in a lift line or have to look far for empty slopes.

At the **Park City Mountain Resort** (page 198), host of the alpine and the parallel giant slalom snowboard races, only 200 of the resort's 3300 skiable acres will be impacted by the Games. Next door, **Deer Valley Resort** (page 198), home of the alpine slalom events as well as the moguls and aerials competitions, will involve but five percent of the resort's 1750 acres. And at **Snowbasin** (page 142), site of the downhill and Super-G races, just 250 of 2950 acres will be devoted to the Games. While the Games will involve the Park City, Deer Valley and Snowbasin resorts, there are 11 other ski areas to enjoy before, during and after the Olympics. These 11 not only reveal some of Utah's most spectacular alpine vistas but offer something for everyone.

North of Park City is **The Canyons** (page 198), a growing resort with more than 3600 acres sprawled across eight mountains for 'boarders and skiers. There are other options within an hour of downtown Salt Lake City, at resorts famous for their ability to capture Utah's famously dry and ticklish powder snow.

For a place where the focus is on skiing, not après skiing, head up Little Cottonwood Canyon to **Alta** (page 89), one of America's "throwback" resorts. Here you'll enjoy legendary snow, spectacularly rugged scenery that falls beneath the towering cliffs of Devil's Castle, and incredibly affordable skiing. Next door, **Snowbird** (page 89) enjoys the same bountiful deposits of Utah's trademark snow. A relative newcomer to the state's ski industry, having arrived on the scene in 1971 compared to Alta's 1938 birthdate, the 'bird packages that snow with killer scenery and some of Utah's steepest runs. A bonus of visiting Alta or Snowbird during this Olympic winter is the *Alta Snowbird Pass*, which allows skiers to visit both resorts with one lift ticket.

North of Little Cottonwood Canyon is Big Cottonwood Canyon and its two resorts, **Solitude** and **Brighton** (page 90). Solitude is an oft-overlooked destination, which is strange because this intimate resort wraps more than 1200 acres of skiing around a charming European-style village. Even when the Olympics aren't in town Solitude defines its name. Finally there's Brighton, whose family-friendly reputation often precedes its renowned snow.

A little farther away from downtown Salt Lake City is the **Sundance Resort**, home to Robert Redford's cozy arts colony. Although Redford starred as an Olympic skier in *Downhill Racer*, he has little interest in the Salt Lake Games. As a result, Sundance, with 450 skiable acres, is a good place to retreat to if you want to get away from the Games' hoopla. ~ Route 92, 17 miles northeast of Provo; 801-225-4100, 800-892-1600; www.sundance-utah.com.

Go north from Salt Lake City and you'll find Snowbasin's neighbors, **Powder Mountain** and **Nordic Valley** (page 142). Powder Mountain averages about 500 inches of snow each winter and offers 5500 acres of skiing. Nordic Valley is a no-frills, no-crowds ski area with just 85 acres.

If you want to leave the Salt Lake area for a day or more, head south three and a half hours to the **Brian Head Resort**, the state's highest resort with a base elevation of 9600 feet. While Brian Head can't offer the same expert terrain as its northern brethren, it has spectacular red-rock scenery and 42 kilometers of groomed Nordic trails. ~ 329 South Route 143, Brian Head; 435-677-2035, fax 435-677-3883; www.brianhead.com.

Really interested in heading off the beaten path to enjoy great skiing? Then head to **Beaver Mountain** (page 142), one of Utah's best-kept alpine secrets. Nestled in the Wasatch-Cache National Forest east of Logan, Beaver Mountain is often overlooked despite receiving 400 inches of snow on average; its 26 trails will keep both experts and novices happy.

With more than 23,000 acres of skiable terrain, you shouldn't have any trouble skiing in Utah during the Games.

Austrian ski academy because coaches didn't think the athlete, who then was slightly built, had a future in ski racing. But six years working as a bricklayer and teaching skiing got Maier in shape; in October 1994 he returned to skiing for Austria.

That said, Maier is not unbeatable in the giant slalom. He edged out Switzerland's Michael Von Gruenigen by just ten points for the World Cup giant slalom title last season, and a mistake on Park City's C.B.'s Run could open the door for Von Gruenigen, American Erik Schlopy, or any number of other skiers to slip past Maier.

Former Olympic gold medalist Bernard Russi was brought in to design the race courses at Snowbasin Ski Area.

The women's giant slalom event will likely be won by a European. But whether it's Switzerland's Sonja Nef, Sweden's Anja Paerson, Austria's Michaela Dorfmeister or Italy's Karen Putzer is hard to say. Germany's Martina Ertl also could find herself on the podium, while a surprise performance could come from Austria's Alexandra Meissnitzer, a silver medalist in the giant slalom and a bronze medalist in the Super-G at Nagano who missed the 1999–2000 season after tearing ligaments in her left knee while training for a race at Lake Louise, British Columbia.

GIANT SLALOM COMPETITION SCHEDULE

Event	Time
THURSDAY, FEBRUARY 21	
Men's giant slalom	10 am–2:30 pm
FRIDAY, FEBRUARY 22	
Women's giant slalom	10 am–2:15 pm

Snowboarding Parallel Giant Slalom

Although similar to skiing's giant slalom races, this event is much more competitive: two snowboarders are on the course at the same time, and while they're really racing against the clock they can't help but compete against the 'boarder on the course next to them. France's Karine Ruby has won more World Cup snowboarding races than any other competitor, so don't be surprised to hear her name called when it's time for medals to be handed out. Yet while Ruby is the defending Olympic champion in the giant slalom, she finished second in the World Cup parallel slalom standings last season to Italy's Carmen Ranigler; America's Rosey Fletcher was right behind her in third place. Still, Ruby garnered enough points in snowboarding's other disciplines to take the overall women's World Cup snowboarding title at season's end.

On the men's side, the story most likely will revolve around American Chris Klug, who needed a liver transplant during the summer of 2000 to save his life from a fatal disease. Five months later Klug climbed up onto a podium at a World Cup race in Canada, and last January he won a parallel giant slalom race in Italy. While Klug finished a respectable 11th in the World Cup parallel slalom rankings, the season's title went to France's Mathieu Bozzetto, who was closely followed by teammate Nicolas Huet; Sweden's Richard Rikardsson came in third.

A story almost as good as Klug's surrounds Austria's Alexander Maier, the younger brother of alpine great Hermann Maier. While Alexander hates comparisons to his more-famous brother, he earned his first World Cup podium at the start of last season with a third-place finish in a halfpipe competition, although his forte proved to be parallel slalom—he rose to sixth place in the overall standings by season's end.

The overall snowboard World Cup title went to Canada's Jay Jasey Anderson, so keep an eye out for him.

SNOWBOARDING PARALLEL GIANT SLALOM COMPETITION SCHEDULE	
Event	Time
THURSDAY, FEBRUARY 14	
Women's snowboarding parallel giant slalom qualifications	10 am–11 am
Men's snowboarding parallel giant slalom qualifications	1 pm–2 pm
FRIDAY, FEBRUARY 15	
Men's and women's snowboarding parallel giant slalom finals	10 am–12 pm

Snowboarding Halfpipe

One of the more difficult events to "score at home," halfpipe involves a scooped out portion of a ski run that resembles a pipe cut in half. Athletes gain points by soaring up the walls of the "pipe" and into the sky, where they make turns and other aerial maneuvers before gravity pulls them back to the snow. The difficulty of the maneuvers and the smoothness of the landings determine the competitors' scores. The "tricks" are judged on their complexity, execution, variety and difficulty of rotations, and height of the maneuvers. Because so many aspects are judged, five judges are used to watch the 'boarders, with one scoring rotations, one amplitude and two overall impression. Points can be deducted for falls, using hands for stability, poor landings and flailing.

Sweden's Magnus Sterner and Stefan Karlsson finished one-two last season in the World Cup halfpipe standings, but that doesn't mean they'll be atop the podium when the halfpipe medals are handed out. While Sterner did lay claim to the overall World Cup halfpipe title at the end of last season, he did so only after watching teammate Markus Jonsson, who finished eighth in the overall rankings, win the last competition of the season, evidence that a hot rider can surprise the leaders on any given day.

Look for Germany's Sabine Wehr-Hasler to rise to the top in the women's halfpipe competition; she reclaimed her World Cup champion status last season and easily outdistanced the rest of the field in the halfpipe rankings, with 4650 points to the 3800 earned by Norway's Stine B. Kjeldaas. Just as Sterner did not win the final race of last season, neither did Wehr-Hasler, who watched as Switzerland's Fabienne Reuteler took that victory.

Challenges to Wehr-Hasler during the Games should come not only from Kjeldaas but also from Great Britain's Lesley McKenna and Japanese teammates Michiyo Hashimoto and Yoko Miyake.

SNOWBOARDING HALFPIPE COMPETITION SCHEDULE

Event	Time
SUNDAY, FEBRUARY 10	
Women's snowboarding halfpipe	10 am–2:30 pm
MONDAY, FEBRUARY 11	
Men's snowboarding halfpipe	10 am–2 pm

Snowbasin Ski Area

Dating to 1939, Snowbasin is one of Utah's oldest ski areas. But it really didn't attract much attention beyond the locals in nearby Ogden until 1995, when Salt Lake City won the bid to host the 2002 Winter Games. With the Games in hand, the Salt Lake Organizing Committee needed a location for perhaps the most glamorous event of the Games—the downhill. Snowbasin's owners agreed to stage the event, along with the Super-G, but only if a land swap could be engineered with the U.S. Forest Service so that they could obtain more property near the resort base for development.

Once that swap was approved, the resort began to blossom into one of Utah's most prestigious; architects began rendering base facilities and on-mountain day lodges. Although the not-quite-two-mile-long men's course Grizzly is somewhat short in length compared to most of the world's other downhill courses, it's considered one of the most demanding because of the hard turns and dramatic pitches Russi included in his layout.

While test events last winter allowed most Olympic competitors to sample Utah's venues, fickle weather—first not enough snow, then too much—kept the world's best skiers from competing on the Snowbasin runs.

GETTING THERE

Snowbasin Ski Area is located roughly 54 miles northeast from the Olympic Village in Salt Lake City. To reach it take Route 15 north from Salt Lake City to Route 84, then head east to the Mountain Green exit. From there, follow Route 167 north to the resort. ~ 801-620-1000.

SIGHT LINES

Viewing either the downhill or Super-G can be tough since the racers whip by so quickly. That's why the higher-priced bleacher seats might not be a bad idea, as you'll be able to view the upper reaches of the courses via large-screen televisions set up near the finish and then be able to watch the racers as they cross the finish.

DINING TIPS

Short of driving all the way to Ogden, your dining options in the immediate vicinity of the ski resort are numbered. But if you don't mind heading to a bar, albeit one with quite a history, not to mention renowned hamburgers, then drive to Huntsville and stop at **The Shooting Star Saloon** (page 112). If you're staying in Ogden and heading back there after the races, try **Rooster's** (page 110) or **Bistro 258** (page 111) on Historic 25th Street, or, for a heavier meal, sample the Teutonic entrées at the **Bavarian Chalet** (page 112).

SNOWBASIN SKI AREA EVENTS

Downhill and Super-G

Speed, nerves of steel and incredible balance are crucial in both of these downhill dashes against the clock. As in the giant slalom conducted at the Park City Mountain Resort, Austria's Hermann Maier is the prohibitive favorite in both the downhill and the Super-G races that will be held on the steep flanks of Allen Peak. If Maier is on top of his art, the fight in both races will be for second and third places. In the downhill, they could go to another Austrian—Stephan Eberharter or Fritz Strobl or maybe Hannes Trinkl—or perhaps to Norway's Lasse Kjus.

When the Super-G—a longer version of the giant slalom—is held, though, a darkhorse home-country favorite for a gold or silver would have to be Daron Rahlves. Although he was an also-ran in the Super-G and giant slalom at the 1998 Nagano Games, Rahlves surprised not only Eberharter but also Maier, and shook the Austrian ski world in the process by winning the Super-G race at the 1999 World Championships in Austria.

Another American who could rise to the occasion by racing on his home soil is Chad Fleischer, whose best finish in a major competition was sixth place in the Super-G at the 1999 World Championships. He does own a silver medal from a World Cup downhill in Sierra Nevada, Spain, back in 1999.

If there's to be a Cinderella story at the Salt Lake Games it would have to be the triumphant return of American Picabo Street. A surprise gold medalist in the Super-G at the Nagano Games, Street was injured a month after those games when she broke her left femur and tore the anterior cruciate ligament in her right knee during a crash. The injuries sidelined Street for nearly three years. Although she returned to competition in December 2000, Street spent last season focusing on regaining her confidence and technique, not driving for the podium. Still, she finished the year ranked 26th out of 55 racers on the downhill circuit and would like nothing better than to win an Olympic medal on American soil.

More likely to reach the podium are Italy's Isolde Kostner, last year's overall downhill champion, Austria's Renate Goetschl or France's Regine Cavagnoud. However, an inspired run could propel American Megan Gerety, who ended last season ranked tenth in the downhill, up onto the podium.

In the Super-G, Street is the sentimental favorite, but the more realistic odds would have to go to Cavagnoud, Goetschl, France's Carole Montillet, Canada's Melanie Turgeon or perhaps Austria's Michaela Dorfmeister.

DOWNHILL AND SUPER-G COMPETITION SCHEDULE

Event	Time
SUNDAY, FEBRUARY 10	
Men's downhill	10 am–11:30 am
MONDAY, FEBRUARY 11	
Women's downhill	10 am–11:30 am
WEDNESDAY, FEBRUARY 13	
Men's combined downhill and slalom finals	10 am–3:30 pm

continued on next page

DOWNHILL AND SUPER-G COMPETITION SCHEDULE cont'd	
Event	Time
THURSDAY, FEBRUARY 14 Women's combined downhill and slalom finals	10 am–3:30 pm
SATURDAY, FEBRUARY 16 Men's Super-G	10 am–11:30 am
SUNDAY, FEBRUARY 17 Women's Super-G	10 am–11:30 am

Salt Lake Ice Center

Fans of the National Basketball Association should be well-familiar with this venue, as outside of the Olympic Games it's known as the Delta Center, the home of the Utah Jazz. Located not far from the heart of downtown Salt Lake City, the ice center will be the venue for men's and women's figure skating as well as short-track speed skating.

The arena, which can seat more than 20,000 spectators for basketball games, is the largest indoor arena within a five-state radius. During the Winter Games the seating will be reduced to just under 11,000.

GETTING THERE

The Salt Lake Ice Center is 3.7 miles from the Olympic Village on the corner of 300 West and South Temple, just on the western edge of downtown Salt Lake City. ~ 301 West South Temple, Salt Lake City; 801-325-2500.

SIGHT LINES

Bottom line: How much you pay for your tickets determines how good a view you'll enjoy during these very popular events, as the higher-priced tickets claim seats closer to the ice.

The problem with staging a figure-skating competition at the Salt Lake Ice Center is that not all the sight lines are perfect—there are some obstructions that could hinder one's view from the, ahem, cheap seats. With this in mind, the Salt Lake Organizing Committee officials tried to overcome this disadvantage by installing large-screen televisions to help improve the obstructed views.

DINING TIPS

Downtown Salt Lake City with its dozens of restaurants (see Chapter Two) is a short walk (or TRAX ride) away from the Delta Center.

SALT LAKE ICE CENTER EVENTS

Figure Skating

In this sport that blends athleticism with artistry, there have long been complaints that national politics influence the judges, who are expected to award points based on how skaters perform a number of required moves as well as some of their own creations. And those complaints will likely continue as long as humans are the judges in a sport where personal interpretation and innovation, not a time clock or scoreboard, determine the champion. Part of the Winter Olympics ever since the first edition in 1924 at Chamonix, France, figure skaters execute dazzling moves—Salchows, loops, flips, triple axels and "Hamel Camels"—on thin blades choreographed to music of their choice. The competition is broken into two segments: the short program, which features required moves and is worth 33.3 percent of the overall score, and the free-skate portion, which is worth 66.7 percent.

Pairs figure skating can be more dramatic than the individual competition since it involves overhead lifts, throw jumps and spins that can bring skaters perilously close to both the ice and each other's skate blades. As with the individual competition, pairs involves both a short program requiring eight moves as well as a longer free-skate program.

Ice dancers, meanwhile, are ballroom dancers on skates, performing a running series of dancing moves across the ice while constantly maintaining contact with their partner. This competition is divided into three portions: two compulsory dance segments, an original dance and a free dance. Each of the two compulsory dances are worth 10 percent of the final score, while the original dance segment is worth 30 percent and the free dance 50 percent. In the compulsory portion, judges look for unison, timing and execution. In the original dance segment, the teams must skate to a prescribed rhythm, such as jive or the blues, and create an original dance to the music. In the free-dance portion, the skaters perform an original program to a piece of music of their choosing.

In the men's figure-skating competition, Russia's Alexei Yagudin was only 17 years old when he finished fifth in men's figure skating at the 1998 Nagano Games—a performance at such a young age that should have sent a message to his competition. Since then Yagudin has won three straight world titles . . . but not the last, which went to teammate Yevgeny Plushenko during the 2001 competition held in Vancouver in March; Yagudin had to settle for silver.

If Plushenko and Yagudin become too focused on their rivalry, America's Todd Eldredge, who was third at the World Championships, could sneak in and grab the gold medal. Others who could figure into the medal mix are the USA's Tim Goebel, fourth at the World Championships, and Michael Weiss, as well as Canadian powerhouse and crowd pleaser Elvis Stojko.

Michelle Kwan has been America's sweetheart on ice, and she's earned that distinction with three world titles, five national titles and an Olympic silver medal. But fellow American Tara Lipinski came away from Nagano with the gold medal. Whether Kwan can finally win the gold she's chased since going to the Lillehammer Games as an alternate could swing on how she fares against her fellow teammates, or against the powerful Russian delegation.

At the 2001 World Championships in Vancouver, the gold medal in the women's competition went to Kwan, but right behind her were Russia's Irina Slutskaya and America's Sarah Hughes, and any one of these three could rise to the occasion in Salt Lake.

The gold medal for pairs competition should come down to the Canadians, Russians and Chinese. While Canada's Jamie Sale and David Pelletier were the 2001 World Champions, Russia's Elena Berezhnaya and Anton Sikharulidze won silver and China's Xue Shen and Hongbo Zhao gained bronze. Americans, meanwhile, will be rooting for Kyoko Ina and John Zimmerman, the U.S. pairs champions, to sneak onto the podium.

Ice dancing is expected to produce a more internationally diverse medal show as Italy, France, Lithuania and Canada all figured into the standings at the 2001 World Championships. The gold went to Italy's Barbara Fusar-Poli and Maurizio Margaglio, with France's Marina Anissina and Gwendal Peizerat going home with the silver. While Lithuania's Margarita Drobiazko and Povilas Vanagas won bronze, not far behind were Canada's Shae-Lynn Bourne and Victor Kraatz.

FIGURE SKATING COMPETITION SCHEDULE

Event	Time
SATURDAY, FEBRUARY 9	
Pairs figure skating short program	6:30 pm–9:30 pm
MONDAY, FEBRUARY 11	
Pairs figure skating free program	5:45 pm–9:30 pm
TUESDAY, FEBRUARY 12	
Men's figure skating short program	5:15 pm–9:30 pm

continued on next page

FIGURE SKATING COMPETITION SCHEDULE cont'd

Event	Time
THURSDAY, FEBRUARY 14 Men's figure skating free program	5:45 pm–10 pm
FRIDAY, FEBRUARY 15 Figure skating dance compulsory	3:45 pm–9 pm
SUNDAY, FEBRUARY 17 Figure skating dance original	5:30 pm–9 pm
MONDAY, FEBRUARY 18 Figure skating dance free	5:15 pm–9:15 pm
TUESDAY, FEBRUARY 19 Women's figure skating short program	5:15 pm–9:30 pm
THURSDAY, FEBRUARY 21 Women's figure skating free program	5:45 pm–10 pm
FRIDAY, FEBRUARY 22 Men's and women's figure skating exhibition	6:45 pm–9:15 pm

Short Track

In this high-speed version of roller derby on skates, he or she who finishes first wins; how long it takes one to reach the finish line does not matter. As a result, strategy plays a substantial role in this event: at the start, the pack of skaters often slowly skates out, rather than making a mad dash around the oval-shaped track. The races involve a series of elimination heats leading up to the finals. There is also a relay component to short-track skating;

YANG AND YANG

The two female Chinese skaters with the same Westernized name, Yang Yang (S) and Yang Yang (A), are not not actually related. In fact, their names are written differently in Chinese and carry different meanings. While Yang Yang (S) means "sunshine," Yang Yang (A) means "flying flag." The "A" and "S" initials after their names mean nothing, having been added only to help Westerners tell the difference between the two.

men compete at 5000 meters, women at 3000 meters. Each team is comprised of four skaters.

The American team will likely be led by a Seattle skater known as Apolo—Apolo Anton Ohno. Although he didn't launch his competitive racing career until 1995, Ohno has quickly developed into America's best male short-track skater. He was 14 years old when he won his first U.S. overall title during the 1996–97 season, a title he successfully defended the following year as well as winning a silver medal in the 500-meter race at the World Championships.

While Ohno's first World Cup win didn't arrive during the 1999 season during a stop in China, he won the overall World Cup title last season.

Two female Chinese skaters with identical names could find themselves sharing the podium during the Salt Lake Games. Yang Yang (S) and Yang Yang (A) between them have accumulated a vast medal chest. While Yang Yang (A) is a four-time overall world champion, Yang Yang (S) was a triple silver medalist at the Nagano Games. If they both compete at the 2002 Games and one of them reaches the top of the podium in Salt Lake City, it could mark the first gold medal China has ever won.

SHORT TRACK COMPETITION SCHEDULE

Event	Time
WEDNESDAY, FEBRUARY 13	
Women's 1500-meter short-track finals	6 pm–9:30 pm
Men's 1000-meter short-track preliminaries	6 pm–9:30 pm
Men's 5000-meter short-track relay preliminaries	6 pm–9:30 pm
SATURDAY, FEBRUARY 16	
Women's 500-meter short-track preliminaries and finals	6 pm–9 pm
Women's 3000-meter short-track relay preliminaries	6 pm–9 pm
Men's 1000-meter short-track finals	6 pm–9 pm
WEDNESDAY, FEBRUARY 20	
Men's 1500-meter short-track finals	6 pm–9 pm
Women's 3000-meter short-track relay finals	6 pm–9 pm
Women's 1000-meter short-track preliminaries	6 pm–9 pm

continued on next page

SHORT TRACK COMPETITION SCHEDULE cont'd	
Event	*Time*
SATURDAY, FEBRUARY 23	
Men's 500-meter short-track preliminaries and finals	6 pm–9 pm
Women's 1000-meter short-track finals	6 pm–9 pm
Men's 5000-meter short-track relay finals	6 pm–9 pm

The Peaks Ice Arena

Once Salt Lake City won the privilege to host the 2002 Winter Games, cities along the Wasatch Front came forward to see what role they might be able to play. For Provo, the answer came in the form of the Peaks Ice Arena that officially opened in October 1999.

With two indoor ice sheets, the 8000-seat arena will serve as the backdrop for preliminary men's and women's ice hockey competition during the Games.

GETTING THERE
The Peaks Ice Arena is located 50.9 miles from the Olympic Village in Salt Lake City via Route 15 and Center Street in Provo. ~ 100 North Seven Peaks Boulevard, Provo; 801-377-8777.

SIGHT LINES
Since all seats are reserved at this venue, higher-priced tickets will garner better views of the action.

DINING TIPS
If you want to flee the Games, then head up Provo Canyon to the Sundance Resort, which has two fine restaurants. **The Tree Room** is a rustically elegant, candlelit dining room adorned with Western and American Indian art from Robert Redford's personal collec-

WESTERN MASTERPIECES

Some of America's Western masterworks will be on display at the **Brigham Young University Museum of Art** in Provo throughout early 2002 thanks to the Smithsonian Institute. Nineteenth-century works by classic Western painters such as Thomas Moran, Albert Bierstadt, George Catlin and Frederic Remington will be on loan from the Smithsonian from January 17 through May 19. Closed Sunday. ~ 492 East Campus Drive, Provo; 801-378-2787; www.byu.edu/moa/museum/index.

tion. Creative menus combine seasonal ingredients—vegetables and fruits, locally grown herbs and edible flowers—while drawing upon various culinary traditions. Game farms provide buffalo, venison, antelope and elk to accompany beef, chicken and fresh seafood, including Utah trout. The restaurant's name stems from the tree that Redford built the restaurant around. Although it died long ago, its trunk still rises through the dining room. Reservations are recommended. ~ Sundance Resort; 801-225-4107. DELUXE.

The less-formal **Foundry Grill** applies regional accents to Southwestern cuisine in a ranch-house setting with big picture windows looking out on Mount Timpanogos. Most dishes are prepared in a wood oven or over a wood-fired grill and rotisserie. If Redford is at the resort and dining here, you'll likely miss him since he prefers a smaller, more intimate dining room off the main dining room. Reservations are recommended. ~ Sundance Resort; 801-225-4107. MODERATE.

THE PEAKS ICE ARENA EVENTS

Women's Hockey

Although women's ice hockey has a short history, that history has focused largely around the rivalry between the U.S. and Canadian teams. At the Salt Lake Games the Canadians will be out for revenge, having lost the gold medal at the 1998 Nagano Games to the U.S. in a 3-1 game that featured two power-play goals by the Americans, whose final score came on a shot by Sandra Whyte into an empty Canadian net. The Canadians had pulled their goalie in the game's waning minutes with hopes of tying the score, but failed to get the puck past the USA's Sarah Tueting. The American victory was a payback for a 4-1 loss to the Canadians in preliminary action.

Heading into the Games, Canada will likely be the favorite, as the team was undefeated in World Championship play heading into the 2001–2002 season. The bracket for the 2002 Games could produce another Canada–USA showdown in the medal round. In Group A, the Canadians are joined by Kazakstan, Sweden and Russia, while in Group B the USA team is joined by Finland, Germany and China.

Though the Canadians and USA are heavy favorites to return to the gold-medal game, the Finns and Russians can't be overlooked.

Men's Hockey

Who will win the men's ice hockey competition? That will be hard to predict until it's determined which National Hockey League players will play for their home countries. While the Czech Republic is the defending gold medal team as well as the 2001 World Champion, the Canadian squad is being overseen by former NHL great Wayne Gretsky, who no doubt would like to see a medal, while the American contingent will be anxious to erase the ugly memory of its rowdy behavior at the Nagano Games.

Fourteen teams will vie for gold at Salt Lake. Earning automatic byes into the final round of the Games' tournament are the top six teams from the 1998 Nagano Games: the Czech Republic, which won the gold medal; Russia, which took home the silver medal; Finland, which won bronze; Canada; Sweden; and the United States. Earning slots in the preliminary rounds were Slovakia, Austria, Latvia and Germany in Group A and Switzerland, Belarus, Ukraine and France in Group B.

Who to watch? The Czech Republic is not only the defending gold medalist but the three-time defending world champion. With goalie Dominik Hasek in the nets and Jamoir Jagr handling the puck, the Czechs are expected to be tough once again. Still, one can't count out any of the other top six teams.

The Americans produced two stories at Nagano—the first was their failure to advance past the quarterfinal round (the Czechs routed USA 4-1). The second was the Americans' trashing of their quarters in Nagano following the loss. Look for Herb Brooks, coach of the 1980 "Miracle on Ice" team, working his team hard to erase those images.

Another story to watch for in Salt Lake will be Finland forward Raimo Helminen, who was named to the team's 41-man Games roster. If he survives roster cuts and actually travels to Salt Lake, Helminen will be making his sixth Olympic appearance. He was on Finland's silver-medal team at the 1988 Calgary Games, its bronze-medal teams at Lillehammer in 1994 and Nagano in 1998, its sixth-place team at Sarajevo in 1984 and its seven-place team at Albertville in 1992.

THE PEAKS ICE ARENA
COMPETITION SCHEDULE

Event	Time
SATURDAY, FEBRUARY 9	
Men's ice hockey	2 pm–4:30 pm,
preliminary rounds	7 pm–9:30 pm
continued on next page	

THE PEAKS ICE ARENA
COMPETITION SCHEDULE cont'd

Event	Time
SUNDAY, FEBRUARY 10	
Men's ice hockey preliminary round	4 pm–6:30 pm
MONDAY, FEBRUARY 11	
Women's ice hockey	
preliminary round	2 pm–4:30 pm
Men's ice hockey preliminary round	7 pm–9:30 pm
TUESDAY, FEBRUARY 12	
Women's ice hockey	
preliminary round	2 pm–4:30 pm
Men's ice hockey preliminary round	7 pm–9:30 pm
WEDNESDAY, FEBRUARY 13	
Women's ice hockey	
preliminary round	2 pm–4:30 pm
Men's ice hockey preliminary round	7 pm–9:30 pm
THURSDAY, FEBRUARY 14	
Women's ice hockey	11 am–1:30 pm,
preliminary rounds	4 pm–6:30 pm
Men's ice hockey classification round	9 pm–11:30 pm
FRIDAY, FEBRUARY 15	
Women's ice hockey	
preliminary round	2 pm–4:30 pm
Men's ice hockey final round	7 pm–9:30 pm
SATURDAY, FEBRUARY 16	
Women's ice hockey	2 pm–4:30 pm,
preliminary round	7 pm–9:30 pm
SUNDAY, FEBRUARY 17	
Women's ice hockey	
classification round	2 pm–4:30 pm
Men's ice hockey final round	7 pm–9:30 pm
MONDAY, FEBRUARY 18	
Men's ice hockey final rounds	1:30 pm–4 pm,
	7 pm–9:30 pm
TUESDAY, FEBRUARY 19	
Women's ice hockey	2 pm–4:30 pm,
classification rounds	7 pm–9:30 pm
WEDNESDAY, FEBRUARY 20	
Men's ice hockey quarterfinal round	1:30 pm–4 pm
THURSDAY, FEBRUARY 21	
Women's ice hockey	
bronze medal game	12 pm–2:30 pm

▼▼▼▼▼▼▼▼▼▼▼
E Center

Population growth in the Salt Lake Valley not only has increased the size and number of suburbs, but it also has demanded additional services for residents. West Valley City officials responded to that need by building the "E Center," a multi-event arena that opened in 1997 and now is home to the Utah Grizzlies of the International Hockey League and the Utah Freezz of the World Indoor Soccer League.

For the Games the 8500-seat arena will stage some of the preliminary games as well as the finals of the men's and women's ice hockey competitions.

GETTING THERE

The E Center is located 10.5 miles from the Olympic Village in Salt Lake City via 215 South to Exit 3500 South; head east about a block to Decker Lake Drive and then head north to the arena. ~ 3200 South Decker Lake Drive, West Valley City; 801-988-8888.

SIGHT LINES

All seats at the E Center are reserved; higher-priced tickets generally equal seats with better views.

DINING TIPS

With Salt Lake City's eateries so close, you'd make a mistake not to head to one of them (see Chapter Two) for dinner. For some wonderful northern Italian entrées, avoid the crowds in the heart of the capital's downtown and go to **Lugano's** (page 77) on the city's south side.

E CENTER COMPETITION SCHEDULE

Event	Time
SATURDAY, FEBRUARY 9	
Men's ice hockey	4 pm–6:30 pm,
preliminary rounds	9 pm–11:30 pm
SUNDAY, FEBRUARY 10	
Men's ice hockey	
preliminary round	7 pm–9:30 pm
MONDAY, FEBRUARY 11	
Women's ice hockey	
preliminary round	11 am–1:30 pm
Men's ice hockey	
preliminary round	4 pm–6:30 pm
TUESDAY, FEBRUARY 12	
Women's ice hockey	
preliminary round	11 am–1:30 pm
Men's ice hockey	
preliminary round	4 pm–6:30 pm
continued on next page	

E CENTER COMPETITION SCHEDULE cont'd

Event	Time
WEDNESDAY, FEBRUARY 13	
Women's ice hockey	
preliminary round	11 am–1:30 pm
Men's ice hockey preliminary round	4 pm–6:30 pm
THURSDAY, FEBRUARY 14	
Men's ice hockey classification rounds	3 pm–5:30 pm,
	8 pm–10:30 pm
FRIDAY, FEBRUARY 15	
Men's ice hockey final rounds	11 am–1:30 pm,
	4 pm–6:30 pm,
	8:45 pm–11:15 pm
SATURDAY, FEBRUARY 16	
Women's ice hockey	
preliminary round	11 am–1:30 pm
Men's ice hockey final rounds	4:45 pm–7:15 pm,
	9:30 pm–12 am
SUNDAY, FEBRUARY 17	
Men's ice hockey final round	4 pm–6:30 pm
Women's ice hockey	
classification round	9 pm–11:30 pm
MONDAY, FEBRUARY 18	
Men's ice hockey final rounds	11 am–1:30 pm,
	4 pm–6:30 pm
TUESDAY, FEBRUARY 19	
Women's ice hockey	11 am–1:30 pm,
semifinal rounds	4:30 pm–7 pm
WEDNESDAY, FEBRUARY 20	
Men's ice hockey quarterfinal rounds	11 am–1:30 pm,
	4 pm–6:30 pm,
	8:15 pm–10:45 pm
THURSDAY, FEBRUARY 21	
Women's ice hockey	
gold medal game	5 pm–7:30 pm
FRIDAY, FEBRUARY 22	
Men's ice hockey semifinal rounds	12 pm–2:30 pm,
	4:15 pm–6:45 pm
SATURDAY, FEBRUARY 23	
Men's ice hockey bronze medal game	12:15 pm–2:45 pm
SUNDAY, FEBRUARY 24	
Men's ice hockey gold medal game	1 pm–3:30 pm

▼ ▼ ▼ ▼ ▼ ▼ ▼ ▼ ▼ ▼ ▼ ▼ ▼ ▼ ▼ ▼ ▼

The Ice Sheet at Ogden

Just as Provo responded to the coming Salt Lake Games by building the Peaks Ice Arena, officials in Ogden north of Salt Lake City offered to stage Olympic curling events. Ogden already had a facility—The Ice Sheet located on the campus of Weber State University—and the Salt Lake Organizing Committee agreed to the city's request.

The Ice Sheet at Ogden, which opened in 1993 for recreational ice skating, hockey and curling, gained experience in staging large events when it was the backdrop for the U.S. Men's and Women's National Championships in March 2000 and then the World Junior Championships last March.

GETTING THERE

The Ice Sheet at Ogden is located 36.6 miles north of the Olympic Village in Salt Lake City via Route 15 to Ogden then Route 89 to Harrison Boulevard. Turn right on Harrison Boulevard and follow it for two miles to the Dee Event Center, which is next to the Ice Sheet. ~ 4390 Harrison Boulevard, Ogden; 801-778-6300.

SIGHT LINES

All seats are reserved here, so the more expensive your ticket, the closer your seat is to the rink.

DINING TIPS

If you're looking for a lively crowd, some good microbrews, and a chance to happen upon some athletes, stop by **Rooster's** (page 110) located on Historic 25th Street. For a more subdued setting and some excellent seafood, walk across the street to **Bistro 258** (page 111).

THE ICE SHEET AT OGDEN EVENTS

Curling

Some call curling, which made its first appearance as an Olympic medal sport at Nagano in 1998, a hybrid of bowling and shuffleboard. After all, the object is to slide a 42-pound "stone" towards a series of concentric circles, called the "house," located 126 feet away. The key is to have your stone stop in the middle of the house, which is known as the "tee," as those stones closest to the tee earn points.

This is where shuffleboard strategy comes to play. Teams alternate sliding their stones towards the tee, and they can either strive to place their stones closest to the tee or opt to knock their opponents' stones out of the house. Also, deft twists of the wrist while the stone is being released can actually impart a curve on the stone as it travels the length of the ice.

Each match consists of ten "ends," which are similar to innings in baseball, except players from the two teams alternate sliding their stones. Each player slides two stones during an end, and once all the stones have been thrown the score is determined.

Sounds simple, right? Well, part of the game involves sweeping the ice in front of the stones as they slide towards the house. This sweeping action not only removes debris from the stone's path but can also melt a very thin layer of the ice, which will reduce friction and increase the distance the stone will slide. Teams can only sweep in front of stones thrown by their teammates.

The sport of curling originated in 16th-century Scotland, where farmers amused themselves in winter by sliding stones across frozen ponds.

In the Olympics the teams meet in a round-robin format. The favorites? Canada long has been a powerhouse, but Switzerland won the men's gold in 1998 while the Canadians took silver and Norway bronze. In the women's tournament, Canada won gold, Denmark silver and Sweden bronze.

CURLING COMPETITION SCHEDULE

Event	Time
MONDAY, FEBRUARY 11	
Men's curling preliminaries	9 am–12 pm, 7 pm–10 pm
Women's curling preliminaries	2 pm–5 pm
TUESDAY, FEBRUARY 12	
Men's curling preliminaries	2 pm–5 pm
Women's curling preliminaries	9 am–12 pm, 7 pm–10 pm
WEDNESDAY, FEBRUARY 13	
Men's curling preliminaries	9 am–12 pm, 7 pm–10 pm
Women's curling preliminaries	2 pm–5 pm
THURSDAY, FEBRUARY 14	
Men's curling preliminaries	2 pm–5 pm
Women's curling preliminaries	9 am–12 pm, 7 pm–10 pm
FRIDAY, FEBRUARY 15	
Men's curling preliminaries	9 am–12 pm, 7 pm–10 pm
Women's curling preliminaries	2 pm–5 pm
SATURDAY, FEBRUARY 16	
Men's curling preliminaries	2 pm–5 pm
Women's curling preliminaries	9 am–12 pm, 7 pm–10 pm

continued on next page

CURLING COMPETITION SCHEDULE cont'd

Event	Time
SUNDAY, FEBRUARY 17	
Men's curling preliminaries	9 am–12 pm,
	7 pm–10 pm
Women's curling preliminaries	2 pm–5 pm
MONDAY, FEBRUARY 18	
Men's curling preliminaries	2 pm–5 pm
Women's curling preliminaries	9 am–12 pm,
	7 pm–10 pm
TUESDAY, FEBRUARY 19	
Curling tiebreakers	9 am–12 pm,
	2 pm–5 pm,
	7 pm–10 pm
WEDNESDAY, FEBRUARY 20	
Women's curling semifinals	9 am–12 pm
Men's curling semifinals	2 pm–5 pm
THURSDAY, FEBRUARY 21	
Women's curling	
bronze medal game	9 am–12 pm
Women's gold medal game	2 pm–5 pm
FRIDAY, FEBRUARY 22	
Men's curling bronze medal game	9 am–12 pm
Men's gold medal game	2:30 pm–5:30 pm

Rice-Eccles Olympic Stadium

Opening and closing ceremonies for the Salt Lake Games will be held in Rice-Eccles Olympic Stadium, which serves as the home field for the University of Utah football team during the fall. Located on the East Benches of Salt Lake City, the open-air stadium is expected to seat at least 56,000 spectators for the two ceremonies.

The stadium sees two days of activity: February 8, when the opening ceremonies are held, and February 24, when the closing ceremonies are staged. These are lavish events, full of pomp and circumstance.

During the opening ceremonies, the lighting of the Olympic Cauldron comes after athletes from the participating nations march into the stadium and signifies the Olympic ideal of peace. While the stadium can seat 56,000 fans, an estimated 3.5 billion people around the world are expected to watch the event on television.

At the closing ceremonies the teams again return to the stadium, usually in a less formal and more gregarious fashion, as they commemorate the end of the Games. Along with honoring the athletes for their efforts, the closing ceremonies feature the passing on of the Games from Salt Lake City to Turin, Italy, which will host the 2006 edition.

GETTING THERE

To reach the Rice-Eccles Olympic Stadium, which is 3.1 miles from the Olympic Village, from State Street in downtown Salt Lake City, take 400 South east to 1400 East. It's located on the University of Utah Campus. ~ 801-581-3295.

DINING TIPS

After the ceremonies, a great, intimate setting to relax over a delicious Italian meal can be found at **Fresco Italian Café** (page 67).

RICE-ECCLES OLYMPIC STADIUM SCHEDULE

Event	Time
FRIDAY, FEBRUARY 8	
Opening ceremony	6 pm–9 pm
SUNDAY, FEBRUARY 24	
Closing ceremony	6 pm–9 pm

Index

Lodging Index

Dining Index

HIDDEN GUIDES

Adventure travel or a relaxing vacation?—"Hidden" guidebooks are the only travel books in the business to provide detailed information on both. Aimed at environmentally aware travelers, our motto is "Where Vacations Meet Adventures." These books combine details on unique hotels, restaurants and sightseeing with information on camping, sports and hiking for the outdoor enthusiast.

THE NEW KEY GUIDES

Based on the concept of ecotourism, The New Key Guides are dedicated to the preservation of Central America's rare and endangered species, architecture and archaeology. Filled with helpful tips, they give travelers everything they need to know about these exotic destinations.

Ulysses Press books are available at bookstores everywhere. If any of the following titles are unavailable at your local bookstore, ask the bookseller to order them.

You can also order books directly from Ulysses Press
P.O. Box 3440, Berkeley, CA 94703
800-377-2542 or 510-601-8301
fax: 510-601-8307
www.ulyssespress.com
e-mail: ulysses@ulyssespress.com

Order Form

HIDDEN GUIDEBOOKS

____ Hidden Arizona, $16.95
____ Hidden Bahamas, $14.95
____ Hidden Baja, $14.95
____ Hidden Belize, $15.95
____ Hidden Boston and Cape Cod, $14.95
____ Hidden British Columbia, $17.95
____ Hidden Cancún & the Yucatán, $16.95
____ Hidden Carolinas, $17.95
____ Hidden Coast of California, $18.95
____ Hidden Colorado, $14.95
____ Hidden Disneyland, $13.95
____ Hidden Florida, $18.95
____ Hidden Florida Keys & Everglades, $12.95
____ Hidden Georgia, $16.95
____ Hidden Guatemala, $16.95
____ Hidden Hawaii, $18.95
____ Hidden Idaho, $14.95
____ Hidden Kauai, $13.95

____ Hidden Maui, $13.95
____ Hidden Montana, $15.95
____ Hidden New England, $18.95
____ Hidden New Mexico, $15.95
____ Hidden Oahu, $13.95
____ Hidden Oregon, $15.95
____ Hidden Pacific Northwest, $18.95
____ Hidden Salt Lake City & Beyond, $15.95
____ Hidden San Francisco & Northern California, $18.95
____ Hidden Southern California, $17.95
____ Hidden Southwest, $18.95
____ Hidden Tahiti, $17.95
____ Hidden Tennessee, $16.95
____ Hidden Utah, $16.95
____ Hidden Walt Disney World, $13.95
____ Hidden Washington, $15.95
____ Hidden Wine Country, $13.95
____ Hidden Wyoming, $15.95

THE NEW KEY GUIDEBOOKS

____ The New Key to Costa Rica, $17.95
____ The New Key to Ecuador and the Galápagos, $17.95

Mark the book(s) you're ordering and enter the total cost here ➯ [   ]

California residents add 8% sales tax here ➯ [   ]

Shipping, check box for your preferred method and enter cost here ➯ [   ]

❏ BOOK RATE   **FREE! FREE! FREE!**

❏ PRIORITY MAIL $3.50 First book, $1.00/each additional book

❏ UPS 2-DAY AIR $7.00 First book, $1.00/each additional book   [   ]

Billing, enter total amount due here and check method of payment ➯

❏ CHECK   ❏ MONEY ORDER

❏ VISA/MASTERCARD _____ EXP. DATE_____

NAME _____ PHONE_____

ADDRESS _____

_____

CITY_____ STATE _____ ZIP_____

MONEY-BACK GUARANTEE ON DIRECT ORDERS PLACED THROUGH ULYSSES PRESS.

ABOUT THE AUTHOR

KURT REPANSHEK has been chasing stories around the Rocky Mountains since 1985, when he arrived in Wyoming as state correspondent for The Associated Press. A freelance writer based in Park City, Utah, since 1993, he has scaled the Grand Teton, paddled portions of the Green, Colorado, Snake and Middle Fork of the Salmon rivers, cross-country skied in the pre-dawn cold to catch sunrise on the North Rim of the Grand Canyon, rode in a four-man bobsled down the Utah Olympic Park track, and skied the men's downhill course at Snowbasin—all in the pursuit of stories. Among the publications that his work has appeared in are *Audubon*, *Sunset*, *National Geographic Traveler* and *Hemispheres*.

ABOUT THE ILLUSTRATOR

DOUG McCARTHY, a native New Yorker, lives in the San Francisco Bay area with his family. His illustrations appear in a number of Ulysses Press guides, including *Hidden Georgia*, *Hidden Tennessee*, *Hidden British Columbia*, *Hidden Bahamas* and *The New Key to Ecuador and the Galápagos*.